THE INGENIOUS MR. PYKE

Also by Henry Hemming

Misadventure in the Middle East
In Search of the English Eccentric
Together
Abdulnasser Gharem

THE INGENIOUS MR. PYKE

Inventor, Fugitive, Spy

Henry Hemming

PUBLICAFFAIRS
New York

For BB

───────────

First published in Great Britain in 2014 by
Preface Publishing
Random House, 20 Vauxhall Bridge Road,
London SW1V 2SA
An imprint of The Random House Group Limited

PublicAffairs books are available at special discounts for bulk purchases in the U.S. by corporations, institutions, and other organizations. For more information, please contact the Special Markets Department at the Perseus Books Group, 2300 Chestnut Street, Suite 200, Philadelphia, PA 19103, call (800) 810-4145, ext. 5000, or e-mail special.markets@perseusbooks.com.

Text set in Bembo Book MT Std by Palimpsest Book Production Limited, Falkirk, Stirlingshire

A catalog record for this book is available from the Library of Congress.
Library of Congress Catalog Control Number: 2014952648
ISBN: 978-1-61039-577-9 (hardcover)
ISBN: 978-1-61039-578-6 (e-book)

First Edition

10 9 8 7 6 5 4 3 2 1

'The fact is, if I may put the point in a somewhat comical way, that I have been literally attached by God to our city, as if to a horse – a large thoroughbred, which is a bit sluggish because of its size and needs to be aroused by some sort of gadfly. Yes, in me, I believe, God has attached to our city just such a creature – the kind which is constantly alighting everywhere on you, all day long, arousing, cajoling, or reproaching each and every one of you. You will not easily acquire another such gadfly.'

Socrates in Plato's *The Defence of Socrates*

CONTENTS

AUTHOR'S NOTE

In what follows direct speech is taken verbatim from either contemporary accounts or memoirs.

INTRODUCTION

February 1948

Mrs Hopkins, the daily help, knew very little about the man who had taken rooms on the top floor, so she was unsure what to make of the note on his door. She could tell you that his name was Geoffrey Pyke. He was just over six feet tall, wore a battered Homburg over his balding pate and walked with the stoop of a man recovering from illness. He was bearded, middle-aged and lean. He had large feet, spoke with a deep and musical timbre and received an unusual amount of post from overseas. As far as she was aware, he was a good lodger, in the sense that he took in few guests, kept to himself and was never late with his rent. But like most of those who encountered this man or heard stories about him – from the fellow residents he passed on the stairs of this boarding house all the way to the King of England – Mrs Hopkins was never really sure who he was.

By the time Geoffrey Pyke had moved to Hampstead, shortly before the end of the Second World War, he had collected an unlikely set of lives. Over the past two decades he had been described as everything from eccentric genius to war correspondent, jailbreaker, bestselling author, educationalist, speculator, mass-observer, advertising copy-writer, political activist, military inventor and scientist, while for those in MI5, the British Security Service, Pyke was thought to be an under-cover Soviet agent who had gone quiet in recent years. In each of these descriptions there was, it would later emerge, at least an element of truth.

The note on his door was brief: 'Please do not wake me.'

Given the appalling weather outside this was not surprising. London was caked with snow and, with so many Londoners unable to get to work, Pyke's decision to sleep in was understandable. But Mrs Hopkins was confused by his curtains being drawn well into the day while his lights remained on, as they had been since her arrival that morning. Something was not right. At around midday she knocked on his door.

Nothing.

And again.

Perhaps she shouted his name before trying the handle, only to find that the door was unlocked.

As usual his room was a mess, a papery metropolis of maps and journals, newspapers, statistical compendiums, letters stamped with the words 'Most Secret' and heaps of notes, many of them on feathery paper topped with a tropical-blue government crest. His bed had been propped up at one end, an attempt to improve his circulation, and elsewhere Mrs Hopkins took in the familiar sight of tabletops, shelves and sections of floor buried beneath strata of sardine tins, biscuit packets, ashtrays, copies of *The Times* and the *Daily Worker*, an occasional dunning letter, cups of lapsang souchong, half-empty bottles and more of that notepaper cobwebbed with his spidery handwriting.

At last she saw him. He was stretched out in a chair by the window, arms loose by his side. His beard had gone and for once he looked indifferent to the world. Next to him there were three sealed letters and a sheet of paper bearing a message.

Outside, Hampstead remained blank with snow and nothing much moved. In the wider world soldiers were still returning from war while refugees tried to make their way home. Society was rearranging itself after six years of armed conflict, genocide and upheaval; it was starting to rebuild and reconfigure according to new indices of fear and hope, but it would do so without this man. Late on Saturday, 21 February 1948, aged fifty-four, Geoffrey Pyke had taken his own life. As *Time* magazine put it the following week, 'it was the only unoriginal thing he had ever done.'

This is the story of a man described in his *Times* obituary as 'one of the most original if unrecognised figures of the present century'. Geoffrey Pyke was hailed by J. D. 'Sage' Bernal as not only a genius but 'one of the greatest [. . .] geniuses of his time'. Lancelot Law Whyte, who helped develop the jet engine, compared him to Einstein, adding that 'Pyke's genius was more intangible, perhaps because he produced not one, but an endless sequence of ideas'. A scientist who worked alongside him felt he 'stood out among his fellows like the North Face of the Eiger in the foothills of the Alps'. For another this was 'the sort of man who would have invented the wheel'. Everyone seemed to agree on the quality of his mind, yet few could understand why he had committed suicide. Fewer still had any inkling that he might have led a double life.

During the Second World War, without any military background or relevant qualifications, Geoffrey Pyke was appointed Director of Programmes at Combined Operations. As one of the 'right-hand men' of its buccaneering chief, Lord Louis Mountbatten, he was responsible for a stream of schemes, feints and military inventions including the idea, known as PLUTO, for an oil pipeline under the English Channel and another proposal whose advantages, for Prime Minister Winston Churchill, were 'so dazzling that they do not at the moment need to be discussed'. Of another plan Churchill wrote, 'Never in the history of human conflict will so few immobilise so many.' Both had at their heart an ingenious use of ice. It was also around this time that King George VI heard about Pyke and became known for his impersonation of Mountbatten's most colourful boffin, which involved exaggerated strokes of the royal chin (at the time Pyke wore a goatee).

That he was the subject of lively stories told by Dickie Mountbatten to his cousin the King hints at a bright and unbuttoned personality. To look at, Pyke was certainly distinctive. Friends described his 'immense natural dignity'. One man compared him to 'a Russian princeling'. For the Nobel Prize-winning playwright Elias Canetti, he was 'like a figure on a Byzantine icon'. By the end of the war there was a rich folklore of stories about Pyke and his various wardrobe malfunctions – it might be his flies getting stuck open, his preference for no socks whatever the weather, or his use of a shoestring instead of a tie. He was capable of standing out in any setting, a fluorescent thread on a hessian sack no matter where he went, and in many ways he cultivated this image of himself as the odd man out. But these tales told to the King were built up around more than the way Pyke conducted himself or his sartorial idiosyncrasies. At their heart was his extravagant ability to solve almost any problem put to him. Stranger still, his solutions seemed to work.

Geoffrey Pyke had a genius for innovation. He was one of the great innovators of the twentieth century, both in the staggering range of his radical ideas and in his technique. He was involved in the birth of – to name just five – a revolutionary kindergarten based on Freudian psychoanalysis, the Mass Observation movement, a pioneering charity, the NHS and the 'Devil's Brigade' – the maverick American-Canadian Commando unit to which today's US and Canadian Special Forces trace their origin, and which provided the inspiration for Quentin Tarantino's 2009 film *Inglourious Basterds* about a band of Allied guerrillas wreaking havoc behind enemy lines. He brought into the world a galaxy of ideas without having any particular expertise or even a university degree. He relied instead on an intuitive and crystal-sharp understanding of what mattered, why it mattered, and what he as a private citizen could do about it.

Thoughout his life, Pyke arrived at the cutting edge of the great issues of the day and, as a consequence, his career – if career is the right word – can be seen as an alternative chronicle of the first half of the twentieth century, an age of extremes in which the possibilities of politics and science seemed to stretch further out to the horizon than ever before. Pyke lived according to the spirit of these times; indeed, he strove to embody within himself the bold idea that it was possible to rewire human society and to produce a world without war or want in which the future and everything it stood for would be embraced like an old friend.

Original, eccentric, ambitious, Pyke liked to get the measure of his audience by making them laugh. He was a gadfly: a perpetual outsider with a nose for what he called humbug. His response to solemnity was to look for the joke, and more often than not this was where he found the seeds of his solutions; or, as he put it, 'It is the concealed truth that makes the jest.' He could be infuriating as well as funny, and at times his company was sobering: indeed, the US Deputy Solicitor-General, Oscar Cox, likened Pyke to 'the voice of Conscience in Spring'.

Although a man of supreme gifts, Pyke was not a household name at the time of his death and for many Britons today the first Pyke who comes to mind will be his cousin Magnus Pyke, the amiable 1970s scientific populariser. Geoffrey Pyke remains, as he was at his death, one of the most original yet unrecognised figures of the twentieth century. His genius was for coming up with radical ideas, not for seeing them through to completion. He had no interest in his legacy, hence there are many parts of his life that have remained unexplored since his suicide. Only now, following the release of previously classified documents by MI5, can this man's extraordinary story be told in full.

In August 2009 most of MI5's material on Pyke entered the public domain. This hoard of documents offers an entirely new perspective on his life. MI5 suspected him of being a German spy in the First World War and, during the next war, while in the employ of Combined Operations, he was thought to have been a senior Comintern official working undercover for the Soviet Union. MI5 even discovered his Soviet code name – 'Professor P.' – and after his death found evidence of a connection between him and Soviet agents Guy Burgess and Anthony Blunt.

The case against him was detailed and substantial. It was based on intelligence drawn from MI5 informants, scraps of overheard conversations, intercepted letters and the results of Special Branch and MI5 observations of Pyke in which he was shadowed through the streets of London. His career in Combined Operations was curtailed, yet at no point did he understand the extent of MI5's suspicions, no charge was ever brought against him and until now the truth of these allegations and of Pyke's real identity have remained a mystery.

This book is as much about whether Geoffrey Pyke was a Soviet agent during his time working for the British government – and, if so, why, how and to what end – as it is an account of the way he thought. Only by combining these sometimes disparate strands of his life can we get a sense of his beguiling, self-destructive genius and the extent to which it was a product of the society that he inhabited. Here was a man who saw the world into which he had been born as a kaleidoscope of challenges, problems and questions, many of which had not yet been asked. For this reason, what follows is arranged around MI5's efforts to understand who he was as well as the great problems he took on during his lifetime, problems which obsessed him, motivated him and ultimately defined him.

In the throes of adolescence Pyke began to believe that he was capable not just of identifying the most urgent problems faced by his generation but of finding solutions to them. Whether it was the design of a new motorcycle sidecar, how to make a fortune by trading copper futures or finding a way to avert the outbreak of war, Pyke was convinced that he could come up with an answer if he came at the question in the right way. It was an approach which he refined throughout his life, and one which he felt could be learnt by anyone. We can all think like geniuses, he insisted, but only if we are prepared to look foolish now and again.

His outlook was particular, bold and exacting and it was not without risks. One of the first problems he set out to solve very nearly led to his death. It was the summer of 1914. The world had gone to war. Geoffrey Pyke was a twenty-year-old Cambridge under-graduate who found himself drawn irresistibly to the impossible.

PART I

HOW TO BECOME
A WAR CORRESPONDENT

On 1 September 1914 Geoffrey Pyke left the offices of one of the country's best-selling newspapers in something of a daze. What he had just suggested to the News Editor of the *Daily Chronicle* was so outlandish, so apparently silly, that he had given little thought to the possibility that it might be taken up. Now, as he made his way through the hurly-burly of Fleet Street, with bodies brushing past and the hum of horse manure buffeting up around him, he broke into a sweat. The thought jammed in his head was simple enough: that as a result of the conversation which had just finished he might be taken outside a foreign jail before the end of the month and shot. Gazing up at the soot-streaked palaces on either side of him, buildings which no longer impressed him as they had done earlier, Pyke wondered if he had made a terrible mistake.

It had begun two months earlier, in July 1914, soon after he had finished his second year at Cambridge where his 'abilities made him conspicuous' and he was thought to be 'extremely clever'. Pyke was taller than most and gangly, with a mat of dark hair set above a playful expression, someone who thrived under pressure and exuded the hard-won confidence of a boy who had been bullied at school before blossoming at university.

After the excesses of May Week – the dancing, the shows and the sunny evenings spent 'ragging' about – he had set off with a friend on a walking tour of Norway and Sweden. Like most of their contemporaries, neither one saw the recent assassination of Archduke Franz Ferdinand in distant Sarajevo as a reason to call off the trip.

His companion was fellow Cambridge undergraduate Philip Sargant Florence, breezy and broad-shouldered, who was three years older than him, half-American and had grown up in an eccentric household. Generally he was hardened to the quirks of others, yet at an early stage in their journey Sargant Florence detected a change in his friend. If some people become a more cautious version of themselves in a foreign setting, Pyke seemed to do the opposite, and in this case Sargant Florence was partly responsible.

They had come to know each other through meetings of the Cambridge Heretics, a debating society that Sargant Florence had

Lionel Pyke QC

co-founded several years earlier and which was famous by then for its lively, free-flowing discussions. Recent speakers included the poet Rupert Brooke and the author G. K. Chesterton, and over the past year Pyke had become an avid member. For him the open-minded rigour of the Heretics' discussions was a revelation, and was a lifetime away from his miserable experiences at Wellington College, the militaristic public school where he had spent two unhappy years before Cambridge. It was also a tonic against the sadness of his life at home where he was never really able to escape the ghost of his father or the all-too-real presence of his widowed mother Mary, who liked to tell her four children that if she could swap their lives for that of their late father she would.

Pyke's father, Lionel, had been a precocious barrister who took silk at the age of thirty-eight before running unsuccessfully for Parliament as a Liberal candidate. He had become Leader of the Admiralty Bar before his unexpected death at the age of forty-four from a respiratory condition. Geoffrey, his eldest son, was five at the time. This was the defining trauma of Pyke's life. It left him reaching for father figures throughout his life, and at the same time it broadened the possibilities of his personality. He could fashion the memory of his father as he liked and even then he was not left with a rigid template of how to behave. The loss of his father seemed to produce in Pyke a Herculean drive: he latched on to new ideas with enthusiasm, and none more so than those outlined in a sensational talk he had heard in Cambridge just days before setting out for Norway.

The Cambridge Heretics had been addressed by the legendary founder of Futurism, Filippo Marinetti, in what was breathlessly described by the *Cambridge Magazine* as 'one of the most amazing meetings Cambridge has ever known'. Pyke had been aware of the larger-than-life Marinetti. Only a fortnight earlier he had included the Futurist's onomatopoeic sound-poem 'Pont' in a special edition of *Mandragora*, the undergraduate magazine that he co-edited. But this was the first time he had seen and heard the Italian in full flight. The effect was like that of a baptism.

Mandragora, May Week 1914

Marinetti's speech to the 'spellbound' Heretics, delivered entirely in French, 'but with such fluency, energy and clarity that few failed to follow his every word', seemed to be a primal howl against convention, sentimentality and the dumb worship of tradition. These were the targets picked off each week by the Heretics. You might think he was preaching to the choir. What set his talk apart was Marinetti's underlying enjoinder to his audience to do more than attack the past: they should revel as well in the possibility of an electrified future defined by machines, speed and the limitless potential of human agency. Only weeks later, in Scandinavia, Pyke launched himself at his new surroundings like a zealous disciple of Marinetti.

Sargant Florence would watch, bemused, as his friend ran up to farmers they passed and ask in puppyish German how a particular machine worked, why it was there, whether it could be improved, and, more often than not, if he could have a go. On one occasion, when the two hikers spied in the distance a team of Norwegian lumberjacks escorting logs downstream, Pyke jogged off to join in. Perhaps he felt there was a better way to move the logs, or maybe he wanted to improve his understanding of the lumberjacks' technique. In any event, he was soon hopping from trunk to trunk, 'caused a log jam, and was almost drowned'.

Pyke was, by his own account, 'very young, and a firm believer that everything was possible till proved the opposite by oneself, and that the madder the scheme, the better the chances of success'. The experience of being abroad for him seemed to slough off any vestiges of adolescent self-consciousness until there was nothing left but playful curiosity.

It was in this spirit, in the Swedish port of Malmo, soon after the lumberjack incident, that Pyke began to run at full tilt towards the end of a quay. Ahead of him was the ferry to Copenhagen. Sargant Florence was on board. Moments earlier it had begun to pull away. Still gathering speed, Geoffrey Pyke reached the edge of the quay and jumped.

It is a moment worth savouring. Suspended in mid-air is a bespectacled young man with a rucksack on his back. The sun angles down on his forehead and the air around him is spiced with the tang of diesel fumes. Passengers on the ferry stare, faces presumably blank as it is not yet clear where the parabola of his jump will take him.

Pyke's leap out over the harbour waters was a typically bold and bravura move, the kind of impulsive act that would have made Marinetti proud. Without any way of knowing how far to jump, or how high, Pyke had plunged himself into this uncertainty, conscious that every second spent dithering would reduce his chances of landing on the ferry. He was not assured of success but the chance of it easily justified the small risk of drowning. Only when he had launched himself off the edge of the quay and begun to fly did he realise – could he realise – that the ferry was out of reach, and rather than land heroically on board he fell like a deadweight into the scum-topped waters of Malmo harbour.

Bobbing about, Pyke yelled at Sargant Florence over the din of the engine to wait for him in Copenhagen. He took the next ferry across the Öresund and arrived in the harbour area of Nyhavn, popular with sailors and prostitutes, where he found his friend amid the purplish shadows of another glorious summer evening. In ways that neither could have foreseen the complexion of their trip was about to change.

Waiting for them in Copenhagen was Sargant Florence's sister, Alix. Elfin, tall and dark, she too was a Cambridge Heretic and doubtless she spent the night bringing both men up to speed on what had been happening in the rest of Europe since their departure. There was Austria-Hungary's ultimatum to Serbia, the Kaiser's support for the Austrians, Russia's backing of Serbia, France's resolve to weigh in, Britain's refusal to rule herself out, and more recently – more ominously – the Kaiser's decision to cut short his own holiday in the Norwegian fjords.

Not long after, on 28 July, these three Cambridge Heretics heard that Austria-Hungary had declared war on Serbia. This was not an elaborate 'newspaper scare'. It was real. It had begun. There followed across Europe more than forty declarations of war and orders to mobilise. In Paris the word heard on every street corner was '*incroyable*'. 'The world is gone mad,' wrote Winston Churchill to his wife. There were drunken celebrations in Berlin, Paris and Vienna as youthful crowds bawled out patriotic songs late into the night. As young men began to be called up, thousands of rushed marriages took place over that sweltering weekend. In Copenhagen, meanwhile, Philip and Alix Sargant Florence took a ship back to Britain. Pyke remained where he was.

Rather than return to London he chose to send a telegram to the head office of Reuters, news agency of the British Empire, offering his services as a correspondent. It was a reckless move: the longer he stayed in Denmark the harder it would be to find a ship back to Britain, and he was not even assured of a reply from Reuters, let alone a positive one.

Reuters, it turned out, was facing the worst crisis in its history. Its arrangement with the Berlin-based Wolff News Agency was on the brink of collapse, which would soon open up enormous gaps in its news-gathering service. Letter codes, whereby Reuters correspondents used code to reduce the length of their telegrams back to London, were soon to become illegal, which would force costs to soar, while the ill-conceived Reuters Bank was in dire straits now that its manager, a Hungarian, had been conscripted into the Austro-Hungarian Army. Shortly before the outbreak of war the company's senior management had decided that only a handful of war correspondents could be sent into the field. Otherwise they must rely on freelancers, known either as 'String' or 'Special' Correspondents.

Just days after making this decision, Reuters received an offer of correspondence from an unknown twenty-year-old in Copenhagen. He was English and appeared to be literate. In that strange hiatus between the outbreak of war and Britain's entry into it, with the shape of the war hanging in the balance, Reuters agreed to take on Pyke as a Special Correspondent.

Pyke would later refer to himself with pride as 'Reuters' special correspondent in Denmark at the time of the outbreak of war'. It was an audacious coup, born of little more than his being prepared to look foolish. But, as he soon discovered, writing the telegram had been the easy part; finding some news was going to be more difficult.

Though Pyke once described Copenhagen as 'the Athens' to which Norwegians flocked 'when their own barren hills did not provide enough intellectual intercourse', his initial experience of Danish conversation was Spartan. 'Woe betide him who finds himself a correspondent on those silent shores,' he groaned. The people of Copenhagen seemed to have perfected the ability to 'answer the most pointed of questions with a discreet evasion, and the most subtle by ignorance'. Instead he looked beyond the city for news, where he learnt that four German warships and a handful of U-boats had been seen to the south. Now he had the material for his first Reuters dispatch. It would also be one of his last.

In London it was noted that: 'Four German destroyers were also reported off Hammerfest, apparently bound for the White Sea. Reuters' correspondent at Copenhagen stated that on the afternoon of August 5 three German submarines were sighted at the southern outlet of the sound. They appear to have taken up their position there as a sort of advance guard.'

This was first-rate news. In Reuters there must have been murmurs of congratulation for those who had given Pyke his opportunity. Now they wanted more.

In a confident and expansive mood, Pyke cast his net wider and over the coming days met Edward Lyell Fox, a young American with a high forehead who was later described by Special Branch as 'a rather seedy individual'. Fox was a twenty-six-year-old Special Corres-pondent with only a handful of pieces to his name, mostly travel and sports. As Pyke would later find out, he was not everything he appeared to be.

At one point in their conversation, no doubt to impress the young Englishman, Fox let on that he was able to smuggle uncensored material into and out of Germany. The implications for Pyke were stunning. There were no British correspondents in Berlin and it was illegal for British, French or Russian nationals to enter the country. Editors on Fleet Street had given up all hope of getting uncensored correspondence out of Germany, and yet 'the desire to know the truth of what was going on at that time in the interior of Germany was intense,' wrote Pyke. 'The floodgates of news had clanged to, and not a word that could be prevented, or had not a purpose in it, was leaving Germany.' If Fox was to be believed, then Pyke had only to find willing correspondents in Germany who could pass their reports to Fox before he took them out to Copenhagen. Pyke would then courier this material to London. On Fleet Street the bidding war would be frenzied. All Pyke needed was a list of correspondents in Germany.

On 17 August, at a quarter to eight in the evening in Copenhagen, Pyke sent the following telegram to Reuters in London (the breaks were added by the censor, who let it pass): 'Have means of uncensored communication interior Germany | literary and telegraphically | send name address of trustworthy intelligent individuals | not press Bureaux | to act as correspondents there.'

If there was a reply he never saw it. By revealing the position of warships in his first Reuters dispatch Pyke had publicised sensitive German naval intelligence. After the publication of this report Germany's Minister to Denmark had made a formal complaint, which had by now percolated through various diplomatic channels. Pyke was told to pack his rucksack and leave. Crestfallen, he sailed to Greenock, Scotland, arriving during the last days of August.

It had been a fascinating adventure, but one which appeared to have run its course. At least, that was the impression Pyke gave for most of the journey home. Yet by the time he reached London his mood was transformed. He had come up with a new plan, one so outrageous that just the thought of it made him smile.

★

Pyke had spent most of his childhood, including the long and unhappy years after his father's death, in an elegant Kensington town house with a white stuccoed facade. It was from this house, several days after his return from Copenhagen, that he set out for Fleet Street. We may never know whether it was charm, luck, personal connections or a cocktail of all three which was responsible, but somehow he had secured an interview with Ernest Perris, News Editor of the *Daily Chronicle*, a newspaper with a circulation exceeding that of *The Times* and *Daily Telegraph* combined.

Like most editors, Perris was at that time in a state of sustained shock after the publication three days earlier of the 'Amiens Dispatches'. These were two frank assessments of the British Expeditionary Force's first engagements of the war – at Le Cateau and Mons – by veteran correspondent Arthur Moore for *The Times* and Hamilton Fyfe for the *Weekly Dispatch*. Ordinarily they would not have been published but both had been approved by the censor, F. E. Smith, later Lord Birkenhead, who even added lines about the urgent need for reinforcements.

The 'Amiens Dispatches' had sent shock waves rippling across the country, undermining some of the popular belief in a swift and easy victory for Britain and her allies. In Parliament the decision to publish these reports was slammed as defeatist. Churchill wrote a furious letter to the publisher of *The Times*. Yet the shock on Fleet Street was as much envious as it was outraged. The *Chronicle*, for one, had recently assured its readers that 'the censorship that we exercise over our news will not affect its value'. The Amiens Dispatches had shown that to be nonsense. Perris needed to strike back with vital news, to let his readers see the war as it really was. He was desperate for a scoop, which was why he was even prepared to meet this callow undergraduate.

'Yes, yes, what is it you want?' Perris began. 'Quickly, please, I've got no time to spare.'

As if to emphasise the point he picked up a pair of telephone receivers and dictated foreign telegrams into each. Next, as Pyke remembered, he 'rang a bell cunningly hid under the edge of the table, glanced about him in all directions at once, first at a row of large clock dials showing the hour in Paris, Berlin, Vienna, Petrograd, Berne, Madrid, Belgrade, Antwerp, and Amsterdam, frowned, looked at the large wall map, gave instructions to a pallid, overworked clerk for yet another foreign cable to go, and repeated, "Yes, quickly, please, I'm busy."

Pyke's plan was ingenious and a little mad, and over the next ten minutes he did his best to explain it.

How to Get a Job as a War Correspondent (as an Inexperienced Twenty-Year-Old)

For many young men like Pyke, who had grown up in upper-middle-class Edwardian London and liked to read, the idea of being a war correspondent had a heroic and at times breathless appeal. In 1912 the journalist Philip Gibbs described it as 'the crown of journalistic ambition, and the heart of its adventure and romance'. The life of a war correspondent seemed to combine the most attractive elements of explorer, spy and best-selling author. Marinetti had been a war correspondent several years earlier in Libya, as had Churchill in South Africa, and by 1914 Pyke described himself as 'absolutely determined to be a correspondent somewhere'.

But where?

On his way back from Denmark Pyke had pored over a map of the world in the hope of finding a newsworthy spot which did not yet have a full complement of correspondents. Yet whenever he found a likely destination his ambition foundered on his almost complete lack of journalistic experience. Apart from a handful of Reuters dispatches, by the age of twenty he had written no more than two short stories, a handful of book reviews, forty-two lines of doggerel and various interviews, including one with the actor Henry Lytton (then playing 'Ko-Ko' in *The Mikado*), all for the *Cambridge Magazine* or *Mandragora*, both of them parochial university publications. Nobody on Fleet Street could mistake him for a seasoned correspondent, and even they were finding it hard to get work.

The novelist Arthur Ransome, a decade older than Pyke, a Russian speaker and the author of books and numerous articles, was unable to persuade any British newspapers to take him on. Indeed, what was sometimes known as the 'Street of Adventure' had been besieged since the outbreak of war by a 'procession of literary adventurers'. There were 'scores of new men of sporting instincts and jaunty confidence, eager to be "in the middle of things," willing to go out on any terms so long as they could see "a bit of fun".' Pyke spoke no foreign language fluently, he had published no books and had left the country just twice. He did not stand a chance.

The problem appeared to be intractable, unless, that was, he could turn it upside down. Rather than look for a way past his inexperience he placed it at the heart of this puzzle. Instead of trying to identify towns or cities where there were not enough correspondents – but where there soon would be – he needed to look for a place in which correspondents would *always* be in short supply and where he might never face any competition.

He looked at the map afresh. No matter how long the war went on there were unlikely to be many correspondents in Reykjavik, surely. Or in Timbuktu, for that matter. 'Suddenly it came to me. We had no correspondents in Berlin. Supreme ass of all asses – of course – Berlin; the very place; no competition; no editor would say with an air of tired resignation that he was already very well served there, and had no necessity for further assistance, though of course he was very grateful, etc. etc. No difficulty at all, except of getting there, and out again.'

Geoffrey Pyke, Special Correspondent in Berlin.

His heart must have lurched at the thought. To produce a single report from the German capital would be the journalistic scoop of the war. Berlin was the last place where anyone would think to go as an English war correspondent, yet there were editors on Fleet Street who would sell their grandmothers for a stream of reliable news from the heart of the German Reich.

Of course, most of Pyke's contemporaries would have dismissed this idea as fantasy the moment it entered their minds. It was thought to be impossible to get into Germany as an Englishman, impossible to move around and impossible to get one's reports out.

Or was it?

Pyke knew that once he was in Germany he could pass his reports to Fox, the American, who could smuggle them back to Fleet Street. All he had to do was get in and out again. While he did not, as yet, know how to do this, he assured Perris that there was a plan but it had to remain secret. Just as he had done in Malmo harbour as the ferry began to pull away, Pyke did not intend to get bogged down in details. He wanted to jump.

In outline, at least, it was an impressive proposition. The thought of an English war correspondent in Berlin bristled with the kind of paradoxical ingenuity which Pyke so admired in others. He liked the challenge of it. 'Glory of glory at having something to do that seemed impossible,' he wrote, 'something necessitating all the virtues and all the vices imaginable, something for which one would have to be alert and cautious, receptive and sceptical, something that would necessitate twenty-four hours' work and twenty-five hours' watchfulness a day, and above all things the colossal humour of the idea.' But it was hard to see how he could actually spirit himself into the country, let alone out again.

For a moment Pyke's idea hung in the air between him and Perris, there to be embraced as a stroke of brilliance or swatted aside as an adolescent daydream. As far as we know, Pyke had given a good account of himself. Having gone up to Cambridge as 'an excessively shy youth' he had rapidly grown into himself, speaking regularly in Union debates before moving on to the Heretics. While he might have had the occasional off-day during his first year at the Union, his speeches became funnier with practice and more fluent. The *Cambridge Review* noted Pyke's 'fine voice', describing him as 'a good elocutionist'; the *Cambridge Magazine* compared his delivery to 'a soft and pleasing song'; while for *Granta*, '[Pyke] probably does some thinking in his spare moments.'

Ernest Perris spoke for the next half-hour, pacing the room, dropping occasionally into his swivel chair and swinging a leg over the arm. He liked the plan, yes, he was intrigued by it, he got the humour of it. Perris enjoyed the idea of having a *Chronicle* correspondent in Germany, in the way that he liked the thought of setting up a practical joke, but it was hard to say whether the young man sitting in front of him would be able to pull it off.

Perris later described his visitor on that day as 'a rather brilliant but erratic youth of twenty-one' (Pyke was twenty), who had, Perris understood, done 'brilliantly at Cambridge, but has always been ill-balanced'. Pyke had in fact scraped through his only Cambridge examination nine months earlier with a Third. While in a time of peace this apparent imbalance might have counted against him, by September 1914 the journalistic landscape had changed. The first scoop of the war had come to the *Daily Telegraph* from an unknown American freelancer after he had overheard the doorman at the US Embassy confirm the German advance into Belgium. Just as Perris needed a scoop, he appreciated that it might come from an unusual source. His main hesitation concerned the idea of sending an inexperienced correspondent into enemy territory on what might later be described as a fool's errand.

Perris offered Pyke the following terms: Perris would publish any material that Pyke could get out of Germany and would pay the standard rate offered to Special Correspondents, but he could not offer Pyke a position on the *Chronicle*'s staff. Nor would the paper be legally responsible for him. It would, however, make a contribution to his expenses.

Pyke accepted.

'Righto!' concluded Perris. 'Let's leave it at that.'

Perris urged Pyke as he left to take care of himself in Germany. If he felt someone was onto him, or had even the slightest suspicion that he was being watched, he must leave immediately. Pyke stepped out of the offices of the *Chronicle* feeling punch-drunk and on his way down Fleet Street began to sweat.

Over the next twelve days he prepared for his journey with the urgency of a man fighting for air. He read up on Germany, Germans and German frontiers. He spent the night in a print shop on Fleet Street. He went to Tilbury with a *Chronicle* employee to meet a sailor. He found the names of men who had managed to get out of Germany and travelled the length of the country to pick their brains: 'some knew a little, most knew nothing, one knew a lot.'

On 12 September, a forgettable and blowy day in London, Pyke said goodbye to his mother, his brother and two sisters, telling them that he had been taken on as a *Chronicle* Special Correspondent and was off to Stockholm. This was true. Perris had accepted him as a Special Correspondent, and, yes, he planned to go to Stockholm. Only it was not the whole truth.

As Pyke waited on the platform at King's Cross for the train to Newcastle, where he would take a boat to Norway, his mind turned again to the mission ahead. If caught, the best he could hope for was to be sent back to England with the German equivalent of a clip round the ear. More likely, he would spend the remainder of the war in prison. Confident that hostilities would be over by Christmas, this did not trouble him – and besides, several months in a German jail might make for an interesting set of articles.

There was another possible ending to this adventure which until then he had contrived to ignore. Pyke knew that what he hoped to do might be construed as espionage. While he had not heard of Englishmen being executed for spying, the war was barely a month old and there was no reason why they might not start with him. Indeed, he might not live to see his twenty-first birthday – the thought of which, he wrote, was 'like a hot iron searing my soul'.

Less than two weeks later Geoffrey Pyke settled down to a cold beer in a café deep inside the German Empire. By then the British intelligence agency later known as MI6, or SIS, was unable to get even one of its agents into the country. This untrained twenty-year-old, incapable of speaking fluent German and thought to be 'unbalanced', had somehow succeeded where MI6 had either failed or had not dared to take the risk. It was a breakhtaking achievement, not least because it had been done entirely on his own initiative. Pyke had defied the received wisdom of the day, according to which Germany was an impenetrable fortress. In doing so he had set himself up for the great journalistic scoop of the war. What baffled everyone who heard about this – as many soon would – was how on earth he had managed to get himself into Germany in the first place.

How to Smuggle Oneself into Wartime Germany

Pyke's first step when facing any problem, including this one, was to set out exactly what he wanted to do. In its simplest form his aim was as follows:

I want to smuggle myself into Germany.

His next step was to imagine a response to that. Not any kind of reply, but the sort of reaction you might expect from an older, wiser voice of authority. It would most likely be along the lines of: *You're mad, you'll get caught.* This was the voice of reality responding to fantasy.

Having set the two against each other, it was time to pull this exchange apart.

It was all very well saying 'you'll get caught', but where would this happen? At the frontier, you might think, where he was bound to be picked out by the guards. But how would they catch him?

If he arrived at a recognised border crossing he might either reveal himself to be an English journalist – which was unlikely – or a German official could work this out for himself. Yet to do so he would need to be on the lookout for people like Pyke. 'Of course, if the Germans were expecting English journalists to come into Germany after the war had broken out – then I should probably get caught. But the point was, were they? Would they be as wide awake as all that?'

Already the chances of getting in appeared to be better than he'd originally thought. What was more, if he entered the country at Warnemünde, a sleepy German port on the Baltic, rather than the Kiel Canal, the guards would be more relaxed. At least, this was what he had heard in Copenhagen, where Warnemünde was referred to as the 'back door' to Germany.

But even if the guards at Warnemünde were not on the lookout for English journalists they might be interested in anyone who looked obviously English, Russian or French.

This led to Pyke's next question: to what extent could he distance himself from these nationalities?

A German suit would help. Yet perhaps his greatest advantage here was an inherited one. Geoffrey Pyke's maternal great-grandfather had been a French Count. His grandfather on the other side was the Warden of London's Central Synagogue. He came from high-born Franco-Anglo-Jewish stock and had grown up within London's *haute juiverie*. Both his parents were Sephardic Jews whose ancestors had settled long ago in southern Spain before being forced to leave after the Alhambra Decree of 1492. They had moved to Holland and later to London, where the Dutch name taken by one, Snoek, was translated as Pike (the 'i' later became a 'y'). Which was to say that Geoffrey Pyke had a naturally dark complexion and, while he did not strike everyone he met as being Jewish, nor did he match a German guard's approximation of a ruddy-cheeked Englishman or indeed a stubbly Frenchman. There was an ambiguity to his looks which might be put to good use. Later on in his life it would work against him.

In theory, at least, he had made a good start. The combination of heading for Warnemünde, his appearance and the fact that the German guards would not be on the lookout for undercover English journalists all boded well. But they did not get him across the frontier.

Many years later, Pyke wrote that 'the correct formulation of a problem is more than halfway to its solution'. Perhaps he had not formulated the problem correctly.

I want to smuggle myself into Germany. You're mad, you'll get caught.

The word 'smuggle' could be improved upon. It implied physical concealment, yet there might not be any need for this. The only reason Pyke was not allowed into Germany at that moment was because of his nationality. Here was the breakthrough he needed. If he could assume a different nationality he would be welcomed into Germany as an Englishman would be in peacetime. He knew that US Consulates across Europe were by then overrun with Americans who had left home without a passport and consequently needed documentation. To claim an American passport Pyke had only to present himself at an American Consulate with valid papers, a passable American accent and a plausible account of his fictional American identity.

He had a good ear and had spent much of the summer with his

half-American friend Philip Sargant Florence, so the accent would be easy. Finding valid papers was more of a problem. Here Perris came to his aid by sending a *Chronicle* employee with him to the docks at Tilbury where they found an American sailor named Raymund Eggleton who was willing to part with his birth certificate – for a small fee.

The final piece in this deceptively simple jigsaw was Pyke's occupation. As a willowy undergraduate he would struggle to pass as a sailor. Pyke was a journalist with a Futurist's interest in machines so he decided to pass himself off as a print-machine salesman. On the remote chance that he might face awkward questions about the print-machine business he spent a night in the bowels of Fleet Street boning up on how these machines worked.

Several days after arriving in Scandinavia he walked into the US Consulate in Stockholm posing as Raymund Eggleton. He wore a German suit, a Serbian felt hat and boots made from Russian leather that would be worn out by the end of the year. But there was a problem with his performance, for he left the consulate without a new laissez-passer.

This was what he had feared more than anything: travelling as far as Sweden only to learn that his fantastic plan was impossible. Others might have turned back. He decided to try again. After depositing a sealed parcel in Stockholm's Grand Hotel, probably containing his English papers, he went to the US Consulate in Gothenburg where he gave his second turn as Eggleton. It worked. He was handed an American passport and several days later he stepped onto the ferry at Falster Island bound for Germany.

You can imagine the explosive compression of nervous excitement that built up in his slender frame as that ship steamed into German waters. After only a few hours it arrived at Warnemünde, the tiny hodgepodge port that he had heard so much about.

Once the ferry had docked he followed the trail of fellow passengers down the gangplank into a newly built wooden Customs shed. Around him he could see *Landwehr* troops in gaudy red and blue uniforms, their guns glinting in the half-light. Up ahead were policemen checking papers. When his turn came Pyke handed over his American passport.

It was in order, and he was waved through. Now all he had to do was get to Berlin and find some news.

While most of the new arrivals from Denmark took the train to Hamburg and continued from there to the capital, Pyke took a seat on a *Bummelzug* heading east to Stettin. These rickety trains stopped every few miles and were notoriously uncomfortable. They were also among the last places in Germany where you might expect to find an undercover Englishman. Though Pyke was travelling on a valid American passport he faced a new and even more potent threat: that someone he encountered might detect his Englishness and raise the alarm, leaving Pyke at the mercy of an angry mob.

By late September 1914 a siege mentality had set in across Germany. 'The people know; they are absolutely convinced that our enemies *forced* us to fight,' explained one German, 'and nothing, no matter what may be the outcome of this terrible struggle, can change that conviction.' In any nation whose people feel that they have been attacked unjustly and know that their borders are closed there is this same tendency to look for the enemy within. Since the declaration of *Kriegsgefahrzustand* – 'imminent danger of war' – issued in late July, anyone who did not look right, sound right, or who merely acted in an unusual manner ran the risk of being singled out and branded as a foreign agent. The American Ambassador to Germany described this febrile atmosphere in which 'people were seized by the crowds in the streets; and in some instances, on the theory that they were French or Russian spies, were shot.'

All this was before England joined the war. The English were loathed in a way that made the Russians and French seem like old friends with whom there had been a regrettable misunderstanding – largely because the German identification with England was so much stronger. War felt like more of a betrayal. *Gott strafe England* – May God punish England – was already an informal greeting between German troops (the response was: 'He will punish them'). The British Embassy was stoned. The American Ambassador was spat at because he was mistaken for an Englishman. (The culprit, a lawyer, apologised when he realised his mistake.) By the time Pyke sat down in a near-empty *Bummelzug* bound for Stettin there was a new bogeyman in Germany: the undercover Englishman.

As the train pulled out of the station Pyke noticed a sluggish, heavyset man heffalumping towards him. It was an off-duty German soldier. He had a pink neck and a half-grown moustache, and rather than keep to himself during the long journey east he had decided to keep Pyke company.

While it was improving rapidly, Pyke's German remained limited. He must have been hoping for a deaf old man to sit opposite him, a Trappist monk, perhaps – anyone, really, other than a German soldier.

After a perfunctory greeting the soldier unfastened his belt and bayonet, swung both onto the rail above, slumped down into his seat and began to talk. Pyke felt a wave of relief. This soldier only wanted to be heard. He must be 'divorced,' thought Pyke to himself, 'which was possible, since he never stopped talking. [. . .] It was twenty-three and a half minutes before he stopped, and then it was only to take a breath.' The soldier seemed to become most agitated when speaking about his commanding officer, referred to variously as *der schweinhund* and *verfluchte schafskopf* – literally, 'the pig-dog' and 'cursed sheep's head'. As the train bobbled along, the invective continued, the flow punctuated by 'spitting at what, from a grammatical aspect, was the crucial point of every sentence'. Pyke nodded sympathetically, making sure to add the occasional '*Ach so*' or '*Naturlich*'.

It seemed to be going well. There was no sign that the Englishman was expected to converse and the soldier looked at ease in his company. Indeed, after an hour or so he wore himself out and fell asleep. Pyke pretended to do the same, but kept one eye on the landscape passing by, noting the freshly dug vegetable patches and ageing postmen. This last detail he saw as evidence of the younger ones having been called up to the front. Such was the news blackout from Germany that even details like these were valuable. Already he might have enough for a short dispatch.

After another hour, as the train began to pull away from a station, the soldier awoke with a start. Bleary-eyed, he asked Pyke if this was Stettin. It was not. Either the young Englishman misheard or he thought it would be amusing to put the soldier out at the wrong station.

'*Ja, ja,*' replied Pyke.

In an explosion of arms and legs the soldier gathered his things and hopped down onto the line. As he did so his trousers fell down. He had forgotten his belt and bayonet. Staggering after the gently accelerating train, one hand holding his trousers up, the soldier yelled up at Pyke to throw them down, but in doing so Pyke accidentally hit the soldier across the shins.

Worried that the disgruntled soldier might cable ahead to Stettin – his destination and the final stop – about this unusual passenger, Pyke knew that it would be unwise to linger there. On arrival he rushed to buy a ticket for the next train to Berlin before turning his attention to food. He had not eaten all day, but the thought of entering a restaurant had become terrifying. In his mind he was unmistakably and unbearably English. He needed some kind of disguise or prop. Yet it was hard to see how he could find one in a railway station.

With a copy of that day's *Berliner Tageblatt* tucked under his arm Pyke strode into the station restaurant and took a seat. The paper worked so well as a disguise that even the waiter took no notice of him. Now he froze at the thought of calling him over.

'I felt horribly uncertain. I was now really in Germany. This was Germany, all around me. This great hall was German, this table was German, and these were Germans all around me. Ugh! What would not they say if they knew I was English?' The train to Berlin left in less than twenty-five minutes but still he could not bring himself to summon the waiter. 'Several times the words rose in my throat, but each time they failed to get further. I tried looking angry, I tried looking pathetic, hungry, helpless, wealthy, hurried, important, all to no purpose. The *ober* [waiter] went busily on.' Perhaps he should wave his arms about, make another face, he could . . .

'Suddenly I heard my own voice ringing out sharp and clear across the room: "*Herr ober.*" The deed was done. It was like jumping into a cold swimming bath.' The waiter came over. Pyke ordered in what he called a 'wisely laconic' manner, tore through his food and caught the *Bummelzug* to Berlin.

After an enervating, sleepless night he woke up to find his carriage full of commuters bound for the capital. They were silent and self-absorbed, yet dotted among them he saw members of the one section of German society he feared above all: teenagers. Pyke's research had left him convinced that the typical German teenager's mixture of childish curiosity and near-adult authority made him or her most likely to detect an impostor. Worse, the Kaiser had recently issued a proclamation urging the youth of Germany to challenge anyone who looked suspicious and where possible have them arrested.

Opposite Pyke was a teenager, his schoolbooks open, whose gaze seemed to wander. Or was this Pyke's imagination? 'I saw by that vacant stare in his eye and the unconscious movement of his lips as he looked at me over the top of his book that he was reciting all the crimes I was to be accused of, the various nationalities I was to be damned with: there are such a lot that lead you straight to Hell in Germany at the present day. Yes, I was sure of it, he would give me no peace until I was safely under lock and key, and booked to face a firing squad – with himself present by special permission – the next morning. He would – He didn't. He got out at the next station. In this manner, then, did I enter into the city of Berlin, a humble traveller by *Bummelzug*.'

Less than a month after telling an incredulous Ernest Perris at the *Chronicle* that he hoped to become the paper's undercover Berlin correspondent, an idea which even Pyke had originally laughed at, this enterprising twenty-year-old had made it to the German capital. None of his family or friends knew where he was or what he had done. To pull off the war's most daring piece of journalism Pyke only had to find a place to stay, write a dispatch and pass it on to the American correspondent Edward Lyell Fox. He was desperately close now.

Any visitor to Berlin in 1914 would have been struck by the city's glorious, teeming vitality. More than any other European capital this was a modern metropolis full of contrasts. Berlin was home both to a thriving salon society and a politically emancipated proletariat. Prussian aristocrats and other vestiges of an imperial past occupied the same energetic space as the pioneering Kaiser Wilhelm Institute for Physics, then run by Albert Einstein, and as many as forty homosexual bars. Berlin was also a terminus for migrants, so there was nothing unusual about the sight of a weary-looking young traveller wandering about in search of a place to stay.

We do not know where Pyke slept, only that it was cheap and was not the Hotel Adlon. Known as the 'American Headquarters', this was where the likes of Edward Lyell Fox were staying. Having found a bed Pyke now faced the problem of finding more journalistic material.

He could write about what he had seen during his journey, about the restaurant and the train. An account of the soldier's complaints could be worked into a longer piece on the reality of life in the German Army, and any of this would have electrified a British newspaper-reading public. But he wanted a broader range of voices. Pyke had made this journey to do more than provide a clipped summary of political developments. Instead, he wanted to gauge popular opinion and give his readers a sense of what ordinary Berliners were really thinking.

While his ability to understand the language was improving, his spoken German remained poor. To survive in Berlin as an undercover correspondent he had to live off overheard scraps. So far as he was concerned, there was only one place to do this.

'The first thing to do in Berlin is to go to a beer café,' he later wrote. 'The second thing to do in Berlin is to go to a beer café; and the third thing to do in Berlin is to go to a beer café. Not to drink beer. No. For even though the beer is light as the fluff off a dove's wing, and is served so cool that the hot moisture of the crowded room causes the sides to drip, nevertheless it is wiser to drink only so much that you shall not be thought an unsociable curmudgeon [. . .] Take a sip here, and listen, a sip there, and listen again; smack your lips occasionally and loudly, and you will be looked upon as a temperate drinker, who enjoys his drink to the uttermost. And also you will hear many interesting things.'

On Fleet Street there was a belief that if the British and French could hold off the German advance until Christmas, the Royal Navy's blockade of German ports would bring the enemy to its knees. By late September, then, Berlin should have been starting to totter. Pyke was expecting food shortages and a prevailing mood of discontent. Perhaps he was in the wrong place.

'I listened to the men talking in cafés. I heard no despair.' If anything, they were 'somewhat boisterous in their lack of it.' Instead the feeling in Berlin could be summed up by the recruitment posters all over the city in which General Wachs roared at passers-by: 'Do not say "Yes – but," say "Yes – SURE!"' Everywhere the spirit was bullish and open and Pyke had no trouble picking up the main talking points. These included rampant Anglophobia and an atavistic fear of Cossacks galloping in from the east. But still no hint of despair. Perhaps the naval blockade was having more of an effect on the German economy?

Having finished off another beer Pyke went to the bathroom to consult the map in his *Baedeker* before making his way across Berlin to the Bourse. Here the beer cafés were jammed with Prussian businessmen having lunch. They had lolling, full-cheeked faces and heads with flat backs. He sat among them like 'Daniel in a veritable den of lions', listening hard, sipping more beer. Yet to his disappointment the one subject these men did not discuss over lunch was work.

Geoffrey Pyke wound his way back to his hotel that evening at the end of his first day as an undercover correspondent in Berlin. He did not yet have enough for the front-page dispatch that he had envisaged, but he was making good progress.

On the morning of Sunday, 27 September 1914, less than a week after his arrival in Germany, Pyke encountered the might of the German Army. He had joined the weekly exodus out of the city centre to Charlottenburg Park, taking with him a packed lunch and two bottles of Pilsner. Having found a quiet spot at the edge of the wood he settled down for what turned out to be an afternoon of military trainspotting.

Two months earlier, in a great centrifugal migration away from the centre of Germany, millions of soldiers had been moved to the

Western and Eastern fronts. Now a fresh landslide of troops was being sent to stem a distant Russian advance. Camouflaged by the trees, Pyke glugged contentedly at his beer as the second great mobilisation of the German Army took place before him. Train after train rolled past at a mandatory twenty miles per hour, each carriage 'packed with row after row of soldiers. They stood at the door, leaning out over one another's shoulders, singing cheerfully and sturdily those wonderful German marching songs that make one's very breathing keep time to them. Each truck sang the same, and right down the train – more than a quarter of a mile long – rose and fell the words of the "Wacht am Rhein." God! with what fervour they shouted it, and yet it was still music.' Little did any of them know that one of the people enjoying their songs was an amateur English spy who was having a picnic.

It was a stirring sight, one that made it hard to imagine Berlin being captured by Russian forces. The irony was that Perris and Pyke had agreed beforehand that the most likely major story during his time in Berlin would be the arrival of Russian troops in the German capital. They had even gone to the trouble of establishing a code for Pyke to communicate via an open channel the direction and intensity of the Russian onslaught. Pyke had allowed this scene to play out in his mind. He would hang on until the eleventh hour, with 'the booms of Russian cannons on the east side of Berlin as I left it by the west', having written a 'dispatch which was to adorn, yes – I confess – I decided it was to adorn a whole page of the morning paper.'

That the News Editor of a major British newspaper was predicting the Russian capture of Berlin for September 1914 is a reminder of the resolute and at times blinding optimism on Fleet Street. The image of Pyke delivering a dispatch in the teeth of a Russian advance hints at something else: his own giddy ambition and a yearning for the kind of affirmation that would come with front-page heroics. It was a sense of recognition he never received at home. Yet this raw ambition was dovetailed increasingly with a growing self-awareness, as suggested by the words 'yes – I confess –'.

When Pyke left Charlottenburg Park later that day the troop trains were still in transit, and the following morning he returned to watch yet more of them pass by, soldiers stuffed in like socks in a drawer, until at last the convoy had rolled past. After making several back-of-an-envelope calculations about how many troops were on the move he took a train back into Berlin. In his hotel room he settled down to write.

It was about six o'clock in the evening. Outside, in the gloaming, lamps were being lit. His first dispatch would take the form of a letter to Perris. He had completed the first paragraph of this note when he heard the door open behind him.

Pyke spun round. Two men were standing in the doorway. They were about six feet away from him. One had bewitching eyes and a long black beard. The other had a fat face with jowls that looked like mutton chops.

'*Bitte, kommen Sie mit,*' said the better-looking one. 'Come with me, please.'

Pyke stood up, positioning his body between the two men and the half-written letter on the desk.

'*Aber wollen Sie nicht Platz nehmen?*' he replied. 'Won't you sit down?' Yet this was far too accommodating, he told himself. He needed a retort worthy of an indignant Raymund Eggleton. '*Wer sind?*' Pyke corrected himself. 'Who are you?'

No response.

Instead the taller one repeated his instruction, adding an unequivocal '*Jetzt.*' 'Now.'

Pyke could only think of the wretched letter behind him. Had they seen it? It was hard to say.

They could not see through the chair's back. If he could get a hand to the note on the desk he might be able to dispose of it. Trying to keep his shoulders still, he extended an arm backwards.

'Where is your authority?' Pyke asked in German, straining now towards the letter.

The senior detective produced a circular metallic emblem. By now Pyke had got a finger to the paper. But he could not get any purchase on it.

Time was running out. The first detective had repeated his instruction for the third time, adding '*Unmittelbar*' – 'immediately.' He had also taken a step towards Pyke. 'It would not be long before he had done another. In four steps he would be touching me. [. . .] He would be on me like a flash. His hands would seize my arm – would twist it back. Ju-jitsu. They teach the police that sort of thing in continental countries.' Pyke had to do something to move the focus of suspicion away from the desk.

With a lurch he strode past the two detectives and out into the corridor, switching off the lights as he went.

Surprised, thinking that Pyke was about to make a run for it – this was his hope the detectives followed him out into the corridor. Yet as he watched them leave he saw one lock the door and drop the key in his pocket. He must be planning to go back – in which case he would find the letter.

With lurid finality, Pyke's mind raced ahead to his execution. He had read countless adventure stories in which the hero was captured, put before a firing squad and offered a blindfold. Usually he refused – before pulling off a daring escape. How would Pyke respond when asked the same question?

As he pictured his final moments the senior detective led him away, before asking him where he had been earlier that day.

He had not been to Charlottenburg to watch troop trains.

'To Potsdam,' Pyke replied. 'To see the pictures. There is a remarkably fine Velazquez there.'

The detective knew the one. In fact, he 'knew everything there was to know about Velazquez. When not arresting criminals he absorbed himself in Velazquez. There was fervour in his voice as he mentioned the name. It was his hobby, so he told me, and it was a pleasure to him to meet somebody who took an interest in the great master.'

Pyke coaxed more out of him and as they continued down the street he felt the detective's grip loosen, until he was no longer being restrained. Was this his chance to escape? Both detectives were armed. It was not worth the risk and, besides, he might yet be able to talk his way out of this situation.

At the police station the wide-eyed Cambridge undergraduate was led into an office reeking of cigarette smoke and sausage meat. Around him was a phalanx of overweight policemen whose bellies seemed to vary according to rank – the fatter, the more senior.

'You'll be shot, you know,' said one.

The room buckled up with laughter.

Pyke rearranged himself mentally, laughed and asked why anyone would think that. Again the room roared.

'This sort of infantile sparring went on for twenty minutes. It was late now, and yet these portly tubs seemed to have nothing to do, except drink beer, eat sausage, turn a roaring gas still higher so that the very sausage began to sweat, and to spit contemplatively and repeatedly.'

The detective with the dark eyes reappeared.

'Herr Pyke,' he began.

The world seemed to stop.

How could he have known Pyke's name? There was nothing on Pyke's person to suggest that he had gone through life with this moniker, in which case the detective must have been tipped off. But by whom?

Experiencing jolts of betrayal amid a rising tide of fear, Pyke was then led outside by the plumper of the two detectives, the one he had come to think of as 'Mutton Chop', and together they took a cab across town. This gave his captor a chance to prattle on about the iniquities of Sir Edward Grey, Britain's Foreign Secretary, until at last they pulled up inside the glass-covered courtyard of the Alexanderplatz Polizeigefängnis, a prison for common criminals. The scene now descended into farce. 'Mutton Chop' did not have enough money for the fare and asked Pyke to pay the cab driver.

He did so and, seeing that he would have no need for money where he was going, tipped the driver extravagantly. Enjoying the look on his face, he then did the same to Mutton Chop, thanking him as you might a porter. Once he had entered the prison his mood became more sober.

His pockets were emptied, he was given a chit for their contents and in the early hours of Tuesday, 29 September 1914, Geoffrey Pyke was shown into an empty cell without any lights. It had slick walls that were cold to the touch. When the door closed behind him he was consumed by a universe of darkness. There was nobody to speak to, only the distant moan of an inmate who had lost his mind. The next day Pyke was left to confront his mortality. His account of that morning remains an extraordinary passage:

> Outside I could hear Berlin throbbing with the noise of motors and trams. I thought of all those people, free, and with lives to lead. I thought of them anxious about relatives at the front, anxious about the next meal, anxious about their own fate in the far-off future, uncertain whether they should marry somebody, cheat somebody, benefit somebody, wondering what would happen to them if they were married, cheated, or what they would do with money if left them, and if it would be necessary to return a kindness if done them by the living. I

envied them their doubt. I solved their problems for them. I lived their lives for them, directing their energies. I married them; I divorced them; I was mother and father to their children; son and daughter to their parents. I gave them fortunes; I helped them spend it. I gave them poverty; I helped them bear it. I gave them politics; I made them socialists. I gave them philosophies, and made them supermen. I gave them a hundred religions, and but one commandment – Thou shalt not kill. I gave them everything they could want and took it away again immediately, that they should know its value. I gave them knowledge of good, and twice as much of evil. I created worlds, in which men lived with intensity, and any tendency towards becoming a moral and mental jelly-fish was followed with death by inanition. I moulded a universe and put in it worlds other than ours, and beings unlike us, and superior to us; I destroyed it. I . . . I awoke with a sob, as my head slipped off my hands, and I fell against the opposite wall.

Which was how Geoffrey Pyke came to be awaiting execution in a German prison cell just two weeks before he was due back at Cambridge to start his final year. Perris at the *Chronicle* would assume that Pyke had been unable to get into Germany and had returned to England. His mother, meanwhile, imagined him to be in Stockholm.

He was imprisoned and alone, and it seemed that nobody who cared about him knew where he was. Before leaving London he had realised that something like this might happen. Pyke understood that to pull off a scheme of this kind he must be prepared to fail, and that given the stakes involved his failure would be spectacular. In setting out for Berlin he had taken an enormous risk. His plan to pull off the great journalistic scoop of the war had met with stunning initial success, and as a twenty-year-old amateur spy he had got further than any professional British intelligence agent would during the entire war. But he had been betrayed. Though he did not know who was responsible, all that mattered just then was that his plan had failed and now he was set to pay with his life.

HOW TO ESCAPE

Teddy Falk was a lugubrious, full-lipped English civil servant who spoke excellent German and liked to say his prayers at night. He was reliable, precise and scrupulously honest, and in the hours after the outbreak of the First World War he made what he later described as 'a terrible mistake'. Falk had been on holiday in Gutersloh, north-west Germany, when the news broke. Others might have made a dash for the frontier, yet Falk chose to surrender his passport to the local authorities for safe keeping. Days later, Britain was at war with Germany and Teddy Falk realised that he had effectively imprisoned himself.

He was arrested, accused of being a British spy – which he was not – and after a spell in solitary confinement was bundled off to Ruhleben Trabrennbahn, a former racecourse in the leafy outskirts of Berlin which had been converted into a camp for those British civilians who had been on German soil at the start of the war. By Christmas Day 1914 what the British press had taken to calling 'Ruhleben Concentration Camp' was home to 4,000 'specimens of *Homo britannicus*', as Falk explained. 'There were whites and coloured gentlemen, Boers, Canadians, Australians, and oddments from outlying corners of the Empire, mechanics, officials, merchants, music-hall artists, musicians, and members of every calling you could imagine, from the estate owner to the lion-tamer, or the person pointed out to me as being a notorious international thief, and the proprietor of a brothel.'

Ruhleben was ill-thought-out, cold, dirty and cramped: a muddy ten-acre enclosure in which there was no possibility of privacy. The food was foul and meagre, which had the curious effect of making the detainees want more of what they loathed. Yet most of the camp's inhabitants threw themselves into their new life with purpose and endeavour. They organised clubs and societies, a prisoner police force, language classes, religious services, musical performances and a roster of sporting events. Later there would be a camp newspaper, a postage system and in time Ruhleben became a self-governing state, a Little Britain in which every inhabitant was determined to make the most of their unhappy situation. Teddy Falk was different; he kept apart.

Teddy Falk during his time in the Militia Battalion
of the King's Shropshire Light Infantry

Since the moment of his arrest Falk found himself stymied by a 'sense of hopeless depression'. He was haunted by the thought that had he reacted to the outbreak of war with a little more nous he would now be fighting on the Western Front. He was also missing his wife, who had been seven months pregnant at the start of his detention. Falk made no effort to hide his gloom and soon became known around Ruhleben as the 'Camp Pessimist'. His reaction to the gossip that flew around Ruhleben on a shivering night in January 1915 was therefore characteristic.

The story was that an Englishman who had sneaked into Germany soon after the outbreak of war had been caught, left in solitary confinement for sixteen weeks – an unheard-of stretch – and was now being transferred to Ruhleben. Falk was just amazed to hear that he was still alive. 'Why the Germans did not shoot him offhand, which they would have been entitled to do, I ignore.' By the end of the war this unhappy civil servant would be glad to know that this man's life had been spared, indeed he would feel a bond of camaraderie with him that only war can produce.

On the night that Geoffrey Pyke was led into Ruhleben there was snow underfoot. The boots he had worn since London had holes in them from the hours he had spent pacing his prison cell, so with every step he would have felt the snow stinging the soles of his feet. This hardly mattered. After he was handed a bowl and a diaphanous, sodden towel Pyke was shown into a dormitory full of men. He found himself surrounded by people for the first time in months and it felt electric. News of his arrival spread fast and he was soon at the centre of a mob of detainees, all of them asking for the latest news from England.

There was a neat symmetry to this. Pyke had set out to report on life in Germany to the English in England; now he was relaying the news from England to the English in Germany. At least, this was what he wanted to do. Having spoken to only a handful of people over the previous four months, and rarely for more than a few seconds, Ruhleben's newest arrival kept tripping over his words.

This did nothing to dull his excitement at being in the company of so many of his countrymen. After the crowd had dispersed even the angriest conversation in the distance was, for him, a lullaby. 'I would lie on my back on my sack, and just listen to people borrowing spoons from each other, or cursing each other for mutual coffee slopping. A universal shout of laughter would make me warm with delight, and a continual cry to someone to shut up or to make peregrinations Hellwards would make me pause over every delectable syllable.'

Later that night the sentries came round to turn out the lights. The hubbub of questions, jokes and stories was replaced by a chorus of snores that 'made the whole loft vibrate'. 'All night long the doors at the end banged, with people going out to the latrines, and every time great flakes of wind-borne snow would rush in, and swirl about, finally settling down evanescent and wet on some huddled form.' It might have been cold and cramped but Pyke's move to Ruhleben had removed from his mind a great weight: he was no longer living in fear of execution. The problem was that, like Teddy Falk, he was not sure how this had happened, or indeed why.

By recording troop movements in Charlottenburg Park and writing these up in a report that he hoped to send back to London, Pyke was guilty of espionage. Had this been established in court at any point after the execution in late October 1914 of Carl Lody, a German agent active in Britain, then he would have faced a firing squad. Pyke was arrested towards the end of September but was never tried.

When asked to explain his transfer to Ruhleben he reached for vague terms about the German Empire tossing him about and 'finally vomiting me, in a fit of either weariness, mercy or disgust, to this day I know not which, into a concentration camp for interned civilians'. *Weariness, mercy* or *disgust*. 'Disgust' was there for effect, along with 'weariness', for letting a prisoner stew in a cell was never going to wear down the German Reich. Given Pyke's fragile mental condition by January 1915 'mercy' seems the most likely explanation.

By then this gregarious twenty-year-old had spent sixteen weeks in a room the size of a billiard table. It had space for little more than a bed and a latrine (made by George Jennings and Co., which became 'my one and only connection with the United Kingdom'), and to begin with he was deprived of exercise as well as company; he had nothing to read, no writing material and was alone with his thoughts.

'I swear to you that to think too much is a disease, a real, actual disease', wrote Dostoyevsky. For Pyke, to think too much and be imprisoned with his thoughts was a kind of torture. 'It is not the months that count in solitary confinement,' he wrote, 'but the quarters of an hour. Every ten minutes is eternity.' Of one moment in that cell: 'I could feel, and know that I was feeling, six hundred different things. I could think, and reverse my thoughts a dozen times before one half-second of time had passed.' He took to reciting Kipling's 'If' and Carroll's 'Jabberwocky' over and over, adding words and syllables or delivering certain lines at the top of his voice – 'ONE, TWO! ONE, TWO! AND THROUGH AND THROUGH . . .' – before dropping to a mousy whisper as if performing some mad Futurist poem – 'the vorpal blade went snicker-snack! / He left it dead, and with its head / He went galumphing back.' He ran through half-remembered conversations with Cambridge friends until they were so real that 'I could almost hear the voices, and could foresee the points where laughter, jibe, criticism, agreement, pause, uproar were to come.' Alone in his cell he delivered barnstorming speeches to the Cambridge Union before taking on a different character to tear apart what had just been said 'with all the sarcasm of a Voltaire'. Extending his arms before him, he imagined rowing down the Cam – he sat at number seven – and in his mind traced the journey along each bend, imagining the coach on a bicycle shouting instructions from the towpath and the echoing clatter of the oars as they passed under a bridge. On finishing these imaginary rowing sessions he would resume his pacing only to find, to his amusement, that he moved 'with that roll peculiar to after-rowing stiffness'.

Pyke was also very hungry. He described how 'real hunger [. . .] has been known to make men think very seriously about the rights of property, and a few have become so unbalanced as to become socialists'. Only later would the gentle sarcasm of this remark become clear. It seems that during these four months of concentrated loneliness the seeds of a political epiphany were sown. It would be several decades before it bore fruit.

By Christmas Day 1914, 'I no longer even had any rooted objection to insanity. I was fast getting to that point where the doubt arises as to whether after all madness is not the true sanity.' By January he was 'sinking fast', 'quickly becoming a broken-down creature' and by the end of the month he was transferred to Ruhleben.

Modern studies have shown that just ten days in solitary confinement will cause most prisoners to experience some kind of mental deterioration. Two months is often enough to induce a severe collapse. Pyke had lasted four months. It is not surprising that he was showing 'signs of mental breakdown'.

On the face of it, then, his transfer was an act of clemency. But there was more to it than that.

In 1916, an MI5 officer was told that Pyke had been transferred to Ruhleben after 'various highly placed persons' campaigned for his release. We know that before the war Pyke had spent 'jolly evenings' in the rooms of Bertrand Russell, the philosopher, and those of Charles Ogden, co-founder of the Heretics and editor of the *Cambridge Magazine*. But none of his English friends petitioned the German government for they had no idea of his whereabouts. Instead, according to MI5, his life had been spared after the American

Ambassador in Berlin, James W. Gerard, a moustachioed New Yorker, 'moved in the matter'.

Gerard certainly had form when it came to extricating Britons from solitary confinement. Before being taken to Ruhleben Teddy Falk had discovered, on his release from isolation, 'that I owed my liberation to the steps taken by Mr Gerard, the USA Ambassador'. In Pyke's case, however, it seems that Gerard not only played a part in securing his release but had also been instrumental in his arrest.

Pyke was addressed by the detective as 'Herr Pyke', so we know that the German police had been tipped off. But by whom? Maurice Ettinghausen, an English bookseller who would get to know Pyke in Ruhleben, explained in his memoirs that this Cambridge undergraduate was 'given away by the American representative in Berlin' – namely Gerard.

How could Gerard have known about Pyke? From Edward Lyell Fox. He was, after all, the only person in Berlin with full knowledge of Pyke's plan. He was also working undercover for the German government.

It turns out that Edward Lyell Fox was both a paid propagandist for the Germans and a government courier, which is perhaps why he was so expert in moving material across borders. The unsuspecting Englishman had inadvertently asked a German secret agent to smuggle intelligence out of the country.

Either Fox tipped off the police or mentioned to Gerard what Pyke was up to. Once it had emerged that Pyke was not an agent provocateur but a harmless adventurer now in danger of being shot, the American ambassador intervened to save his life.

Pyke knew parts of this narrative but not all of it, and certainly had no inkling that Fox was working for Germany. In those first few weeks in Ruhleben he tried to forget about his time in Berlin and concentrate instead on his new surroundings and the forgotten pleasures of conversation – which led to an encounter with a depressed civil servant named Falk.

Teddy Falk described Pyke as 'overgrown, tending to stoop, short-sighted, but extremely observant'. He was unlike anyone he had ever met, 'a pessimist and a cynic in affairs which concerned the heart and the soul, but in things material he was the most imaginative optimist I have ever come across.' Pyke had also shown himself to be remarkably resisilient.

Though Pyke had described himself as an atheist since the age of thirteen, either he looked Jewish in the eyes of the camp staff or it emerged that his parents were, for on his first night he was taken to Ruhleben's only Jewish barrack, 'the oldest and dirtiest stable in the compound'. As there was no room on the ground floor he was given a mattress in the loft. When Gerard, the US Ambassador, was taken on a tour of Ruhleben and shown this makeshift dormitory he 'recoiled with a shudder'. The beams were so low that Pyke was unable to walk around upright. 'The atmosphere was as thick as cheese,' he wrote. 'The whole place stank, and you could take the air, and cut it into chunks, throw it about and stamp on it, and yet it seemed about the same viscidity as mud.' For journalist Israel Cohen, one of the lucky ones on the ground floor, the loft with 'its little windows, its stifling atmosphere, its dismal light and its fetid smells, gave the impression of a veritable "Black Hole of Calcutta."' Two weeks after his arrival in the freezing, stinking loft of Ruhleben's Jewish barrack, Pyke contracted what was described by a fellow detainee as 'double pneumonia'.

In the days before antibiotics pneumonia was a far more deadly disease than it is today, and had contributed to the death of Pyke's father Lionel fifteen years earlier. His son was up against both pneumonia and the apathy of the camp's medical staff.

Known as 'Dr Von Aspirin', for his habit of prescribing patients two aspirins regardless of the symptoms, the Ruhleben camp doctor refused initially to see Pyke. Instead he told the men nursing him that his office was open every morning between nine and ten, and that the patient was welcome to visit him then. The patient, of course, could not move. Only when the camp commandant heard about Pyke's condition was Dr Von Aspirin ordered to see him.

'The doctor's mentality as regards myself when he arrived was, Is he dead? If not, why not? He gave me two aspirins, and remarked that I was too ill to be moved, remarking a little later in the week that I wasn't ill enough. He had me both ways. He never came to see me again.'

After ten days Pyke's fever fell away. He had survived, but at a price. For the next two weeks he convalesced in the loft, gazing up at the low-slung beams, and as he considered his predicament he became overwhelmed by what he called a sense of 'misery and futility'. It was unlike anything he had experienced before. This feeling was unrelenting, suffocating, and soon he was desperate 'to do something – anything – to avoid more of it'. His friends in the loft tried to lift his spirits: they 'did everything that human kindness and superhuman ingenuity could devise, but nevertheless I felt stifled, crushed, comatose'. Yet it was hard to see what Pyke could do.

Escape was out of the question; indeed, by the time of his arrival in Ruhleben this belief was so entrenched that even the subject of getting out of the camp had become taboo. As most detainees agreed, Ruhleben was exceptionally well guarded and its location hundreds of miles from neutral territory made it impossible to get home. The era of daring getaways, they told each other, had finished with the Napoleonic Wars. This was a new kind of war, they went on, a more scientific war in which escape was no longer technically possible.

The population of Ruhleben included men like James Chadwick, the physicist who would later win a Nobel Prize, and John

Masterman, who went on to direct the Double Cross operation during the Second World War: intelligent, reasonable men who were full of imagination. There was no good reason to doubt their collective wisdom. But as he lay in the cold and stinking loft, Pyke himself dared to think that these people were wrong. Perhaps escape from Ruhleben was merely a problem, and as such there was bound to be a solution.

'Before a problem can be solved it must be detected,' he later wrote, and 'it is easier to solve a problem than it is to spot what *is* the problem (as the whole history of science and technology shows). Almost any fool can solve a problem and quite a number do. To detect the right problem – at least so I have found – requires what [H. G.] Wells calls the daily agony of scrutinising accepted facts.' This attitude had spirited him into Germany. Now he hoped it might get him out. His motivation this time was altogether different: he was drawn not by the intellectual thrill of confounding expectations, though this remained satisfying, but the fear he had that his body could not survive a full winter in Ruhleben.

His fellow detainees were right, he told himself, insofar as it *was* a scientific war. This called for a scientific escape. If he approached the question in a suitably scientific manner, scrutinising every assumption within the camp and testing his theories by gathering evidence and conducting experiments, he was confident of being able to find a way out.

To almost any other Ruhleben detainee the case against such a fantasy was overwhelming. By March 1915 not one Briton had escaped from Germany. Pyke's idea was radical to the point of being absurd. Indeed, it was so daring that he resolved not to mention it to anyone. 'When men have nothing to do all day long but talk, they become so garrulous that it becomes impossible to keep even the slightest and least important bit of news locked up inside one.' If his fellow inmates learnt that he was plotting an escape it would be only a matter of hours before the authorities overheard the gossip. Yet for all this, Pyke began to toy with the idea of taking on a co-conspirator: preferably one who spoke German.

Soon after Pyke's arrival the camp authorities gave the detainees permission to take their daily constitutional in the grassy no-man's-land between the two fences that surrounded the camp. Pyke described the scene out there as 'like a bank holiday crowd on Hampstead Heath, only more crowd and less holiday and no Heath', and it was in this area one morning that Pyke bumped into Falk. The civil servant looked 'very gloomy about something'. Pyke, also feeling down, unburdened himself. As he did so he noticed Falk's eyes light up.

According to Pyke the atmosphere in Ruhleben was characterised by 'what seemed to me an insane belief in the inevitable fact of our muddling through somehow'. It was rare to hear anyone suggest that they were feeling depressed or low. Pyke's decision to do so marked him out in Falk's opinion as a fellow 'realist', and from that day on they took their daily walks together. During one of these Falk mentioned that he spoke fluent German.

On the face of it, they made an odd couple. Falk was a married man in his late thirties who had spent his early years in Bradford; Pyke was a twenty-one-year-old bachelor who had grown up in a salubrious pocket of west London. Falk was a devout Christian, Pyke was an atheist raised by an observant Jewish mother. Falk was an ex-serviceman; Pyke had a mistrust of all military men. Yet Falk was someone who kept the full details of his past to himself. Though born in Bradford, his parents were both German and his mother was Jewish. It is unclear whether he was raised as a Christian or chose to convert to that religion, but this may shed some light on the affinity he felt for Pyke, a young man he later described as 'essentially English, and at the same time essentially Jewish'. Falk was not only English and Jewish, but German as well and latterly Christian.

Ruhleben was a place which lent itself to personal reinvention, a levelling environment in which much of one's life until then could be made to feel peripheral. Pyke and Falk were drawn together mainly by their conversation. Both relished debate and were habitually sceptical. At the same time they complemented each other: Pyke was an optimist in material matters while Falk was more negative. In their discussions the younger man came to be the voice of fantasy while the older one represented reality, a duality which made their exchanges loud and lively. It was not long before Pyke realised that Falk would make the perfect co-escapee. Less clear was how he should bring this up. He simply could not tell whether Teddy Falk would ever countenance such a thing.

If Pyke misread the signs and was rebuffed there was every chance that Falk might spread the word about what he was planning. Their relationship began to resemble a courtship. 'We were both very careful, and approached the matter delicately. It was quite a month before I dared even get on to the subject,' recalled Pyke. 'At first we used to discuss the state of affairs prevailing outside; and then, when wandering round the camp, I pointed to a part of the fence and remarked, "That's not very carefully guarded, is it? Look how slack that sentry is. One might be able to get out there if One was fairly sharp about it." "Yes," Falk would reply, "but what would One do when One had got out?"'

That would be it for the day. The next morning the discussion might edge forward onto what One might do if One got onto, say, a train. Was One required to show a passport? Pyke tracked down an inmate who had recently been allowed to take a train into Berlin and who explained in the course of a long conversation that you were not required to show your papers on every German train. Pyke passed this on to Falk the next day.

They carried on like this for some time, creeping forward in their imaginary escape, until at last Pyke crossed the Rubicon. He changed the 'One' in their conversations to 'I'. Falk 'made no sign of having observed the change.'

This was remarkable. Here was a man whose response to the outbreak of war had been to hand in his passport, and who had at home a wife and a young child, a child whom he had never seen. Now it seemed that he was prepared to risk his life by attempting an escape.

'The next morning we were both a little shy,' wrote Pyke. 'Both of us had experienced the effect of waking up in daylight immediately conscious of our last night's plan as a new factor in life, and neither of us was quite certain as to whether in the other this feeling had not overswamped the determination of the preceding evening.' In a testy mood, Falk ran through a list of objections to the scheme. 'By admitting that he had been foolish the night before,' felt Pyke, Falk was offering him a way out. He did not take it. Instead he demolished each of Falk's objections. Their courtship was over. Bound together by the intimacy of conspiracy, the two inmates began to plot their route back to London.

Several months later, at about seven o'clock one summer's evening, with most detainees out on the exercise ground, Geoffrey Pyke and Teddy Falk met as agreed in front of Ruhleben's main grandstand. Both wore suits cut in a German style. Neither one said very much. In silence they scanned the horizon with nervous intent. It was a clear, warm evening and the sky was blank and blue. Beyond the fences they could see poplars by the riverbank, and from time to time a train mumbled by on its way to Berlin. The conditions were perfect. Their escape would begin in less than thirty minutes.

'I felt artificially calm about the whole matter,' wrote Pyke, ever the optimist, 'and more of a captive than ever. The sun was getting low, though it would be another two hours before it set. Something very terrible was going to happen to me, and quite soon. In half an hour's time Falk and I would either be shaking in the grip of a couple of German soldiers, or the possibility of a totally new life without horizon would extend before us. It was like waiting for reincarnation, with the alternative of death.'

Falk, the pessimist, was coping less well. 'In view of the danger of the undertaking, I confess that I felt qualms when the date fixed came nearer and nearer.' Indeed Falk 'loathed' the idea of escape, given that the likelihood of being tripped up by 'some unlucky coincidence' was in his mind, 'infinitely greater than the possibility of success'.

'Far more courage was needed from him,' agreed Pyke, 'than from me, for he thought he was going to his death, whereas I was by then so confident that I should be in London in three weeks, that I arranged the whole thing so as to be home in time for the school holidays of my younger brother and sister.'

For Wallace Ellison, a Ruhlebenite who had agreed to join their escape party, the fear of capture had proved too much. 'I had a strong presentiment – I can give it no more definite name, that three were one too many for such an enterprise.' He had pulled out the day before, which had only compounded Falk's anxiety. A much greater concern was how many German sentries would be trying to stop them.

In March, when Pyke had first resolved to escape, the idea of doing this was outlandish mainly because up to that point nobody had tried to escape from Ruhleben. Things had changed since then. A fifty-two-year-old engineer from Dumfries had spent fourteen days on the run before being picked up near the Dutch frontier and hauled off to Berlin's Stadt-Vogtei Prison (where Pyke had spent a few days). None of the detainees had heard of him since. During the past ten days there had been a further five attempts to get out of Ruhleben, each of which had failed. Not only did this confirm the prevailing belief that escape was impossible, it had led to fifteen extra sentries being posted to the outer fence just before Pyke and Falk hoped to break out.

Pyke did not share this news with Falk. Instead he 'behaved extremely caddishly', as he put it, by keeping it to himself. He was convinced that his friend would pull out, given his concern for his wife and child. This strikes a different note in our understanding of Pyke. Even as it suggests a certain ruthlessness, it is a reminder of just how desperate he was to get out. His body had not fully recovered from his pneumonia, a situation that he might have kept from Falk, and he was increasingly uncertain that his lungs and heart could withstand much longer in Ruhleben. So he kept this information from Falk and instead assured him that he would be able to spirit them both out of camp.

'You make it safe first,' Falk had said long ago, 'and I'll come.' It had always been Pyke's responsibility to find a way out of Ruhleben, whereupon Falk would take over. During the past few weeks Pyke had finalised his plan. It involved just one implement – a piece of stiff wire – which was now in his pocket, along with money and as much food as he could easily conceal.

Half an hour had elapsed, and it was time to set the plan in motion. Slowly, neither too fast nor too slow, the two men entered the exercise ground between the two fences. The barriers on either side of them were eight feet tall and topped with barbed wire. Armed sentries patrolled 250-yard-long beats and beyond the outer fence was a stretch of open ground watched over by further sentries armed with rifles and equipped with searchlights. It was an impressive set-up, well thought out and meticulous. But there were flaws.

Pyke had noticed that during the day the sentries' attention was focused on the outer fence – the only barrier between the exercising detainees and the world beyond – while at night, with everyone back in their barracks, the guards concentrated on the inner fence. So to escape one would ideally cross the inner fence by day and the outer fence by night. This was an elegant solution: it had the pleasing symmetry of a pared-down mathematical equation and the advantage of taking you over the open ground by night when it was poorly lit. It was also totally impractical.

You would need to hide in no-man's-land while day turned to night and, naturally, the camp authorities had done their best to make that impossible. Not only was the area between the fences patrolled at all times, but the solitary building in this interstitial zone was regularly checked by passing sentries.

That building was a tiny wooden kiosk, six feet across at its widest point, which was used to store athletics equipment. Even if a detainee did manage to hide in there one night he could not escape because it was locked from dusk until dawn. Or so it seemed.

As Pyke and Falk milled about with other prisoners on the exercise ground they heard a bell. It was 7:45 p.m.: time to return to their barracks. The two men joined a column of inmates trudging back to their huts – but at the last moment broke away towards the kiosk.

It had begun.

Having pulled away both men expected to hear the shout of a sentry or the crack of a rifle, as thunder follows lightning. But there was nothing.

Reaching the kiosk, they nipped inside and pulled the door shut. Still nothing.

'I felt a natural calm,' wrote Pyke, 'as if I was observing the workings of fate through a telescope.' Any moment now the sentry would open the door for his final inspection of the kiosk before bolting it shut for the night. According to Pyke's plan not only would he and Falk be able to deal with the bolt, but when the sentry opened the door they would be invisible.

Pyke had noticed that the sentries were lackadaisical in the way they bolted the door. Rather than push the bolt right along and pull it down they merely threw it halfway across. He had also noticed a hollow knot in one of the door's timbers. Using a piece of stiff wire he had found that one could open the bolt from inside the kiosk. But Pyke's greatest discovery was to do with the position of the window in relation to the entrance.

The small building shook as the door swung open. Standing in the doorway was a uniformed German sentry, so close that Pyke could see the colour of his eyes. They were pale blue and flecked with gold. For a moment nothing happened. The evening sun cast the sentry's face in a sickly, jaundiced light. The smell of athletics equipment filled the air like a reminder of childhood and each of the three men in that tiny hut was still like a statue. The sentry's gaze registered nothing – it was as if he could not see Pyke and Falk.

In the weeks following his recovery from pneumonia Pyke had been reminded – we do not know how – of the optical effect of a bright light behind a solid. He realised that if you were to look into this kiosk late on a summer's evening, given that the only window was on its western side and the door was on the east, it would be very hard to make out what was beneath the windowsill, in the way that when the sun breaks the horizon it is difficult to focus on the landscape immediately below. This was not to say that you would be invisible if you crouched beneath the window, as Pyke and Falk now did, but you would be hard to see. The more pertinent question, and the one on which their escape now hinged, was whether a German sentry might *expect* to find two detainees hiding there.

'If you are going to turn your hand to out-manoeuvring or out-cheating a person or persons, you should have very definite ideas as to their mentality,' wrote Pyke. Rather than study the bars to your cell, consider the mind that made them. To the best of his knowledge, the sentries at Ruhleben were the kind of men for whom the idea of trying to hide out in this hut was so idiotic as to be beyond even the eccentric Englishmen they were required to guard.

Trusting in all this, Falk and Pyke remained stock-still beneath the window. Their bodies were partly covered by scraps of netting and anything else that had been to hand. They were not obscured, but the combination of the sun and the sentries' habitual lethargy might be enough to make them invisible.

The German withdrew. The door closed with a *whoomph*. The bolt was dragged roughly across and the two detainees listened to the sound of the sentry's boots crunching over the gravel.

The first part of Pyke's plan had worked. It had been utterly audacious, simple and brave. Now the two men remained motionless on the floor of the kiosk while a band of sunlight moved sleepily up the wall, the colour becoming fuller and more golden, until it reddened and began to fade. At 9:30 the camp's electric arc-lights came on with a wide-awake hum and a bugle sounded for the change of sentries.

Time to move.

The next stage of Pyke's plan was clumsier. They had to get from the kiosk over the outer fence and across the open ground beyond. He had been unable to find an ingenious way under or around this fence and instead had taken to conducting experiments along its perimeter to find the least noisy place to climb over. To do this he had disturbed the fence, as if by accident, to see how the sentries reacted.

The results had been strange. Rattles of about the same intensity in the same place elicited different responses at different times. He concluded that some of the sentries were more switched-on than others. Since then Pyke had worked out which sentries were less attentive, when they were on duty and where. Based on this he was confident that the sentry now operating the searchlight over the area by the kiosk was either lazy, sleepy or hard of hearing.

He had also established that during the sentry changeover the no-man's-land between the fences was unguarded for approximately one minute. Pyke and Falk picked themselves up and took off their boots so that they could move more quietly over the gravel. Pyke produced his piece of stiff wire and slipped it through the knot in the door before working the bolt back towards the hinge. The door swung open.

In front of them the exercise ground was whitish and empty. Wide-eyed, strung out, the two detainees bolted the door behind them and padded over the gravel towards the outer fence before clawing their way to the top of the wire. For Falk 'the rattling wires seemed loud as cracking whipstocks to my ears, but it was only my bad conscience'.

Still no shots, no shouts.

They had both made it over the outer fence when they saw the spike of a sentry's helmet heading towards them. Again it was time to put their faith in elementary optics. Trusting that at night the eye is better at picking out movement than familiar shapes, they lay very still near the fence. Falk watched as the new sentry 'walked on, for we were already in the shadow, and the glare of the lamps in his eyes rendered it impossible to see far into the outer gloom, as Pyke had discovered previously'. Again their escape depended on one of his small-scale experiments.

Now they had to reach the safety of the woods beyond, which required crossing the open ground without being picked up by the sentry's searchlight. The trick was to move without flailing your limbs. To do this, Pyke had developed two bespoke crawls: the 'crab-crawl', which allowed you to 'proceed in one direction, and yet keep one's eyes fixed on a sentry in any other'; and the 'caterpillar', which, despite its name, was the faster of the two, and 'depended on lifting the knee at a certain point in the movement.'

Both were fine in theory but difficult to practise in Ruhleben where privacy was impossible and even the latrines lacked dividing walls. Pyke's solution was characteristically simple. He practised his crawls in full view of the guards and his fellow detainees. When asked why he was writhing about on the floor he explained that these were exercises for a weak heart which had been suggested to him by Dr Sörgersund, a Danish doctor whom he had invented.

Once the relief sentry had moved on a little, the two suited escapees began to crab-crawl across the open ground. Soon their elbows were aching and their brows wet with sweat. A searchlight beam swung lazily across the open ground. It would be on them in a moment. With a spurt both men propelled themselves over the last stretch, reaching the woods just before the beam moved harmlessly past.

Pyke and Falk had escaped from Ruhleben, and had done so scientifically. Every detail of this escape was rooted in Pyke's refusal to take any assumptions for granted, whether it was the idea that the kiosk was too small to be used as a hiding place or that it was impossible to crawl across the open ground without being seen. This scepticism had led to hypotheses, experiments and proofs and now both men appeared to be free. If the lesson of Pyke's journey into Germany was to think without fear of failure, then getting out of Ruhleben underlined the importance of challenging what you were told. Falk was in awe of how Pyke had done this, praising his 'positive genius' for an escape based on 'sheer hard thinking and acute observation'. But they were not yet out of the woods – in every sense.

As the two men caught their breath, Pyke noticed in the near-distance the flickering dart of a flashlight. It was a little man and his dog. Too old to fight, this patriotic Berliner and his companion would do their bit for the *Vaterland* each night by patrolling the woods beyond the camp, never taking the same route twice. This unpredictability placed them outside Pyke's meticulous plans.

Keeping low, the two Englishmen hurtled through the undergrowth. 'How the twigs underfoot cracked! It was as though a thousand squibs had been let off.' Having made it to the other side of the trees and away from the flashlight they saw to their horror a fresh set of fences.

There seemed to be nothing to do except try to scramble over. At the first fence Falk used Pyke as a step, yet this left the younger man stuck. The problem, according to Falk, was the size of Pyke's feet. They were 'exceptionally large' so he was unable to scale the wire mesh. 'Seeing him in difficulty,' wrote Falk, 'I put my hands through the netting and clenched them. Pyke stepped on to my knuckles and climbed over.'

They took on the second fence in a similar fashion, only to spot a third. As if caught up in an allegorical fable, this third and final fence was 'the biggest we had yet come across. It was something worse than tall.' The barbed wire ran along a series of brackets set on a cruel overhang. Again the Londoner presented himself as a climbing frame for the Yorkshireman who scrambled over 'with a great deal of difficulty', before it was Pyke's turn. He sent himself shooting skywards, but on reaching the top was unable to hoist his leg over. For a moment he was suspended in the wire like a fly in a web, suit torn, legs akimbo, stuck in a no-man's-land between detainee and fugitive. The summer before he had leapt out over Malmo harbour to catch the departing ferry and again, for an instant, it was unclear how this would end. This was becoming a refrain in his life. The thrill of a challenge often proved irresistible. He seemed to live without any fear of the future or indeed of failure; he was someone who jumped first and made calculations later. On this occasion gravity was against him and he came crashing down on the wrong side of the fence.

With his heart thumping against his chest Pyke picked himself up and again clambered up to the barbed-wire overhang before falling back down. On the other side of the fence Falk looked on in despair, telling his friend how exposed they were and what an easy target they would make for a passing sentry. This last remark – like pepper under Pyke's nose – seemed to power him up to the overhang. 'I had got to the top; I had got over the strand of wire that leant back; I had not an ounce of strength left. I could do no more. I just held on, balancing myself. Below me was my friend; he was looking up at me and his face was singularly intense, and I saw that the boot blacking had left a smudge below his mouth. He must be saying something, for his lips were moving. It was odd, for I could hear nothing. Then suddenly his face grew larger, and I began to dream. I felt him catch me, and in a moment I had come to.'

Shattered, full of adrenalin, the two men jogged away from the fence towards the banks of the canalised River Spree where they put on their boots and tried to walk along the towpath as if nothing had happened. Yet before they could relax they saw ahead the glow of what looked like a cigar. 'Was it a constable?' thought Falk. 'It was too late to fly. To walk on was the only chance. I called out a cheery good evening as we passed a gentleman in white flannel trousers. He responded, stared, and vanished. Would he give the alarm?'

They could not risk it. The two panicked fugitives slipped off the towpath and for several hours made their way through back gardens and allotments before reaching Charlottenburg Park, where Pyke had watched the troop trains ten months earlier. With dawn coming on they found a sheltered sandpit and settled down to rest. Falk said his prayers and fell asleep, yet Pyke remained awake.

At the speed of an express train he began to process the events of the last few hours, until at last he lay down with his hands behind his head, 'watching the stars fade away in the face of the first glimmering of the first day'. He later described those moments in his life when he had identified a problem, solved it and realised his solution as 'rare beatitudes which nothing can excel'. Here was one of these. The confidence which had been leached out of him during four months in solitary confinement was flooding back, and in this new mood Pyke began to feel that anything was possible: he might even be able to slip out of Germany undetected.

HOW TO BECOME INVISIBLE

One of the first questions that Pyke had asked himself after making the decision to escape, in March 1915, was how to get out of Germany as fast as possible. But really this was the wrong question. For it was precisely what the German authorities would expect him to ask when pondering his first move. If he and Falk were to slip out of the country unnoticed they must confound expectations at every turn. The police would anticipate them taking the fastest train to nearby neutral territory – Holland, Switzerland or Denmark – which was why they had to do the opposite.

They could travel away from London towards Romania, or aim for a non-neutral country, such as Austria-Hungary, and from there continue to Italy, which at that stage of the war was neutral.

This was the first plan that Falk and Pyke agreed upon in Ruhleben, and with the aid of an out-of-date school atlas they had worked out a route to the Austro-Hungarian frontier, only to read in a German newspaper that several army units had been stationed nearby. The territory they had hoped to walk through would be saturated with soldiers, so the plan was abandoned.

Next Pyke had turned his attention to the Baltic coast and developed what became known between Falk and him as 'The Baltic Scheme'.

Some of the options Pyke and Falk considered as they planned their escape

His idea was to move to the coast as slowly as possible – preferably on foot – before stealing a boat and sailing to Falster Island in Denmark. This idea also had to be scrapped after they read in a newspaper that for security reasons it was no longer permitted to moor small boats off the Baltic coast. Pyke, however, found it hard to let go of the scheme.

'I repeated to myself countless times, "Well, if we can't get boats there, we must take boats with us," without quite grasping the meaning of the phrase. [. . .] How to take boats with us? Then I saw it – portable canoes.'

He had seen an advertisement for portable canoes in a magazine that was lying around the camp. Rather than attempt to sneak out of Germany undetected, he and Falk, perhaps with some other escapees, could leave in broad daylight posing as friends on a canoeing holiday. Indeed, the more of them in the canoe, the better. With half a dozen canoeists they could pretend to be a *Gesangverein*, or singers' club, and paddle out of the country singing patriotic German songs. Pyke even put his mind to choosing a name for this club, one so German that it would make even the most patriotic German baulk. By then it was late May 1915, and earlier that month a German U-boat had torpedoed the SS *Lusitania* off the coast of Ireland, sparking outrage around the world at the loss of more than 1,000 civilian lives. He would call their club the *Lusitania Verein* – the Lusitania Singing Club.

All he needed now were fellow canoeists. Wallace Ellison, an economics lecturer at Frankfurt University, doubled up with laughter when he heard the plan, as did Falk, before telling Pyke to grow up. Yet over the following days Falk and Ellison both fell in love with the idea and in early June they agreed to go ahead with it.

Again, there was a catch. The advertisement for portable canoes had disappeared. Though Pyke searched through every bin in Ruhleben, he did so in vain. The *Lusitania Verein* was dissolved before it could sing its first song.

In the days that followed a crippling sense of doubt set in. They had spent two months trying to find a route out of Germany but had failed so far. Pyke's response was to instil in himself a new steeliness. He urged himself to 'go forward from one discouragement to another automatically as if by instinct', to become emotionally less attached to his ideas. He also questioned the level of his ambition. Perhaps their plans were too modest; it was time to be more brazen and consider 'something utterly and hopelessly mad and impossible'.

At this point Pyke turned to his great boyhood passion: detective fiction. It was no good coming at the question of how to get out of Germany with the mentality of a Sherlock Holmes, that icon of enlightened Victorian rationality, who, in Pyke's opinion, would last no more than a few minutes in wartime Germany. They needed to adopt the approach of that suave chameleon Arsène Lupin, the literary creation of Conan Doyle's contemporary Maurice Leblanc.

Lupin was a very different detective from Holmes. He was dashing, duplicitous and reckless: a gentleman-thief and trickster. 'The great charm about Arsène is you never know quite who or where he is. It is just the opposite with Holmes. Arsène hardly ever is so puerile, so banal as to think of the idea of disguising himself. He simply becomes two people at once. He is simply the prince of criminals and the chief of police at the same time, and nobody can say whether the chief of police took to crime, or the prince of crooks to guarding the property of the public. And the whole thing works beautifully.'

The key to solving this problem, Pyke realised, was to reformulate his original question. Rather than ask which disguise would allow him and Falk to travel unnoticed from Ruhleben to neutral territory, the question should be: how would we like to appear in the eyes of those who meet us? The difficulty was that they needed different characters for different situations. Pyke asked himself what Lupin would do. That was easy. He would invent a string of characters and in the eyes of his beholders be each of them *at the same time*. There was no need for costume changes; instead they would simply alter their accounts of who they were.

It would be an extreme test of their ability to play certain parts and improvise. Neither man was an actor, but both agreed to the plan. If escaping from Ruhleben had been a scientific exercise, then extricating themselves from Germany looked set to be theatrical. Pyke was about to be given a crash course in being two different people at the same time, or how to lead a double life.

On the morning after breaking out of Ruhleben the two fugitives woke up in a sandpit in Charlottenburg Park feeling hungry and sore. Having brushed each other down, they stepped out of the undergrowth onto Spandauer Strasse and began to walk towards the centre of Berlin. The performance had begun.

For both men, moving freely down a pavement like this felt exquisite and doubtless they would have preferred to say nothing and merely marvel at the sensation of being unencumbered by the sight of wire fences and sentries, but to do so might have marked them out. Instead they started to play the parts of two friends discussing last night's beery antics. As they came within earshot of several passing pedestrians, Pyke exclaimed hammily in German, 'And what happened then?!'

'Oh,' Falk replied, 'she got furiously angry and . . .'

He carried on like this until the passers-by were out of earshot, before starting up again as the next set of Berliners approached.

But then what?

Well, let me tell you, she . . .

This staggered conversation became gradually more absurd until both men were creased up with genuine laughter, which of course made their performance all the more plausible. Feeling confident, they agreed to take a tram into the centre of Berlin rather than walk. It was only when the tram had set off that they realised their mistake.

Next to them was a clutch of men in military uniform, including one who stared at Pyke's clothes with myopic intent. He glanced at the soldier's shoulder strap and saw a red 'E' on a yellow background: the insignia of the 'Elisabeth Regiment'. The two escapees were standing next to a group of Ruhleben sentries whose job it had been the night before to prevent their escape.

The sentry continued to stare. Pyke looked away. The passengers swayed this way and that like wheat in the breeze as sunlight flooded into the carriage, until at last the sentry appeared to lose interest. Pyke and Falk had agreed beforehand that they must never take an unnecessary risk, and at the next stop they got off to board the following tram.

In the city centre, Falk led Pyke at a brisk march to a smart-looking restaurant, whereupon, as they crossed the threshold, both men transformed themselves again.

'My dear sir,' began Falk in a bullying tone, 'to tell you the truth, I did not enjoy inspecting your unfinished jerry-built houses at such a ridiculous hour.'

Pyke did his best to look embarrassed and accommodating.

'We both look like low-lifes,' Falk steamed on, 'and besides, a 5 per cent mortgage in wartime is a poor investment.'

Having previously been two old friends they were now property developers back from an early-morning inspection of one of Pyke's building sites.

'Waiter,' Falk bellowed with the disdain of a pompous *Junker*. A man appeared. 'Show us the lavatory, and then we'll have breakfast.'

And what would they like for breakfast?

'Omelette?' Falk enquired. The waiter nodded. 'Good,' he said. 'Omelette for two then.'

Pyke might have been surprised by just how well Falk was playing this part, but in truth this was a character he knew well. His wife, Helena von Recklinghausen, came from a high-born German family, and no doubt this character was a composite of the various relatives he had got to know.

In the washroom they kept up the act with Falk doing most of the talking. Yet back at the table Pyke felt his lack of sleep starting to catch up with him. He found it hard to think of anything other than the strange, and at times hallucinatory, quality of the scene unfolding before him. 'Everything looked different, even when it was but half consumed, and I felt perplexed that I saw nothing in the faces of others to show that they too recognised the change that had come over the world. It was our first real meal for the greater part of a year; our first meal with a tablecloth. This was our first waiter for that time. One wanted to hit him on the shirt front to see if it was real.'

Before he could do this, the waiter came over with a basket of bread. Pyke's eyes lit up, and at once Falk saw what was about to happen. 'Before Pyke could stretch out his eager hand to grasp the tempting rolls I abruptly told the waiter to remove them. "I never eat bread before noon now that the country is short of it, nor shall you in my company," I said. We had narrowly escaped a pitfall. Neither of us had the police-stamped bread-ticket to produce which the waiter would have demanded.'

In silence the two fugitives tore through their ham omelette, followed by two cafés au lait, before Falk paid, using some of the money he had amassed in Ruhleben. Over the last few months he had set himself up as the camp's unofficial money-transfer agent without arousing any suspicion. Detainees would give him small sums to transfer to their wives back in England. Falk kept the money and sent a postcard to his banker, instructing him to transfer the amount from his account to the inmate's wife. 'Before long,' he wrote, 'my pocket-book was well lined with notes.'

Having finished their breakfast, the Englishmen lit up cigars and in a cloud of smoke strolled out of the restaurant into a balmy Berlin morning. It was time for another change of character. As they continued away from the restaurant, unknown to any of the passers-by, they metamorphosed again. This time it was into a pair of well-heeled friends about to embark on a walking tour – for which they would need camping gear.

Their shopping spree began with two umbrellas – 'great big fat things, that looked as if a boy of twelve had tried to roll them, in deference to parental orders, and had done it as badly as possible on purpose' – before they moved on to Wertheim's, Berlin's palatial answer to Selfridge's and Bloomingdales. Here they ordered rucksacks, felt-covered aluminium water bottles, dark green Loden cloaks, a collapsible cooker (Pyke spent forever deliberating over which one to buy), an aluminium knife, a clothes brush, a spoon and fork, an electric flashlight, handkerchiefs, several hunks of chocolate and, most important of all, a luminous compass.

As well as being the most valuable item on their list the compass was the most suspicious. Anticipating this, Falk had prepared a letter from an imaginary brother at the front asking him to find one. In Wertheim's optical department the British civil servant produced his fake letter and asked the assistant in a befuddled tone 'whether he had any notion what kind of a thing a luminous compass was, as I had no idea what they looked like'. He was duly given one.

The two Englishmen then began an anxious wait while their purchases were packed up. It was, for Falk, 'like sitting on hot coals'. The cashier announced the total and Falk paid. At which the girl looked up and said, 'Name and address, please?'

Pyke's heart almost stopped.

Without missing a beat, Falk conjured up both.

'Blumenthal, Luetzow Strasse, 21.'

Pyke was astonished by the speed with which his companion had done this.

The two men staggered out of Wertheim's laden with gear before making their way across Potsdamer Platz. Yet before they had crossed the square they noticed in the distance a familiar-looking figure. It was the Ruhleben Camp Commandant, Baron Von Taube. Whether or not he noticed the two men weighed down with camping gear

74

on the morning after two of his detainees had broken out, he did not make the connection.

Eager to get out of Berlin as soon as possible, Pyke and Falk continued to Potsdamer Bahnhof where they did not buy tickets for the frontier – that was too predictable – but for the Harz Mountains in central Germany.

The carriage was full, and to deflect attention from Pyke, whose deficient German remained their Achilles heel, Falk chatted enthusiastically to his fellow passengers while his companion did his best to look absorbed by a book he had bought in the station. Its jacket illustration showed a team of German soldiers cheerfully bayoneting a huddle of pathetic-looking British Tommies. Arsène Lupin would have been proud.

Goslar lies at the foot of the Harz Mountains and remains to this day a popular hiking destination, so there was nothing unusual on the afternoon of Saturday, 10 July 1915 about the sight of two Berliners struggling under the weight of their brand-new camping gear. Both were whey-faced and whip-thin. One was apparently 'a compact bourgeois Jew – by name Blumenthal' while his younger friend, much taller, was a bespectacled Gentile dubbed 'Herr Referendar – a kind of assistant under-magistrate' who suffered from a weak heart and had worked himself into such a frenzy over the last few weeks preparing for his exams that he was often too exhausted to talk. In case the Ruhleben authorities had told the police to look out for two men travelling together, one of them tall and Jewish, the other short and Christian, Pyke and Falk had swapped religions.

Having stocked up on supplies – ham, cheese, cocoa, chocolate, sausages, eggs, dried soups, matches, string and soap – they went for dinner in Brusttuch, which was, and still is, the grandest hotel in Goslar. There followed a feast which began to wash away some of the depressing memories of their months in Ruhleben, a meal which they were both enjoying until the proprietor came over to ask politely about the food and whether they planned to stay for long in Goslar. Blumenthal explained that, with regret, they had to leave before sunset. Confused by this desire to hike after consuming an enormous meal, the proprietor suggested that they should spend the night in the hotel. Blumenthal thanked him but explained that their holiday was so short and they were so keen to sleep under the stars that they must refuse.

A bed that night would have been heaven, but, as one needed valid papers to stay in a German hotel, it would have brought their escape to an end.

They paid for their meal and slipped out into a warm, bustling street. A sharp climb took them out of Goslar to the saddle of a pine-clad hill where they paused to watch the sunset. Before them a timeline of valleys plunged into the distance and, as the sky became an imperial purple and the insects began to cluster, they were free for a moment from the nervous reality of their new lives as fugitives. With the sky gently darkening they found a sheltered spot where they cooked ham and eggs on their new gas stove before wrapping themselves in their Loden cloaks and smoking long into the night. For the first time since leaving Ruhleben both men experienced 'a feeling of delicious security'.

They awoke the next day to the sound of birdsong while 'a bright sun streamed through the fragrant dew-spangled pines'. During the next twelve hours Falk and Pyke managed to cross most of central Germany by train, often sharing a carriage with off-duty soldiers to whom Falk cheerfully read out excerpts from his newspaper. That night they reached the mountainous Teutoburg Forest, which stretched like a wooded flyover across north-west Germany towards the Dutch frontier. Holland, neutral throughout the war, was their destination.

After reading in a newspaper that since the outbreak of war the Teutoburg Forest had become deserted, they had decided to use this woodland like a ladder in a game of Snakes and Ladders. It would take them undetected to within striking distance of the Dutch frontier. For the first few days the plan worked magnificently. Amid heavy rain, the two Englishmen squelched down empty forest trails and encountered nobody. But in some ways it worked too well, for it was so quiet that they became overly confident. They soon agreed to take a short cut which would involve leaving the forest for a few hours. As they ventured down a quiet country lane, away from the protection of the trees, they began to talk in English. Not long after that they heard behind them a crack.

It was a boy on a bicycle who had just run over a twig. Having crept up on them and apparently overheard their conversation he now raced off towards the nearest village, turning occasionally as if to memorise their faces. The two Englishmen shot off in the opposite direction.

This was bad, they agreed – it must never happen again. In future they would march by night and leave the forest only when absolutely necessary. For several days this new regime seemed to work, until their sixth day on the run when they chose to spend the day resting up near a bilberry bush.

Soon after settling down they heard in the distance the cheerful clamour of children rushing towards them, yet before they could move away they were surrounded. Their mistake was not that they were hiding by a bilberry bush but that bilberries were in season. 'Fugitives please note,' Falk later wrote, 'avoid ripe fruit when selecting hiding places.'

For the next hour the children played by the bush and ate its berries before a little girl caught sight of the two stubbly men. She stopped.

'Got many bilberries, Elsa?' asked Falk in his gentlest voice.

She put her finger in her mouth and giggled, before being joined by a fellow berry-picker.

'Well, Gretel, and what about you?' Falk persevered. 'Have you got many?'

One by one the children came to stare at the strange-looking men sprawled out on the forest floor. Nobody knew quite what to do, and after more nervous laughter the youngsters ran off.

Again the two men fled, heads buzzing with the impossible calculations of the fugitive. How would these children describe what they had seen? Would they be believed, and if so what would be the likely response? The same went for the boy on the bicycle. Perhaps the hotel proprietor in Goslar had alerted the authorities, or had they already been contacted by Wertheim's? By now, surely, the Ruhleben camp commandant had tipped off the police. There were times when it could feel as if the entire German population might be after them. Yet there were other, more pressing problems to consider. One was the deteriorating condition of Pyke's heart; another was their dwindling supply of food, a situation that Pyke hoped to remedy with the help of Arsène Lupin. He asked himself what Lupin would do in this situation. That was easy. As a gentleman-thief, naturally, he would thieve.

In the days after the bilberry-bush incident Pyke tried out a new character, that of petty thief. His first haul was modest: some unripe potatoes from a field. But soon he graduated to lowly farmsteads where he scavenged for scraps of food left outside and filled their bottle from water-butts. Falk preferred to keep watch, admitting, 'I lacked the nerve for this kind of enterprise.'

Pyke found his new task exhilarating. After only a few days he was 'extremely addicted to stealing'. 'Burglary is the most absorbing work imaginable. Every instant you are ready to see an irate owner in a night-cap issue forth, shouting and bellowing, and then comes the great moment when one has to decide whether to crouch down with not a finger moving, as rigid as a rock, every particle of white, even one's hands, covered up, trusting to luck that he will not see you, or whether to bolt as hard as possible into the darkness, trusting to luck that he will not catch you.' It was hard to say whether his enjoyment stemmed from the satisfaction of providing himself and Falk with food or whether there a part of him which relished the thrill of deceit in the name of a worthwhile cause.

Of course, this was not without risk, and only two days into Pyke's new career as a petty thief he and Falk made their third mistake: they forgot to wind on their watches one night. Having found a cottage with a sizeable water-butt, Pyke crept towards it, thinking it was about midnight. When he had almost reached the building the door swung open and an angry-looking woman strode out.

'The idea that I always followed on these occasions was the Red Indian dictum that anything that moves is twice as easily seen as anything still.' He froze. Yet she continued in his direction. In another few seconds she would be upon him. At this point Falk decided to intervene.

As Herr Blumenthal, Falk came bouncing out of the undergrowth, full of bluff bonhomie. The woman turned in fright. 'In suave tones I explained that we were members of the Imperial Pedestrian Touring Club, slightly belated and very thirsty. "Well, you look a gentleman," she replied, "but to tell you the truth I thought your friend had come to steal my cows." Pyke withdrew into the shadows under cover of this conversation. With a cheerful "Good-night" I followed him leisurely.'

Now they were in a spin. Unsure of the time or their location, they walked on in what they hoped was the direction of Holland. Down deserted country lanes, where their greatest fear was a silent gendarme coming up behind them on a bicycle, they looked for a place to hide. But the road only became wider and the landscape more congested until they arrived at the outskirts of Saerbeck, a town they had been at pains to avoid.

It was now past midnight and rather than turn back they agreed to march on. Having sliced clean through this town they found no shelter on the other side, and instead walked into Emsdetten, an even larger town. Again they did not break their stride in case anyone noticed the hesitation. 'How our boots echoed in those silent, cobbled streets!'

They encountered no gendarmes in Emsdetten, no nightwatchmen, dogs or insomniac vigilantes, but walked without a word through to the country west of the town where they found a wood in which to sleep. It was here, less than a day later, that Falk and Pyke separated for the first time since leaving Ruhleben.

Their objective for the night was simple: they had to cross the mighty Max-Clemens Canal, just under a mile away. Yet to swim this canal they would need all their strength and by now both men were flagging. Between them they had just one slice of sausage, a lump of cheese smaller than a matchbox and two biscuits, all of which had to last until Holland, some fifteen miles away.

Pyke offered to get fresh supplies in Emsdetten, a plan that Falk described as 'suicidal, in view of his extremely defective German'. He offered Pyke his share of their rations but the younger man would not budge. Finally Falk volunteered to return to Emsdetten. It was a terrible risk, one that flew in the face of every principle which they had agreed upon, but there seemed to be little choice.

Using a Gillette safety razor and a drop of water Falk gave himself a crude shave before Pyke licked him clean, straightened his tie and reshaped his hat.

'You'll do nicely now.'

'If I'm not back in three or four hours,' replied Falk, 'you must crawl on as best you can.'

'You'll get caught right enough,' Pyke teased. 'See you in prison later.'

With that, Teddy Falk walked into Emsdetten. All was not as he had hoped. It was a Catholic holiday which meant that almost every shop was shut. As Falk roamed the streets with a look of growing consternation on his face, a crowd of boys began to follow him, peppering him with awkward questions. Again it was the children of Germany who seemed alive to the fact that something about these two men was not quite right.

Falk was about to give up when he came across a shop run by a Protestant family. Behind the counter was 'a buxom dame' who stared in silence. He began by asking for four pounds of chocolate.

'Four pounds!' she exclaimed. 'Surely you can't eat all of that?'

'Not at all,' Falk replied. 'The truth is, it's my fiancée who is so fond of it, and, well, I want to spoil her. Now,' he said, producing a notebook, 'let me see what my housekeeper wanted. Ah,' he went on, 'sugar, margarine, soup squares, and cheese. Do you have any sausages or ham?'

The woman shook her head.

'No – what a pity. And nowhere else in town?'

No again.

'This dreadful war. Your husband is at the front, of course?'

He carried on like this in the mounting certainty that as soon as he stopped, her interrogation would begin. At last he paused for breath. She asked what his business was in Emsdetten.

'My business, madam? I have been sent by the government to repair the canal locks. Yes, a pound of sugar and one of margarine, please.'

'Which canal?'

'Why, the one to the west, a few miles out.' The Max-Clemens Canal. 'You never heard of it? Remarkable how few people I meet on my journeys seem to know their native towns well. I'll take two pounds of that cheese, please.'

'It's strange that nobody ever mentioned the canal to me in all these years that I've been here,' the woman said.

Falk had almost everything he needed and was about to pay when he saw a packet of biscuits. Could he buy these without a bread ticket? He stared longingly at the biscuits before musing out loud, 'I'd like to take my children some of these home . . .'

'I thought you just said you were engaged,' came the reply.

She had got him. He had indeed said that he was engaged and now he was talking about children. It was a rare slip from this light-footed civil servant. Most people at a moment like this would feel a flush in their cheeks and perhaps clam up, but not Teddy Falk.

Instead, with just a hint of melodrama, he leaned forward, grabbed the counter with both hands and whispered: 'She's my second one. But don't you tell anybody. And now for the bill, please.'

This seemed to work.

'Where should I send the parcel to?' she asked, perhaps testing him one last time.

'Madam,' he said, pausing for thought, 'in these days those who cannot fight at the front must help by assisting to economise labour. Although my physician has beseeched me not to over-exert my feeble frame, I intend to carry that parcel home myself, heavy though it is. I wish your husband a safe return home.'

Perhaps it was the mention of her husband that did it, for as Falk left the shopkeeper gave him a cigar.

The two fugitives ate well that evening and later that night arrived at the Max-Clemens Canal. No wonder the shop-keeper had sounded so confused. The canal had lain derelict for years. All that remained was a grassy trough that they were able to walk across easily.

★

In spite of just having had a substantial meal and being close to the Dutch frontier, both men were starting to fray at the ends. After twelve days on the run Falk found himself haunted by what he called 'that hunted feeling'. When he was playing the part of Herr Blumenthal he was confident and calm, and could improvise his way out of most situations, yet in those longueurs between performances he experienced a creeping sense of paranoia. Pyke's discomfort was physical rather than psychological: his heart seemed to be getting weaker every day. For different reasons each man was becoming addled and reckless, and on the night after crossing the Max-Clemens Canal, as they marched through the rain, the two fugitives made no attempt to talk quietly. Instead they entered into a full-blooded debate on 'the respective merits of our universities, the probable duration of the war, the progress of religious thought, or women's suffrage'. Indeed, they were enjoying their conversation so much that they failed to notice that the road had become increasingly well kempt. Nor did they pause to investigate the wall of light one had seen beyond the trees or the strange humming sound. Instead they carried on, their voices a talisman against the unfamiliarity of their setting, the darkness and the rain, only to turn the corner and find that night had become day.

Before them a startling scene was illuminated by a concentration of electric arc-lamps. What had been a hum was now a roar. Fifty yards away was a cordon of armed sentries, bayonets glinting like shark's teeth, guarding an enormous factory. In their attempt to slip out of Germany undetected Falk and Pyke had walked up to one of the world's largest munitions factories. The road before them led directly and irresistibly towards it and they knew that to pause, even for a second, would be to invite suspicion. So they continued, like two cartoon characters who have run off a cliff, until they reached the sentries guarding the factory.

'Good evening,' Falk grunted at one of the uniformed men.

No reply.

They carried on past the soldiers into the heart of the factory complex. The sound of the plant was thunderous now. On either side of them was a dystopic sprawl of bright-lit huts, barracks and chimneys. They were surrounded by munitions that would soon be raining down on their fellow countrymen but were unable to stop and stare. Instead each man summoned up an artificial calm and continued along the road until they arrived at a barrier blocking their path.

For Falk, it was all over. 'This must be the end of our journey, I felt. We had had no time to consult when a figure stepped forth, and apologising for delaying us flung open the barrier.' They marched on in silence before being enveloped again by the night.

The sentries must have mistaken them for two engineers coming off duty. Later that night they settled down in a dank copse, perhaps wondering to themselves what they had to do to get caught.

Pyke woke up the next morning amid the sound of pounding hooves. He was also aware of a jabbing pain in his abdomen. It was Falk digging him in the ribs.

'Get your legs in, you fool,' Falk whispered. 'There is a squadron of cavalry all around us.'

Pyke pressed his body deep into a clump of sodden heather and lay still as the damp spread through his clothes. Beyond the undergrowth horses and men were busying about. 'There was nothing exciting about this. There was no dramatic suspense. If you were caught, you were caught, a truism that seemed to cover everything. The ground was still just as wet, the air just as cold, and the heather roots just as rough as before these gentlemen on horses made their presence heard.' Indeed, he was so unmoved that he fell asleep.

When Pyke came to again the cavalry squadron was still there. There was no way out of this, he told himself, before starting to picture the interrogation that was bound to begin. Who would ask the questions? Probably the man issuing orders, 'a very stiff frightful Prussian' who had just shouted:

'Section A will now send a man to see if this copse is clear of the enemy.'

He was referring to the copse they were in.

It was not very big.

Pressing himself deeper into the heather, Pyke watched as a mounted soldier advanced into their wood. He was 'a bored young farmer, his belly encircled with a belt with "Gott mit uns" inscribed on it', *God with us*, who was carried about by a 'beautiful jet-black beast'. Like hobbits hiding from a ring-wraith the two Englishmen pulled their loden cloaks over them and pressed themselves harder into the undergrowth. The mounted soldier passed by within several metres of them before carrying on out of the copse. After this the squadron gathered itself up and rumbled off into the distance as if to war.

That night the wind picked up and the two men marched into what felt like a typhoon. The landscape looked different now. It had become a chopped-up, muddling mess, a dismal matrix of fields and patches of pine about a kilometre square, delineated by barbed-wire fences and ditches. They were on edge now. At the slightest sound, anything at all, they would drop to the ground as if felled by machine-gun fire.

Pyke's condition was getting worse. Walking felt like rowing through molasses and every twenty minutes Falk stopped to let him catch his breath. He would count down the ten-minute break while Pyke lay very still 'with the one wish that the last of the ten minutes might never come. In a few minutes the earth became spongy and it was even harder to go on. I remember keeping my eyes on Falk, and wondering why one should walk on one's feet instead of one's hands.' He was listing now. Nothing was quite as it seemed as they entered the Gildehauser Venn, a peat bog notorious for swallowing up travellers who strayed from the path. In this anaemic, moonless gloom a silvery puddle could become a sandy hump, and back again. Was the light ahead the dawn coming on or the nearby town of Ochtrup? The world had become monochrome and empty, a ghostly hinterland, and Pyke could no longer tell where they were going or why, which way was up, how this would end, when all at once he felt his heart 'give a sickening leap, as if it would break itself against my ribs, and the sky and heath had disappeared. Great masses of earth were being hurled about, and one hit my head so that it almost fell off my neck.'

He appears to have had a mild heart attack.

Falk was just behind. 'He suddenly pitched forward on to his face and lay motionless. I believed him to be dead. What was I to do? In one brief hour dawn would be upon us, and with it detection was certain unless – I could conceal the corpse, remove all means of immediate identification, and march on.' Elsewhere he wrote: 'I shall never forget the terror of that moment. The deathly silence of the night, & the prostrate figure outstretched on the cart track.'

According to Pyke, the German-born Yorkshireman made the grim decision to abandon Pyke's corpse and carry on to freedom but had not gone far when he remembered from his days as an Assistant District Commissioner in Nigeria that the jaws of those men he had seen executed always dropped. Pyke's had not. Perhaps he was still alive. Falk raced back to see his friend's eyelids twitching in the breeze.

Pyke came to, Falk helped him to his feet and together they carried on into the night. Yet the Gildehauser Venn seemed reluctant to give them up. At one point Pyke had to use his rope to haul Falk out of a quagmire. Finally, just before dawn, they escaped its clutches, and again the landscape changed.

With the night starting to run out, for it was the height of summer, the two Englishmen crossed an ornate wooden bridge which led into landscaped parkland. By their calculations they were less than three miles from the Dutch frontier. Any moment now, they told each other, they might encounter the initial cordon of sentries. They continued through the darkness of a wood with Pyke leading the way, 'for my sight and ears were keener. Every ten paces we would stop and listen. We could never hear anything, but we always did stop nevertheless. I never knew whether my fingers would touch a sentry or if I might have the luck possibly to touch his rifle first. The idea came to me that I might touch it so gently that he would not notice it, and then I should stand still, trying not to complete the step I should be in the process of taking, trying not to breathe.'

The wood was interrupted by a railway line and, as there appeared to be no sentries, they crossed using a version of the crab-crawl before passing over a road on the other side in a similar fashion. Immediately they admonished themselves for their sloppy technique. When it came to the actual frontier, they told themselves, they must take more care.

Just then they saw that the trees were starting to show up against a pewter-coloured sky. Dawn was coming on. In a mad rush they looked for a suitable place to hide but could only find a dip marked by several low-hanging firs. It was not ideal, but it would do. As the sun broke the horizon they hunkered down in anticipation of what they told each other might be the last day of their lives. It was 23 July 1915. Fourteen days after leaving Ruhleben in the most scientific manner possible, Pyke and Falk had smuggled themselves theatrically and fortuitously to within half a mile of the Dutch frontier. They had saved one another's lives on more than one occasion. Now, less than a day after Falk had almost drowned in a peat bog and Pyke's heart attack, they faced their greatest challenge yet.

The two men spent much of the next day swimming in uncertainty. It was impossible to say precisely where the frontier was, whether the sentries on duty would be sleepy *Landsturm* or snipers with orders to shoot on sight, or if they should expect live wires, ditches, dogs, automatic alarms or bells on wires. Indeed, there was little they could do other than sit still and wait for the night.

Nearing sunset Pyke described his mood as 'rather garrulous'. Both he and Falk laughed at the sight of a grim-looking reaper scything a nearby field – surely he had come for them. As darkness fell they heard the sound of German soldiers in the distance singing a marching chorus.

'The new guard coming on duty,' said one fugitive to the other.

'There sounds enough of them. Looks cheerful for tonight.'

They agreed to set out in fifteen minutes. As the tension grew, Pyke chatted nervously about what he planned to do back in London. Not wanting to tempt fate like this, Falk changed the subject. He began to talk about his teeth, and how many days he had gone without brushing them, when Pyke heard the crack of a twig.

'Instead of turning round, I put my hand up to my hat, which was fixed in the twigs, and holding it steady, turned my head round inside its brim . . . Behind me, so close that I noticed the texture of his trousers, was a soldier, who was holding aside the branches and stooping down over us . . .'

'My God,' faltered Pyke. 'It's all up.'

The soldier continued to look down at Falk and Pyke. He was a large man, made to seem larger by his position above them. In one hand he held a rifle. In the other he steadied a bicycle. He stood very still and said nothing. For a moment the three men looked at each other, puzzled, curious and a little afraid to different degrees, before the soldier asked in a guttural German accent what they were doing.

For Pyke this was too much. His imagination spun away from the scene until he was back in his green-walled cell in Berlin. Falk, meanwhile, metamorphosed once again into Blumenthal, the bourgeois Jewish Berliner.

'Well, Herr Doktor,' he beamed at Pyke. 'It's about time we were going on.' Turning to the soldier: 'It's a bit late, isn't it?'

With Tiggerish confidence Falk bounced to his feet and made to leave.

'What are you doing here?' the soldier asked again, firmly.

Falk gave him everything he had – the Imperial Pedestrian Touring Club, their walking holiday, his friend's exams, the exhaustion resulting in Pyke not being able to speak so much and the line about both men being unfit for active military service. The soldier looked unimpressed. Neither before the war, nor during it, had the German-Dutch frontier been a popular hiking destination. Even if it had been, these two looked like vagrants, not hikers. To Pyke, in his gloom, Falk's story sounded like one of those improbable, rambling lies that you tell a teacher, in which you rattle along at great speed 'until a full stop is reached in the middle of a sentence, and you wait for the verdict'.

Pyke could not wait. He knew all too well about being arrested in Germany and wanted to get the next part out of the way. 'I ached with the thought that I was nothing but a fatuous dreamer after all; that it was impossible for anybody ever to escape the great arm of Prussian organisation; that I might have known they'd catch us here.'

'That is no satisfactory explanation as to why you are in Holland,' said the soldier.

Silence. Constellations of calculations exploded in each man's mind.

Was this a trick?

'I have no business in Holland of any sort,' Falk wavered. 'This is Germany.'

'Not at all,' the soldier replied. 'What's more, you will have to come with me to see the frontier section Commandant at Losser; you are probably smugglers.'

Losser was in Holland – the neutral territory they had been aiming for all along.

More stupefied silence and anxious looks between Falk and Pyke, Pyke and the soldier, the soldier and both of them, Falk and the soldier and back once more to Pyke.

'If you don't believe me,' he said, 'look at this.' He removed his helmet to reveal the red cockade of the Dutch military.

At this Falk leapt up, grabbed him by the lapels and began to rock him back and forth, pleading, 'Is this really Holland?'

Only when the soldier failed to push him away did both Englishmen realise that they were safe. 'No German soldier can be shaken by a tramp,' explained Falk.

'You see that red-roofed cottage over there?' The soldier pointed at a building some fifty yards away. 'That cottage is in Holland. The rain from its roof drips off into Germany. We call this the three-posts corner.' Now his expression became quizzical. 'How did you get through the German sentries along the road and railway line? They shot a Russian officer who tried to get across last month'.

Their answer was simple and implausible: they had crawled over the German-Dutch frontier the night before without a moment's thought. The railway line and road that they had crossed absent-mindedly had been the actual frontier. The German cavalry unit which had almost ridden over them as they hid beneath their loden cloaks had probably been a border patrol.

Despite its bizarre conclusion, Falk and Pyke had pulled off the first escape from German captivity of the Great War. There would be seventy-two attempted getaways from Ruhleben in total, all of which except this and two others would fail.

Realising what they had done, the two escapees turned to each other in shock. Had this scene played out today they might have embraced – perhaps there would have been tears. Instead, they shook hands. 'To him I feel only as those who have been hunted for together, who have lain shuddering in hiding with a price upon their heads, can feel,' wrote Pyke. They were bound together by a hard-won complicity and the knowledge that each one owed his freedom and his life to the other. The two 'realists' of Ruhleben had used science and detective fiction to find a way out of Germany, and in doing so had developed an acute understanding both of one another and the society which they had just left. Their escape was a monument to counter-intuition and the intellectual bravery it requires. As well as doing the opposite of what had been expected at every turn they had had the courage to contemplate escape in the first place, without which none of this would have been possible.

For Pyke the last two months had been the final test in a year-long, self-taught apprenticeship in the art of solving problems. He had learnt to set aside the fear of failure or ridicule and to endure what H. G. Wells had called the 'daily agony' of scrutinising accepted facts. He had come to appreciate the importance of asking the right question and ensuring that his wording was correct. He had also come to understand something about theft and the nature of disguise. Each lesson was rooted in the landscape of his mind for the rest of his life. Indeed, this adventure tells us more than any other about the man he would later become.

Olde Daalhuis, the Dutch soldier, led them away from the firs and when they reached the frontier post he asked cheekily if they wanted to meet the German sentries.

'No,' came the emphatic reply.

In Overdinkel they picked up beers and cigars for the journey to Losser.

'*Gott strafe England*,' teased the Dutch sergeant as they walked in – 'May God punish England.' Satisfied that they were not smugglers, he made them coffee and sandwiches before finding them a hotel for the night.

'Oh, the joy of that first bath!' exclaimed Falk. 'Our host, Mr Smid, looked after us in a most exemplary manner, and we slept that night in feather beds, rising next day to find clean underwear in our rooms.'

That morning, with a pathetic fallacy that would almost certainly be edited out of a novel, the sun shone after a fortnight of heavy rain. Falk went to church to give thanks for their deliverance, Pyke began to write up their escape, and later that day they took the train to Amsterdam.

By now both men had run out of money so Pyke wired Ernest Perris at the *Chronicle*. No doubt he was astonished to hear from him and sent over 'a generous cheque'. Before that arrived they persuaded the British Consul to lend them £10 to secure a room in the Hotel Doelen. Although this happened to be where most of Amsterdam's German intelligence agents were based, the two fugitives would not be there long enough to arouse their interest.

That evening Pyke and Falk were picked up by a group of fellow Britons who took them out for a slap-up celebratory meal. The following day Pyke sent his cable to the *Chronicle*. At the start of the war, as Reuters' Special Correspondent in Copenhagen, Pyke had dreamt of writing a dispatch for the front page of a national newspaper. Now he was in that rare position of being not only the author of front-page national news but also its subject.

The Daily Chronicle

MONDAY, JULY 26, 1915.

A 'DAILY CHRONICLE'

CORRESPONDENT'S

ESCAPE FROM RUHLEBEN

TRAMP BY NIGHT THROUGH THE ENEMY COUNTRY.

SUFFERING IN A PRISON CELL.

We received last night the following cable from Mr Geoffrey L. Pyke, who started out from England shortly after the war broke out, in order to study economic conditions in Germany.

AMSTERDAM. July 25.

After ten months of imprisonment in Germany I rejoice to announce that I have escaped, and at last find myself in hospitable Holland.

[*continues for another 1,500 words*]

There followed a strangely stilted report of his escape, including details he contradicted in later accounts, such as a line about Berlin being 'mainly peopled by women'. The story published by the *Chronicle* was in fact a heavily edited version of Pyke's 3,000-word telegram. It was the young journalist's first experience of news being shaped to fit an agenda, and it left a dent in his relationship with Perris.

Another problem was the consequence of the meal that Pyke had enjoyed on his first night in Amsterdam. The men who had taken him and Falk out were journalists working for the *Chronicle*'s rivals. Either they reneged on an agreement not to report the escape or Pyke had failed to lay down guidelines. In any event, what should have been a sensational scoop for the *Chronicle* was anything but, as Perris discovered to his dismay over the next few days.

The Times.

MONDAY, 26 JULY, 1915.

CIVILIANS' ESCAPE FROM RUHLEBEN.

FORTNIGHT'S TRAMP TO HOLLAND.

The Manchester Guardian

MONDAY, JULY 26, 1915.

ENGLISHMEN ESCAPE FROM GERMAN CAMP.

AMAZING 'WALKING TOUR' FROM BERLIN.

THE SCOTSMAN

MONDAY, JULY 26, 1915.

PRISONERS ESCAPE.

ADVENTUROUS JOURNEY FROM RUHLEBEN.

Daily Mail

MONDAY, JULY 26, 1915.

ESCAPE FROM RUHLEBEN.

The Daily Telegraph

TUESDAY, 27 July, 1915.

DARING ESCAPE
FROM
RUHLEBEN CAMP.

JOURNALIST'S ADVENTURE.

The Aberdeen Free Press.

TUESDAY, JULY 27, 1915.

FIGHT FOR FREEDOM

AN ESCAPE FROM RUHLEBEN

FUGITIVES' ADVENTUROUS JOURNEY

The story of their escape went around the country like a rumour in Ruhleben, and two days after it broke Falk and Pyke took a mail packet from Holland back to England. Falk watched for the coastline and when it came into sight began to cry. Pyke, retracing the journey that his ancestor Moses Snoek had made in the eighteenth century, was below deck, being seasick. At Tilbury there was a telegram waiting for him, not from his mother or an overjoyed relative, but from Robert Donald, Editor of the *Chronicle*, who had written to congratulate him on his safe return. It was a gesture that Pyke never forgot, yet it would take more than this to repair his relationship with the newspaper.

In the days that followed, Pyke and Falk were received by the Prime Minister, Herbert Asquith, and for an instant they became celebrities. Yet for those working in a secret government department, one that did not officially exist, the story of their escape jarred.

Like most well-informed Britons, the staff of what would soon become MI5 were certain that escape from Ruhleben camp was more or less out of the question. The idea that two bedraggled Englishmen, including one who did not speak fluent German, had travelled incognito from Ruhleben into the centre of Berlin seemed to be impossible. To then make it all the way to the Dutch frontier was inconceivable, and subsequently to crawl into Holland, as these two claimed to have done, was truly beyond belief. Their escape did not add up, unless, that was, they had been helped along the way.

PYKE HUNT, PART 1

By the summer of 1915 Major Vernon Kell was on the lookout for a different kind of German spy. Kell was a lantern-jawed asthmatic who kept a parrot at home and, since its inception, had been Director of MO5(g), the War Office department later renamed MI5. He had started the war on a high after the dramatic arrest of twenty-two suspected German agents, many of them employed by Nachrichten-Abteilung, or 'N', the German Admiralty's intelligence service.

Since then the landscape had changed. Kell's department was now up against both 'N' and its military counterpart, Sektion IIIb, an adjustment reflected in the new wave of German spies being sent over to Britain. With the war no more than a year old, the latest agents tended to be non-Germans who had spent time inside a German jail, travelled on an American passport and posed as salesmen. When Geoffrey Pyke returned to England in July 1915 he was a non-German who had spent time in a German jail and had posed as a salesman while travelling on an American passport. It was not long before Kell's department made the connection.

The Department of Prisoners of War was the first to ask MO5(g) about Pyke after he had failed to appear at a routine Home Office appointment. 'We do not appear to have any papers about "Pike",' came the reply.

Had the Security Service checked the spelling they would have found a bulging Personal File devoted to this young man. It contained copies of telegrams he had sent from Copenhagen the previous year, evidence of his illegal entry into Germany disguised as Raymund Eggleton, and an account of an MO5(g) investigation into Pyke's uncle, who had cabled his nephew about his grandmother's health – a telegram which was thought to be a coded message.

Instead his Personal File went unopened and, while there were those in Kell's department with grave suspicions about the nature of Pyke's so-called 'escape', there were no grounds on which to have him arrested or to ask for his letters to be opened. As well as being medically unfit for military service, Pyke could not be called up now that he had been imprisoned by the enemy. Instead, he was left to finish his university degree – at least for now.

Cambridge felt like a very different city to the one Pyke remembered from before the war. By September 1915 its undergraduate population was a quarter of what it had been; his college, Pembroke, was dominated by an Officer Training School, and the streets were filled with convalescent soldiers, many of them missing limbs or suffering from the effects of poison gas. It was impossible to escape the war, and rather than lose himself in his law degree Pyke found his mind wandering back at the slightest provocation to Ruhleben. In his spare time he wrote about his experiences. He sent food parcels to his fellow detainees, including one with a false bottom that contained a detailed account of his escape; unfortunately the recipients were so excited by the food that they failed to look for any hidden compartment.

Keeping an eye on him at Pembroke was his tutor, W. S. Hadley, who recognised a change in Pyke. It worried him. Towards the end of that Michaelmas term Hadley took an unusual step. He contacted the local Chief Constable about Pyke, explaining that he was 'not a desirable person to have here' and that the police should keep an eye on him.

This is strange, largely because Hadley mentioned nothing specific about Pyke's behaviour. Nor did he attempt to have him sent down. Clearly the university rules and the laws of the land had not, to his knowledge, been broken. Instead we are left the outline of a vague animus. For this patrician figure of authority there was something about Geoffrey Pyke – and he was either unwilling or unable to put his finger on precisely what – that made him suspicious. Perhaps it had its roots in his intelligence combined with the unusual nature of his escape, or maybe his Jewishness changed the way Hadley thought about him.

Whatever it was, the Chief Constable did nothing about Hadley's note until he read, several days later in a local newspaper, about a public lecture that Pyke had given in aid of the Ruhleben detainees. It was an account of his escape, a talk that he would give repeatedly over the coming years. What concerned the Chief Constable was not the lecture but its introduction.

Eminent literary critic Sir Arthur Quiller-Couch had told a full house at the Guildhall that what Geoffrey Pyke might go on to say 'neither included nor suggested any controversial matter. If it did, that platform would be no place for him, and if he only guessed or believed that it did, he would not be there, and he imagined that in spite of things foolishly said from time to time, they were a united nation.' The room had thundered with applause before Pyke stood up to speak. As far as the newspaper report allowed, he did not suggest any 'controversial matter'. Yet for the Chief Constable the possibility that he *might* have done was enough in itself.

'You must remember,' wrote the historian A. J. P. Taylor, 'that the civilian enthusiasts for the First World War developed a hysteria almost wholly absent in the second.' Even in Cambridge, with its tradition of dissent and religious nonconformity, public expressions of anything less than outright patriotism were rare. Britain had been gripped by a desire for collective discipline and displays of public unity and the mere suggestion that one was capable of delivering 'controversial matter' was serious.

The Chief Constable in Cambridge decided to contact the Home

Office about Pyke. He followed up his initial call with a letter to the Inspector of the Constabulary asking for Pyke's correspondence to be monitored. The matter was passed on to MO5(g), where Vernon Kell organised a warrant for Pyke's post to be opened.

Pyke was described by the Cambridge Chief Constable – who never met him – as 'a very unsettled sort of person'. Add this to Hadley's account of him as 'not a desirable person', or Quiller-Couch's warning that he might deliver 'controversial matter', and a picture emerges of an individual who was hard to place, singular and irregular. For those in the Home Office, the Police and the Security Service this, together with his dubious 'escape', was more than enough to warrant a letter-check.

It revealed almost nothing, for Pyke was no longer living at home. Only when fresh reports came in from the most unlikely quarter did MI5 realise where this young man was and what he might be up to.

Admiral Denison could not believe his eyes. This retired naval officer, who had spent more than three decades at sea, had witnessed a feat of sailing in Falmouth Harbour so astonishing that it raised his hackles. Earlier that day a man who claimed to have no 'previous knowledge of yachting' had asked him, as Senior Naval Officer at Falmouth, for permission to take his yacht beyond the harbour limits. Denison then watched in disbelief as this novice succeeded 'in manoeuvring, single-handed, the 10-ton yacht in Falmouth Harbour; but to anybody with a knowledge of yachting this feat is so remarkable, if not impossible, as to throw considerable doubts on the whole story'. This was not the only problem that Admiral Denison had with Geoffrey Pyke's story.

Pyke had also claimed that the yacht was his, but did not produce proof of ownership. Then there was his letter of introduction from Admiral Charles Napier, apparently a family friend from his father's days as Leader of the Admiralty Bar, which he had failed to show Denison 'until the day he left (15 June), and it would appear that he had then completed the business on which he was engaged and for which it is possible this introduction was to be used as a cover'. Cover for what, exactly?

On 21 June 1916, Denison's report on the suspicious behaviour of 'Geoffrey Pike' as he sailed out beyond the harbour limits – perhaps to deliver material or pick up fresh instructions – arrived on the desk of one of MI5's longest-serving officers, Reginald 'Duck' Drake, head of 'G Branch', who was responsible for cases of suspected espionage, sedition or treason. This time the misspelling of Pyke's surname was corrected straight away.

Drake found the report 'disquieting'. He began by asking the Chief Constable in Bodmin for more information on Pyke's 'movements and associates at Falmouth, and if possible, his present whereabouts'. In his letter he included an outline of Pyke's escape from Germany, stressing that this story contained 'awkward gaps in material points, so much so, that there are suspicions that his "escape" was effected with the collusion of the German authorities'. After this, Drake contacted the country's best-known detective.

Basil 'Spycatcher' Thomson was the flamboyant head of Special Branch and the Criminal Investigation Department (CID), a man whose career had included stints as an Iowan farmer, Governor of Dartmoor Prison and Assistant Prime Minister of Tonga. Though notorious for taking credit where it was not due – before the end of the war Drake would refer to him as a 'dirty dog' – 'Spycatcher' Thomson was a fine detective.

Drake set him to work on Geoffrey Pyke, asking him to find out precisely what this 'unsettled' undergraduate was doing in Falmouth and, in particular, whether he had recently visited Harwich. German agents working for 'N' had been known to visit major ports and seeing that Pyke had been acting strangely at Falmouth, 'whence he disappeared under circumstances rather suspicious', evidence of him at Harwich would be enough for an arrest.

Even before Thomson could begin his investigation, Drake received further intelligence from Cornwall where the MI5 District Intelligence Director, whose purview included Falmouth, had reported the suspicious 'movements of a boat owned by *PIKE*'. Again the word 'suspicious' was left undefined, the ambiguity only adding to its potency.

Two days later Drake heard back from 'Spycatcher' Thomson after he had completed a long interview with Perris at the *Chronicle*. Thomson felt as though he had the measure of Pyke, describing him as having done 'brilliantly' at Cambridge and someone who 'boasts of having no nationality; he is a friend of Bertrand Russell; is concerned in the editorship of the *Cambridge Magazine*; and is probably a Sinn Feiner and everything else that goes with that class of mind. His father is a K. C. who does not at all share his son's views.'

This was largely because Lionel Pyke had been dead for seventeen years. Otherwise this section of Thomson's report on Pyke reads like an MI5 checklist of undesirable anti-war affiliations, which only confirmed their initial suspicions. Bertrand Russell, for example, was known to MI5 as a pacifist and a prominent member of the Union of Democratic Control (UDC), one of many organisations campaigning against either military conscription or the war itself, all of which had become more of a worry in light of the new German policy of *Revolutionierungspolitik*, designed to slow down the British war effort from within. One of the few mainstream publications fully sympathetic to Russell and those of his ilk was the *Cambridge Magazine*. Thomson was absolutely right about his involvement.

Pyke's formal title was London Advertising Manager, yet he appears to have had an informal editorial role as well in a magazine that had changed beyond recognition from the light-hearted university publication for which he had written before the war. By 1916 it was leaner and more internationalist with a nationwide circulation of 20,000. Its output was later described as 'a dazzling display of Dissent at its most aridly intellectual level'. Thomas Hardy, for one, 'read the

Magazine every week', as it would 'enable one to see England as bare and unadorned, her chances in the struggle freed from distortion by the glamour of patriotism'.

The *Cambridge Magazine* – and the same could be said of Pyke – was not just anti-war but opposed to the principle of defensive nationalism on which war had been waged. Pyke's claim that he had no nationality was not a rejection of his country so much as a protest against the idea which permeated parts of Fleet Street whereby Germans were all inherently militaristic and should be fought to the last man. The *Cambridge Magazine* pushed for a negotiated armistice rather than a knockout blow, on the grounds that this would make for an enduring peace. Pyke later acknowledged that this stance marked him out as 'almost a traitor to my country'. Yet he did not waver. Tellingly the fear of being called a traitor was not enough to change his political position.

While Thomson's report gives us a fascinating glimpse of the man Geoffrey Pyke was becoming, it supplied MI5 with little to get its teeth into – but for one detail. Perris had revealed that Pyke 'intended going to Scandinavia' and 'in the meantime he meant to learn how to manage a boat, and for that purpose was going down to Cornwall'.

What was he planning to do in Scandinavia? Why had he told Perris? More importantly, how did the boat fit in?

As Drake considered his next move, two Cornish policemen tracked down Pyke to St Mawes, a fishing village across the water from Falmouth, where they began 'secret observations'. Every day they watched Pyke leave his boarding house, walk to the harbour and take out his yacht. As Perris had suggested, he seemed to be in training. One night the two policemen stole onto his boat in the hope of finding incriminating material but they came away empty-handed.

Unlike Admiral Denison, however, the local policemen were less than impressed with Pyke's seamanship. 'With reference to his handling the Yacht, I have seen him sailing it on six occasions,' wrote

PC Tonkin, 'and I think that he has no practical knowledge of sailing her, and it is only by good luck that he has not come to some misfortune.'

Otherwise there was little to report. Drake told them to keep an eye on him, as Pyke was 'quite likely to do something foolish as he loves notoriety', and 'should he transgress in any way, he should be prosecuted immediately'. Yet before Drake's message could reach Cornwall the two policemen had a breakthrough.

On the morning of 6 July 1916, just days after the start of the Battle of the Somme, the bloodiest battle in British history, these two Cornish policemen watched Geoffrey Pyke leave St Mawes, noting with hopeful precision the colour of his bag (yellow) and the initials on his case (those of his father). They then called on the guest house where he had been staying.

'Whilst Mr Pyke was out in his yacht, yesterday,' the landlady explained, 'a telegram came for him. When he came in, he read it and said that he had to go to Scandinavia in a few days' time and that he would be leaving this morning.' Perris was right. Pyke really was planning to go to Scandinavia. Even more remarkably, he appeared to be acting on instructions.

By the time this report arrived with MI5 in London, Pyke had been gone for three days, and even when leaving Cornwall he had somehow attracted further suspicion. A signals officer at St Anthony who knew nothing about the allegations against him contacted MI5 to report this young man's 'suspicious' behaviour.

This left Drake in a spot. He did not know why Pyke was heading to Scandinavia, with whom he was in contact, nor was he aware of how far he had travelled. All he knew was that Pyke must be stopped.

On 13 July 1916 the following directive was issued to all British ports, the Foreign Office, the Home Office, the Permit Office, Scotland Yard, the French High Command (GQG), Glasgow Police and MI1c (later known as MI6 or SIS).

P Y K E, Geoffrey

British subject, of Jewish origin, age 21.

Early in the war he was interned at Ruhleben, from whence he managed to escape. Latterly he has been staying at St Mawes, Cornwall.

He left St Mawes by the Bristol-Manchester train on the 6th instant. His present whereabouts are not known.

He should not be allowed to leave the United Kingdom.

At some point in the weeks that followed, Pyke attempted to leave the country but was stopped. Nothing survives from this incident apart from the covering slip on the CID report which includes an angry scribbled note, probably from Thomson:

'Couldn't this youth be nailed down by use of the Military Service Act?'

Pyke on board his yacht

'He is unfit for service,' went Drake's reply.

So why was Pyke trying to get to Scandinavia? It is possible that he hoped to sail into northern Germany, perhaps to write another article for Perris or to gather material for a second book: in the space of less than a year this twenty-two-year-old had become a best-selling author.

Pyke's account of his German adventure, *To Ruhleben – And Back*, was published by Constable in January 1916 to critical acclaim. He had written it in his spare time during his first term back at Cambridge. Just two months after publication it had gone into its fourth impression and an American edition had come out with Houghton Mifflin. Later that year a 'Popular Edition' came out; a new cloth edition followed in 1917; and eventually it would be described as 'one of the First World War's best sellers'. More recently, eighty-seven years after its initial publication, this book was reissued by the American publisher McSweeney's.

'He writes extraordinarily well,' went the *Punch* review, describing *To Ruhleben – And Back* as 'a piece of expansive writing'. *The Times* called it 'a very fine story of a great and perilous adventure'. 'The narrative of his escape is indeed thrilling,' according to the *Chicago Tribune*. 'Very exciting and very well told,' wrote the reviewer in the *Manchester Guardian*. '"Thrilling" has become a kind of courtesy epithet to apply to an adventure well described,' began the review in *Country Life*, where it was Book of the Week, 'but we can apply it sincerely to Mr Geoffrey Pyke's book. Mr Pyke not only had the pluck and the resource to carry out a nerve-shattering enterprise; he also has the ability to relate it brilliantly.'

The book belonged to the literary *zeitgeist* while at the same time transcended it. By 1916 the British reading public was swamped with war novels, some of which would be read for years to come, like John Buchan's *The Thirty-Nine Steps* and *Greenmantle*, while the others were formulaic romps centred on a self-deprecating, plucky hero who made light of the worst situations. *To Ruhleben – And Back* had elements of all this but was more expressive, better written and contained the rudiments of a *Bildungsroman*. It also had the considerable advantage of being true.

The only drawback was that Pyke's language could be too showy. But, as the critic in *Punch* put it, the author was 'too young and too clever (both charmingly venial faults) to write simply'. The *Spectator* echoed this. 'If sometimes his irreverent cleverness is a little oppressive, we may remember that he was only in his second year as a Cambridge undergraduate when the war broke out.'

If the language was occasionally too much, the story that Pyke told was imbued with personal modesty. Only Teddy Falk knew the truth of their escape and, as he would later write, Pyke failed to allude in this book to his 'indomitable doggedness' or his 'great courage in combating the physical distress caused him by a weak heart'.

This all adds to our image of the man Pyke was starting to become, one who had the imagination and gall to think of smuggling himself into an enemy nation as well as the courage to actually do it. He also had the modesty to downplay his own physical bravery, and the literary nous to write a best-selling book in less than two months. Though he had been subjected to four months of solitary confinement in Berlin and had almost died in Ruhleben for want of medical attention, he was prepared to campaign for a negotiated peace with Germany – even if this meant being cast as a pariah in the eyes of his family. In short, he was becoming a principled adventurer who seemed to be unencumbered by the need to conform.

The year after Pyke's attempt to leave the country the Security Service's interest in him spluttered back to life when the Detective Superintendent at CID asked angrily why someone like Pyke, who had escaped from Ruhleben, should be allowed to edit a 'pro-German publication' such as the *Cambridge Magazine*. Vernon Kell's response was to summon 'Spycatcher' Thomson again.

He asked him to find out where Pyke was living. Thomson ordered an observation to begin on Pyke's family home in Kensington, and several days later it was established that Pyke had left home the previous year after an explosive row with his mother.

Their quarrel arose out of Mary Pyke's reaction to her youngest son Richard's decision to become a conscientious objector. Rather than risk the social stigma of having a child who chose not to fight, she had co-opted relatives and friends into talking him down. Pyke loathed the idea that his mother would rather her younger son fought against his will than that she should be the subject of social disapproval. After a noisy argument Pyke left home for the last time. Yet as we shall see, this row belonged to a broader and more troubling sequence of confrontations between Geoffrey and Mary, and that for some time Pyke had been looking for an excuse to leave home.

Having worked out where Pyke was *not* living, MI5 discovered that he had been put up for membership of a new club that they were keeping tabs on. The '1917' was a Soho members' club described by Virginia Woolf as 'the centre of life'. Her husband called it the 'zenith of disreputability'. Named after the February Revolution of 1917, which led to the collapse of the Russian monarchy, the club's appeal went beyond traditional Bloomsbury and attracted figures like Ramsay MacDonald, Siegfried Sassoon and Henry Nevinson, as well as Bertrand Russell, Maynard Keynes and a full house of Stracheys and Sitwells. Which is not to say that the 1917 was ostensibly glamorous. One member described the 'overpowering aroma of stale cat'; Virginia Woolf complained about how ugly everyone was (she found most people ugly). 'Each time the door at the 1917 Club opens, a fresh deformity enters. I sit in a corner and stare in a kind of trance, as though one had fallen to the bottom of some awful pit in a nightmare. And they're all quite young – the coming generation – which makes it seem worse.'

Well known among these younger habitués of the 1917 was Geoffrey Pyke, author, escapee, undercover correspondent, minor Bloomsberry (as members of the Bloomsbury Group were sometimes known) and key member of staff at the anti-war *Cambridge Magazine*. Owing to his modicum of fame, when the news of his engagement appeared in the *Daily Sketch* it was accompanied by a photograph of his fiancée – which was cut out and added to his ever-expanding MI5 Personal File.

DAILY SKETCH.
SATURDAY, MAY 25, 1918.

Margaret Chubb on her engagement to Pyke, photograph by Hoppé

Pyke had only met Margaret Chubb for the first time five months earlier. A doctor's daughter from Kent, she had read History at Oxford before taking up a position in the War Office as Deputy Assistant to the Chief Controller of the Queen Mary's Army Auxiliary Corps. She was level-headed, brave and beautiful and, without meaning to, had shattered Pyke's resolve to avoid marriage.

As a teenager he would often quote Bernard Shaw to his siblings, indeed there were times when Shaw was the equivalent of a distant father-figure with a penchant for epigrams. In particular, Pyke liked to repeat Shaw's opinions on marriage, telling his brother and sisters that it was a dotty Victorian institution in need of reform. So everyone was surprised to hear about his engagement – including, it seems, Pyke himself.

Several weeks after Margaret had accepted his proposal she found him drawing up a list of reasons why they should not get married. It was in his nature to doubt, and to rationalise this doubt with himself before presenting it to anyone else, yet on this occasion Margaret was able to talk him round.

Several months later, on 8 June 1918, they were married in a London register office. Mary Pyke was not invited. After a honeymoon in the English countryside – Pyke was still on MI5's blacklist so even if he had wanted to he would have been unable to leave the country – the newly-weds set up in a small flat on Bouverie Street, just a stone's throw from the offices of the *Chronicle*. For perhaps the first time in his life Pyke described himself as content. His wife was everything that his mother was not: university-educated, balanced, loving, undemanding and employed. She had a calming effect on him, and this appeared to be a marriage of equals. Both husband and wife shared a manifest sense that British society was about to enter a post-war age in which everything they took for granted could be recast, traditions sundered and the rules of life written again. But it was not until they had a child that their role in this became clear.

During the Great War, MI5 never found evidence of Pyke doing anything more suspicious than making plans to go sailing off the Scandinavian coast. There was certainly no proof that he and Teddy Falk had escaped from Ruhleben with German assistance. Nonetheless, his name was retained for some years in a 'Special File' of those banned from travelling overseas.

It would be just under twenty years before he came to the attention of MI5 again and, though the world was coloured then by a new set of concerns, their suspicions about this man were dogged by some of the same prejudices. For the British Security Service it seemed that the problem with Geoffrey Pyke was not so much his irreverence, his cleverness or his Jewishness – though the combination of all three did little to endear him – it was the sense that they never quite knew what he was going to do next.

HOW TO RAISE YOUR CHILD
(AND PAY FOR IT)

———————

Pyke's reaction to the birth of his son David in the summer of 1921 was to book himself an appointment to see a psychoanalyst. Although Dr James Glover became 'so charmed and so overwhelmed that the analysis fell apart', Pyke came away with what he wanted. He had gone to Glover for a Freudian insight into a problem that had been troubling him for years, namely, how to give your child a truly enlightened upbringing. Many parents may ask themselves a similar question as they face parenthood for the first time. Few will go as far as Pyke in their pursuit of an answer. It was not that he felt the responsibility of being a parent more than anyone else, rather that he was starting from scratch. As he adjusted to his new life as a father, to the responsibility, the wonder and the occasional sleepless nights, his overriding desire was that his son's childhood should have nothing in common with his own.

Although he wrote so much during his adult life – to a degree that suggests a compulsion, graphomania – among the millions of words that Pyke committed to paper almost none refer to his upbringing or to his mother. His younger brother Richard compensated for this omission with his first book, *The Lives and Deaths of*

Roland Greer, published in 1928, a *roman à clef* that focused to the exclusion of all else (including a plot) on the relationship between the four Pyke siblings as children and their mother Mary, barely disguised in the novel as 'Myra'.

Lionel and Mary Pyke, seated, with their
eldest daughter Dorothy

Written in the wake of Mary's death, while Richard underwent psychoanalysis, it is a stark and often unforgiving portrait of a woman unable to reconcile herself to widowhood. 'What had been even in favourable circumstances a hasty temper and a shrew's tongue were transformed by grief, a sense of isolation, and a hatred for all women who were not bereaved, into savage misogyny and a lashing speech that knew nothing of conventions. Half of her was dead, and four ghosts stayed to mock her. As ghosts they haunted her; as at ghosts she lunged at them; like ghosts they left her no spiritual peace.' In time she grew to love her children, but it was a bullying, paranoid kind of love, that of a dictator towards the masses. 'Myra was consumed by the feeling that she must fight. It was only thus that her love found an outlet. And fight she did – relatives and servants, strangers and tradesmen; brothers, sisters, mother, children.' Richard described her 'hurricane shakings' and the memory of her 'fist flourished villainously under his nose, her teeth clenched, her eyes flashing crazy passion, and her face dark red with murder'. His elder brother bore the brunt of this. For Richard the most explosive relationship in that household, the one that seemed to embody its immanent tension, was between Mary and Geoffrey – or Myra and Daniel.

In the book, Daniel is 'irresistibly impelled by his mother's widow-hood and his cruelly exploited ambition to fill a father's place, and to assume responsibilities from which he should have been exempt for many years'. As well as being told, from the age of five, that he was the man of the house, Daniel became Myra's 'only formidable opponent, if not her equal'. In one exchange, aged fourteen, Daniel / Geoffrey physically restrains his mother 'with an expression of utter horror, such as he might have worn if forcing himself to touch a mutilated corpse'. Keeping hold of her, 'he pushed his elbows outwards and forced them up, thus twisting her wrists round and holding them down'. On wriggling free Myra began to beat him 'on the side of his head as hard as she could'. Richard later described to a friend how his 'mother chased them round the dining-room table with a carving knife, and once held Richard out of a third-floor window to frighten him into good behaviour'.

The effect of all this on the four siblings was profound. As a teenager, Pyke maintained that he would never have children for nobody should endure what he had gone through. From an early age the Pykes began to distance themselves from their mother and took to 'playing at pork butchers and drawing crosses' in the face of her growing religious conservatism. The more she urged her sons to provide her with Jewish daughters-in-law the stronger their determination to do otherwise. Mary's elder daughter converted to Christianity, broke all ties with her mother and left home in her early twenties; both of her sons became committed atheists; one refused to talk to her for the last years of her life.

The Pyke siblings: (left to right) Dorothy,
Richard, Geoffrey and Evelyn

For Richard, this troubled and at times violent upbringing also had the effect of oversensitising all four children. 'Not only could their emotions be roused far more easily, but they were roused to a far higher pitch, and far oftener, than should have been.' As well as echoing Mary's Manichean mood swings the children became familiar from an early age with inconsistency and contradiction. If, as F. Scott Fitzgerald wrote, 'the test of a first-rate intelligence is the ability to hold two opposing ideas in mind at the same time and still retain the ability to function', then the Pyke children were precocious.

Of course it was hard for Mary to raise four children in the more straitened circumstances which followed Lionel's death. Her neuralgia came and went and she was tragically unable to resolve herself to the death of her beloved husband. Perhaps it is unfair to highlight her violent outbursts and the way her children turned against her. But she made mistakes, and for Pyke one of the most egregious was her choice of where, aged thirteen, he should go to school.

By then, Pyke's atheism and lack of discipline were causing his mother real concern. After five happy years boarding at St Edmund's, Hindhead, a preparatory school in Sussex, Pyke was not sent to a Jewish day-school in London, where so many of his cousins went. Instead his mother packed him off to Wellington College, the 'military Lycée' in Berkshire which embodied the sporty, strict, empire-building ethos of a nineteenth-century public school, and where, at Mary's insistence, Pyke was to be treated as an observant Jew. He was forbidden from attending lessons or playing sports on the Jewish Sabbath, he had to wear slightly different clothes from the other boys and kosher food was prepared for him at every meal. All this in a school where there had never before been a practising Jew.

He later recalled the sensation of 'running as fast as your panting breathing will allow you, with a rabble of respectable people thundering and shouting after you. You have only got to see a real man-hunt once in your life, for all your sympathy to go to the hunted.' This strange spectacle, he added, 'can always be seen at any really good public school'.

Like sharks scenting blood, packs of teenage boys will pick up on the slightest difference in their ranks and even without his Jewishness paraded like this, the young Geoffrey Pyke was the odd one out at Wellington. He was taller than most and brighter. He was no good at games. None of his family had been in the military. His father was dead. He loved to read. He did not live in the country and had never shot an animal. The bullying that followed was relentless and at times systematic. As well as opportunistic attacks – his brother referred to 'malicious devils' brandishing 'wetted towels' – there were moments when whole sections of the school chased him along the corridors yelling 'Jew Hunt!' or just 'Pyke Hunt!'

After two miserable years, Mary took him out, and until the age of eighteen Pyke was tutored at home before going up to Cambridge in 1912.

Five years later he was asked to give a talk at Wellington about his escape from Ruhleben. Having run through the first set of lantern slides he described his arrest and the moment when he was told that he would be shot in the morning. The young Wellingtonians were rapt. 'Yet when things were at their worst in Germany,' he told them, 'even when I was quite certain I'd be taken out and shot as a spy, I was never quite so unhappy, never so completely miserable as I'd been when I was a boy here at Wellington.'

It was not just the bullying and the casual anti-Semitism which had worn him down, so much as the unimaginative teaching and relentless emphasis on discipline for discipline's sake. George Orwell, briefly at Wellington soon after Pyke, described the school as 'beastly'. The author, politician and publisher Harold Nicolson, another contemporary, described being 'terribly and increasingly bored' there. 'One ceased so completely to be an individual, to have nay but a corporate identity.' Nicolson later 'blamed the Wellington system for retarding him mentally and socially'. Naturally Pyke did not want his son to endure anything similar. So where to send him instead?

Perhaps this was the wrong question. The problem might not be with Wellington *per se* but the English educational system as a whole.

The early 1920s was later described by Evelyn Waugh as 'the most dismal period in history for an English schoolboy'. The expression 'spare the rod and spoil the child' was not yet a historical curiosity and in schools up and down the country the ghost of Dr Arnold stalked the battlements. Arnold was the Rugby schoolmaster who had done more than any other to change the character of so many English schools – until 'an English public schoolboy who wears the wrong clothes and takes no interest in football, is a contradiction in terms', as Lytton Strachey had pointed out several years earlier. 'Yet it was not so before Dr Arnold; will it always be so after him?' The assumption for most British parents was that yes, it would. The character of these institutions appeared to be entrenched, the people running them had little incentive to change and it was hard to see why or how things would evolve.

As he had done in the face of those who believed that no Englishman could slip into Germany undetected, or that escape from Ruhleben was impossible, Pyke challenged these verities. In the months after David's birth he reached a pivotal realisation. To give his son the education he wanted for him he must set up his own school. Of course he had no experience of teaching and only an amateur interest in educational theory. Even if he was able to get down on paper a convincing outline of a radical new establishment, it was hard to see how he could persuade any parents to offer their children for this scholastic experiment. This was a risk he would have to take.

Over the following months he developed the blueprint for a new kind of school, one that would go further than existing progressive models such as Bedales, Abbottsholme, The King Alfred School or St Christopher's in Letchworth Garden City, and take in children at a younger age. It drew on the painful lessons he had learnt growing up and combined them with ideas filleted from Rousseau, contemporary philosophy, psychology and Freudian psychoanalysis. Underpinning it all was his ardent belief that each of us arrives in the world as a scientist in the making, that as children we are naturally inquisitive and will conduct experiments in order to understand the world around us. This new school would be revolutionary and scientific. It would also be hugely expensive to set up. If David Pyke was to have the ultra-modern upbringing his parents wanted then they would have to raise a lot of money, and fast. In many ways this was an even greater challenge.

Pyke and his son David in 1922

Pyke's job at the time was poorly paid and precarious. He had been employed by the *Cambridge Magazine* since 1916, and while he had always seen this as a cause as much as a livelihood, identifying with its internationalist anti-war perspective, the demand for such publications had evaporated since the Treaty of Versailles. In 1922, Pyke was asked to dispose of its most valuable asset, a weekly survey of the foreign press. He sold it to the *Manchester Guardian*, and later that year the magazine folded. Very soon after, another pillar in his life began to totter: Mary Pyke told her children that she was dying of cancer.

Having refused to see her during the previous five years, Pyke now visited her in the nursing home – in body if not in spirit. He had cut her out of his sentimental attachments with such finality that now it was as if he was seeing her for the first time. Mary did not seem to notice. Indeed, as she lay there surrounded by her four uncomplaining children, her sense of family, as Victorian as it was Jewish, was at last satisfied. Over the days that followed her face greyed, the cancer spread and the daily dosage of drugs was increased. Her stream of complaints about the nursing staff petered out, and on 18 August 1922, aged 57, she died.

Her corpse was taken to Willesden Green Cemetery where just one exception was made to the orthodox Jewish ritual. Following her instructions, Mary Pyke was buried wearing her wedding ring. Pyke found the funeral shocking and lonely, and would later urge his son to stay away from his, describing it as 'a silly business'.

The death of his mother and the end of the *Cambridge Magazine* produced in Pyke an overwhelming urge to get away, and the next month his passport application was finally approved. He had been removed from MI5's Blacklist. Yet this was not in response to fresh intelligence which exonerated him from suspicion – indeed, five months later MI5 would refuse a request from the Passport Office to remove him from their 'Special File' – but he was free to leave the country and did so at once, setting off with Margaret for the Swiss Alps.

Geographically, emotionally, sexually, they had never felt so free. Though married and in love, neither claimed a proprietorial hold on the other. Even if this went against the gospel according to

Shaw, who wrote that 'a real marriage of sentiment [. . .] will break very soon under the strain of polygamy or polyandry', the Pykes professed a looser sexual morality, not in a bohemian spirit of laissez-faire but as part of what they saw as a more scientific approach to life.

The Pykes on honeymoon

The word 'scientific' had a particular resonance by then. Once confined to machines and laboratories, there was a fashionable new sense that a scientific perspective could be applied to everything. Science could do away with all traditional assumptions – indeed, the word had come to stand for a youthful rejection of what one's parents had taken for granted. Shaw envisaged a society dominated by scientifically minded 'engineer-inventors'; H.G. Wells referred to 'scientific samurais', the men and women of tomorrow who would rise to the top by dint of their ruthless intellectual technique, slicing through a thicket of outdated prejudices. While there was nothing new about this urge to cast off Victorian certainties – journalists, novelists and playwrights had been doing this since the turn of the century – by the early 1920s this project had a pronounced urgency. The blind slaughter of the trenches seemed to be evidence of what happened when society was run according to traditional precepts. The Soviet Union, dazzling in its potential, suggested that it was possible to reinvent an ancient nation along more scientific lines. This was not to say that a scientific attitude must always be left-wing, only that it implied starting from scratch. For the likes of Geoffrey and Margaret Pyke, science allowed for a modern perspective on everything from sexual morality to warfare, the education of children and, of course, the business of making a lot of money quickly.

In late 1922, having sublet his Bloomsbury flat at 41 Gordon Square to Maynard Keynes, the renowned economist who had recently made and lost a fortune in currency trades, Pyke began a meticulous and what he called 'highly scientific' study of the financial markets. This was where he hoped to make his money. While it is tempting to imagine him discussing some of his ideas with his new tenant, Keynes, the economic heavyweight of the twentieth century, there is no evidence of this. Nor did he consult any of his cousins who worked in the City, preferring instead to come at this subject as an outsider, a scientific samurai in search of an original insight.

The Pykes had moved from Gordon Square to Cambridge where they got to know one of Keynes's protégés, a brilliant yet hormonally charged undergraduate named Frank Ramsey. Earlier that year, aged nineteen and already a member of the Cambridge Apostles, perhaps the best known of all university secret societies, Ramsey had produced the first English translation of the philosopher Ludwig Wittgenstein's *Tractatus Logico-Philosophicus*, a feat made even more remarkable by the fact that he was then studying mathematics (and would later be awarded a stunning First). Ramsey was owlish and precocious, a prodigy for whom the solution of philosophical and mathematical problems came easily. Social relations were more confusing, and none more so than those which involved women.

Frank Ramsey

During the first few months of 1923 Ramsey saw the Pykes daily and at the same time became a close friend of Pyke's brother Richard, then reading Economics at King's College. Indeed, Ramsey got to know Geoffrey and Margaret so well that they asked him to become David's godfather – meant in a strictly non-religious sense for the Pykes and Ramsey were determined atheists. Whether or not Ramsey accepted, he was keen to maintain his close relationship with the Pyke family. By that stage of his life Frank Ramsey had become infatuated with Margaret Pyke.

Unaware of his feelings, the Pykes invited him to come away with them over Easter to Lake Orta, in the foothills of the Italian Alps. Noting with approval that Pyke claimed no 'proprietary rights' over his wife, so that if she 'announced she was going off with someone else he would be pleased because she was going to be happy', Ramsey accepted.

Pyke's study of the markets was acquiring greater focus. He had homed in on commodities futures and in particular the metals market, where he studied the relationship between the prices of tin, copper and lead as if they were the movements of the Ruhleben sentries. He wanted to know everything about them. He drew graphs charting their fluctuations and discussed these with friends from the London School of Economics. Yet by the time he set off for Italy no patterns had emerged and he appeared to be no closer to generating the fortune he needed for his pioneering school.

In the romantic setting of Lake Orta, Ramsey's feelings for Margaret became overwhelming until at last he decided to act. One hot afternoon the two of them went out together on the lake before settling down to read. Unable to concentrate on his book, Ramsey gazed over at Margaret, thinking to himself how 'superlatively beautiful' she looked in her horn glasses. At last he broke the silence.

'Margaret, will you fuck with me?' he asked.

Either she did not hear or, more likely, could not believe what he had said. Ramsey repeated the question.

'Do you want me to say yes or no?'

'Yes,' he exclaimed, 'or I wouldn't ask you!'

'Do you think once would make any difference?' she asked.

'I don't know, perhaps that is the question[.] I haven't thought it out,' he admitted. 'I just want to frightfully.'

Margaret was both open-minded and inoffensive. She said she needed time to think it over. Ramsey's response was to tell her that his psychoanalyst had warned him that if he did sleep with her he would probably be unable to perform. Relieved at having got this off his chest, Ramsey then went for a walk by the lake feeling 'awfully pleased at having some chance'.

On his return Margaret's response was a polite no. But this was not a total rejection. Back in Cambridge he kissed her for the first time and 'then came a wonderful afternoon when she let me touch her breasts, partly (I discovered) because she thought it was genuine curiosity'. Sadly we do not have Margaret's version of events.

Just before setting off for Austria that summer to find Ludwig Wittgenstein and talk him out of philosophical retirement – a trip that would change the course of twentieth-century philosophy – Frank Ramsey went to stay with the Pykes. He was dismayed to find that Margaret ignored him entirely, until 'Geoff told me as it were fortuitously that he probably only had two years to live and I understood M's behaviour and felt full of love for G and pity.'

There are no other references to Pyke's life-threatening illness except for a note he wrote around this time explaining how the news of his death should be relayed to David. 'The adaptation should be *gradual* and unaccompanied by any shock.' His son 'will tend to feel it tragic just so much [. . .] as the matter is treated tragically by those [with] whom he comes in contact'.

This tells us something about how the news of his own father's death was conveyed. Even at the end of his life, those close to Pyke suggested that he had never fully recovered from the shock of losing his father and it seems that the way this news was handled played a major part in this. As for his illness, all we know is that by the time Ramsey returned from Austria several months later Pyke had recovered. Yet Ramsey's infatuation with Margaret had, if anything, become worse.

The young philosopher decided to clear things up with a letter. 'I wrote and asked her if (1) I might caress her breasts (2) see her private parts (3) if she would masturbate me.' Margaret was not won over by this bullet-point approach – indeed, she found Ramsey's letter deeply upsetting – and for now he was forced to keep his distance.

Meanwhile Pyke put the finishing touches to his financial model. After months of painstaking research, he had developed a 'tentative hypothesis' about the relationship between the prices of copper and tin, two staples of the London Metal Exchange. He had found an inverse correlation between the two prices. Put simply, if the price of one went up, the other tended to go down. Within any futures market a mathematical relationship of this simplicity was the philosopher's stone. If accurate, he stood to earn a fortune.

Using money he had been left by a relative and some of the proceeds from his book, in the second half of 1923 Geoffrey Pyke took the greatest financial gamble of his life. As a newcomer to the metals market he gambled his savings on the basis of a home-made financial model.

During March 1924 three versions of an unusual advertisement appeared in successive issues of the *New Statesman and Nation*. 'WANTED—', each one began, 'an Educated Young Woman with honours degree – preferably first class – or equivalent, to conduct the education of a small group of children aged 2½–7, as a piece of scientific work and research.' The successful applicant, it went on, would receive a 'liberal salary'.

Pyke's financial model had worked. During the first six months of trading he was said to have earned £20,000 (more than £600,000 in today's money); Ramsey noted that Pyke 'now made £500 for every £1 the price rose, and so expected to make much more'. To generate these spectacular returns he had acquired debt, some of which was unsecured by real assets, but this was in the nature of this kind of speculation and in itself was not worrying. Far more important, just then, was the business of finding the right head teacher for David's new school.

The notices in the 'Staggers and Naggers' worked in the sense that they caused a stir. By 1924 the supply of teachers far outstripped the demand, so to have a teaching position advertised in this way was remarkable. Several readers of *Nature*, where a similar version of the notice had appeared, assumed that it was the work of white-slave traders planning to sell the unwitting applicants into bondage. Others were intrigued by the lines about preference being 'given to those who do not hold any form of religious belief', and that work would be preceded by six to eight months of paid training. Training in what, exactly?

Nathan Isaacs, a precocious and self-effacing German Jew who had fought for the British during the war and been gassed at Passchendaele, found his curiosity piqued by a different line. The advertisement had called for a woman who had 'hitherto considered herself too good for teaching'. Isaacs thought immediately of his wife, Susie.

She took one look and dismissed it as the work of a crank. Yet in the weeks that followed she spoke by chance to Dr James Glover, the psychoanalyst who had tried to analyse Pyke and was now on the school's board. He suggested that at the very least Susie should meet with Pyke. She looked at the advertisement again.

Susie Isaacs, then thirty-nine, was a wiry Lancastrian with thick blonde hair and a pale complexion who had a habit of jutting out her chin when animated. She was intelligent, bookish and driven. She had a rebellious streak. After her mother had died when she was six, she was raised by her father, an imposing Methodist preacher, who took her out of school when he heard that she had become a Fabian and an atheist. Following his death in 1909, independent at last, she went to the University of Manchester and was awarded a First in Philosophy before taking her Master's degree at Newnham

College, Cambridge. The following year she married the botanist William Brierley, but the marriage soon broke down, whereupon she went to London to develop her interest in psychoanalysis and write what would become a bestselling introduction to psychology. In 1921 she was psychoanalysed in Vienna by Otto Rank, a follower of Freud (whom she had hoped to be analysed by), before giving a lecture later that year that would change her life.

It had taken place at the Workers' Educational Association, in London, and in the audience had been Nathan Isaacs, ten years her junior. He pursued her, and soon they fell in love. Though the teacher-student dynamic never really disappeared, they became a tight fit intellectually, with Nathan more accommodating and perhaps lighter on his feet. Even if it meant that her teaching position had to end, Susie agreed to marriage.

Several years later they both went to meet Pyke for the first time. The three of them clicked almost immediately. The subject of that first conversation ranged from the boundaries of self-understanding and repressed sexual urges to the impact of childhood on one's adult psyche. Each one was fluent in the language of psychoanalysis, and over the following months Pyke 'lived almost as one of us', wrote Nathan, who went on to call him 'undoubtedly an educational genius!' Susie's feelings were more complicated.

As ever, Pyke did not imagine that he had all the answers. He wanted Susie and Nathan to help fill in the gaps and provide fresh angles on the existing problems, and out of these passionate, lively conversations during the summer of 1924 came Susie's appointment as Principal of the new school. Several months later, on 7 October, the three-year-old David Pyke was joined in a gabled former oast house in Cambridge by nine boys between the ages of two and four. Girls would soon follow. It was the first day of term at Malting House School, one of the boldest experiments in pre-school education anywhere in the world.

★

Imagine yourself to be one of those children. What would you have noticed as you began to explore the new school for the first time? For one thing, a lack of classrooms. Instead you would have ventured into a vast play area dominated by a piano (which you could play whenever you liked) and a space beyond filled with nothing but cushions and mattresses where you could take a nap. You would have also found that all the shelves and cupboards had been lowered to be at your height, something you had probably never seen before. Otherwise you might have been amazed by the piles of books, bulbs, beads, shells, counters and wooden blocks for you to investigate whenever you liked, as well as the mechanical lathe, two-handled saw, Bunsen burners, gramophone player and tools for dissecting animals – all of which you could use with the minimum of super-vision. As you would soon find out, from an improbably early age children at the Malting House were to become familiar with both the principles and reality of scientific experimentation.

The area you would have been most intrigued by – the one which children at Malting House spent more time in than any other – was the garden. Following Rousseau's idea that the most beneficial child development takes place outside, in nature, which was why early Malting House literature referred to the children as 'plants', the garden had been transformed over the summer into an edenic playground. You could climb the trees and look after the hens, rabbits, mice, salamanders, silkworms and snakes. You were given a garden plot to look after and could make bonfires to see how different matter burned. You could also clamber over a state-of-the-art climbing frame, which had been shipped in from abroad, or jump around on the lopsided see-saw with adjustable weights (to illustrate mechanical balance). If all this failed to capture your imagination you could always play in the giant sandpit which was sometimes flooded and turned into a pond.

If you were a particularly observant child, you might have noticed that in each room, at a level which you could not reach, there were books which the adults liked to write in. The Malting House was a scientific experiment as much as a school, and as such everything was to be recorded. Which child played with what, when, how, and the questions they asked, all of this was jotted down during the day and typed up later on. Too often in the past, felt Pyke, judgements about child development had been made first and supporting evidence found later. He wanted to spin this round. His school would be an environment in which almost all adult influences were removed, leaving children to be observed in their 'natural' state. This decision to record everything would be significant, and explains why Malting House went on to have such a lasting impact on British education. Yet what really distinguished it from other pre-schools and explains why it attracted the brightest toddlers in Cambridge, including the grandson of the Nobel Prize-winning chemist Sir Ernest Rutherford and the children of the philosopher G. E. Moore, had to do with what happened when a child asked a question.

Early on in the school's history one of the children asked the name of the funny-looking box into which adults sometimes talked. He was not told that it was a telephone. Instead it was *suggested* that *together* they call it 'a telephone'. Great emphasis was placed on allowing the children to feel as though they were discovering the world for themselves, even if they were often being steered towards the correct answers. Having worked out what to call it one of the children asked what it was for. The staff at Malting House never responded to a question like this with a straightforward statement of fact, and instead had been drilled to say, 'What do *you* think?' or, their favourite, 'Let's find out!' So rather than being told what this so-called 'telephone' was for, the children were asked to think of all the practical uses to which it could be put.

Here was another thread in the school's philosophy: discovery must be allied to utility. This was probably inspired by H. E. Armstrong's theory of heuristics, in which effective learning was associated with discovery as well as action. Rather than be told that it was important to learn, say, how to write, because that was what you were meant to do, the children were encouraged to see that writing would allow them to send letters to their friends or let the cook know what they wanted on the lunch menu. (Once they had learnt how to write they ordered almost nothing but chicken.) Later they would be encouraged to budget these weekly menus, do the washing-up, make their own clothes or repaint tables and chairs. As well as helping them to discover the world for themselves, there was a desire to give the children as much autonomy as possible.

On the day that one of the children asked about the telephone, it was agreed that this strange box could be used to invite their friends from outside the school over for tea. Now that they had an incentive to master it, they set about calling these friends and learning how to keep records of their numbers. Without any timetable to get in the way, they spent the rest of the day tackling further questions about the telephone, at one point following the wire which came out of it round the school and out to the street. Later they went on an outing to the local telephone exchange to meet the operator and solve the riddle of why there was a female voice stuck in the receiver.

Wherever possible, the direction and speed of learning was generated by the children. Indeed there were no 'teachers' at Malting House, just 'co-investigators'. It was a learning environment without timetables or formal instruction, one in which curiosity and fantasy were rewarded. The contrast to most 1920s kindergartens was acute. At Malting House each child was seen as 'a distinguished foreign visitor who knows little or nothing of our language or customs', as Pyke put it. 'If we invited a distinguished stranger to tea and he spilled his cup on the best tablecloth or consumed more than his share of cake, we should not upbraid him and send him out of the room,' he explained. 'We should hasten to reassure him that all was well.' In other words, there were to be no punishments, a reminder of the influence of Freud on the school.

Sigmund Freud's theory of psychoanalysis was seen by those in Bloomsbury and beyond as the defining scientific discovery of the age. At its heart was the idea that we bury in our unconscious the memory of shocking or traumatic experiences, only for these memories to resurface later as nervous conditions. The effect of Freud's theory could already be seen in contemporary literature, philosophy and the treatment of post-traumatic stress, yet by 1920 nobody had thought to apply Freudian psychoanalysis to education. Around the time of David Pyke's birth in 1921 this began to change. The Institute of Psychoneurology's 'Children's Home' had opened in Moscow – Stalin's son Vasily was one of the first pupils – and later that year A. S. Neill's Summerhill school opened in Germany. Like the innovators behind both of these institutions, Pyke wanted the children at his school to come away without traumatic memories to suppress, nor any association between punishment and either sexuality or the natural function of their bodies. Yet by 1924 neither Summerhill nor the Moscow institute had written up the results of their endeavours. By recording everything at Malting House, Pyke had gone further than either school. His was the first valid experiment into the idea of reorganising education in the light of Freud.

The lack of structure and discipline at Malting House was not without problems. Though the children there were brighter than most – the average IQ in 1926 was 131 – a surprising number showed signs of psychological imbalance. Susie Isaacs later described their initial intake as 'the ten most difficult children in Cambridge'. Her account of 31 October 1924, is typical: 'B., as on one or two previous occasions, hit me in anger. I tried passive resistance, but he went further, and hit me several times, hard, stinging blows with the open palm, and was gleeful when he thought he had really hurt me and "made me cry".'

She concluded with studied detachment: 'The method of remaining passive did not appear the answer.'

'I must say I can't make out the point of it,' wrote James Strachey, one of Freud's first translators, who had married Pyke's friend Alix Sargant Florence and had a niece and nephew at the school. 'All that appears to happen is that they're "allowed to do whatever they like". But as what they like doing is killing one another, Mrs Isaacs is obliged from time to time to intervene in a sweetly reasonable voice: "Timmy, please do not insert that stick in Stanley's eye." There's one particular boy (age 5) who domineers, and bullies the whole set. His chief enjoyment is spitting. He spat one morning onto Mrs Isaacs's face. So she said: "I shall not play with you, Philip," – for Philip is typically his name [Philip was also the name of Strachey's brother-in-law] – "until you have wiped my face." As Philip didn't want Mrs Isaacs to play with him, that lady was obliged to go about the whole morning with the crachat upon her.' Though Strachey never visited the school, and loathed Susie Isaacs for her sometimes serious manner, his account was not too wide of the mark.

As well as spitting a great deal, the children would often gang up on one of their classmates and shout 'funny face' at them before locking him or her in the henhouse or shutting them out of the school altogether. The victim might change from day to day, but the urge to do this was constant. As well as upsetting the child who had been singled out, this was becoming expensive. The children who were locked out tended to break a window on their way back in. Others had developed a taste for smashing plates when things did not go their way. The school's Freudian approach ensured that adults could not censure a child if they did this, or indeed if they took too much interest in another's turds or genitals. The Malting House was rapidly becoming known around Cambridge as a 'pre-genital brothel'. Pyke and Susie had hoped that if this behaviour was simply ignored it would lose its appeal. They were wrong.

Towards the end of the first term Pyke's educational experiment had reached a critical point. Over the past seven weeks valuable insights had been gained into what happens when you give a pack of two-to-four-year-olds almost total freedom. The number of stories and imaginative games they invented shot up. The children had also begun to show the kind of scientific curiosity that Pyke and Susie had predicted. But by now they were in open rebellion against the adults. It was becoming the law of the jungle and for the first time in the short history of Malting House it seemed as though this bold venture had run its course.

Pyke saw things differently. After all, it was no more than a case of identifying and reformulating the problems they faced: solutions were bound to follow.

How to Tame a Group of Wild Children

Pyke began with the question of how to prevent the children from ganging up on each other without explicitly forbidding it, for this would do little to curb the original desire. Rather than ban it, he turned it into more of a game. How? By volunteering himself to be 'funny face'.

Over the days that followed Pyke spent many hours locked in the Malting House henhouse as one of the children's prisoners – a strange echo of his solitary confinement in Berlin.

It worked. The game lost its sting and when he suggested that those children who had shut him up should take a turn in the henhouse they rapidly lost interest.

There was also the problem of 'spitting or excremental talk'. Again it contradicted the school's principles to punish the children for this, so instead he instructed the staff to withdraw their help as soon as it began, and in some cases they 'explicitly requested that there be no more such talk, and only one child in the lavatory at a time'. If a game became violent, rather than stand idly by, the adults would immediately start a different game. Pyke also introduced a handful of guidelines: children must be punctual; material had to be put away after use; nobody was to endanger themselves or others.

These sound like tiny adjustments, none of them commensurate with the crisis at Malting House, but together they worked. Susie noted with approval that 'the individual aggressiveness of the children has grown much less' and, several weeks later, that there was a new 'pleasure in co-operative occupation'.

Something else changed at Malting House towards the end of that first term. Whether or not any of the children noticed, there was a different chemistry between two of the adults. Just as the school was a testing ground for experimental attitudes and ideas, these two individuals had long believed that marriage was not an expression of exclusive physical ownership and that 'the sexual act', to quote one of their Cambridge friends, was really 'like a kiss' and 'merely a demonstration of affection, more violent, more pleasurable but essentially of the same nature'. But neither had yet put this attitude to the test.

That summer, in Vienna, Frank Ramsey had lost his virginity to 'a charming and good-natured prostitute' and had been psychoanalysed by one of Freud's disciples, Theodor Reik, in the hope of ending his obsession with Margaret Pyke. As Lytton Strachey gossiped to his brother James, Ramsey had left Vienna thinking he was 'cured of such wishes. On returning and meeting her, however, he was more bowled over than ever, but asked her to go to bed with him – which she declined.'

Ramsey's infatuation was now common knowledge around King's College. Pyke even joked about it with Ramsey's mother – which Ramsey resented terribly. Maynard Keynes warned Ramsey around this time that the rumours about him and Margaret Pyke could damage his chances of being offered a fellowship at King's, advice which might have helped drive him into the arms of the undergraduate Lettice Baker.

Rather amazingly, Baker was then sleeping with Pyke's brother Richard, still one of Ramsey's close friends. It seems that this Cambridge prodigy made a habit of falling for women who were sleeping with one of the Pyke brothers. Margaret was at last off the hook, but this gave way to a new complication in her life: her husband and Susie Isaacs had begun to have an affair.

Pyke had become overwhelmed by the fantasy of having found in Susie the complete modern woman, similar to Margaret but more combative and one who understood the pain of losing a parent at a young age. They were drawn together by the music of their conversation. The psychoanalyst John Rickman described Pyke and Susie in full flight as like 'watching a fine exhibition of ballroom dancing, the movement of their minds was in such close touch that it seemed as if a single figure moved in the intellectual scene, she skilled in philosophical method followed his sterner logic, he yielded to her more subtle psychological intuition'. The longer this dance went on the closer they became, until their intimacy in conversation felt like an open infidelity. 'Geoffrey turned more and more to Susie as a confidante,' Nathan later wrote, 'as to one who was more important to him than anyone else, as to the woman he had been looking for and hoping for all these years. Susie wasn't less drawn to him, let us say.'

They slept together for the first time in late 1924, and while Susie admitted later that 'she didn't feel any overpowering longing for intercourse, she was quite ready for it'. By March 1925 the Director and the Principal of Malting House were 'in full and open love with one another', with Susie describing her 'very real love' for Pyke. Rather than wink at this infidelity, Margaret gave it her 'blessing and active encouragement'. Nathan, however, remained in the dark for now.

Sexually it was a disappointment. Pyke later conceded that 'he had not been a very satisfactory physical lover', and if his brother's novel is anything to go by, we may have some idea why. In *The Lives and Deaths of Roland Greer*, Richard Pyke described his fictional self being unable to 'rise to the occasion' and having 'secret difficulties' in 'sexual matters'. He added that his elder brother 'understood too well' these difficulties 'because they were his own too, though he overleapt them by a *tour de force* – a method which cannot be imparted'. Either this *tour de force* could not always be relied upon or he and Susie naturally grew apart: after a year of the affair she 'decided to go no further' and by the start of 1926 their relationship was no longer physical.

Even then, as Nathan, the unlikely chronicler of the affair, recalled, 'the draw they were exercising on one another was more powerful than ever'. To most observers it seemed as though their liaison had ended amicably and that the school would not suffer, but there was a storm on its way. It would test not only the fragile nature of their relationship but the very existence of the school they had made together.

By early 1926 the Malting House experiment was in full bloom. Having overcome those initial difficulties it was now winning international plaudits from leading educationalists of the day such as Jean Piaget, who would soon pay an approving visit, as well as Melanie Klein, the psychoanalyst and expert in child psychology. Klein even performed at Malting House one of the first psychoanalyses of a British child on David Pyke, then aged four. Yet they were at cross purposes throughout. David had recently been given an old bus conductor's tray and was determined to sell Klein a ticket for his bus. She was only interested in finding out whether he had seen his parents having sex, which he might have done, only not with each other.

As the prestige of Malting House grew, so did Pyke's stock within Cambridge. The physicist and engineer Lancelot Law Whyte later described him as one of the leading lights of 1920s Cambridge, alongside Sir Ernest Rutherford, Peter Kapitza and E. M. Forster. He was a playful conversationalist, an entertaining bauble on the tree of academic life who 'looked like an Assyrian king' and was, if nothing else, a doer in a city full of thinkers. 'Philosophers have only interpreted the world,' wrote Marx, 'the point is to change it.' Pyke did not just talk over tea on the High Street about the possibility of making a fortune on the stock market – because it looked so easy – or the need to revolutionise education by applying the lessons of Freud. This thirty-three-year-old *did* these things – and they worked. None of it seemed to be a fluke. His success was the result of his small inheritance, dazzling self-confidence and a capacity for laborious research.

Pyke taking a break during one of his many Swiss holidays

By now his Cambridge social circle had expanded beyond undergraduate friends such as Philip Sargant Florence, then on his way to becoming a renowned economic theorist and whose children were at Malting House, or his editor at the *Cambridge Magazine*, C. K. Ogden. Newer Cambridge friends included the film-maker Ivor

Montagu and the couple at the end of the Malting House garden, Phyllis and Maurice Dobb, he a young economist at Trinity College. There was also crystallographer J. D. 'Sage' Bernal and his wife Eileen, who had recently become involved in Pyke's financial operation, as well as J. B. S. Haldane, the legendary biologist who had joined the Malting House board, and his wife Charlotte, well known for her literary salons.

It is interesting that at least five of these new friends either joined the Communist Party, worked for Soviet intelligence or did both. A decade later there would be nothing remarkable about having so many Cambridge friends who subscribed to dialectical materialism and saw the USSR as a beacon of radiant utopian possibility. But during the mid-1920s it was unusual – in the General Strike of May 1926, in which the Moscow National Bank aided some of the striking miners, almost half of the city's undergraduates were thought to have been involved in efforts to break the strike.

Although he had a number of Marxist friends there is no evidence that by 1926 Pyke shared their political views. Since his political epiphany in Berlin he had remained close to the Fabianism of Sidney and Beatrice Webb and Shaw, and had corresponded with all three, but he did not give himself the time to take any of this further. If nothing else, he was 'intensely distracted' both by the school and the newfound complexity of those financial dealings on which Malting House depended.

In the early days Pyke had been making straightforward directional bets on whether the price of a certain metal would rise or fall, guided by his hypothesis about the relationship between copper and tin. As with comedy, the key to this was timing. Generally he got it right but occasionally he lost money. To reduce the scope for error Pyke had concocted a new trading system. He was now making what traders today will call 'relative value arbitrage trades' using 'advance-dated double options'. Even by modern standards this is an exotic trade. At the time it was pioneering. Rather than bet on whether the prices of copper and tin were going up or down, he now predicted the deviation between the two. As he later explained in court, 'it no longer made any difference whether prices went up or down as long as they did not separate or separate in one direction.' Compared with his earlier dealings this was 'immensely less speculative'. He increased his margins accordingly and used some of the new profits to employ a team of researchers in offices off Chancery Lane. This was all going well until he realised that he would soon be facing an enormous bill for income tax.

Having poured his profits into either the school or increasing his holdings in the metals market, he was unable to pay. He sought the advice of a barrister: D. N. 'Johnny' Pritt KC, later described by a Soviet defector as 'one of the chief recruiting agents for Soviet underground organisations in the UK'. Pritt assured Pyke, in answer to his question, that it was perfectly legal to alter his operation so that he was no longer trading as an individual but through a series of companies. This would turn his taxable income into a capital gain, meaning that there would be less tax to pay. But there was more to this plan. If he set off these gains against losses incurred by buying options on the companies' shares from the shareholders then he could reduce the money he owed to almost nothing.

Pyke duly set up two companies, Orcus and Siona (a misspelling of 'ciona', a stationary sea creature which sits on the bottom of the ocean and feeds off passing plankton), and began to buy options from his shareholders at exorbitant prices. Whether or not Pritt knew that each of the shareholders was an acquaintance of Pyke by one remove, or an employee, is unclear. The new system worked. Pyke no longer faced a crippling tax bill, while his sway in the metals market continued to grow. Had he settled up with just one of his three brokers on Christmas Day 1926, when he was said to hold a quarter of all tin reserves in Britain, he would have walked away with a trading profit of over £20,000. But he saw no reason to do this.

Though he never visited the trading ring of the London Metal Exchange he was by now so well known there that he had a nickname, 'Candlesticks', after cabling in a trade from the Swiss town of Kandersteg. Even the editor of *Metal Bulletin* had heard of 'Candlesticks' and was 'certainly impressed by his market activities'. Less impressed, however, was a group of heavyweight American copper producers.

In October 1926 there was a historic meeting of the world's most powerful copper magnates. Between them they controlled up to 90 per cent of the global copper supply with mines in Africa, South America and across the United States, yet they did not control the price of copper and, as they resolved at this meeting, that needed to change.

The United States was entering a period of frenzied financial speculation. With the largest bubble in American finance beginning to form, these copper producers wanted to take steps to protect themselves against price shocks, which were usually caused by the activities of lone speculators. Using the Webb-Pomerene Trade Export Act of 1918, originally designed to boost the American war effort by granting immunity to certain export companies from standard anti-trust regulation, they formed a cartel of historic proportions. Copper Exporters Incorporated (CEI) was later described as 'the most formal cartel in the twentieth century in American industry'. It was powerful and coordinated and had been formed with the sole aim of stabilising the copper price. The best way to do this was by flushing out speculators like 'Candlesticks' in London. First the CEI needed greater control of the market, which would take a little time. Having started out with ambitions to do nothing more than pay for his son's enlightened education, the scale of Pyke's success had turned him into a target.

★

Just before this copper cartel came into being, Pyke reached a momentous decision. David was now approaching his sixth birthday and in a year or so would need to go to a new school, unless, that was, Malting House could be adapted to accommodate him and other children of his age. Pyke decided to turn the school into an international institute for educational research which could care for children all the way through to university. It had always been in his nature to take ideas to an extreme, and now he would do the same to his groundbreaking school. So he began to spend.

Pyke appointed Nathan Isaacs as the school's researcher-at-large on £500 a year, telling him to 'run away and read and write' on questions like 'Why do children ask "why"?' At enormous expense, he hired stenographers to record every word the children spoke. He also lavished more than £1,000 on advertisements for the school's first scientific appointee, and arranged for a selection committee made up of Sir Ernest Rutherford, J. B. S. Haldane and Sir Percy Nunn. When the *Daily Express* heard that a science teacher had been employed by a kindergarten they sent their Crimes Reporter to investigate. This type of prurient interest in the school persuaded Pyke of the need to publicise his work in a sympathetic light.

During the summer of 1927 he commissioned a promotional film from a prestigious production company which specialised in battle scenes and wildlife documentaries. Despite their obvious qualifications for the job, they found the task somewhat challenging. 'In all our experiences of photographing every kind of wild creature, not excepting cultures of bacilli, the problem of photographing children in their wild state proved the most difficult to tackle,' grumbled one cameraman. 'Whereas animals can be more or less localised and controlled by food, and bacilli must remain within the confines of a test-tube or petrie-dish [*sic*], no such artificial fixity could be obtained with the children.' Eventually the children lost interest in the cameras, and were recorded dissecting Susie's recently deceased cat – 'It fair

makes you sick, doesn't it?' a cameraman whispered to his producer
– as well as starting a bonfire that got out of hand and burnt the school
canoe. 'Even Geoffrey Pyke was a bit upset about that.' Ten days later
they had enough material to cut a half-hour-long film.

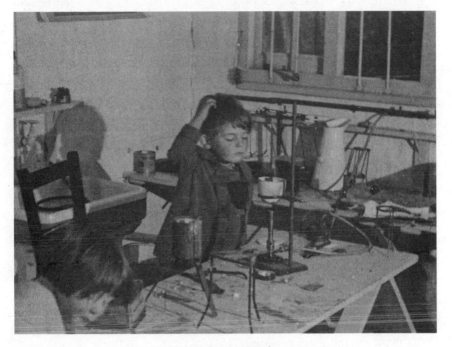

Two young scientists at Malting House

'Remarkably interesting and altogether delightful,' was the
Spectator's verdict on *Let's Find Out*, after initial screenings in
Manchester and London, where 500 people came to watch it in the
Marble Arch Pavilion. The children appeared to be:

> 'having the time of their lives, wading up to their knees trying
> to fill a sandpit with water, mending a tap with a spanner, oiling
> the works of a clock, joyously feeding a bonfire, dissecting crabs,
> climbing on scaffolding, weighing each other on a see-saw,

'Co-investigator' Susie Isaacs with the children of Malting House

weaving, modelling, making pottery, working lathes – in fact doing all those things which every child delights in doing. At Malting House School children's dreams come true. The school is equipped with the most extensive apparatus, which will stimulate the natural curiosity possessed by every child. [. . .] There is no discipline. There are no punishments. Children may hit one another so long as they only use their hands, but I believe quarrels are rare and, though it seems almost unbelievable with the unending opportunities which must occur, there has never been an accident of a serious nature. The children are left to form their own opinions, tastes, and moral codes. After having seen this film, on the photography of which the British Instructional Films are to be congratulated, I came away wishing

with all my heart that my own dull schooldays had been as theirs
are, and that education could be made such an adventure for
every child.

Much of this was an accurate reflection of the radical educational
experiment Pyke had set up. For most children it really was as if
their dreams had come true. But as a promotional film there was no
mention of any of the school's difficulties.

'Moulds are wrong,' Pyke had once said, 'and shaping is wrong,
whatever it may aim at.' Yet his belief that every child was a scientist in
the making had permeated the school, and although he scoffed at the
idea of parents pressing their cultural inheritances onto their children,
he was gently moulding his son and the other children at Malting House
into idealised versions of himself: free-thinkers with scientific outlooks
who could one day reminisce on healthy and non-traumatic childhoods.
There was nothing wrong with this, perhaps, but it illustrates one of
the small slippages between theory and practice at Malting House.

A more telling gap had opened up between how the children were
supposed to react to a life without rules and how they actually reacted.
Beyond a certain age it was clear that some children needed clearer
boundaries.

'We want to be made to do definite things as they are in other
schools,' one seven-year-old complained at a fractious staff meeting,
having just threatened to hit one of the grown-ups. This same child
was asked why he wanted to be made to do definite things.

'Because we don't do anything otherwise. After all, what's a school
for?'

He was then asked to draw up a timetable, which he did, before
summing up his feelings as follows: 'I want to be made to do what
I want to do.' This perfectly embodies the sometimes paradoxical
nature of our relationship with rules, no matter how old we are.
These children wanted boundaries, boundaries of their own choosing,

but boundaries all the same, and they wanted them to be enforced. This went against the school's philosophy.

Another problem, though less obvious, was the extent of Pyke's largesse. Even he would later admit to managing the school during this period 'extravagantly' and 'irrespective of money'. Although he continued to spend within his means, his liquidity was greatly reduced. While he was not in debt, he had never been so vulnerable financially.

Having gained control of most of the world's supply, the CEI cartel squeezed up the price of copper from £54 a ton earlier that year to £60 by October. Pyke had never seen the price behave like this. Nor had he ever pitted himself against an international cartel. It would be a severe test of his market prowess.

Earlier that month he had bought a large quantity of copper and, later, a sizeable holding of tin. The market was up. According to his model, the next move should have been to sell his copper on the basis that the price would soon drop. But he did not. Second-guessing the cartel, he hung on to the copper, thinking that the CEI was only interested in growing or stabilising the price, a decision he later described as a mixture of 'imbecility and commercial rashness'.

The order of subsequent events is hard to reconstruct. Either the cartel flooded the market with copper or one of Pyke's brokers got wind of his exposure and began to offload, with other brokers following suit. Most likely, it was a combination of the two. The price of copper plummeted, followed by the price of tin and lead, leaving Pyke with no choice but to hold on to what he had in the hope of weathering the storm. With the metals market in freefall one of his brokers asked for cover. Hopelessly over-leveraged and with very little liquidity, Pyke had no way of providing it short of selling up. Doing so, of course, would merely depress the price further and worsen his position. As he stalled, his other two brokers came in for cover. It was at this point in the history of Malting House that Susie Isaacs resigned.

The difficulties between her and Pyke had become more pronounced over the last ten months. It had begun with trifles over missed appointments and the ghost of a disagreement about who was taking more credit for the success of the school. Periods of calm would be punctured by rows in which both hurled torrents of half-remembered slights at each other before apologising and carrying on as if nothing had happened. The subtext to this was the way in which their affair had ended. Pyke resented the idea that Susie had both started it and finished it, which seemed to induce in her a scintilla of guilt to add to any feelings of inadequacy she might have had owing to their difficulties in bed. When she heard that Pyke had gone to Switzerland to see another woman after the end of their affair she had felt a pang of jealousy. All this had the strange effect of making her not only more tolerant of his unreasonable behaviour in between rows, but angrier when they came to argue.

'I don't want to hurt you,' he told her, after she had begun to cry. 'But I've been hurt too. There's a limit to endurance. You've pushed a knife in me and screwed it round!'

She had done no such thing, but when the world appeared to be collapsing around him Pyke looked for a scapegoat. Susie was the obvious target.

By now Nathan knew about the affair and, following Susie's resignation, he sent Margaret a sixty-eight-page letter in which he described himself as 'quite naturally displaced' and 'full of admiration for Geoff'. 'I've no resentment against Geoff,' he went on, feeling only that his judgement had gone awry. The crux of the problem, he explained – Pyke's greatest asset and at the same time the source of his self-destruction – was 'the free play of that magnificent instrument, his mind. [. . .] More than anyone else I know [he] needs to be on his guard against the very powers of his mind.' Magnificent it might have been, but it was hard to see how even Pyke could find a way out of the mess he was now in.

A family portrait taken shortly before Pyke's financial crash

The first decline and fall of Geoffrey Pyke was halting and slow; it lasted nearly two years and by the end there seemed to be no further to fall. Unable to provide cover to his three brokers, Pyke's trading companies had all gone into liquidation by the start of 1928. As sole guarantor he faced claims against him of £72,701, more than £2.2 million in today's money. He had no way of paying it back.

Pyke did everything possible to save Malting House, making advance payments to the staff and disappearing to Switzerland for two months to delay the issue of writs. Cambridge friends rallied round and donations came in from parents as well as the likes of Siegfried Sassoon, Victor Rothschild and Victor Gollancz. But it was not enough.

After the school received a glowing write-up in the *New York Times*, Pyke applied for a grant from the Laura Spelman Rockefeller Trust with a covering letter signed by a group of worthies later described as 'possibly the greatest galaxy of academic figures of the day ever assembled for a private fund-raising scheme'. It was to no avail.

The year after his personal financial crash Pyke was declared bankrupt, and in January 1929 the public bankruptcy hearings began. Lawyers acting for the brokers picked over his activities in what felt like a protracted judgement on his life and on the school into which he had poured at least £11,000 – referred to witheringly in court as his 'great scheme'.

Certainly there were problems in the conception of Malting House. At least one of the children there, Jack Pole, who went on to become a renowned historian, would look back on his time there with bitterness. Yet for the majority of children this was a sunny, magical period that could only be appreciated once it had passed. One teacher wrote of the school that she had 'never seen so much pleased concentration, so many shrieks and gurgles and jumpings for joy as here'. It was in the field of educational theory, however, that the impact of Malting House was most keenly felt on account of the mountainous records kept from the start. As Pyke had always hoped, the school became a starting point for further research. What he may not have appreciated, given the unhappy end to their relationship, was that most of this analysis would be done by Susie Isaacs.

Her study of the Malting House data formed the basis of her books, *Social Development in Young Children* and *Intellectual Growth in Young Children*, which secured her reputation as arguably 'the greatest influence on British education in the twentieth century'. The same data provided the impetus for Sir Percy Nunn's Department of Child Development at the University of London that went on to play a key role in the development of primary education in post-war Britain.

Yet for the barristers in the Bankruptcy Court in 1929 the only question that mattered was whether the school had played a part in Pyke's tax-reduction scheme. Without full details of his accounts, it is impossible to say one way or another. What does become clear from the transcript of his examination is that Pyke was determined not to be pinned down. He was in escapologist mode. Even when the most damning evidence was read out to him about the tax advice he had received from the Soviet stooge D. N. Pritt, he would not yield to its meaning. Pyke was on top of his facts and light on his feet, exceptionally so. He infuriated his examiners by picking apart their questions, at one point informing a barrister that the question he had just been asked was in fact a statement delivered with a questioning lilt. Another time he asked the barrister to improve the wording of his inquiry.

'Quibbling again?' came the reply.

'Accuracy,' said Pyke.

'No, quibbling again.'

'No, one meaning to one question.'

And on it went.

At one point he was accused of presenting the court with a 'tissue of falsehoods', and there is no doubt that he was obscuring some key details in the arrangements between him and those shareholders from whom he had bought share options at inflated prices. Yet before the truth of this could be established, at the end of a particularly long session, Pyke collapsed.

Owing to the bankrupt's 'indisposition', described elsewhere as a 'sudden illness', the hearing was adjourned until the following month. Only days before he was due in court again Pyke wrote to say that he was ill. The date of the hearing was pushed back once again and the night before he was due to appear, 22 April 1929, Pyke might have tried to kill himself.

A note signed by two doctors shortly afterwards described him as 'dangerously ill and in my opinion [he] may not live through the night'. There is no further clue as to what happened, only the possibility that he had attempted suicide. The session was adjourned once more and Pyke was moved to a nursing home in Muswell Hill, from where a signed affidavit was sent to the court describing the patient as 'suffering from paranoia (bordering on insanity), amnesia, fits of melancholia and incapability of severe mental effort', so that 'he will not be fit to attend to any business or legal affairs for at least twelve months'.

While there is a minute chance that Pyke had either fooled or persuaded a doctor to write this note, now that the barristers were closing in, this was almost certainly a genuine breakdown. Since he had been struck by what was thought to be pneumonia in Ruhleben he had experienced periodic bouts of chronic inertia accompanied by an overpowering sense of melancholy, so bad that there were times when he could not get out of bed. The strained circumstances of watching his life fall apart might have induced or exacerbated one of these episodes.

In July 1929 Margaret Pyke confirmed to the court that her husband was 'bordering upon insanity'. In the same month the school's scientific appointee sued him for unpaid wages. It was also around this time that Malting House closed its doors for good.

Geoffrey Pyke was bankrupt, he was being sued, his experimental school had closed, he was living in a nursing home and had been described as borderline insane. But still he had not reached rock bottom. During the winter of 1929, with the global economy entering meltdown, his wife left him.

We will never know all the reasons for this. Pyke's affair with Susie must have played a part in their separation, and there is the possibility that Margaret had an abortion in the years after David's birth, and that it was Pyke who had first suggested this. Yet we know that she was never again in a relationship with a man, and that rather than get divorced they remained amicably separated for the rest of their lives.

In a potted biography of Margaret Pyke published long after her death the reader is told that 'her husband died in 1929'. He did not. And yet, a version of Pyke came to an end. During his first thirty-five years as an energetic Futurist in love with the scientific method, Geoffrey Pyke had tricked his way into and out of an enemy nation and had tasted life as a correspondent, best-selling author, minor Bloomsberry, financial speculator and radical educationalist. He had ridden waves of desire and rejection, jealousy and lust, living throughout as if with one layer of skin removed, and as a parent he had staked everything on the possibility of providing his son with an upbringing that was better than his own. His life was characterised by a propensity for taking enormous risks to achieve the seemingly impossible. Here was someone who inhabited the world as if it were an enormous game in which the rules were still being worked out. Now that game seemed to be over. In many ways it helps to think of this moment in his life as a death, for if he was to return to the stage he would need to do so as a man reborn.

PART II

HOW TO RESOLVE AN EPIDEMIC OF
ANTI-SEMITISM, A ROYAL SCANDAL AND
THE THREAT OF FASCISM

By the time Adolf Hitler became Chancellor of Germany, in 1933, Geoffrey Pyke was living in a damp, ramshackle cottage in the Devil's Punchbowl, deep in the Surrey Hills. He had become a recluse, or what his mother would call a *luftmensch*, literally 'a man in the air', a dreamer who does not concern himself with material things and appears to be drifting along without any purpose. Yet that would soon change.

It was Margaret Russell, a cousin of Bertrand and friend of Pyke's from his days at the 1917 Club, who had helped to arrange his tenancy at the cottage. Its ceilings were famously low, a reminder perhaps of the Jewish barrack at Ruhleben, and there was neither running water nor electricity. But at twelve shillings a month the cottage was, if nothing else, affordable. During the four years since his financial collapse Pyke had survived on handouts from friends, what little remained of his inheritance and the occasional commission to write advertising copy for Jack Beddington at Shell, where others such as John Betjeman and Ben Nicholson were also helping to reinvent the brand. Yet the money was never enough and for the first time in his life, as the Western world ground deeper into economic recession, this unemployed bankrupt experienced the imprisoning austerity of poverty.

Since his breakdown in 1929 Pyke had drifted apart from his Cambridge friends and lost some of his *amour propre*. He wore a beard and went about the cottage in a dilapidated elephant-grey Homburg hat. He wrote and read more than before. He considered his purpose in life. When his mood was up he played Mozart records at full blast, yet when it was down and descended into one of those deadening lulls with which he had become familiar, there were times when he felt unable to move.

His son, David, was now at the Dragon School in Oxford, and during the holidays lived mostly with his mother at Balcombe Place in West Sussex. This was home to the remarkable women's rights campaigner Lady Denman, who had recently appointed Margaret the Secretary of her National Birth Control Council. This was at a time when birth control remained an outré subject. David later recalled being driven in Lady Denman's chauffeured Rolls-Royce from Balcombe to his father's cottage. Sometimes he arrived to find him accompanied by Marjorie Edwards, aquiline and attractive, who cooked for him and typed. Otherwise his father's only companion appeared to be his dog, Judy.

Though he was cut off geographically and saw less of his friends, Pyke remained in touch with the world beyond through newspapers delivered to the nearby village of Thursley. It was through these that he read with growing interest about the political developments in Germany. The rise of fascism was a subject that seemed to matter to him more than any other, and in particular the treatment of German Jews.

Just after the end of the Great War, Hitler had confided to a friend that he found German anti-Semitism much too 'emotional'. He felt that it would never amount to anything more than short-lived pogroms. Instead he wanted to give this medieval superstition a more 'scientific' backbone – to produce what he called, in a chilling phrase, an 'anti-Semitism of reason'.

In the two years after Hitler became Chancellor a mass of discriminatory laws were passed aimed at belittling, excluding and vilifying German Jewry. Pyke read in the newspapers about new laws that prohibited Jews from working in the civil service, state-run schools, universities and hospitals; soon German Jews would be unable to use public swimming pools in certain cities, employ Germans under a particular age, marry or have an affair with a non-Jew, fly the German flag or refer to themselves as citizens of Germany. Yet for the most part this statutory discrimination during the first two years of Hitler's reign elicited little or no international outrage.

In part, this was because these laws had failed to inspire any popular torrents of anti-Semitism. When Goebbels called for a nationwide boycott of Jewish businesses immediately after Hitler's accession the response of the German people was apathetic, to say the least. In the months that followed, almost every attack on Jewish shops was orchestrated by the state. Just as Oswald Mosley failed in his attempts to transform British anti-Semitism into a wild, out-of-control force, it seemed that most Germans viewed anti-Semitism as a Nazi tic which they were largely prepared to ignore.

It was hard to see why this might change, especially given the standing of Jews in German society. When Hitler received his Iron Cross, it was on the recommendation of a Jewish officer – one of more than 100,000 Jews in the German Army. German Jews had enjoyed full legal equality with their fellow citizens since 1869 and were far more assimilated than their counterparts in Russia or Eastern Europe. Yet by the end of 1934 Pyke had become fixated by the issue of Nazi anti-Semitism. It concerned him, and that it did so was a telling reflection on his own relationship to Jewishness and just how much it had changed.

In his best-selling book *To Ruhleben – And Back*, published in 1916, Pyke not only omitted the fact that he had been held in Ruhleben's Jewish barrack but made a point elsewhere in the book of describing the tenacity of German teenagers as 'frightful', 'intense' and 'Semitic in its persistency'. In print, at least, Pyke had learnt to ape some of the casual anti-Semitism of Edwardian England. Seven years after publication, his brother Richard looked on in embarrassment as Pyke rowed with a Jewish barber who had suggested that he looked Jewish. It was more than coincidence that this argument took place with both brothers en route to their mother's funeral.

Pyke's prickly relationship with his own Jewishness was bound up with those complicated feelings he had about his mother. For as long as he could remember, Jewishness and Mary Pyke were inseparably intertwined, so to cut her out of his life implied the need to cauterise his Jewish identity. Jewish ritual, Jewish dress, Jewish culture, the gossipy provincialism of the well-off West London Sephardic community in which he had grown up: all this reminded him of his mother and as a young man he wanted nothing to do with it. Only in the years after her death did this change.

By 1935 Pyke could describe himself, without drowning in qualifications and parentheses, as an Englishman and a Jew. In notes from a meeting with Sir Isaac Woolfson, an interview which he hoped would be confidential, he said, 'I have been told – and I find it true of myself – that a Jew can keep everything but a joke' (before assuring Woolfson that he would try not to make him laugh).

This self-identification as both Englishman and Jew changed the way that Pyke read the news from Nazi Germany. He saw these developments from the perspective of both the oppressor and the oppressed. Those years spent running away from his own Jewishness had given him an understanding of the mindset which could make a person chase someone down the corridor yelling 'Jew Hunt!' – as had happened to him at Wellington. He could play the bumptious Little Englander as well as the Jewish intellectual and understood that 'the Jews among all the persecuted are probably the only people who marry and breed with the consciousness that their children and grand-children and great-grandchildren will probably be persecuted'. The difference here, and it is crucial, was that Pyke did not see this as inevitable.

By late 1934 he was convinced that Nazi anti-Semitism was a problem of such minatory potential that it must be solved. His frantic attempts to do so would change his political perspective for ever, stinging him out of his early retirement, whereupon, as the journalist Claud Cockburn put it, he 'zig-zagged across the 1930s like forked lightning'.

How to End Anti-Semitism

First of all, why? Setting aside everything we know today, why, by late 1934, was it important to end Nazi discrimination against German Jews?

His answer was rooted in two historical parallels, the first of which was the execution of 'witches' in medieval Europe. Witches were believed to possess the magical ability to harm others, and, in a surprisingly similar way, the Nazi attitude towards Jews was rooted in the idea that the members of this minority had a threatening, unnatural power which allowed them to outperform their Gentile neighbours. 'Belief in contemporary Germany that the dangerous quality ascribed to Jews is transmitted to their children, who must therefore in school be separated from other children, belief in the extraordinary power which so small a proportion as the 1 per cent Jewish population in Germany is accused of possessing, bears a striking resemblance to the dangerous powers ascribed to witches.' Who was to say that the modern-day Germans would not have the Jews expelled or murdered, as their ancestors had done to so-called witches? As Pyke later explained in the *New Statesman and Nation*, things had become so bad in the Middle Ages that in some European towns 'the guilty were roasted in a specially prepared oven'. He was bold enough to imply that something similar could happen in modern-day Germany.

The strength of his conviction came from a second historical parallel, that of the Turkish government's genocidal assault on Armenian Turks during the Great War. More than a million men and women may have been murdered. Pyke was interested in what had happened in the years immediately beforehand. The Turkish government had, he explained, 'bamboozled' its people with propaganda. At length, the people of Turkey had been told that Armenian Turks were not only different but dangerous, and mass persecution did not begin – could not begin – until Turkish society had been sold this myth.

'One thing is clear,' wrote Pyke. 'Our susceptibility to myths is a world danger. Because the application of science to human behaviour has come so late the myth is regarded as less dangerous than the bacillus. It is doubtful whether such a belief is justified.' In the same way that the Turks had been bullied by their government into thinking of Armenians as dangerous and different, it seemed as though the Germans were being bamboozled into seeing Jews in a similar way. Pyke's fear was that, as had been the case in Turkey, this might be a prelude to genocidal assault.

At the time this was a hysterical analysis. It was certainly not one you would find rehearsed in the mainstream British press. Germany was one of the most modern nations on Earth, a land of dynamic theatre, art and poetry. Scientifically and industrially it was one of the most advanced polities anywhere in the world. A parallel involving Turkey or indeed medieval Europe seemed far-fetched. Yet Pyke was convinced by the logic of his analogy.

He had identified the problem. Now for the solution.

Again he reached into the past, fixing upon the 1735 Witchcraft Act, 'an event which may come to be regarded as one of the three or four most significant events in the history of the race'. It was, he went on, 'perhaps the first result in the Christian era of the impact of science on social behaviour'. Rather than dismiss witchcraft as superstitious nonsense the predecessors of modern-day scientists had *shown* it to be so. Once it had been made clear that the myth of witchcraft made no sense the laws prohibiting it were soon repealed. Why not do the same for the myth of anti-Semitism?

Only the year before, Pyke's great idol, Bernard Shaw, had said on the subject of the Nazi discrimination against Jews: 'It is idle to argue against this sort of insanity.' He was right, in the sense that you would achieve little by arguing *against* it. Instead, you should demonstrate how it worked. Rather than attack the myth, explain how it was made. Or as Pyke put it: 'The answer to those who try to incite us is not, "What you say is untrue," but "Aha, I can tell you why you say that."'

His solution was to 'demilitarise' the Nazi myth of anti-Semitism by showing the world how it worked. The effect would be like having a magic trick explained – everyone would feel a bit silly for not having seen what was going on earlier. Pyke proposed an international centre devoted to exploring and exploding the myth of anti-Semitism. The work must be done by academics, for 'people will take from them what they won't take from their own political leaders', and the findings would be taught in schools. Eventually anti-Semites would go the way of flat-Earthers: they would be seen first as wrong, then old-fashioned and finally mad. 'Let a man be thought to be deranged and you isolate him as no prison can do,' noted Pyke, words which had particular weight from someone who had spent four months in solitary confinement and had since been declared borderline insane.

While organisations such as the World Alliance for Combating Anti-Semitism aided its victims and pushed for boycotts of German goods, and the British government was offering sanctuary to those German Jews who excelled in science and art, none of these measures addressed the taproot of this largely Christian affliction. This is what set Pyke's solution apart. In Germany the Nazis would soon open a *Forschungsabteilung Judenfrage* – a 'Research Department for the Jewish Question'. Pyke was proposing the opposite. As a Jew he would launch an institute devoted to the 'Nazi Question'.

He was realistic about what it could achieve. At no point did he believe that its findings would bring about a Damascene conversion for the Adolf Hitlers and Alfred Rosenbergs of the world. Yet he held out the real hope that its work could affect 'the marginal convert', the ordinary German, 'the man who unless something is done may tomorrow become an anti-Semite'.

For the diplomat and politician Sir Andrew McFadyean, this idea had to it 'a touch of genius', though Pyke was perhaps less impressed by his own handiwork. All he had done was look to the past for analogies.

Socrates once warned that the advent of writing and reading would lead to 'forgetfulness in the learners' souls, because they will not use their memories'. The solution to this problem had been hidden in plain view. As Pyke saw it, he was merely the first one who had gone to the trouble of looking for it. As McFadyean went on to say, what really made this solution remarkable was that nobody had thought of it before.

At the start of 1935, with most of his debts written off, Pyke began to raise money for a myth-busting scientific institute devoted to the study of anti-Semitism. The initial response was hesitant. Professor David Keilin, Quick Professor of Biology at Cambridge, assured Pyke that as a Jew he had found the most effective response to

Jew-baiting was not academic analysis but 'commonsense and sense of humour'. The Marquess of Reading, the first practising Jew in the British cabinet, explained that for similar reasons he was unable to lend his name to the scheme. Indeed, many of those English Jews first approached by Pyke suggested that an institute like this might in fact make matters worse. These were men who had learnt to think of anti-Semitism as if it was rain during an English summer: a regrettable fact of life which should be endured, laughed at and otherwise ignored. They were in a minority.

After six months of fundraising Pyke had the backing of Lord Lytton, the Fabian leader Sidney Webb and prominent English Jews such as Lord Melchett, Sir Robert Waley-Cohen and Sir Albert Beit, all of whom provided money, advice and further introductions. The largest cheque, for £200, came from Victor Rothschild, the twenty-four-year-old polymath and heir to a banking dynasty, who had helped Pyke earlier with Malting House. Neither man could have guessed the decisive role that Rothschild would later play in Pyke's life when serving as an MI5 officer.

By July 1935, with the project still gathering momentum, Pyke met another secular Jew devoting himself to the future of the Jewish people. Chaim Weizmann was a Zionist who had played a part in the genesis of the Balfour Declaration of 1917, and as such belonged to the long tradition of Jews on the religious periphery, from Herod to Herzl, who have changed Jewish history. Before rushing off to the 1935 World Zionist Conference in Lucerne, Weizmann gave Pyke a tip. To win over reluctant English Jews he must get the backing of at least one overseas Jewish community. Weizmann suggested South Africa, adding that he had a number of contacts there. Pyke agreed, renewed his passport and in September set off for Johannesburg.

One of his first introductions was to General Smuts, the former South African Prime Minister who had helped found the League of Nations. Smuts was taken by the idea and agreed to lend his name to what Weizmann called a 'really good cause'. For the next four months, Pyke was on the drawing-room circuit, delivering stump speeches to South African Jews about the need for a scientific institute devoted to the study of anti-Semitism in the face of worrying Nazi discrimination. He finished each talk with the same plaintive line: 'Do you know of any better proposal, more practical, more immediate? If you do, I will chuck this and work for that. But if you do not, I ask you to promise to give as much as you possibly can.'

Pyke was in his element. He had spent much of his adult life presenting or defending unusual ideas to thoughtful strangers. He was a powerful, lively speaker who liked to punctuate his most serious passages with moments of comedy – usually inspired by Shaw. He revelled in reversal. Resistance, he told himself, was due to a lack of imagination, and it was essential to tease the audience into seeing the world upside down.

The response to Pyke's South African fundraising was overwhelming, and in January 1936 he returned to Britain with pledges worth £8,000. Admittedly these had all come on the condition that he raise a further £72,000 elsewhere – which was what he planned to do in Britain and the United States. Yet in the months that followed the project's momentum began to fade. Pyke found himself unable to secure the necessary four- or five-figure sums, and, as progress slowed, several South Africans withdrew their support.

Perhaps there was another way of doing this? Could he not produce a scientific analysis of anti-Semitism by himself?

In a letter to *The Times* in the summer of 1936, concerning the connection between anti-Semitism and the laws against witchcraft, Pyke hinted that he might do just that. He followed up in September with an extended piece in the *New Statesman and Nation* which read like the précis of a book. By November he had written a deconstruction of anti-Semitism that ran to more than 100,000 words. But just as he began to revise his manuscript, his attention was dragged elsewhere.

Before he could finish this book or work out where he had gone wrong with his fundraising, Pyke became caught up in the solution of first one problem, then another, each one incrementally more urgent than the last. This was how his grasshopper mind worked. He was, he once wrote, 'a mere dreamer of brilliant ideas'. Steering a solution through to completion was always less attractive than the magical prospect of identifying a fresh problem and solving it.

Dr Alfred Blunt, Bishop of Bradford, was not afraid of controversy. At a regional Diocesan conference on 1 December 1936, this forthright bishop asked his fellow clergy whether the new monarch, Edward VIII, was fully aware of the religious significance of his role as Defender of the Faith for, if he was, 'some of us wish that he gave more positive signs of such awareness'.

This was a none-too-subtle reference to the possibility of the King marrying his mistress, Wallis Simpson, a twice-married Baltimorean with milky skin and a lean, unforgiving face. Blunt's remarks lit the touchpaper on the greatest royal scandal of the twentieth century. Though the story had been kept out of the British press until then, by the end of the week newspapers were jammed full with opinion pieces on the subject and photographs of the couple taken during the summer. The interest was such that people would queue in the street to buy the evening paper. It was a perfect storm of national introspection, touching on issues of class, sex, monarchical deference, British identity, religious propriety and the constitutional implications of this marriage. There was also a hunger to find out how this romance would end and how the rest of the world had reacted to the news.

'Society is suspended in mid-air,' the King told Alfred Duff

Cooper, a member of the Cabinet, holding up a chair to make his point. 'Nobody knows what is right.' Nobody knew, and yet everyone had an opinion. The King's Private Secretary assured the Prime Minister, Stanley Baldwin, that 'there is little doubt what the opinion of the people would be'. The Labour leader, Clement Attlee, was confident that his feelings matched those of his entire party, 'with the exception of the intelligentsia who can be trusted to take the wrong view on any subject'. 'I do know public opinion in this country,' insisted Baldwin, later described by the King as 'the Gallup Poll incarnate'. All the same, Duff Cooper remarked, 'it was curious how everybody who had sought the views of taxi drivers, hairdressers, hospital nurses, clerks or servants had heard exactly what they wanted to hear, that is to say their own opinion'.

Observing all this from his cottage in the Devil's Punchbowl, Pyke had an idea. Less than a week after the Bishop of Bradford's speech, with the country apparently divided between those who thought the King should marry and others calling for his abdication, Churchillians against Baldwinians, Cavaliers against Roundheads, Pyke wrote a letter to the *New Statesman and Nation*.

Under the heading 'King and Country' he called for 'the anthropological study of our own civilisation of which we stand in *such* desperate need'. One of the reasons why the King's potential marriage had turned into a crisis was that nobody quite knew what British public opinion was, and to what extent the press had reflected it or 'evoked and moulded' it. 'Anthropologists and psychologists all over the world are studying the reactions of primitive tribes to sexual situations,' Pyke wrote, so why not study the British tribe and its reaction to the Simpson affair, a sexual situation if ever there was one? Already it was clear that within this particular tribe many were 'unable to tolerate the image of a Queen – whose chief function together with her Consort would be to be an object of idolisation – who has previously been married to two men who are still alive.'

A comprehensive study would build on observations like this to provide a mass of information about how the British thought and felt, which unconscious motives drove them in times like these and how politicians or newspaper editors were able to exploit them.

Perhaps a similar study could begin in the United States, if for no other reason than to understand how Americans were responding to British hostility towards 'that woman'. Pyke's worry was that some of those on the other side of the Atlantic might interpret this antipathy towards Mrs Simpson as 'an aspersion on themselves', leading to anti-British feeling that could manifest itself 'on some future occasion' in a 'refusal to co-operate and perhaps a revengeful suspicion of motive'. Although there was at least a correlation between this idea and the American refusal three years later to join Britain against Nazi Germany, the thrust of Pyke's letter lay elsewhere. He had called for an anthropological study of the British and, for once, he got exactly what he asked for.

The magazine which carried Pyke's letter went on sale in London on a glum, cold morning, several days after the abdication of Edward VIII and only hours before his younger brother Bertie was sworn in as King George VI. In a house in Blackheath this letter was read with a mixture of excitement and anxiety by a group of Surrealist poets led by a *Daily Mirror* reporter, Charles Madge, and a young film-maker at the GPO Film Unit, Humphrey Jennings. Over the next few days both wrote to the *New Statesman and Nation* to say that they had been thinking along very similar lines to Pyke.

Their letter was seen in early January by Tom Harrisson, an Old Harrovian and self-taught anthropologist then labouring in a Bolton cotton mill while observing the local working class. He had picked up a copy of the magazine to admire his first (and last) published poem, 'Coconut Moon', a choppy Surrealist ode to his sweetheart, 'Zita', who had since run off with another man. It had appeared just below Madge and Jennings's response to Pyke's letter. Harrisson immediately contacted Madge and Jennings, and the trio wrote to the *New Statesman and Nation* with what was effectively a manifesto for what would become Mass Observation (M-O). Out of this suitably surreal juxtaposition of letter and poem, the kind of accidental textual bricolage which Madge, Jennings and Harrisson enjoyed so much, a new movement was born.

Acknowledging their debt to Pyke's call for an 'anthropology of our own people', Madge, Jennings and Harrisson explained that their study of the British tribe would take on subjects like 'shouts and gestures of motorists', 'the aspidistra cult', 'bathroom behaviour', 'female taboos about eating' and, tellingly, 'anti-Semitism'. Along with their underlying emphasis on gathering mountains of raw data, on observation and analysis as two distinct stages, this inclusion of anti-Semitism suggests a greater debt to Pyke. They would have read his piece several months earlier on anti-Semitism, and as former Cambridge undergraduates it was also likely that they knew about Malting House. M-O was to focus on what British people did as much as what they said. The children at Malting House were 'under trained observation out of school hours as well as in them' and 'practically all that they do, and much of what they say, is recorded'.

M-O went on to become a unique and influential organisation dedicated to social research, and was employed during the war by the Ministry of Information. Pyke's letter brought it into being. It is just about possible to call him the father of M-O, though he was an errant father at best, one who wanted nothing to do with the child's upbringing. Madge kept him abreast of major developments and they corresponded briefly, but thereafter Pyke was never directly involved. By the time the three M-O founders had written their manifesto Pyke had moved on: indeed, by that point he had set himself a problem which made the Abdication crisis feel like an interesting but essentially parochial distraction. The question Pyke now sought to answer seemed to affect the very future of European civilisation.

Early in 1937 Pyke travelled up to London to take 'preliminary soundings of opinion' on an idea which seemed to him so obvious that he was amazed to learn that nobody else had yet thought of it. Imagining he would be gone for no more than a week he left his dog, Judy, with his landlord, and kept the cottage open. But one meeting led to another and more than two years later Pyke had still not returned to the Devil's Punchbowl. Judy, presumably, spent the rest of her days with the landlord. No doubt Pyke missed her, but there was nothing he would not sacrifice for the sake of the cause he had taken on.

The scheme that would come to dominate his life was an attempt to change the way we give, a redefinition of voluntarism in the face of the fascist threat. Its target was Spain. The year before, a 'Popular Front' coalition of left-leaning parties had won the Spanish General Election by a whisker. A clique of army officers led by General Francisco Franco had subsequently risen up against the government and the country had spiralled into civil war. What followed was savage and complicated, a bloody maze of reprisals and score-settling, with neighbours turning on each other as a mosaic of regional and sectarian tensions was uncovered.

From afar it was something else entirely: a war of opposites in which democracy was pitted against fascism, atheism against religion, the proletariat versus the bourgeoisie. As the journalist Martha Gellhorn wrote, 'it was one of those moments in history when there was no doubt'.

This grand narrative played to the throttled aspirations of Pyke's generation, one which had grown up during a military apocalypse and had since lived through an economic meltdown of unparalleled proportions. For many this either suggested or confirmed that liberal democracy was not the answer. As support for the fascist and communist alternatives grew, so did the bitter enmity between the two camps. Within each was an irresistible and mounting sense that they were not only trying to lead humanity to the promised land but at the same time preventing it from being dragged down to perdition by the enemy. It was a millenarian age, an age of extremes, and in Spain the forces of good and evil seemed to be sharing a battlefield for the first time. This feeling was shored up by the idea that Franco's 'Nationalist' rebels were being armed by Germany and Italy, while the left-wing 'Republican' government was backed by the Soviet Union.

In this sense, what had just begun in Spain appeared to be the first act in a new kind of struggle, an international civil war in which fascists all over the world would eventually line up against anti-fascists. If you were opposed to Mosley's Blackshirts you were also at war with Franco's Blueshirts, Mussolini's Blackshirts, Hitler's Brownshirts, Pelley's Silvershirts in the United States or even O'Duffy's Greenshirts in Ireland. Allegiance was determined not by nationality but by personal politics. 'Never has there been a period when patriotism, in the sense of automatic loyalty to a citizen's national government, counted for less,' wrote the historian Eric Hobsbawm. Pyke was physically unable to fight, an impotence which might have inspired his activism, but there was never any doubt in his mind about which side he belonged to.

In the weeks after the outbreak of the Spanish Civil War, Baldwin's Conservative government made the decision not to intervene, sparking the Aid Spain Movement, an alignment of charitable committees, organisations and other voluntary groups, 'a *de facto* Popular Front' geared towards providing the Spanish Republicans with everything the British government would not – except for arms. From the Cambridge Scientists Anti-War Group to the Basque Children's Committee or Bloomsbury's For Intellectual Liberty, these popular anti-fascist groups staged a crescendo of rallies and fundraisers across the country during the second half of 1936. Aid began to make its way to Spain and by the start of the following year 'Spain Shops' were sending money to the Republican government and British medical volunteers were making the journey to Spain. So were some 500 brave, idealistic young men who formed the British Battalion of the International Brigades. It seemed as if everything that could be done was being done. Or was it?

How to Get Aid to Spain for Free

In late 1936, Pyke had asked the mechanic who was fixing the clapped-out Armstrong car outside his cottage how much this vehicle was worth. The mechanic had explained that just then the second-hand car market was in a terrible state. The country was 'covered with dumps of old motor vehicles of all types' which could be 'bought for a song'. But rather than being bought, reconditioned and put back on the road, most were broken up and sold off to scrap merchants. A growing proportion of this scrap metal was even ending up in Germany where Nazi rearmament had created a buoyant market.

Over the weeks that followed, Pyke combined three basic observations: in Britain there were heaps of cheap second-hand vehicles, the sale of which was inadvertently boosting Nazi rearmament; there was popular support for the Spanish Republicans among British factory workers; and in Spain there was a need for costly ambulances and transports. Out of these came an idea.

If he could get his hands on some of these old vans and trucks before they were scrapped and have them transported to engineers who identified with the Republican cause and were willing to volunteer some of their spare time, then perhaps these vehicles could be reconditioned, turned into ambulances and sent out to Spain, all for very little money. He could provide material aid at a fraction of the retail cost. Factory workers would be doing out-of-hours pro bono work in aid of the Spanish Republicans. Or, to put it another way, the British labour movement would be fighting fascism with labour, not with capital.

It was a beguiling concept, and one that could easily be extended. Perhaps there were factory owners who were prepared to credit workers' overtime towards the cost of goods produced on their premises. Either Pyke would supply the raw materials to the workers, or volunteers would put in extra hours knowing that their employer would donate goods to the value of their labour (as well as donating the use of their machines and premises).

His plans for an institute devoted to the study of anti-Semitism had collapsed due to lack of funds, a failure which reflected in part the cause's unfashionability. This new scheme was different. It required very little funding and was inspired by the political cause célèbre. Having come up with the idea it seemed that all that Pyke needed to do was publicise the scheme and coordinate the efforts of hundreds of willing volunteers.

Voluntary Industrial Aid for Spain (VIAS) was formed in February 1937 with Pyke as Honorary Secretary and almost no funds to its name. He turned for help first to Sage Bernal and his partner, the art collector Margaret Gardiner. They gave a cheque for £15 which allowed Pyke to take rooms at No. 32 Great Ormond Street in Bloomsbury, a flat that would double up as Pyke's home and the VIAS headquarters.

His next step was to canvass further opinions, as he always did when approaching a new subject. He sought out Cambridge friends like Maurice Dobb, J. B. S. Haldane, the classicist F. L. Lucas, Kingsley Martin at the *New Statesman and Nation* and Harold Laski at LSE. All agreed that the idea was valuable and that he must first win over the trades unions. With no experience of the labour movement, Pyke went to Bernal for introductions and by the end of the month had cobbled together a VIAS Advisory Committee made up of fourteen high-powered union men and for added respectability the Labour peer Lord Faringdon.

Once the inspiration for Evelyn Waugh's 'Lord Parakeet' in *Decline and Fall*, Faringdon, a camp and flamboyant figure, had swapped the studied nonchalance of the 1920s for the campaigning seriousness of the 1930s. As well as being Treasurer of VIAS, after the bombing of Guernica he would open his home to the children of Basque refugees. Yet even Faringdon's involvement in Pyke's committee failed to mask its political character. It was, as Pyke would admit, 'hardboiled', with key figures like Joe Scott, Harry Adams and Jack Tanner either close to the Communist Party or card-carrying members. At the time this seemed unimportant. The idea behind the new 'Popular Front' mentality was that left-wing groups should pull together in the face of the fascist threat. But, as Pyke soon discovered, not everyone saw it like that.

Using new VIAS headed stationery he wrote to a high table of trades unions leaders explaining the concept, and persuaded Kingsley Martin to publish appeals in the letters section of the *New Statesman and Nation*. While eight of the unions he contacted agreed to become involved, others confessed that they could not agree to it until VIAS had the blessing of the all-powerful Trades Union Congress (TUC).

Depicted by the cartoonist Low as a lumbering carthorse, the TUC was slow to agree to anything, let alone an initiative dreamt up by a bearded bankrupt who had never done a day's manual labour. Pyke met with various officials, including the TUC General Secretary, Walter Citrine, most of whom, 'failed to respond with any trace of enthusiasm that I could detect'. In a letter to Bernal, he bemoaned this dilatory progress and 'the complexity of the organisation of the Labour movement'. Little did he know that while he was writing that letter Citrine was busy contacting the eight unions which had agreed to Pyke's plan to highlight what he believed to be a dangerous flaw.

The Amalgamated Society of Woodcutting Machinists agreed with Citrine that the voluntary manufacture of goods – no matter how worthy the cause – set a 'very dangerous precedent'. Perhaps more alarming for Citrine was the political character of Pyke's committee. The TUC leadership had resolved to avoid any endeavour which had communist associations, and in this regard, as one of his staff put it, the make-up of the VIAS Advisory Committee was 'rather unfortunate'. Which was why the TUC formally rejected VIAS.

For Pyke, this was an obvious moment to abandon the project. In terms of time and money, he had lost very little, and it was now clear that it was going to be extremely difficult to get this scheme up and running. Letting go of the idea at this early stage was also prudent given his financial situation, which was now 'desperate'. As he explained to Bernal and Gardiner, he was facing 'complete destitution. I come under no insurance or other scheme, and though apparently intelligent, have no prospect of a job'. He did not like asking for money and had begun to exhaust the generosity of friends. But he kept going. Indeed, he redoubled his efforts to promote an organisation which depended entirely on voluntary aid.

He was driven by the failure of his anti-Semitism work and, perhaps more than this, what he felt to be the inadequacy of the Left's response to the Spanish Civil War. Pyke was convinced that VIAS could do a better job of converting the popular sympathy for the Republican cause into actual aid. In the tone of his letters, as well as the quantity, it is clear that he was exasperated by other charities' lack of imagination. Why didn't they ask their members for ideas and labour, rather than just pressing them for more cash? It annoyed him on account of the seriousness of the fascist threat. Everything that *might* be done *must* be done. 'To forego any reasonable experiment – social or mechanical which may help the Spanish people – is to betray them.'

Why did he keep going? Because by the end of 1937 Geoffrey Pyke had gone to war; he was at war with fascism and as such he had no choice but to keep fighting.

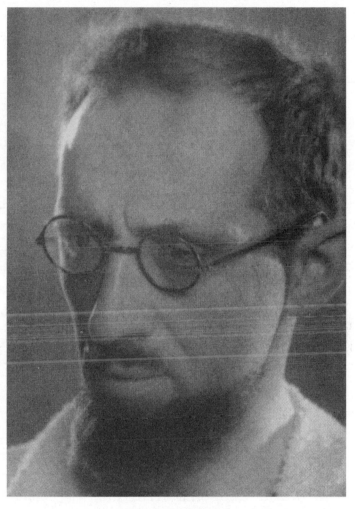

Pyke in the early 1930s

In spite of TUC opposition and limited funds, Pyke's brainchild began to fulfil some of its extraordinary promise. Over the coming months workers in factories dotted all over the country signed up to the scheme and formed VIAS cells. By October 1938, the charity had shipped to Spain some twenty-five vehicles including two mobile blood-transfusion units, and by the end of the war as many as seventy reconditioned vehicles had been donated. As well as mattresses for Basque refugees, ampoules of anaesthetic, anti-tetanus serum and novocaine they also sent microscopes. Employees at R. & J. Beck Instrument Makers, in Kentish Town, worked extra shifts on Sunday mornings until they had earned enough credit to send crates of microscopes out to Spain. Legend has it that while the ship carrying the first batch was torpedoed, other crates made it through and these instruments were thought to be the finest in Spain.

Every VIAS cell was different. The one in Cambridge, led by the sinologist and embryologist Joseph Needham, managed to produce just one reconditioned motorcycle, and even that was a struggle. Needham described the Sunday afternoon when the enormous Harley Davidson they had been working on shot out of the garage and crashed through a nearby fence, causing extensive damage. The Manchester cell, by contrast, was getting through so many motor-cycles that they had to start using space behind the nearby Eccles Trade Council building.

Pyke's charity was a triumph of small-scale voluntarism, and its founder was in no doubt that its 'real capital' was the energy and frenetic enthusiasm of its volunteers. In some cases this led to greater politicisation. One of his workers recalled the effect of this work on his colleagues. 'They were starting to understand how vital it was for the working class to help one another, no matter what country they lived in.' This was the Popular Front as it should have been. Those on the British Left were uniting to produce material aid which was going to those who needed it in Spain.

One of the VIAS 'social entrepreneurs' next to a reconditioned
truck before it was sent to Spain

Just as these factory cells were run by volunteers, so was the
charity's headquarters on Great Ormond Street. Pyke described those
young men and women who came in after work as 'social entrepreneurs' (long before the term became popular). They wrote letters,
coordinated shipments and did battle with the notoriously chaotic
VIAS card-index system. At the centre of this vortex of good intent
was Pyke: drawn, balding, bespectacled, often in sandals and eschewing
formal dress as he padded around the flat. Yet for all his commitment
to the cause, he was a terrible manager.

Pyke's style was circuitous and often labour-intensive. He tended
to spend too long looking for a joke, analysing a joke or exploring
apparently blind alleys. 'I have not yet trained myself to keep my
papers neatly,' he added, conceding elsewhere, 'I am very conscious,

from my experience, that I am not the man to run this, as, psychologically, I am an habitual procrastinator'. He could also be impatient. There was an asperity to his urgency to aid the Republicans and he made no secret of his desire that VIAS should function with all the efficiency of a cut-throat capitalist operation. In a paper prepared for the Spain Campaign Committee of the Labour Party he described his charity as 'damnably inefficient', asserting 'with complete confidence in the accuracy of my description, that if we had to face in direct opposition a German Fascist concern of the same size, we should be simply wiped out of the way'.

Out of this underlying dissatisfaction came the desire to apply himself more widely. For one of the first times in his life he had teams of workers awaiting instructions and, after reading about some of the issues faced by the Republicans, he began to design small-scale practical solutions to particular problems which were then sent out to VIAS cells. In other words, Pyke began to invent and his inventions were realised.

On learning that many of the roads leading to the front line in Spain were too rough for ambulances he designed a motorcycle sidecar capable of carrying a wounded soldier.

When he heard about the difficulty of getting hot food to the front, he produced plans for a separate sidecar which could keep rations warm by using the heat of the engine.

Knowing that there were problems with the Republicans' trains, he developed plans for a pedal-powered locomotive in which the motive force came from an engine room of cycling men.

When he was not inventing, he would look to the past for solutions to contemporary problems. With fuel in short supply and fields to be sown, Pyke sent out instructions to his volunteers that they should look for discarded horse ploughs hidden in hedgerows. These could be restored and sent out to Spanish farmers.

He also read about a variety of moss which had been used during the Great War in lieu of cotton bandages. Self-sterilising, highly absorbent and readily available both in the Scottish Highlands and parts of Spain, sphagnum moss was described by the War Office in 1919 as 'one of the most valuable and cheapest surgical dressings for the relief of suffering in the case of sceptic wounds and surgical operations generally'. Since then, curiously, it had been overlooked. Anyone can forget, Pyke allowed, but a collective failure to find out what had been forgotten was, in his opinion, unforgivable. Using his VIAS network Pyke distributed a guide to collecting and preparing sphagnum moss. He gave talks about this neglected material in Paris and London, all of which may have contributed to its use several years later, during the Second World War, when even the young Princesses Elizabeth and Margaret were reported to be gathering sphagnum moss from the moors surrounding Balmoral.

For a year and a half VIAS provided material aid to the Spanish Republicans at a fraction of its retail cost. There were enthusiastic write-ups of its work in the *Daily Worker*, *Left News*, *Tribune* and *Manchester Guardian*, and even *The Times* mentioned VIAS motorcycle-ambulances on their way to Spain. The Spanish Minister for Foreign Affairs, Julio Álvarez del Vayo, who had helped to purchase arms from the Soviet Union, praised the work of VIAS. Yet by the winter of 1938, with Franco in the ascendant, its activities started to slow.

Since his decision to take on Nazi anti-Semitism four years earlier a new version of Geoffrey Pyke had emerged. Similar to his 1920s iteration, he was intellectually adventurous, unafraid of extremes and always on the lookout for sloppy assumptions. He took great care to formulate his questions correctly, and when searching for solutions would conduct small-scale experiments or seek inspiration in newspapers, conversations, films, songs and anything else that he could find. He would also mine the past for historical analogies. What had changed was that he was now capable of mechanical invention, and in a political sense he had come alive. Yet for the British Security

Service there would soon be a question mark over how far he had taken this newfound political awareness.

But he was not the complete inventor, at least not yet. Pyke might have perfected the ability to identify problems and come up with bold solutions, but he had failed to master the next stage – how to have his radical ideas taken up at the highest level. At times he would complain that it was everyone else's fault, and that he lived in 'a country whose deepest social belief is, perhaps, that nothing should ever be done for the first time'. While there was some element of truth in this – the 1930s in Britain will not be remembered as a decade of epic scientific advance – the real problem was that he had not yet understood that resistance to innovation was and is innate. 'Wisdom is like gold,' he had written, 'it is useless if no one will accept it from you.' Pyke was perfectly good at finding this gold. Now he needed to improve his ability to sell it – which was why his next challenge was so apt.

HOW TO PREVENT A WAR

By the summer of 1939 Peter Raleigh was a man in need of an adventure. He had gone up to King's College, Cambridge, several years earlier, where he had fallen under the spell of the historian and fellow Kingsman Eric Hobsbawm, then a senior figure in the Cambridge Student Branch of the Communist Party. 'His quality of mind was such,' wrote Raleigh, 'the speed of his appreciation of a situation so extraordinary, his analysis of it so impeccably unemotional, that he was a natural guru for young Communists. He was also rather a nice man.' Under Hobsbawm's guidance Raleigh had become a probationary member of the Party, and in an ill-fated attempt to gain full membership had staged a fundraiser in aid of the Spanish Republicans. It included a sideshow called 'Shoot the Dictator', in which visitors took it in turns to take potshots at caricatures of Mussolini, Hitler et al. In a momentary lapse, Raleigh had added to this rogues' gallery a portrait of Stalin. He was taken aside by a 'rather foursquare earnest man', Dr Arnold Kettle, and told 'with gentle solemnity' that perhaps he was not cut out for Party membership.

Several months later, in June 1939, Peter Raleigh returned to the

Bloomsbury flat in which he had been staying, the home of a doctor who had volunteered in Spain, where he was told that he had a visitor. Raleigh was then introduced to a gaunt, wiry man in glasses and a threadbare suit.

It was difficult, he found, 'not to be mesmerised by Geoffrey Pyke's head', and in particular 'the shiny bald scalp with its in-built crease, a sort of adult fontanelle' and the 'tufty black beard waving uncertainly at the end of the chin'.

The combination of Pyke's appearance and the way he spoke – an opening salvo of questions and jokes followed by streams of ideas and observations that would wash over you, the meaning apparent and beguiling, leading up to a moment of high seriousness in which it felt as if you were being let in on a tremendous secret – all this made him come across as both 'Mad Scientist and conspirator from *The Secret Agent*'. Raleigh was entranced. 'Without knowing anything of what was to be asked of me, I volunteered myself for whatever Geoffrey had in mind.' It would be some time before he realised what this was, and that unwittingly he had agreed to smuggle himself into Nazi Germany as part of a private attempt to avert another world war.

How to Give Germany 'the Facts'

Fifteen months earlier, in March 1938, German troops had marched into Vienna in the wake of the *Anschluss* between Austria and Nazi Germany. In the weeks that followed Hitler had turned his attention to the Sudetenland, a little-known section of western and north-western Czechoslovakia. With the indignation of a man who had succumbed long ago to an enveloping victimhood, the German Chancellor declared in speech after speech that the Sudetenland belonged to Germany – until the Sudeten 'issue' had become the Sudeten 'crisis'. The danger was ample. If Hitler ordered his troops into Czechoslovakia, as well he might, British, French and even Soviet forces might come to the aid of the Czechs. A single order from Hitler could trigger another war.

This remained the situation on the morning of Monday, 29 August 1938, which began in London with a dribble of rain. On opening his curtains in Great Ormond Street Pyke looked out onto a flat, cloudy day.

'Waking up, with me, has always been a slow process,' he confessed. Rather than get up, he decided to go through the day's newspapers in bed. On page nine of the *Manchester Guardian* he read an article that would change his life.

The paper's former Berlin correspondent had written: 'If the main facts of the conflict between the Sudeten Germans and the Czechs and of the international situation as a whole were known to the German public Hitler would no longer be the "Fuhrer and Chancellor". The fear of war is greater amongst the German people than amongst any other, and if they knew that Hitler has been, and perhaps still is, as much as considering a war of pure aggression, then neither his eloquence nor his measures of terroristic coercion would avail him any longer.' This was a revelation. If the author was to be believed, then Hitler would lose the support of the German people once they realised, as so many Europeans had, that he was leading them to war. One can imagine a smile spreading across Pyke's face.

'For me the world changed with that sentence. One response filled my mind: "Why not tell them? Tell them that Hitler is leading them to war."' 'I forgot to ask myself whether anyone would take it on himself to tell the German people. I felt only the necessity of their being told: told at once and loudly and repeatedly and by the right people.' 'The civilian population of Germany should be bombed,' he went on, 'NOT WITH BOMBS – which is about the best way to unite them against us – but with leaflets, etc., containing the truth. A continual stream of messages (issued, too, as publicly as possible in this country) giving to the Germans *facts* which have been concealed, that there is no hope for them or us while Hitler and the Nazis are in power.'

Again he had identified the root of a problem in that lacuna which lies between the reality of a situation and how it is perceived. His task now was to reduce the gap, and in a Platonic sense show Germany the world beyond the cave. But he would need to move fast.

Pyke's first attempt to give the German people 'the facts' took the form of a message to be sent to the workers of Germany from a body representative of the British labour movement to say that Hitler was leading them to war. Again he failed to persuade the TUC to help, but on this occasion won over an affiliated body, the National Council of Labour. In late September, the night before Prime Minister Neville Chamberlain flew to Munich for the last time, this organisation released a version of Pyke's message. It was featured on the BBC News and appeared in the next day's *Manchester Guardian*. But this was much too little, too late.

Though an agreement was reached the following day in Munich, and the immediate threat of war was diminished, Hitler remained in power and so did Chamberlain. Another international crisis was bound to flare up sooner rather than later. Over the weeks that followed, Pyke plunged himself once again into the question of how to prevent a war with Germany. He rejected the idea that conflict was inevitable, or that these events were beyond his control. Instead he chivvied himself into approaching this problem as if he was a newcomer to the situation, or, as he put it, being a Jew he had to think like an Ishmaelite, adopt the mentality of an outcast and reject 'the common assumptions of the time as to what is feasible and what is not'.

Late in 1938 Pyke had his breakthrough. He had been intimidated, he realised, not by objective difficulties but by Nazi propaganda and, to a lesser extent, by the thought of sounding ridiculous. This, of course, ran counter to his dearly held belief 'that among the first duties of a citizen (of the modern world) is a willingness to make a fool of himself. But for this belief it is, I think, doubtful whether the idea in my mind of a private attempt to prevent the war would ever have passed into action. For men do not think purposefully of what they believe they can never hope to do and they do not do what they have never thought of.' Pyke now had in mind a scheme that was 'not only practicable' but 'ridiculously practical providing we tackled it professionally'.

His plan was radical and dangerous – far more so than broadcasting a message to the German workers – and would be hard to implement. It depended on persuading at least ten German-speakers to enter Nazi Germany under false pretences and stay there for anything up to a month while carrying out undercover work on Pyke's behalf. This was not an easy sell.

For the Director of SIS, Britain's foreign intelligence agency, the recent failure of his organisation to penetrate Nazi Germany had nothing to do with funding or motivation. 'The fact of the matter,' he wrote in 1938, 'is that during the last twelve months or so, things have become very difficult indeed in Germany.' One of the only SIS agents in the country, Baron de Ropp, had recently been moved to Switzerland because of fears for his safety. For years, there had been no British agents in the country – indeed, the situation was so bad that SIS was by then forced to rely on aerial photographs for its military and industrial intelligence. If, by early 1939, it was too dangerous to send even one professional intelligence agent into Nazi Germany, then dispatching a team of amateurs was senseless.

Yet for Pyke the risk was easily outweighed by the consequences of success. If he could find enough people who were willing to enter Germany on his account, and his plan actually worked, then war might be forestalled and millions of lives would be saved. With that in mind, Pyke began to look for recruits.

★

He started by contacting senior figures at the Workers' Educational Association, Toynbee Hall, LSE and University College London (UCL), asking them if they knew of any adventurous German-speakers who might be willing to go on a paid expedition to Germany. If so, they should write to him. In spite of the risks, almost immediately the letters and telegrams began to arrive at Great Ormond Street.

One of the first to get in touch was Cedric Hentschel, a lecturer at UCL whose German and Polish parents had named him after *Little Lord Fauntleroy*, and whose students liked to rhyme: 'The Lectures of Hentschel / Are really essential; / No other teacher / Knows so much about Nietzsche', although it was Byron, really, where his expertise lay. Amy Cunningham, at LSE, was a friend of Hentschel whose teaching methods were described by colleagues as 'unorthodox' – sadly we do not know why. She too wrote to Pyke, as did Edith Lamb, the daughter of a trades-union official whose only weakness, worryingly, was her ability to speak German. John Gilbertson, a miner's son who taught German at a boy's school, was a better linguist but would not be able to travel for another few weeks. Stanley Smith was another man who taught German and was on holiday when he heard about the scheme. 'The thought of augmenting my modest salary as a teacher with activities of a kind reminiscent of Ashenden [Somerset Maugham's fictional British spy] appealed strongly,' not least because he had recently become engaged and was saving up for a ring.

As well as Peter Raleigh, the Cambridge undergraduate who, for Pyke, 'by a short head is perhaps the most brilliant of the team', the amateur spymaster was contacted by a teacher from Bradford; a young architect; a manual worker who was unable to travel until his broken finger had healed, and six or seven others, mostly young teachers and lecturers in German Studies, each one patriotic, curious and quietly courageous. A Miss Crowther was typical. She reminded Pyke of the formidable Lysistrata in Bernard Shaw's *Apple Cart*. 'Apparently rather gentle, but as firm as a rock underneath. I think if she came up against a Gestapo agent that the Gestapo agent would get the worst of it. Yorkshire accent. No nonsense about her. Full of beans and enthusiasm. I suspect wanting a little adventure and a laudable desire to be of use and to do her bit. The obstacle: an aged widow mother.'

More mysterious among the team of Pyke's potential recruits was Fred Fuller, then living in Paris, whose ability to speak German was never questioned, and Marjory Watson, a stout, sallow-looking woman in her late thirties, who was apparently eking out a living as a German translator. Watson had once been described to the police as 'a drunkard and a bad character'. More recently, in April 1939, Special Branch had referred to her as a 'woman suspected of being a Nazi agent'. MI5 had subsequently labelled her 'unsuitable for employment in any capacity under the War Department'. It would later emerge that they were right about Watson's unsuitability, but for the wrong reasons.

It was a fascinating group, a neat cross-section of the coming generation in Britain whose members hailed from across the gamut of social and geographical backgrounds. But it was hard to see how this band of well-meaning linguists could possibly thwart Hitler in his attempts to take Germany to war.

Pyke gave nothing away, to the extent that most of his young recruits did not even realise they were part of a larger team. Instead, they were kept apart from each other and merely told that they would be paid to visit Germany and interview ordinary Germans. If the answers to their questions matched certain criteria, a more complex operation would begin. Given the risks involved, some of these young recruits might have pulled out in the face of such opacity, but they reported to a man who seemed to have mastered the art of charming evasion. Pyke could bat away most enquiries with a self-deprecating authority which the young linguists found winning.

'Most of us, I suppose, regarded Pyke at the time as a harmless eccentric who had given us a paid opportunity for a holiday with a difference', wrote Smith, later recalling Pyke's 'mischievous eyes twinkling behind his spectacles', and how he held court 'in his seedy office-cum-flat in Great Ormond Street' where the filing system was 'stacked fruit trays from floor to ceiling'.

Cedric Hentschel was equally taken by Pyke, and was even moved to poetry:

> With his gaunt frame and square-cut beard
> He had the air of a Russian princeling.
> His voice, silky and insinuating,
> Came from some orient top-drawer,
> A contrast to his shabby clothes,
> To socks mismatched or simply lacking.
> In a fine baritone he would hail me as *Ceedrick*,
> The lengthened vowel conferring extra status.

Hentschel and the others were now ready to go, but there was a snag. Their Svengali had disappeared. On 26 July, Stanley Smith went to meet Pyke, as had been arranged, only to be told that he had flown to Paris.

In France we know that he stayed at the Royal Hotel, off the Champs-Élysées, and that he was away for two nights. The flight, at £6.6s., was expensive. Pyke's reasons for going were less straightforward.

On his return, he explained that he had gone to see an exiled German statistician and had pumped him for advice on which questions to ask the German people. As Pyke wrote to Norman Angell, the Nobel Prize-winning author and campaigner, whom he had also seen in Paris, his journey had been 'amply worthwhile'. It had also led to several changes in their operation.

In the days after his Parisian trip, Pyke instructed each of his linguists to visit at a certain time a house in Brixton or one in Hampstead where they were met by a German émigré introduced only as 'Professor Higgins'. Following the successful film of Shaw's *Pygmalion* the year before, this reference would not have been lost on them. In that version, Professor Higgins was played by Leslie Howard. Yet nobody seemed to know the identity of the man Pyke had playing the part.

Smith described him as 'a 34-year-old German refugee'. Others remarked on his blond hair. 'We had to converse with him,' Smith explained, 'and during the interview put ten questions to him and memorise the answers, which we then had to pass on to Pyke – or Uncle Geoffrey as he preferred to be called for the purposes of the exercise.' It was a task at which Smith excelled, recalling every answer with schoolmasterly ease.

You might not think there was anything unusual about Pyke asking his linguists to do this – but for the fact that they had done so already. Just before his trip to Paris, Pyke had told Hentschel and Cunningham to test their fellow linguists like this. Now he was starting again. Everyone was to be put through their paces by this anonymous German émigré.

In another respect this episode jars. Throughout his life Pyke had shown himself to be wary of delegating responsibility, and would do so only after long consideration. This refugee was a stranger to him. His name does not appear in any of Pyke's letters, address books, notes or diaries until after his trip to Paris, whereupon it appears more than any other.

August began in London with a downpour of rain. With the newspapers full of speculation about whether Japan would join the Axis, thunderclaps rang out around the capital like the sound of collapsing buildings. None of this dampened the collective desire to enjoy the coming Bank Holiday, and on Friday, 4 August, with the weather improved, some four million holidaymakers left the capital. The next day, lost among the crowds, Stanley Smith and Amy Cunningham began separate journeys to Nazi Germany. Soon after, Cedric Hentschel and Peter Raleigh did likewise. High above Great Ormond Street, in his latest incarnation as amateur spymaster, Pyke was left to contemplate their fate, and the broader question of whether his scheme stood any chance of success. The answer to this depended, to a large extent, on the quality of the idea behind it.

Pyke's plan, in full, was to send a team of up to two dozen linguists into Nazi Germany to carry out a Gallup-style survey of German attitudes to war. He had read in the *Manchester Guardian* that most Germans did not want Hitler leading them to war. He planned to prove it with a scientific survey of German public opinion. If the results were as expected, they would be publicised at the highest level. Initially he had envisaged their release through a major newspaper syndicate or news agency – at one point he had in mind the American Institute of Public Opinion, or the BBC – yet by the time Smith and Cunningham set out for the Hook of Holland Pyke was certain that he could get the survey results to the White House for US President Franklin D. Roosevelt to use in one of his weekly 'international' speeches.

There were two things one could say about Hitler's response to the results of this survey: it would be furious and public. 'You would then have got the attention of the whole world – the German people to some extent included – focused on this question: "How far are the German people behind Hitler – or not?"' Details from individual interviews could be leaked in later speeches, reinforcing the notion that Hitler did not have his country's full support.

Even if most Germans proved to be against Hitler taking them to war, and Pyke's 'conversationalists' were able to complete their survey without being picked up by the Gestapo – and were somehow able to get their results out of the country (a problem that remained unsolved) – what were the chances of the survey results having the desired effect? What difference would it make if you could prove that most Germans did not want war?

By the summer of 1939, one of three things needed to happen to prevent a war with Germany. Britain and France could agree to turn a blind eye to Hitler's eastward expansion. The Polish government might accept Hitler's demands regarding the status of Danzig. Or Hitler could back down from military confrontation, as it could be argued he had done at Munich, on the basis that the resistance to war was too great either within Germany or without.

Already the first two options looked unlikely. British foreign policy continued to gravitate away from appeasement and there was even the possibility of an Anglo-Soviet pact. Nor did the Polish government show any desire to accept Hitler's demands; for Sir Edmund Ironside, inspecting Polish forces in July 1939, 'the whole nation has made up its mind to fight' with Poles everywhere gripped by a 'mad spirit of optimism'. Pyke's plan was aimed squarely at the third option: the idea that Hitler might come to see an invasion of Poland as a political mistake. A successful survey, if publicised internationally, might at the very least cause him to hesitate. In itself this would buy time for Germany's putative enemies, Britain and France, both rearming at speed. It would also provide a shot in the arm for the German opposition, which remained hamstrung by an inability to gauge its collective strength. For those millions of Germans still ambivalent about the possibility of war, the idea that it was imminent might push them into a state of opposition. Pyke also believed that the survey would make it harder, if hostilities broke out, for the British government to caricature the German people, as it had done during the last war, as a nation of bloodthirsty Huns, and that this might shorten the conflict or make post-war reparations less severe. Unknown to Pyke, those German generals manoeuvring behind the scenes to avert an invasion of Poland would also benefit by gaining time, as would Adam von Trott and the Swedish businessman Birger Dahlerus, both trying to stave off the threat of war through high-level informal diplomacy. All this, however, was predicated on Pyke's team being able to steal what he described as the 'most carefully guarded of all the Nazi secrets' – German public opinion.

Here was a plan which drew on all Pyke's obsessions: gathering masses of data; operating undercover; solving political problems using a scientific method; disregarding popular assumptions; understanding the importance of public opinion; combating fascism by any means; putting one's faith in untrained amateurs; and not only identifying a looming crisis but doing one's utmost to avert it. Above all, this was characterised by breathtaking ambition. 'It was a private attempt to prevent the war', he wrote. 'It is true that it only stood a faint chance of success, but that, I think you'll agree, was not a reason for not making the attempt.'

It did not take long for the German border guards to sense that something about Amy Cunningham was not quite right. After being asked how much money she was carrying – fourteen English shillings, ten German Marks and a handful of Registered Marks – the LSE lecturer was escorted out of the main hall and handed over to a sour-faced German woman.

'I noticed that she had on a long white garment, and round her waist a belt with a bundle of twelve or so keys,' Cunningham recalled. 'She took me into a building, went along a little corridor [. . .] there were about eight small doors, all very similar. She unlocked one of them and told me to go in. She then locked the door behind us.'

'Take off your clothes,' she ordered.

Just weeks earlier, Pyke had asked various experts on Nazi Germany about the practicality of his scheme. Of these the best informed was undoubtedly Sir Robert Vansittart, Permanent Under-Secretary at the Foreign Office for most of the 1930s, and by 1939 part of MI6's top-secret Z Organisation, sometimes referred to as 'Vansittart's

Private Detection Agency'. Pyke had outlined his scheme, to which Vansittart's response had been emphatic.

'Ridiculous,' he had said. 'The Gestapo will have them all within twenty-four hours.' Amy Cunningham, it seemed, had lasted only a matter of minutes.

As instructed she removed her clothes and watched, naked, as the guard picked through her bag, something she did with stony exactitude. At one point she removed the mirror from Cunningham's compact to check for hidden material. There followed a 'very thorough' bodily examination, and 'when she was quite finished, she promptly washed her hands with much swishing. This annoyed me really more than the actual examination.'

'It must be very unpleasant for you to have to undress foreigners,' Cunningham snarled.

'On the contrary,' came the reply.

There was a pause, before the woman's arm swung up in a Hitler salute. Cunningham was free to enter the Third Reich.

Neither Stanley Smith nor Marjory Watson had any such trouble at the frontier and were soon wandering the streets of Frankfurt-am-Main, unaware of each other, as they began to look for potential interviewees. One of Pyke's greatest worries was that nobody would talk to them. 'It was even part of the general opinion of the time, that foreigners were watched, their contacts with the population noted and those to whom they talked, later questioned.' He had asked his amateur spies to send him coded postcards giving an indication of their progress. Each was to be addressed to 'Uncle' and sent to one of four different correspondents in England, all friends of Pyke, who would forward the messages to Great Ormond Street. If they were finding it impossible to engage ordinary Germans in conversation then they were to complain in the postcard that the trip was 'boring'. If the interviews were going well, the holiday was 'interesting'.

'Quite an interesting town,' went Smith's first postcard. The following day: 'It is an interesting old town'. 'This seems to be an interesting place,' began Amy Cunningham's card the day after she checked into the Hotel National. But still no word from Hentschel.

'My dear Cedric,' wrote Pyke, 'you have disappeared into the blue. What is Germany like? It ought to be most interesting to see at first hand. [. . .] We have not had a single word from you. Do the young women of Germany leave you so little time that you cannot even spare a moment to send us some postcards?' At last one arrived: 'Life continues strenuous,' he managed, 'though interesting.'

'It was not difficult to get Germans to talk,' explained Smith. 'For all their harsh and commanding exterior, [they] are sentimental enough underneath and love talking about their families.' Cunningham was amazed at 'how much they have to get off their chests'. 'I had ridiculously over-rated the difficulty of making contact with the German population,' wrote Pyke. What had made this easier was that each of his undercover pollsters was not just another tourist, but the embodiment of a lovable German stereotype – the eccentric Englishman abroad.

Before letting them go, Pyke had urged each member of his team to play up to their national caricature. Each one should 'go grumbling incredulously to everyone, refusing to believe what he was told or to take "no" for an answer, to display an undue and obsessive concern with his own comfort, to behave as if his own habits were fixed and sanctioned by the universe and that it was the place and concern of other people to contribute to their satisfaction.' As he saw it, 'providing our behaviour did not go beyond the limit of credulity as conditioned by the behaviour – real, exaggerated or mythical – of our ancestors who had travelled in Germany, we were safe. We had something more than safety. We could use the myth positively. It could be used to give us elbow room – one might almost say *lebensraum* – to make contact with Germans of every class.'

Inspired by this advice, Raleigh had arrived in Germany carrying a full set of golf clubs. After 'a tender farewell' to his on-off girlfriend (and future wife) Ros, daughter of the *Manchester Guardian* Editor, C. P. Scott, he had made the relatively short trip to Frankfurt where he planned to play a lot of golf. But it was raining, so instead he sought out the nearest cabaret bar. Here he conducted an interview with one of the bar's hostesses, who was 'very intelligent' and, on account of the army officers who frequented the place, particularly 'well informed on politics'.

Raleigh soon found that cafés and bars were the best place to pick up strangers, the only problem being that he was required to drink 'endless coffees or beers. Leaving the café table for the loo was both physically necessary and a means of jotting down answers to questions. But the sheer number of beers involved – given that 53 per cent, or whatever the percentage was, of those we interviewed had to be men – meant that I rarely got to bed sober.'

'You *are* a disgusting pig not to have written,' ran Pyke's first note to Raleigh, in which he disguised himself as a rather Wodehousian 'Aunt Marjory'. 'David Allen' – code for Pyke – 'tells me that he may be going abroad for a few days holiday almost any day now. He asked me where you were and I told him you were in Frankfurt. He says he has half a mind to go somewhere like that, so you may hear from him. [. . .] At any rate, you monster of iniquity, the purpose of this letter is to say that we are dying for news of you, even if it is only a picture postcard of yourself drinking flagons of German beer.'

Pyke sent this clumsily coded message just two days after Raleigh had set out for Germany (it crossed with his first postcard back to Pyke). Evidently time was passing slowly in London. The amateur spymaster was desperate to be in the thick of things and, as he waited for news, he began to wonder if he could slide unnoticed into Germany as he had done twenty-five years earlier.

★

On the day that Raleigh received Pyke's note, he had a strange encounter at breakfast. It began when he engaged a young German in conversation, only to find out that he was in fact a fellow English tourist. There was something familiar about him: a lively intelligence and an adventurousness which Raleigh might have recognised in himself.

'Do you know a man called Geoffrey Pyke?' he tried.

Stanley Smith replied that he did. Both men smiled. As they had both begun to suspect, they were part of a larger team. While they agreed that it would be a mistake to operate for long as a pair, Smith and Raleigh decided to go to the golf course at Bad Schwallbach now that the weather had turned. They spent the rest of the day scooping balls out of bunkers under the watchful eye of the golf professional while conducting undercover interviews with club members.

Amid the 'sweet-smelling pines', which kept getting in the way of Raleigh's drives, there were moments when the threat of war felt inexorably distant. This sunny reverie was broken only by 'the rasp of the Messerschmitt fighters chasing their tails in the blue sky above'. War was close – but not so close as to keep Pyke out of the country.

Just before 13:00 on 13 August, a group of Pyke's conversationalists met, as instructed by postcard, at the thirteenth green of Frankfurt's main golf course. They saw a lanky figure advancing down the fairway. He was carrying a canary in a cage. It was Pyke. To Smith, he looked 'as strange as a unicorn'.

'It should have been no surprise that Geoffrey's dress was the opposite of what most would expect,' reflected Raleigh. 'Whereas in London you found him walking the streets in wrinkled trousers, shapeless jacket over, maybe, a pyjama top with what looked like a bootlace at the neck, and sandal-shod feet, here on a sultry August day on the golf-course he wore the smartest of dark city suits.'

The canary was his disguise, an eye-catching prop to deflect attention.

It had worked like a charm, and earlier that day Geoffrey Pyke had been welcomed into Nazi Germany posing as a canary buff.

The following day he sat down in a Frankfurt café with five of his conversationalists to discuss their findings. If Pyke had ever received any kind of espionage training, he must have forgotten it. Meeting like this in public with all his agents was not the work of a professional agent. 'I suppose the best that could be said about this was that the Gestapo, if around, could hardly believe that we constituted any sort of threat to German security', wrote a bemused Raleigh. Or was this by design? Pyke's preference in disguise was always to hide onself in plain view and to behave as if incapable of subterfuge. If the Gestapo was looking for people who hid, they must be out in the open. Besides, he was feeling impatient and could not wait to hear the initial results of his survey.

In less than a week, each of the five Frankfurt conversationalists had questioned as many as ten Germans a day, making sure to vary the age of their interviewees as well as their occupation, gender and social background. They had tried to shoehorn into each exchange ten distinct questions, always in a set order. These covered everything from where the subject got their news to whether Germany would win a future war; did they want Germany to win; whether Britain should stand up to Hitler; how the Nazi government treated the workers, the Jews, the Church; whether territorial conquest justified another war, and, a tricky question, was the interviewee prepared to rise up against Hitler? 'I only once reached that question,' confessed Raleigh.

The technique was demanding and risky, yet the survey's success depended on it. Several months earlier Pyke had been granted permission by Dr Gallup, founder of the eponymous survey and head of the American Institute of Public Opinion, to imitate the Gallup technique 'as closely as is possible in a totalitarian state'. In return any profits from the publication of Pyke's survey would go to Gallup.

It made poor financial sense, but Pyke needed this Gallup connection to reinforce his survey's credibility and to make it hard for the Nazi regime to discredit its results. In a broader sense, the German government would find it difficult to criticise the idea of attaching political weight to public opinion. Hitler had used plebiscites to rubber-stamp everything from Germany's exit from the League of Nations (95 per cent approval) through to the *Anschluss* with Austria (99.7 per cent approval). Just as the plebiscite had become a recognised political tool in recent years, so had Gallup surveys. Mass Observation, which Pyke had helped to bring about, had also come to the fore with the publication that year of the bestselling Penguin Special *Britain by Mass-Observation*. Public-opinion polls had never been so fashionable, so scientific and so plausible – which was why Pyke was thrilled by what his team had found.

According to their survey, most Germans did not think Hitler's desire for territorial conquest justified war. This was remarkable. Nor did they think that war was imminent. 'Though they admitted the political situation was dangerous,' explained Raleigh, 'they seemed to have perfect faith in the fact that [. . .] Hitler didn't want war and could obtain what he wanted without precipitating one.' Equally surprising, and key, was the high proportion of those interviewed who were either fed up with the government or professed no opinion. Ambivalence about the Nazi regime – given its nature and the effort required to be anything other than supportive – suggested that these subjects were closer to being anti-Nazi in sentiment than pro-Nazi. A surprising number of people wanted a war just to see Germany lose, as this would mean the end of Nazi rule. Others opened up about their dislike of anti-Semitic discrimination, one man confiding in Smith that he had recently been playing the Violin Concerto in E Minor by Mendelssohn, a banned Jewish composer. 'If that's bad music,' he had told him, 'then it's a bad government.'

Of course, these were the results Pyke *wanted* his conversationalists to find. There is the small possibility that his team deliberately exaggerated their findings. But given the long and detailed reports later produced by each one, and the memoirs they wrote, this seems unlikely.

After several more days in Frankfurt, Pyke returned to London eager to flood Germany with more pollsters. Earlier that summer he had spoken to various statisticians, all of whom had agreed that he needed the results of at least 1,000 interviews, preferably 1,500, for his survey to be statistically valid. So far he had just under 100. If he was able to add more members to his team, and they carried on at their present rate, then in a matter of weeks there would be enough data. But there was still the problem of getting the results out of Germany.

How to Get the Results Out of Germany (with the Help of Josef Goebbels)

There are so many of us out here in Frankfurt that we should form a team and challenge the local golf club to a match.

This was the gist of what Peter Raleigh had just said. We do not know the precise wording, only that he was sitting on the terrace of the Frankfurt Golf Course and was talking to Pyke, and that on hearing this remark the older man had begun to laugh – yet almost immediately his face froze.

'I felt as epileptics must do when they are about to have an attack, a condition of great but generalised tenseness. I knew that a revelation was coming into my mind, and that the details were falling fast into place. I concentrated on the horizon and in another breath or two my mind was quite clear and I felt as loose and content as I imagine people do when they have received [. . .] religious revelation.'

Pyke's idea was ingenious, if a little far-fetched. It is interesting mainly for what it tells us about his intellectual technique, and how quickly he was able to develop a new idea.

His first step was to take Raleigh's joke seriously. Then he extrapolated it. Having imagined his pollsters forming a team, he pictured them taking on every golf club in the area.

What would happen next?

It would be a magnificent PR opportunity for the Nazi regime. 'A lot of flap' could be made about England and Germany's shared love of sport and fair play, as evidenced by this series of golf matches.

Then what? Pyke's pollsters could exploit Nazi interest in this sporting exchange by inviting a team of German golfers back to England. Crucially, they would have to make sure that both teams left from the same airport. This would guarantee the presence of official German photographers and camera crews at the airport. In turn, this would more or less rule out the possibility of Pyke's pollsters being strip-searched, so they could bring out the survey results on their persons. Better yet, it would mean that if the Nazi government ever came to question whether this survey had actually taken place, which he hoped they would, Pyke could casually refer to those Nazi publications which had run the story.

This tickled him. Indeed, the idea 'that the Nazi regime itself had been compelled to bring out of Germany without knowing it the truth about the feelings of the German people would make it ridiculous. It would be an excellent jest. A jest which would achieve an important political result. The laughter would be a double weapon. It would concentrate attention. And it would make them [the Nazis] less paralysingly terrible.'

Laughter played an increasingly prominent part in the way Pyke came up with new ideas. This plan had its roots in a moment of laughter, while at the same time it made use of the political power of laughter when directed at someone or something. Pyke had trained himself to pause every time he laughed and to consider what had set him off. Indeed, laughter was becoming, for him, a gateway to innovation, for, as he wrote, 'it is the concealed truth that makes the jest'.

In the days after Pyke's return to London, on 15 August, a German teacher called Lal Burton was dispatched to Hamburg – 'I find it all interesting here' – and Edith Lamb was cleared by Professor Higgins. Two more were to go to Bremen; Fred Fuller was in Berlin where he teamed up with one of the only recruits never vetted by Higgins, and on the day that London experienced two mock air-raids, with Spitfires swooping down on a fleet of corpulent French bombers, Stanley Smith's fiancée was given the all-clear to join him in Germany. Two days later she arrived in Frankfurt laden with cigarettes, money and a list of instructions for Pyke's team – all of which she had 'memorised perfectly'. None of these, however, could prepare the linguists for what happened next.

Marjory Watson had been enjoying her evening until a 'pale, wild-looking young man' burst into the restaurant and began to shout. She had been conducting an interview with six Frankfurters who had all agreed that territorial gain did not justify another war, and had even come round to her point that the average Briton enjoyed greater political freedoms than their German counterpart. These were typical of the views she had already heard. The conversation had then moved on to rather less combustible questions, like the quality of the wine grown in the Rhineland, only for the young man to fly into the room and shout: 'We have the non-aggression pact with Russia. Ribbentrop is going there on Wednesday to sign it!'

It was late on Tuesday, 21 August. Earlier that day talks on a putative military alliance between Britain, France and the USSR had collapsed and now Germany and Russia were to sign a pact of non-aggression to complement the recently finalised economic agreement. Fascism was to unite with communism or, as one Foreign Office official quipped, 'All the isms are wasms.'

Watson experienced the passivity of extreme shock. 'There was an almost tangible spirit of excitement spreading amongst the people assembled round the table, and the hostility to my country, latent a moment before, was now alive in each pair of eyes that encountered mine. The wireless was turned on, and amidst a breathless silence the clear, even tones of the announcer made that momentous pronounce-ment, which was followed by the playing of the Deutschland and the Horst Wessel song. I felt quite stunned with horror, but tried to look as though the news was of but little importance.'

Her companions began to speak over each other in their excite-ment. War was out of the question . . . Their children would not be sent to the front . . . England was finished . . . Germany could do what she liked in Poland . . . The wound of Versailles would heal at last as Germany took her rightful place in the world . . . One by one they made their excuses and left to celebrate.

The following morning Watson observed the crowds gathering around news-sheets pinned to kiosks and reading with 'what I can only describe as gloating chuckles'. The national mood was trans-formed. 'The word "England" seemed to be on everyone's lips, and the attitude taken showed me beyond the possibility of doubt that any more work along the lines I had been investigating would not only be useless but actually dangerous.'

At half past three in the morning, several hours after the announce-ment of Ribbentrop's trip to Moscow, Pyke drove to the offices of *The Times* to buy that day's first edition. Anxious and confused, he returned to his flat and by dawn had composed a series of telegrams to be sent later that morning. He climbed into bed at about six, with a telephone alarm set for nine.

It rang. He came to. He called Sir Robert Vansittart, latterly of the Foreign Office and MI6, who mentioned that he had been up until two in the morning. Pyke chose not to share his own bedtime, asking only that they should meet as soon as possible. Vansittart suggested they talk as he was driven in to work, which was why, at just past ten o'clock, Pyke clambered into the back of Vansittart's chauffeured car. He was now sitting next to one of the few men in England who could help him extricate from Germany both his conversationalists and their results.

'I found him full of the same charm as I did last year – a charm which is quite peculiar to him,' wrote Pyke in his diary. 'Most unlike a Foreign Office official. Far from holding himself in and making a demonstration of his reserve, he has all the appearance of giving himself with enthusiasm to whatever is in his mind at the moment.' Vansittart 'agreed straight off as to the value of the work and the value of the material', before offering to instruct the British Consul in Berlin to contact Pyke's conversationalists, collect their results and have them sent to London by diplomatic bag. Pyke agreed, and suggested also that he be appointed King's Messenger in order to fly out to Berlin and make sure that the survey results made it into the diplomatic bag. Vansittart refused, perhaps realising that there was more to this suggestion than the bearded man was letting on.

At the Foreign Office, Pyke was handed over to a different kind of official – the opposite of Vansittart, 'typically Foreign Office' – who worried about endangering the British Consul in Berlin and only agreed to Vansittart's instructions with reluctance. The telegram had been sent to the British Consul, but still Pyke could not bring himself to order his conversationalists home. Only after calling R. T. Clark, News Editor at the BBC, a man with the inside line on most political crises, did he accept that for the safety of his team he must now scuttle the operation.

Back at Great Ormond Street Pyke sent the telegrams he had prepared the night before to Hentschel in Wiesbaden, Fuller in Berlin, Brook in Bremen, Burton in Hamburg, Cunningham and Raleigh in Frankfurt (to whom he sent money as well). Each member of his team was told to get his results to the British Consul before leaving Germany immediately. He then cabled his network of English correspondents – Ridley, Webber, Hicks and Dowdall – telling them to telephone if any messages came through before taking a moment to write to his son, David, then eighteen and soon to win a place at Cambridge, to see if he would ask his mother to leave London. 'She will listen to you.' But not to him.

Later that same day, in spite of not being appointed King's Messenger, Pyke made the decision to fly out to Berlin. He contacted his friend Sidney Elliott at *Reynolds News* to see if he would give him press accreditation. He wanted to be the paper's Berlin correspondent. Twenty-five years after his first attempt with the *Chronicle*, Pyke hoped to have another go at being an undercover war correspondent in the German capital. Clearly this episode still rankled.

Yet before he could find a flight, messages began to arrive at Great Ormond Street. His plans went on hold. Lamb, Hentschel and Raleigh were together in Frankfurt. The others had already left. For a moment, receiving one telegram out of chronological order, Pyke imagined Raleigh to be missing, which led to 'a momentary loss of consciousness from shock. Owing to Peter's youth and appearance, I identify him with David, and the idea of his being in any danger is quite unendurable to me.' Perhaps he also identified Raleigh with a younger version of himself, having been the same age when he first set out for Germany. Raleigh was not missing, but he was not heading for home either.

The night before he should have returned to London, Peter Raleigh, in Frankfurt, had met the Mexican Consul in 'a rather dreary night-club' and had promised to play table tennis with him the next day. 'Which is how I found myself in a grand suburban villa playing ping-pong with this tiny man whose chest hardly cleared the table, while outside in the garden confidential documents burned slowly in a brazier and flakes of ash rose into the still afternoon air.' Having never received the message about getting his results to the British Consul in Berlin, Raleigh merely shoved them in his pocket and made for the frontier.

Just before entering Holland the train stopped for German police to search everyone's belongings. Raleigh was in trouble. Thinking fast, he took out his wallet where he found a picture of 'a former girlfriend posing on a Cornish beach in a two-piece bathing costume'. He slipped this into his passport and hopped off the train with the survey results in his pocket. One of the soldiers on the platform stepped forward and asked to see his papers. Opening Raleigh's passport, he saw the picture of the ex-girlfriend.

There followed a colourful conversation 'about the pleasures that were to be found in life', before Raleigh was waved through to the station café where he sipped patiently at a cup of tea while the inspection continued on board. Once it had finished the train began to pull off, at which point Raleigh ran back on with the survey results still in his pocket.

Pyke's relief at the safe return of his team was little short of parental. 'I felt so delighted that I almost kissed her on the spot,' he wrote of seeing Edith Lamb. 'The more I see of Stanley [Smith], the more I admire his qualities and like him.' Lamb had become 'full of quiet self-confidence'. Cunningham, on the other hand, appeared to have been 'knocked out' by the experience. The change in Raleigh was most compelling. 'I find his posing delightful. He will not, I think, be capable, like my David would, of saying quite frankly that he felt pleased with himself. I shall tease him gently so as to introduce him to the idea that one's emotions are as much fact, and as little to be ashamed of, as a brick wall.'

That night, as the conversationalists swapped tales of Nazi Germany, of close shaves with men and women who might have been with the Gestapo, or those who had guessed what they were up to – they would never know for sure – all agreed that once the results had arrived back from Berlin they should be publicised as soon as possible. War might erupt at any moment, but as they knew from Munich the year before, the crisis might just as easily blow over. None of them was sure what the next few weeks could hold. Nor did they have any inkling that their operation had come to the attention of MI5.

On the day that Ribbentrop flew to Moscow, a young woman in Golders Green remarked to her neighbour that 'there will be no war'. This was hardly unusual. All over the country similar and opposite views were exchanged, but this woman claimed to know that there would be no war because she was 'in the Secret Service'. Her neighbour happened to be friendly with someone else who worked for British intelligence, and who soon established that this young woman was not part of MI5 or SIS. He also discovered that she was receiving letters from Germany, which raised the indelicate possibility that she was working for a different 'secret service'.

For most of the 1930s, MI5 was a small and often unloved government department which suffered periodically from cuts. Its greatest coup over the last few years had been the infiltration and exposure of a Soviet spy ring in the Woolwich Arsenal. While MI5 did not possess the resources to follow up every lead this case had presented, it managed to prosecute the ringleader, Percy Glading, who turned out to be a Soviet agent. What piqued their interest in the woman from Golders Green was that she had a friend in common with Glading.

She had told her neighbour that she could be contacted during the day on Holborn 6119. This number was passed on to B.2.b, the MI5 Counter-Espionage section, where the subscriber was found to be a man who had come to MI5's attention several times over the last few years – Geoffrey Pyke.

In February 1938, on the second day of criminal proceedings against Percy Glading and his accomplices, a welder had gone to the police with what appeared to be an important tip-off. The summer before, he had seen Geoffrey Pyke in the offices of the Amalgamated Engineers Union where he was frequently in conversation with 'Communists, particularly J. R. Scott and J. R. Longworth'. Of these two, the welder went on, Scott 'was in very frequent telephonic communication with Glading'.

The welder had been following the Glading trial in the press where he had read about the shadowy 'Mr Stevens' – to whom Glading seemed to report. Stevens's identity was a mystery, one which the welder thought he had solved. He wondered 'if Pyke was identical with "Mr Stevens" and if Scott had acted as intermediary'.

Later that month another member of the public came forward as a result of the Glading case to raise concerns about Pyke. This time it was an insurance agent who had gone to Great Ormond Street to discuss Pyke's cottage in the Devil's Punchbowl. 'As I was about to enter I heard PIKE read aloud, as if dictating, "We have been attacking the AEC and we are now working on Negretti and Zambra." PIKE asked me when I entered what I wanted and appeared disturbed at my appearance. There was nothing to show to whom he had been speaking, no typist, no report that he could have been reading aloud and no apparent telephone.' This insurance agent 'received a bad impression' and decided not to insure the cottage. Only when he read about the Glading trial did he think that Pyke might somehow be mixed up in all this.

So what was Pyke up to? Was he recording a secret message, or rehearsing a report to give in a cell meeting? Who was the 'we' he referred to, or indeed the AEC, and Negretti and Zambra?

'AEC' was either the Associated Equipment Company, which made buses and lorries, or 'AEU' – the Amalgamated Engineers Union –

either misheard or wrongly transcribed. The other names are perhaps more revealing. Negretti and Zambra was the name of a company which specialised in gun-sights, aviation gauges, thermometers and flow meters, and whose principal client by 1937 was the Air Ministry.

At the time, most Russian espionage activity against Britain was geared towards the capture of scientific and technological intelligence. Glading had provided his Soviet handler with the blueprints of specialist military instruments, and, in the year that he was convicted, Mihel Kaptelsev, a Soviet agent attached to a trade delegation, had tried to acquire technical information from a Vickers Armstrong employee. His replacement, Aleksei Doschenko, another Soviet agent, did almost exactly the same thing, approaching a worker at Rollston's aircraft factory. Negretti and Zambra was precisely the kind of company that Soviet agents might be told to 'attack'. Was this what Pyke was up to? Indeed, was he using his charity as a front to conceal these activities?

Pyke certainly understood that Voluntary Industrial Aid for Spain (VIAS) might be mistaken for a Communist front organisation, and went out of his way to refute the idea. He characterised it instead as 'a strong autonomous body to the right of the CP [Communist Party]'. One trades union official described him as 'particularly anxious that [VIAS] work should not get into the hands of the Communist organisation'. Of course this proves nothing. By definition a 'front' organisation must conceal its agenda.

At the very least, Pyke's charity had clear Communist associations. It was later described as 'closely linked' to the Aircraft Shop Stewards National Council, a militant ginger group set up by a Comintern agent, and we know that three of its most energetic figures – Harry Adams, Joe Scott and Jack Tanner – belonged to the Party and moved as one. This hints at the idea that Pyke's charity might have been subverted to a Communist agenda, without him necessarily being involved.

MI5, however, was in no doubt that VIAS was 'under Communist control' but they had no concrete evidence. Their interest in Pyke was stepped up after these two tip-offs from members of the public and his case was taken up by Jane Sissmore, the legendary MI5 officer later described by Soviet agent Kim Philby as being almost without exception 'the ablest professional intelligence officer ever employed by MI5'. Sissmore began by asking for Pyke's passport papers, presumably in the hope of identifying suspicious patterns of travel. Nobody got back to her, other cases came up and the trail went cold.

Although Pyke wondered occasionally if the 'English *sicherheits polizei*', i.e. MI5, 'were listening in on the telephone conversations and opening the letters of all the organisations which by helping Republican Spain were trying to stem the Fascist tide', in other words, organisations like VIAS, the reality was far less impressive. Staff and funding continued to be in short supply, and for almost a year Pyke fell off the MI5 radar. In 1939 he appeared in an SIS report on Spain, which remains classified, before being linked to the woman in Golders Green who boasted of belonging to the 'secret service'.

This had come to the attention of MI5 in late August 1939, by which time this secretive government department was readying itself for war and moving to a new location. Evidence of the suspicious remark was filed away and forgotten about, in part because it concerned Communist networks at the time when the Soviet threat was not a top priority.

MI5's longtime Director-General, Vernon Kell, the parrot-owning asthmatic who had asked in 1916 for Pyke's post to be opened, had recently assured representatives of the Deuxième Bureau, the French equivalent of SIS, that '[Soviet] activity in England is non-existent, in terms of both intelligence and political subversion'. This was reflected in the fact that MI5 had just one officer working on Soviet espionage at the start of the war.

Within the Foreign Office, MI6 and to a lesser extent MI5, there was a gently dismissive attitude towards the idea that the fabric of British society might be riddled with Soviet spies. Thinking like this could be taken as evidence of a touchingly antique paranoia. The suspicion that had hung for a moment over Geoffrey Pyke was probably proof of nothing more than the public's tendency to see 'reds under the bed'.

The mood in London on 30 August 1939 was lively and industrious. Windows were being busily blacked out, barrage balloons had begun to bob up and down and heaps of sand were appearing on street corners, there to fill sandbags or put out fires once the bombs had begun to fall. Meanwhile, in the offices of the BBC German Service, a group of men went over their script for the last time.

Broadcasting as 'Peter Salter' and 'Stanley Fry', Peter Raleigh and Stanley Smith proceeded to describe their 'holiday' in the Third Reich. Both men would later become well-known BBC foreign correspondents. Raleigh made his name in the Algerian Civil War while Smith, then known as Patrick Smith, was for many years the BBC's man in Rome. Yet their first BBC broadcast proved to be their least accurate.

Stanley Smith hamming it up in Nazi uniform while
on holiday in Germany, 1936

Peter Raleigh, in 1940

The script they read from had been liberally supplemented and redacted by a man introduced to them as a Foreign Office official. In fact he was Sir Campbell Stuart, Director of Propaganda to Enemy Countries, and from the moment he met Pyke and his young charges he took against them, dismissing Smith and Raleigh as '"pink" Cambridge undergraduates ['pink' meaning left-wing here], Grammar School boys, I should think of a scholarly disposition, but undoubtedly naive to a degree'. He described their script as 'quite unsuitable' and decided 'to rewrite it almost entirely'. Raleigh and Smith remembered things differently, recalling only that this crusty official told them to describe England on their return as 'stiff with uniforms and sandbags' – which it was not.

Two days later German forces poured into Poland. 'One of my personal complaints against Hitler,' wrote Raleigh, was 'that he paid no attention to our broadcast.' The following night a storm of strange, bullying intensity swept over the capital, and the next morning, as tens of thousands of Sunday services began all over the country – vicars welcoming the faithful, announcing the first hymn, organ pipes starting to blast – the Prime Minister declared in a weary voice that Britain was at war with Germany.

The scheme was effectively over. This courageous band of linguists, along with Professor Higgins and Pyke, had been just days away from releasing their preliminary findings, and their results were astonishing. Using a modified version of the Gallup technique, based on 232 completed conversations, they estimated that just 16 per cent of the German population felt that territorial conquest justified war. If there was a conflict, incredibly, just over a third of those interviewed wanted Hitler and Germany to lose. Only 19 per cent imagined Germany was capable of victory if facing an alliance of Britain, France, Russia and Poland, while more than half the German population felt the Nazi Party was unjust in its treatment of society, failing to treat rich and poor alike. Sixty per cent of those Germans they spoke to disapproved of the government's attitude towards Jews.

Even today, given what we know, these results are startling. They are the result of the only serious attempt to gauge public opinion in Nazi Germany on the eve of war and are remarkable both for their content and for the fact that they were gathered at all. Pyke's amateurs had managed to work undetected in an environment so hostile that it had scared off all professional British intelligence agents. His idea that the members of his team would not be found out if they presented themselves as indisputably and eccentrically English – friendly, loud and even pompous – had worked perfectly.

The extended accounts of their interviews provide a detailed and at times moving portrait of a nation sleepwalking towards the brink. We meet the crooked timber of German humanity, from reluctant garage workers and gregarious road sweepers through to tailors, innkeepers, waiters and lawyers, students and teachers, steel workers, shoemakers, artists and decorators, pianists and violinists, librarians and bookbinders, salesmen and farmers; Catholics, Nazis, communists and socialists. They are generous, they are funny, they are serious, they are hospitable. There is a wide-eyed woman with enormous hands who urges Raleigh to feel her biceps; the secretary who was only interested in talking about the speed of her touch-typing; the middle-aged businessman who read *The Times* every day; those Germans who pretended not to hear when greeted with 'Heil Hitler!' through to the ball-bearing factory-worker with his political views lifted straight out of the Nazi newspaper *Der Stürmer*. At times this disparate group seemed to be united by nothing more than a willingness to share their thoughts with a friendly English tourist.

But there were aspects of this survey and how it came about which did not add up. Why did Pyke fly to Paris in late July? Who was the mysterious 'Professor Higgins' and why did he play such an important role? Was Marjory Watson a Nazi agent, as MI5 suspected, and how did the likes of Fred Fuller and Kenneth Spencer, his contact in Berlin, come into Pyke's orbit? Moreover, where did the money come from to fund this elaborate operation?

With only a handful of people aware of the survey, and most of them sworn to secrecy, these were not questions that Pyke was required to answer. Instead, in the days after the outbreak of war, he turned to the future. The question he asked himself now was familiar: how should he fight fascism? With the nation at war he knew that there was 'no hope for private organisations and still less for private individuals like myself'. Perhaps it was time for a different approach.

Meanwhile in MI5, now that the Soviet Union was in league with Nazi Germany, the focus of their counter-espionage activities had begun to shift. London was fast becoming a hub for Soviet espionage, on a scale that the Security Service would not understand for years, and it would soon become clear that somehow Geoffrey Pyke was caught up in it.

PYKE HUNT, PART 2

In the early hours of a cold February morning in 1940 a volunteer police constable cycling through Bloomsbury heard a strange sound. He squeezed on his brakes and paused to listen. The streets were empty, unlit and silent, apart from this electronic fluttering noise. It sounded like a message being tapped out in Morse code. The policeman made a note of the building from which it came and pedalled back to the station as fast as he could. Fifteen minutes later two officers from Special Branch were parked outside the house, straining to hear more of those tell-tale sounds. But they were too late. The street was again dark, deserted and still.

A report of this incident was passed on to MI5, followed by a list of those living in the house from which the suspicious noise had come. The British Puppets Model Theatre had an office on the ground floor. It was probably safe to rule them out. The publisher Mervyn, later Lord, Horder was also based in the building; as were a compositor, an architect and the cartoonist Arthur Ferrier, then drawing the glamour cartoon strip 'Our Dumb Blonde' for the *Sunday Pictorial*; while the occupant of rooms on the second floor was none other than Geoffrey Pyke, now described by MI5 as 'a known Communist'.

Two Special Branch officers were dispatched to investigate. They spoke to the housekeeper at No. 32 Great Ormond Street, a Mrs Lipschitz, who explained that Pyke was 'in the habit of listening to foreign broadcasts even in the early hours of the morning'. But it was hard to imagine why these broadcasts would sound so much like Morse code.

Whatever was going on in Pyke's rooms, it did not stop, and three weeks later more suspicious noises were reported from his flat. Again 'investigations failed to produce any evidence of transmitting, and the case was closed'.

By this stage of the war the country had been plodding for more than six months through what was known as the Bore War or, in America, the Phoney War. After the devastating German invasion of Poland, London had not been flattened by the Luftwaffe, as so many had predicted. Indeed, there was a cautious sense that this might not happen after all. Noticeably fewer Londoners carried around their rubber gas-masks and waves of evacuees had started to return to the capital. But all this began to change in early April 1940 after German forces launched Operation *Weserübung*, their assault on Denmark and Norway. Not long after there was, in the case of Geoffrey Pyke, what MI5's Colonel Malcolm Cumming called 'an interesting, or possibly even significant, development'.

MI5's Lady Superintendent, the 'rather terrifying' Miss Dicker, had received a job application from a would-be secretary that came accompanied by 'a glowing testimonial from no other than Geoffrey Pyke'. Equally intriguing was the identity of the woman who had suggested that the applicant should get in touch with MI5: Philippa Strachey, sister of one of Pyke's oldest friends, James Strachey. The woman who hoped to work at MI5 was one of Pyke's undercover pollsters, Marjory Watson.

'The plot thickened considerably,' Cumming went on, 'with a look-up on Miss Watson, who, we find, is the proud possessor of a fat "Personal File" here.' Watson's file made out that she was a Nazi agent. Very soon MI5 would learn that during the 1920s she had belonged to the British Union of Fascists, had claimed to be 'on excellent terms with a large number of Nazi officials' and 'never ceased from spreading German propaganda'. Meanwhile Pyke was supposed to be a Communist. Was their collaboration the strange fruit of the Russo-German pact? Was one duping the other? Or had MI5 and Special Branch simply got their wires crossed?

'In view of this rather curious link-up,' remarked Cumming to MI5's liaison with Military Intelligence, 'I think you will agree that we ought to try to get to the bottom of Master Pyke's activities.'

Malcolm Cumming was later described by a colleague as 'a short man, not overly endowed with intellectual skills but intensely loyal to MI5. Like the policemen in John Buchan novels, he seemed as likely to be chasing the hero as the villain.' He now recommended that Watson be asked to fill out the standard questionnaire for potential MI5 secretaries, 'in the hope that we might glean something from it', before contacting SIS to see if 'Master Pyke' was working for them.

Meanwhile the complexion of the war changed further. The *Wehrmacht* had now achieved stunning victories not only in Denmark and Norway, but in Belgium, Holland and France. These had been so resounding that many observers were convinced that there must be an explanation beyond the purely military. Perhaps the Germans had had help from Fifth Columnists – Nazi agents hidden among the population of those countries under attack who passed intelligence to the advancing forces or committed small acts of sabotage. In Britain, as the threat of invasion grew during May 1940, so did the feeling that the country must be full of undercover fascist agents. With the population starting to be gripped by spy fever, a telephone operator in a City of London shipping firm listened in to a conversation she found so suspicious that she went straight to the police.

An unidentified man had called up Marjory Watson, then working as secretary to the Managing Director of the United Baltic Corporation, which for years had run routes between London and the Soviet Union.

'You see some of our members are now in power,' the man had told her. 'I wanted to get in touch with you to see if you would go to America to continue instructing.'

Watson had replied that she was 'in a new position but it was quite interesting'.

The man said that he would 'bear her in mind' before asking 'if she had seen anything of "Siegfried"'.

She had not. 'But his duties at the BBC are very awkward,' she went on, 'and I will get in touch with him if possible.'

To this, the man said that he was doubtful of Siegfried being 'absolutely trustworthy'.

The telephone operator made a note of the man's number. It was Holborn 6119 – to which the only subscriber was Geoffrey Pyke.

This raised all sorts of questions. Who did Pyke mean by 'our members'? In what way were they 'in power'? What sort of 'instructing' did he want Watson to continue in America and, if this was a continuation, what instruction had she implemented so far? Perhaps these comments related to the group he had mentioned in 1937 'attacking' the specialist arms manufacturer Negretti and Zambra? Then there was 'Siegfried' at the BBC: why was his work 'awkward'? What made him untrustworthy? Indeed, why was there the need for trust in the first place? More to the point, who was he?

Following further enquiries, Cumming at MI5 found out some of the details regarding Pyke's undercover poll. He also discovered that, according to Sir Campbell Stuart, Pyke had been trying since then to launch an alternative version of this poll using American conversationalists, and that this would require him to travel to the US. This could explain his line about going to America, but Cumming also learnt that he had been denied permission to visit the US after the idea had been torpedoed by SIS who were worried that Pyke's under- cover work would interfere with their own. Nor did Pyke work for them. In which case, why was he still talking about going to America?

By the end of May 1940, Cumming understood the following about Geoffrey Pyke: he was a 'known Communist' connected to a convicted Soviet agent, Percy Glading. His rooms had on several occasions been the source of what sounded like Morse code transmis- sions, and he was somehow connected to a woman in Golders Green who claimed to be part of a secret service (which was not British). Now he appeared to be in some form of trust or conspiracy with a different woman, Marjory Watson, possibly a Nazi agent and appar- ently a fascist, who had worked with him on an undercover poll of German public opinion and had since tried to get a job at MI5 with his help. Now they and others were 'in power' and planning to go to America. It was all as clear as mud.

Even if he had the inclination, Cumming no longer had the time to unravel Pyke's activities. MI5 was tottering around him. The Security Service was by then dealing with an average of 8,000 requests each week, an unprecedented figure, most of them from government departments seeking security clearances. It was also suffering from increasingly doddery leadership. For Christopher Andrew, MI5's official historian, its administration was 'close to collapse'. Cumming had little choice but to leave Pyke's case until there was fresh intel- ligence. He would not have to wait long.

One of the reasons MI5 was struggling to cope by May 1940 was the flood of reports coming in from members of the public convinced that they had seen a German or Italian behaving suspiciously. 'Collar the lot!' was, ultimately, the response of the new Prime Minister, Winston Churchill. Soon thereafter the Chiefs of Staff ordered the internment of every male 'enemy alien' between the ages of eighteen and seventy and by the end of July 27,000 men had been interned. Most had no pronounced political outlook, while some were openly fascist or indeed anti-fascist. One of the latter was Pyke's friend 'Professor Higgins', the blond-haired German refugee who had appeared – a *deus ex machina* – to help with the undercover poll.

Pyke was convinced that Higgins could not be a Nazi agent. Instead he saw him as 'a much persecuted German political refugee of the finest character'. He began to campaign for his release.

One of the first letters he wrote was to an elderly Tory MP, Leo Amery, an erudite, free-thinking Conservative known as the 'pocket Hercules' who had recently made the most important speech of his career. During a heated parliamentary debate on the military fiasco which had followed Germany's invasion of Norway, Amery had quoted the words of Oliver Cromwell with eloquent force, directing them at the Prime Minister, Neville Chamberlain: 'Depart, I say, and let us have done with you. In the name of God, go!' Three days later Chamberlain had resigned and Churchill, Amery's contemporary at Harrow, someone he had once thrown into the school swimming pool, became Prime Minister. Amery was appointed Secretary of State for India – he had hoped for something more – and just over a month later he received a 'very agitated letter' from Geoffrey Pyke.

Amery had met Pyke the year before, and remembered him as 'a strange creature, Mephistophelian in appearance but with a brilliantly original mind'. He had taken to this wild-haired intellectual and was happy to help. On receiving Pyke's letter, he wrote to the Parliamentary Under-Secretary at the Home Office, Osbert Peake MP, urging him to have Higgins released.

Pyke did not stop here. After contacting Amery he dispatched letters to Sir Robert Vansittart and Sir Richard Acland MP, both of whom also wrote to Osbert Peake, before Pyke wrote to him personally, stressing in oblique terms that Higgins was 'the *only* man in a position to perform the task which may be demanded of him. It is, therefore, of the utmost importance that he should not be sent to Canada', where many 'enemy aliens' were being dispatched.

We know that he called Amery's office repeatedly during the months that followed, as well as Peake's. The name 'Higgins' appears in Pyke's notebooks more than any other and is invariably underlined or is the first item on a to-do list. Higgins later expressed to Pyke his 'deep gratitude for your unceasing efforts on my behalf', and his diaries and correspondence suggest that they were indeed unceasing. Pyke also sent Higgins money, a succession of regular payments, usually of £4 or £5, a respectable sum, which is curious given how short of cash he himself appeared to be.

Higgins was not the only German refugee whose release Pyke campaigned for. He also wrote to the Commandant of Onchan Internment Camp, on the Isle of Man, about a young Jewish German refugee named Heinz Kamnitzer, introducing himself as someone who had not only escaped from an internment camp but had smuggled messages into and out of them, all of which gave him 'deep sympathy with the Commandants of Internment Camps'. It was an ill-judged ice-breaker and Captain Sidney Kraul was not amused. Nor was he inclined to believe what he had just read, given who it had come from.

By the most unlikely coincidence Kraul had also been interned in Ruhleben in 1915 at the time of Pyke's escape. Like most detainees, he had convinced himself that escape was impossible without German assistance. Now a man whom Kraul imagined to be a traitor wanted to organise for one of his internees a magazine subscription to what Pyke light-heartedly described as that 'organ whose dangerous revolutionary tendencies relieve the tedium of the lives of many London bankers': the *Economist*.

Kraul said no, before going to the trouble of forwarding this letter to MI5.

'Pyke is well known to us,' came the reply, 'and, for your guidance, we would suggest that extreme caution must be used in any dealings you may have with him.'

Never one to give up easily, Pyke continued to campaign for this refugee's release and the words 'Kamnitzer' and 'Heinz' appear in his notebooks almost as frequently as 'Higgins'. Years later Pyke was made godfather to Kamnitzer's son. What's strange about this is that he had only ever met this refugee on two occasions before launching his campaign to have him released.

How can we explain Pyke's almost obsessive interest in the plight of these two refugees? One of the first mentions of Kamnitzer in Pyke's notebook may provide a clue.

It was made in late June 1940 and at first looks like any other. There is Kamnitzer's name, misspelled once, followed by the address of his internment camp. But several details stand out. One is the colour of the ink. It is a distinctive burnt umber which appears nowhere else in Pyke's papers. The line of the script is also thicker than usual, which suggests that this entry was written using someone else's pen.

Then there is the spelling of the name Kamnitzer. The first attempt, in Pyke's distinctive handwriting, is 'Chamnitzer'. This is crossed out and beneath, in a very different hand, a more scrupulous hand, is the name 'Kamnitzer' next to the full address.

That Pyke wrote 'Chamnitzer' shows that he was not copying his name from a letter but taking it down in conversation. The different ink suggests that this was not over the phone but face to face and that he had borrowed a pen from his interlocutor. We can also speculate that he was speaking to a man who pronounced the 'K' of Kamnitzer in such a way as to make Pyke think of the 'Ch' of Chemnitz, the east German town. There is a subtle difference in pronunciation between the two. The 'Ch' of Chemnitz is a sound you do not often hear in English, one that would come more naturally to a native German speaker.

So it seems that this name might have been given to him by someone who knew Kamnitzer well enough to pronounce and spell his name correctly and who was probably not English. Less clear is why Pyke kept at this task for so long and to what extent it was a favour for a helpless refugee or a job he had been asked to carry out.

In a letter to Higgins, Pyke discussed the prospect of his release and mentioned 'all those interested in the matter'. In Pyke's notebooks the text of a telegram reads: 'Higgins all possible steps would be taken meanwhile facilitate release.' Neither line supports the idea that Pyke was working alone and was acting out of nothing more than personal friendship.

At last, after a year of campaigning, Pyke's hard work paid off. He had asked Amery to contact the General Secretary of the Fabian Society, John Parker MP, about Higgins, and had again mentioned it to Sir Stafford Cripps who brought the matter to the attention of the Home Secretary, Herbert Morrison. Higgins was duly released. Several months later Kamnitzer was also freed, and again Parker was one of his referees along with Pyke's friend Sir Richard Acland.

We are left with the same troubling questions: was Pyke's interest purely personal or was he working on behalf of others, and if so, whom? Perhaps we should do what Pyke would do at a moment like this. We need to reformulate the question. Who would want to see Higgins and Kamnitzer released?

'Professor Higgins', the man who had vetted most of Pyke's pollsters, was in fact a hardened communist 'cadre' who operated under the Party cover-name *Blonder Hans* or 'Blond John'. His real name was Rolf Rünkel. He was a senior intelligence operative for the German Communist Party (KPD). Based on clues in his past, as well as gaps in his record at the Comintern archive in Moscow, it seems that early on in his career Rünkel was recruited by the NKVD, the Soviet security service. Certainly by the time of his release from internment on the Isle of Man, in 1941, the Gestapo had Rünkel on a list of known communist saboteurs operating in the USSR who should be tracked down during Operation Barbarossa.

Rünkel was a shortish, powerful-looking man who walked with the metronomic gait of somebody accustomed to carrying out orders. 'The blond beast', as he was known to his cell-mate on the Isle of Man, embodied for some the most formidable kind of communist. There was a detachment in the way he described his vision of a Soviet Germany, an ideological clarity which knew little of compromise. 'Certain words were missing from his vocabulary,' that same cell-mate wrote, 'words like pity, tolerance, freedom. The only purpose of his existence was to make the world ripe for Communism, and if, to achieve this ideal, a few millions more or less had to die, so much the worse for them.'

The son of a university professor, Rünkel had grown up in a small town outside Essen and in the late 1920s had joined the secret apparatus of the KPD, the AM-Apparat or M-Apparat. He worked for the Party in Breslau and Berlin, and may have gone to Moscow several years later for his training. At the time, the Soviet Union had its sights firmly set on Germany, with Berlin the Comintern's centre of European operations. Soviet agents working in Germany for the NKVD or its military intelligence counterpart, the GRU, were given logistical support by German communists and, according to one former communist, by 1930 there was a consensus in the Comintern 'that a Soviet Germany was "in the bag".'

This was not wishful thinking. The KPD won six million votes in the 1932 elections. Had its leaders ignored instructions from Moscow and brokered an alliance with the other great force on the German left, the SPD, their coalition could have taken the Reichstag. But Moscow's 'Class against Class' line forbade this and instead Hitler came to power.

The KPD was forced underground and Rünkel was moved by the Party to Lower Silesia where he worked in an illegal network for a year before fleeing to Prague following the arrest of others in his KPD

Bezirksleitung – Party district leadership. The Europe through which he travelled was a continent in flux. It was becoming once again a deracinated age and this suited Moscow perfectly. Cadres like Rünkel could now enter parts of Europe which might otherwise have been off-limits.

In Prague, Rünkel was appointed head of Intelligence and Analysis in the KPD's *Abwehrapparat* – the intelligence section – and became a close assistant of Wilhelm Koenen, the most senior KPD figure in Prague. 'Professor Higgins' was also close to the NKVD agent Herbert Lessig, chief of Soviet intelligence in Czechoslovakia, and there is a chance that Rünkel might have spied on Koenen for Moscow at around this time.

Otherwise his work involved vetting refugees, maintaining Party discipline and, during the latter stages of 1938, helping to spirit KPD members out of Czechoslovakia before the start of the Nazi occupation. Here he ensured that where possible the Party's political rivals, often SPD refugees, would end up in the hands of the local Gestapo, soon to be taken over by Adolf Eichmann, the Nazi bureaucrat later described by Hannah Arendt as the embodiment of the 'banality of evil'.

Rünkel then became one of the first communists to be smuggled out of Prague, in December 1938 – a sure mark of his seniority within the intelligence *Apparat*. He went first to France, where he was arrested and forced to sign a document pledging never to return. In March 1939 he arrived in London and moved in with Koenen, now leader of the German communist exiles in Britain. They lived in a Brixton safehouse which had been supplied by someone who was almost certainly a 'closed' Party member, Lord Faringdon – still Treasurer of Pyke's VIAS.

Shortly after his arrival in London this devout communist, by then responsible for the imprisonment, detention and probable execution of many socialist rivals, took on the part of Professor Higgins in Pyke's survey. He later resumed his work in the Records Department of what would become the Czech Refugee Trust Fund (CRTF), a government-funded body which supplied aid and visas to Czech refugees, where again he did everything he could to ensure that his fellow German communists were brought out of Czechoslovakia at the expense of those affiliated to the SPD.

If Rünkel had scruples about this work then he kept them to himself. He was a professional communist and, as former Party member Charlotte Haldane put it: 'In the case of all non-Russian professional Communists, the Stalinist system requires a discipline and a loyalty apart from and above all loyalties to the Party member's fatherland or nation.' He could be warm and charming but remained utterly committed to the communist cause.

Rolf Rünkel, otherwise known as 'Professor Higgins' or 'Blonder Hans'

It is easy, then, to imagine who would have wanted him to be released. The same goes for the other man on whose behalf Pyke campaigned with such tenacity, Heinz Kamnitzer. He had fled Germany in 1933, aged sixteen, after his father was taken to Buchenwald Concentration Camp, making him one of the first and youngest Jewish refugees to arrive in Britain from Nazi Germany. After two years he moved to Palestine and 'made aliyah', something his parents, both committed Zionists, had always hoped for. Yet his time in the Middle East did not end well. After working for a period as a carpenter in Palestine he lost his job, joined the illegal *apparat* of the Palestinian Communist Party and was forced to flee when he heard that the police were onto him.

By late 1936 Kamnitzer was in London once again, surviving this time on a small stipend from the Palestinian communists. His services as a Party cadre were also sought by the German Communist Party and in 1938 he was forced to choose between the two, ultimately allying himself to the latter.

By this stage Kamnitzer was living in Lawn Road Flats, the modernist block in Hampstead which also housed Arnold Deutsch, the cosmopolitan, charismatic Soviet agent then running Kim Philby. NKVD records show that during his time in London, Deutsch recruited some twenty Soviet agents and had contact with almost thirty. We do not know the identities of all those agents, and, while Kamnitzer may well have been one of Deutsch's agents, there is nothing which has been declassified to confirm it.

To whom did Kamnitzer and Rünkel matter? They mattered to the KPD and to Moscow, which casts Pyke's campaign for their release in a rather different light.

At the time, most of the details of Kamnitzer's and Rünkel's backgrounds were unknown to MI5. They were unaware of Deutsch's activities and had no idea that Lawn Road Flats was a hub for Soviet espionage. Yet they knew where Kamnitzer's loyalties lay, noting that he 'associated with British and alien Communists' and was one of the editors of *Inside Nazi Germany*, an anti-war newsletter later described to Special Branch as 'the publishing house of the Comintern in Great Britain'. It was only after Kamnitzer's 1941 release from internment, to which MI5 raised no objection, that intelligence came in to say that this young German was 'a fanatical Communist' whose 'whole life is, in the widest sense of the phrase, bound up in Party work'.

Rünkel was different in that MI5 knew more about him, and sooner. From late 1939 they had suspected him of being an NKVD agent. The following year his internment-camp commandant described him as 'a fervent communist' who 'is stated to have been and still is a member of the Russian Secret Police'. A subsequent tip-off suggested he was a leading member of the N–Dienst – the intelligence service of the KPD in exile in Britain. MI5 even had a detailed account of his modus operandi in the CRTF, including a list of men whom he had denounced. So it was hardly surprising that after his release from internment Rünkel was placed under surveillance by Special Branch, which was how MI5 began to connect him with Pyke.

'I have now definitely arranged about a "residence" for you to come to directly you are released', wrote Pyke to Rünkel shortly before he was freed. Not only did Pyke arrange a place for Rünkel to stay, he also paid his expenses upon his release and employed him to perform 'private secretarial duties'. Pyke would later offer Kamnitzer an almost identical job.

Rünkel's 'residence' was the home of Bobby Carter, an architect who had recently joined the Party. It was a pretty, delicately proportioned house on Keats Grove in Hampstead, which was, explained Pyke, 'unfortunately, now rather full, and you may have to sleep down in the air raid shelter for the first few days until we have discussed what you'd like to do and where you'd like to go and so on'.

Pyke also mentioned that he had arranged this accommodation 'after consulting my cousin'. Yet there is no evidence of him being in touch with any of his cousins at the time. He then told Rünkel that he had been consulting with 'mutual friends' about his future. 'We know how devotedly you worked at forestry and how you enjoyed it, but we all now feel that you should devote your energies to something even more useful to the public interest. At any rate for a month you will be my guest and this will give time to discuss and make all arrangements.'

Again there is a clear sense here that Pyke was acting as a conduit between Rünkel and others. Or is this a case of seeing 'reds under the bed'?

Rünkel had played a crucial role in Pyke's survey and had asked for no fee, so naturally the Englishman would have felt indebted to him. What's more, Pyke knew first-hand about the helplessness of being detained in a foreign country during a time of war. It is at least possible that Pyke was doing this out of friendship and was simply unaware of Rünkel's past. As a professional intelligence agent, it is not inconceivable that Rünkel was capable of keeping this from his well-meaning English host. Their 'mutual friends' might have been just that – friends they had in common.

Rünkel became a popular fixture at No. 2 Keats Grove and was adored by the Carters' children, who called him 'Uncle Rünkel' (he would later name his son after the Carters' boy, Tom). While it was accepted there that Rünkel might disappear for up to a week on 'work', nobody pressed him too hard about these unexplained trips.

'B[obby] and I always thought that probably he was a Communist spy,' wrote Carter's wife, Deborah, 'but we had learnt not to ask questions.' Her use of the word 'learnt' hints at the closed, secretive nature of life at the extremes of the British Left. You 'learnt' not to ask too many questions and to trust that while you might all be pulling in the same direction there were those with connections and duties which you could never understand, nor should you try to. For a movement rooted in an egalitarian ideal, life within the Party could be surprisingly hierarchical and prone to conspiracy. Being in the penumbra of all this, as the Carters were, was like belonging to the congregation in a medieval church; Rünkel was a man of the cloth.

As well as Rünkel's going off for unexplained trips, Deborah Carter recalled their houseguest being shadowed by Special Branch. 'Two plain-clothes men stood outside our house until Rolf went to work.' Every day they 'followed him to the bus and got in too and stayed outside the office where he worked until 5.30 when they knocked off and went home.' Subtle it was not. Yet Rünkel did not find the experience too troubling, and was soon cheerily pointing out his two shadows to friends.

When Pyke heard about the two detectives trailing his friend he did not exactly panic – rather, he complained to the police. This led to a long interview with one of the men investigating Rünkel. Pyke followed up with a letter in which he offered to send him copies of Shaw's *Pygmalion* and *St Joan* 'where there is a dramatic and I think you will agree sympathetic portrait of some of your distinguished predecessors – and their methods'. The policeman's response was to tell MI5 that there was probably a stronger connection between Rünkel and Pyke than had previously been imagined. Again, Pyke hardly comes across as an experienced secret agent.

Towards the end of 1941 Special Branch's observation of Rünkel was called off. Following Germany's invasion of the Soviet Union, the shape of the war had changed and with it the scope of communist activities across the Continent, which provided the British authorities with new targets.

At around the same time that Special Branch ended its observation, one of MI5's informants was told by a reliable source that throughout Europe communists had been instructed to 'see to it that any revolutions or mutinies would lead not only to the downfall of Hitler, but to universal revolution in Europe'. In Britain, the source went on, the 'next important step' was 'the penetration of the Communists into the key positions of propaganda (the BBC), the Civil Defence, war industries and the Army'. Already there were 'some signs of good success in this direction, which in the coming weeks and months will be improved upon'.

MI5 received this intelligence in November 1941. Unbelievably, as the German Army drove deep into the Russian steppe, orders were issuing out of Moscow concerning the political shape of Europe after Hitler's defeat and the need for communists to infiltrate important British institutions. As the MI5 controller of this source added, with stony understatement, 'I consider this to be not uninteresting.'

Over the twenty-two months leading up to the receipt of this report, starting with the debrief of an ex-GRU officer, MI5 had been given momentary, tantalising aperçus into the demi-monde of Soviet espionage. They had been told about Soviet moles in Whitehall, the inner workings of *rezidenturas*, Russian courier systems, methods of payment, letter codes, false identities and 'decomposition' work. They knew that the NKVD claimed to have had 'great success' in Britain during the 1930s, and that when a former Soviet intelligence agent was told that the CPGB was treated like any other British political party he was 'genuinely astonished' and 'most emphatic that the existence of the Communist Party organisation is a very real danger'. One senior communist later said it was a 'colossal joke' that the Party was not closed down at the outbreak of war since Hitler and Stalin were in league with one another at that point. But MI5's approach continued to be libertarian and hands-off. It had a characteristically English preference for watching and waiting rather than stamping out any subversion in its infancy.

Soon after this report was filed Pyke wrote to the Aliens War Service Department, the body responsible for granting work permits to 'enemy aliens', stressing the 'complete reliability and trustworthiness – and a much rarer quality – discretion' of Rolf Rünkel, 'in my opinion a first-rate example of a person fit to be employed in work affecting the security of this country in the war.' Kamnitzer, meanwhile, applied for a job at the BBC. MI5 would soon remark on the uncanny number of German communists applying for positions at the Corporation's German Service. Other communists were trying to find employment in trades unions or government departments, and so was Geoffrey Pyke.

In early 1942 he set out to join a military command at the heart of the Allied war effort. On the face of it, this was bizarre. The idea of a bearded, 'pink' civilian with a bulging MI5 Personal File offering his services to the British military was little short of cartoonish. Pyke would never succeed – unless, that was, he could offer them something that proved impossible to turn down.

HOW TO DEFEAT NAZISM

On an insipid day in February 1942, Geoffrey Pyke approached the sentries standing outside No. 1a Richmond Terrace, the headquarters of Combined Operations, and asked to be let in. His chin was invisible beneath a goatee beard. He wore a wrinkled Homburg and no tie. Filing in and out of the building before him went bluff, clean-shaven officers from each of the three military services, some of whom must have done a double take at the sight of this scarecrow-like figure. Pyke was hoping to speak in private with the most senior man in the building, Commodore Lord Louis Mountbatten, the great-grandson of Queen Victoria, later described by his biographer as 'intensely elitist' and 'proud of his royal birth'. Pyke was a suspected communist whose recent journalism included the article 'Are Tories Sadists?' What he hoped would be his passport into Mountbatten's office was a document that he had written twenty months earlier. It contained his proposals for how to turn the tide in the war against against Nazi Germany.

Neither Pyke nor anyone in Combined Operations could have predicted what happened next. Indeed, it would take a wild imagination to guess that by going to Richmond Terrace on that day Pyke would set in motion a train of events that would lead to the creation of today's US Special Forces.

How to Turn the Tide in the War Against Nazi Germany

This was the question that Pyke had asked himself back in 1940, as German forces powered north through Denmark and Norway. Britain was on the back foot. The problem faced by the government, as he saw it, was: '*How* can a weak and undeveloped power hold and put pressure (near to home) on a strong and already developed power?'

As well as putting pressure on the enemy, this weaker power needed to strike by the end of the year, but could not call upon large supplies of manpower and physical resources – 'because you won't get them and we haven't got them'. In short, the question appeared to be: 'how to do something with nothing which would be so offensive as to be serious to the enemy almost at once.'

Pyke wrote this at the start of May 1940, at a time when it was widely accepted that most of Norway was under German control.

Or was it?

The next stage in Pyke's reasoning was so important that he set it out in capital letters:

IN A FULL MILITARY SENSE THE GERMANS DO NOT OCCUPY THE COUNTRY. THEY ARE "OCCUPYING" THE POPULATION, NOT THE COUNTRY (with exceptions noted). THIS MEANS THAT THE GERMANS HAVE NOT TIED UP IN NORWAY AN UNDULY LARGE ARMY.

Fine, but could you not say the same historically of any occupying force? It will always be impossible physically to occupy every square metre of enemy territory. Yet the implications in Norway were special. This was the most sparsely populated country in Europe. By 'occupying' no more than its tiny population, German forces controlled a minuscule proportion of the country's land mass.

Pyke reformulated the problem again: 'Providing always that it can be done simply enough, *we should compel the Germans to occupy the country [Norway], completely in a full military sense*, thus immobilising more men and material than are immobilised at present.' As it stood, Germany had all the advantages of controlling Norway for a fraction of the potential cost. This led logically enough to Pyke's next question: 'What are the factors that would compel the Germans (within the limits imposed on us by our military situation elsewhere and assumed above; i.e. only very small calls for help from Navy, Army or Air Force) fully to occupy Norway and to put in a fairly large amount of men and material?'

The answer: they must be made to feel that their military superiority was threatened. 'The Germans had complete mastery on land. They had partial mastery in the air. Our mastery on sea was incomplete. If we had complete mastery of one element we could perhaps use it to modify and even disrupt his superiority in the others.' So which element land, air or sea?

This appeared to be the next question, unless, of course, there was a fourth military element, one which did not exist, in the sense that it had not yet been thought of as a military element. This might sound pointless, like searching for a fourth primary colour. Nonetheless Pyke paused to consider it. Remaining open to questions like this no matter how silly they might sound was a rudimentary part of his technique. 'The mathematical physicists have given us the correct pattern of thought. They are always taking as a hypothesis what seems absurd, excluding the appearance of absurdity from their minds, and then asking what happens if it were so, irrespective of whether it *seems* to be so. I am not a mathematical physicist. I can hardly add. But there had been enough popularisation of their thought for everyone to know *how* they think.' In which case, absurd as it might sound, *was* there a fourth military element to consider in addition to land, air and sea?

Pyke cast his mind back to a conversation he had had recently with the renowned military strategist Basil Liddell Hart. In relation to the Spanish Civil War they had agreed that control of the Spanish Pyrenees would have given one side a distinct advantage. Pyke had been reminded of this conversation by a report in the *Evening Standard* which had mentioned a strategically important road in Norway. No car could move along it 'without being bombed or machine-gunned', and nor could anyone escape the road because the surrounding country was buried beneath snow. 'Note the obvious implication,' he wrote. 'They were tied to the road.' (Note also that Pyke had once again taken inspiration from a detail in a newspaper.)

What tied them to the road? Snow. It was an immobilising factor, or at least it appeared to be. Was there a way of reimagining snow from a military point of view, and seeing it as an opportunity rather than a hindrance?

In theory, yes. If you could find ways of moving through, into or over the snow which your enemy did not possess then you would have a military advantage. '*Mastery of the Snows* was the next, and one of the key formulations of the problem. It was no mere phrase. It was susceptible to almost arithmetic definition. It meant three things. (1) the ability to go up steeper slopes than could the enemy. (2) to move more quickly than he could, even on the flat, and (3) the ability to move cross-country.' You would need a force of guerrilla troops armed with specialist vehicles allowing them to outrun, outclimb and outmanoeuvre the enemy; 'to travel fast and far, not through but *on* the snow, over and down the slopes of the Norwegian mountains, able to carry arms for attacking, explosives to destroy bridges, tunnels, railway tracks, hydroelectric stations, etc., etc., equipped to maintain themselves in any part of the country, however high and desolate, to launch frequent attacks on vital objects simultaneously or in quick succession.'

Pyke envisaged this force attacking 'like pernicious gadflies' – elsewhere he compared them to 'a cloud of mosquitos'. When possible they could ski silently downhill towards their targets, an image which gave Pyke an idea for this force's motto: 'The Assyrians came down like the Wolf on the Fold.' Their snowmobiles should be agile and light like skiers – for 'how often could an aeroplane hit a skilful skier zigzagging rapidly down a hill?' Petrol tanks for refuelling could be disguised as felled trees. The vehicles might be designed to throw up clouds of snow to act as screens. 'Principles of attack should be: (1) complete surprise (2) complete confusion (3) complete distraction' and, most importantly, 'never be brave where foresight and intelligence can be used instead'.

Twenty-five years after smuggling himself out of Germany, Pyke had applied his principles of escape to military insurgency. Outnumbered and outgunned, this tiny force would confound the enemy's expectations in its style of attack and the way it had turned the inhospitable snowy conditions to its advantage. It was an idea that owed everything to a single conceptual reverse. Pyke had challenged himself to think of snow as a fourth military element rather than a natural hazard. Just as prehistoric man must have thought to himself one day, as he rowed across a choppy sea, that perhaps his enemy, the wind, could become his friend – and without this it would have been impossible to imagine a sail – Pyke had done nothing more than reverse an everyday assumption.

The logic here was compelling, but without the revolutionary snowmobile it was merely science fiction. Pyke maintained that the machine he envisaged was 'no more an invention than the tank in 1915 was an invention. The tank was an adaptation to a military problem of an already existing mechanism: the Holt Tractor and the Diplock Caterpillar.' A snowmobile such as the Armstead Snow Motor, with a Ford tractor engine set above two helically flanged cylinders to control its direction and speed, could easily be adapted to the strategic needs of guerrilla warfare in Norway, 'similar to the adaptations which animals make to their environment and to competition with one another'.

The Armstead Snow Motor

Pyke concluded that 'with relatively slight help from home and without protection from the air, a small force from a maximum of about 4,000 down even to a handful – say 50 or 100 men – for six months could compel the enemy to devote continuously resources of men and material 500 to 1,000 times as great as those which would be needed from us'. The goal was simple: 'Make every one of the 125,000 square miles of Norwegian territory not already fully occupied in the complete military sense of the term, an area from which dangerous surprise attacks may be launched.'

Yet this must not be a prelude to full-scale invasion. 'Far from wanting to drive the Germans out of this area we want, under certain conditions, as many as possible of them to come in [. . .], to treat the Nazis in Northern Norway as Pharaoh treated the ancient Jews. On no account must we let these people go [. . .]. We want the enemy to keep his head in the halter. But, I submit, if he should succeed in taking it out, we should not be so foolish as to put ours in, merely because the halter is empty.'

His proposal was ambitious and radical, a masterpiece of counter-intuitive military thought which combined a series of small technical innovations within a single daring strategy. It was elegantly paradoxical. Britain would strike while on the back foot, 'military ju-jitsu', in Pyke's phrase. 'Consider the *political* consequences of having won the war *without* the use of overwhelming weapons. Let us show the Germans, and indeed the world, that we can beat them even when we are *weaker*.'

Four days after the start of Blitzkrieg, 14 May 1940, as German forces fought their way through the Low Countries and France, Pyke finished his paper and had it typed up in double-spaced, narrow-columned text (designed to make it easier to read). He then dispatched copies to a group of individuals who might be able to act upon it. Pyke had always been willing 'to make a fool of himself', as he reminded Liddell Hart in his covering note, and it would soon become clear which was more foolish: his strategy, or the idea of an amateur like him suggesting such a thing.

One of the men to receive a copy of Pyke's paper, just days after his legendary speech in the House, was Leo Amery MP. This well-turned-out Tory might have been politically poles apart from Pyke, but the two men came together in their intellectual curiosity and the way they talked about the future. Amery was an un-conservative Conservative, an amateur futurologist who had recognised as early as 1904 the military importance of air power; in the following summer he would propose that when the Imperial War Cabinet was unable to meet in person its members should gather virtually by using television and radio, effectively presaging the modern-day Skype conference. (This plan was dismissed out of hand by Churchill's curmudgeonly scientific adviser, Frederick Lindemann.)

In Pyke, Amery had found someone who thought along similar lines to himself, yet with the ambition and scientific rigour which he lacked. He was 'impressed by the remarkable originality and inventiveness of his mind', and was not only sympathetic to Pyke but loyal. Amery's experiences with his tearaway son, John, whose anti-communism would soon morph into fascism, had made him more patient, and he never tired of Pyke's demands, unlike other politicians who dealt with him. Perhaps he also detected in Pyke a certain vulnerability following a remark he had made earlier in the war. 'He told me', wrote Amery, 'that he was a Jew and that he saw no prospect for Jews in the future except suicide.' Amery was Jewish himself and had helped to draft the Balfour Declaration. This comment left an impression.

Pyke described Amery as 'the sort of person who does not easily come into things, but that when he does, he bites', which was what happened here. Pyke's proposal 'very naturally appealed to me as a skiing enthusiast', explained Amery, who took it to the War Office, the Admiralty and to Sir Walter Monckton at the Ministry of Information. For now it would remain out of Churchill's hands. 'I am bothering the Prime Minister with so many things just now that I really cannot at this moment approach him on Pyke's behalf.'

Monckton felt that he was not the right person for this and after being pressed by Pyke – with whom 'it seems to be all my time or none, and all it cannot be' – he passed the proposal on to Churchill's scientific adviser, Frederick Lindemann, soon to become Lord Cherwell. A lifelong bachelor, fastidious, teetotal and vegan, Lindemann could be prickly and difficult to get along with. Though by no means a great scientist, Lindemann's skill was his ability to explain scientific concepts to non-specialists. Having long ago befriended Churchill he was now one of his most trusted advisers. His reaction to this scheme would be pivotal.

Over the next month Pyke sent an array of follow-up notes, left messages with secretaries, attended meetings and by late June 1940 had managed to get his proposal onto the desks of Lindemann, the First Lord of the Admiralty, A. V. Alexander, and Major-General Bourne of the newly formed Combined Operations.

None of them wanted anything to do with it. 'Mr Pyke has here a number of fairly commonplace ideas,' began Lindemann in his damning response; 'he clothes them with so much garrulous, pseudo-scientific blather that the reading of it becomes extremely wearisome.' Pyke had added to his initial plan two unrelated schemes, one for a grenade with hooks to catch onto tank tracks, the other for setting the Thames on fire using floating petrol mines and underwater petrol tanks. 'Others have thought of this,' Lindemann sniffed. 'Mr Pyke is able to dash off reams of this pretentious nonsense. I suggest that he would be better employed annoying the enemy instead of us, by feeding their espionage with bogus information.'

Bourne at Combined Operations, or more likely a junior officer, gave Pyke's proposals a little more thought before ruling that they were 'not considered practicable'. Although the snowmobiles had not been designed, let alone built, Bourne felt that they would be difficult to land and the Norwegian terrain was too precipitous for them. Alexander at the Admiralty echoed this strange conclusion, doubting 'the circumstances he has in mind would enable these vehicles to be usefully employed'.

Pyke had come up against what Evelyn Waugh later called the 'measureless obstructive strength' of military bureaucracy. 'Unless all my skiing friends have informed me wrongly,' protested Amery, 'the main characteristic of all the upland regions of Norway is precisely the fact that they are not precipitous, but undulating.' He disagreed too with the idea that getting the snowmobiles into Norway was unrealistic. This changed nothing.

The strategic proposal had been rejected not in strategic terms but on mechanical and logistical grounds. It seemed that Amery was the only one to have grasped Pyke's premise that it might be militarily useful to think of snow not as 'a *quality of weather* like cold, rain and mud, which must be endured with whatever protection water-proofs, sheepskins and gumboots, etc. can provide', but as 'a medium like the air and sea which, if we can master it, can be made in a positive sense to serve the very ends of war'. Having mastered snow you might find a situation in which – as Lenin almost said – 'The worse the weather for the enemy, the better for us.'

Pyke claimed to be unsurprised by this rejection. 'You won't get it done,' Bernal had warned him, adding that he was appalled by the sclerotic attitudes he had encountered in Whitehall. 'I, with an official position, have for months been trying to get things done that – believe it or not – are even simpler. I have failed. And so have all of our type. You will find that the simplest and most obvious statements that you make, remarks that you would think at this stage would be taken as axiomatic – will be challenged, referred to and fro, back and forth, at best hundreds of letters will be written: – nothing will be done.' 'The whole country,' Pyke later wrote, 'and by no means least the administration, were saturated, and had been for years, with the defensive spirit, not to say the spirit of surrender, the *inherent* result of the Baldwin-Chamberlain epoch of appeasement.'

The proposal was mothballed. Though Amery renewed their correspondence in February 1941, this came to nothing, and it was not until September of that year – shortly after Rolf Rünkel had begun to work as Pyke's secretary, and with the Soviet Union suffering terrible losses in the German onslaught – that Pyke sent Amery a revised and expanded proposal. It described how this guerrilla force could be deployed in the Italian Alps or Romania, where it could target oil refineries, as well as Norway, where targets would include the country's hydroelectric plants.

Amery sent a copy to General McNaughton, then Commander of the Canadian Corps, and to Field Marshal Sir John Dill, Chief of the Imperial General Staff. Just as the shape of the war had changed, so had the military mood, and on this occasion Pyke's idea was not rejected out of hand.

It was also around this time that Pyke moved into the flat of Cyril Ray in Albany, off Piccadilly. Spritely and brave, Ray was a *Manchester*

Guardian war correspondent who would later be mentioned in dispatches when covering the Allied advance into Europe and remains one of the only British journalists to receive an American Army citation. According to MI5, Ray was also 'a Communist'.

Earlier that year he had been embedded with the Fifth Destroyer Flotilla, the 'Fighting Fifth', then under the command of Lord Mountbatten – who had made a deep impression. For years afterwards the two would exchange Christmas cards and, after Mountbatten's death, Ray labelled him 'perhaps the greatest Englishman of the century, and all the more so for not being of English blood'. Pyke listened carefully to what Ray had to say about Mountbatten. 'I heard things about him that made me say "Ecce Homo".' He even looked up a book co-written by Mountbatten back in 1931, *An Introduction to Polo*. What gave him hope was that this aristocratic young naval commander appeared to be hungry for new ideas, whether they concerned polo tactics or anti-submarine measures.

Having been struck down over Christmas with pleurisy, as he had been several times in recent years, by February 1942 Pyke was back on his feet and on the attack once again. He asked Amery if he would take his proposal to Mountbatten. 'I feel that, and I think you'll agree, it is most desirable this should be dealt with by Lord Louis himself. The resistance to new conceptions is so strong that if it is dealt with by any member of his staff it *may* not stand the same chance. Could you ask him if he would 1) read the memorandum himself, then 2) see me, himself? Is this a feasible request?'

Amery wrote to Mountbatten at once, and just three days later they sat down together for dinner in Amery's house, whereupon he began to explain Pyke's proposal with the pent-up enthusiasm of a man who feels he has been right all along. He referred occasionally to the 'brilliant' inventor behind it, and at the end of the meal Amery handed his guest a copy of Pyke's proposal. Later that night, Mountbatten wrote him a letter.

Lord Louis Mountbatten

'Many of the descriptions of him are merely lazy attempts to foist on the public a stock figure from the waxworks', Pyke would write of Mountbatten. To look at, he was magnificent: tall, handsome and stag-like. Yet beneath the glossy exterior was a man who sometimes struggled to belong. He had been born a German prince: however, owing to his grandparents' morganatic marriage he was a Prince of Battenberg rather than of Hesse, the former more junior than the latter. As a teenage naval cadet during the First World War he watched as his father, the First Sea Lord, was forced to step down on account of his German ancestry. He was a victim of the same xenophobic spirit which had contributed to his family's decision in 1917 to follow their cousins in the British royal family in anglicising their name. His Serene Highness Prince Louis Francis Battenberg, then aged seventeen, became plain old Lord Louis Mountbatten, second son of the suitably British-sounding Marquess of Milford Haven.

After the war Mountbatten would appear in the press as an occasional sidekick to his cousin, the Prince of Wales, and for a moment was known as a playboy. But again the shoes do not quite fit. He would turn up to dances in large crowds and leave early to go home and read. He was cuckolded by his wife, Edwina Ashley, one of the world's richest heiresses, to whom Mountbatten bemoaned his inability to flirt or 'excite you more than I fear I do'. Instead he devoted himself to his naval career, determined to emulate his father and become First Sea Lord.

For many in the Admiralty, where his nickname was 'Master of Disaster', he was thought to lack 'sea sense'. According to his biographer, Philip Ziegler, his technical abilities as a naval captain were never more than second-rate. But he retained what Wallis Simpson called 'extraordinary drive' coupled with a knack for keeping his reputation spotless, and by the start of the Second World War Lord Louis Mountbatten was just where he wanted to be: at the helm of a ship.

Although he had three destroyers go down beneath him, which

might suggest a degree of recklessness – he was known to get carried away in the heat of the moment and to have a lust for speed – by the summer of 1941 he was thought to be having a 'good war'. This spin had as much to do with skilful public relations as it was a reflection of his qualities as a leader. For all his lack of sea sense, Mountbatten was a decisive, forward-thinking commander with huge charisma. He could put anyone at ease and exuded throughout his life the breezy self-confidence of a man who slept well at night. One of the men to recognise these abilities as a leader was Churchill.

The Prime Minister saw that he was popular both with his naval ratings and the British public and in October 1941 summoned the 'Master of Disaster' to Chequers. Over lunch he explained that he wanted him to take over Combined Operations, the military command responsible for Commando raids on occupied Europe.

Mountbatten was unimpressed, and described himself as 'damned annoyed' at the job offer as he was about to take command of the aircraft carrier HMS *Illustrious*, then being repaired in the US.

'You fool!' Churchill shot back. 'The best thing you can hope to do there is to repeat your last achievement and get yourself sunk.'

The Prime Minister explained exactly what the new job entailed. 'All the other headquarters in this country are thinking defensively, *your* job will be to think *offensively* – to restore the offensive spirit.' Mountbatten was to plan and launch a crescendo of raids against the European mainland, with the objective of preparing the ground for D-Day, set to be the world's largest-ever amphibious assault. Combined Operations was to determine which landing craft to use, how to supply an army operating in occupied territory, what level of air cover should be provided and where to make landfall. This was no ordinary desk job.

Mountbatten accepted, and over the following months he immersed himself in his new task, often sleeping in his office, and by the end of the year this hitherto small and unloved command had been transformed. When he took over there were just twenty-three people working at Combined Operations headquarters, including messengers and typists. By the time he sat down to dinner with Amery he had a staff of more than 300.

In his letter to Pyke that night, Mountbatten described the proposal as 'very interesting', adding that he would pass a copy on to one of his officers, whom Pyke should go to see. 'When I return he will make a report to me and I shall then be in a position to judge what our next steps should be.'

It would be wrong to say that Pyke now had a foot in the door at Combined Operations. But he had at least established the existence of a door and the possibility that it might open.

'Major Parks-Smith reminded me a little of what the Prince of Wales must have been like in the last war,' Pyke confided to Amery, of the Combined Operations officer he went to meet. 'Very charming, modest and doing his best, but not, I should say, an outstanding intellect.' Pyke had watched as the major read his proposal. 'Like Mephistopheles, striving by art and artifice for possession of his mind, I saw his open face light up with complete understanding. Major Parks-Smith then suddenly rose as if he were about to come to attention. He needlessly lifted a bundle of papers from his desk; and with emphasis put them down again. He then resumed his seat. Unconsciously he was expressing the fact that he had made up his mind. Later on came the words, "I must go to the CCO and tell him this is important".'

The CCO was Mountbatten, just back from Scotland. Yet rather than invite Pyke in to meet him he arranged for a captain in Combined Operations to see him next. Several days later he was called back to meet a colonel, then another colonel, followed by two brigadiers, including Mountbatten's Chief of Staff, Geoffrey Wildman-Lushington.

Pyke seemed to enjoy this. 'They knew, only too well for my liking, that they were but agents, and their principal might cancel the bargain at any moment.' By the same token he knew that he was there to pitch himself to Mountbatten through these ambassadors, a task he relished. Selling oneself was an art, he insisted, later referring to that moment in his life as 'what my biographers will no doubt call my most mature period'. Indeed it was, and this artistry was about to be put to its greatest test.

The first time Pyke set eyes on Mountbatten was at a meeting in Combined Operations to discuss whether or not this proposal should be taken on. As directed, Pyke got up before 'a vast gathering of nabobs and experts' and was asked 'to expound the whole project at great length'.

Though he prided himself on being able to sell himself in an interview, Pyke had 'very little' experience of meetings like this, and was not always very good at judging the collective character of his audience. Nor was he an academic or professional scientist who had devoted his career to the study of snow, snowmobiles or guerrilla warfare. Rather, he was an unemployed forty-eight-year-old, a civilian who had begun to read up on these subjects in his spare time less than two years ago. Yet his research had been comprehensive, he had an excellent memory, he 'bore himself with immense natural dignity' and could command attention when he spoke thanks to his 'superbly resonant voice'.

Standing up before a blur of khaki, Pyke ran through his proposal for what must have felt like the hundredth time. He fielded questions, and at last Mountbatten asked for a show of hands. Pyke's pulse must have quickened. In the next few seconds he would find out whether Combined Operations was prepared to pursue his idea.

For the men in that room what, if anything, was the appeal of Pyke's plan? Part of its attraction lay in the novelty of the scheme. By February 1942 German forces were continuing to drive deeper into

Russian territory; Rommel was apparently unstoppable in North Africa; Greece and Crete had recently fallen; and the Japanese were rampant in South-East Asia. Pyke's plan outlined a daring British offensive in a war which had been dominated until then by German victories.

It also proposed a new kind of military unit. At the start of the war there were just two British organisations devoted to guerrilla warfare: MI6's Section D and MI(R). Neither was capable of operations on the scale that Pyke envisaged: instead, one was to operate 'stay-behind' parties to harry any occupying Nazi forces in Britain; the other specialised in individual acts of overseas sabotage. During the summer of 1940, SOE had come into existence, as well as the Commandos, whose activities were coordinated by Combined Operations. Both performed small-scale attacks against occupied Europe, the Commandos concentrating on coastal areas and SOE carrying out sabotage work further inland. Though he was unaware of this division, Pyke had proposed, by chance, a hybrid unit: a Commando force performing SOE-style sabotage in what was seen as SOE territory.

As well as bringing into existence a new kind of force, this plan would divert enemy troops away from France, which was another attraction for those in Combined Operations given that they were preparing for D-Day. Indeed, the strategy of drawing enemy troops up to Norway, described by Hitler as a 'zone of destiny', would soon become an established principle in Allied military planning. Later that year, in the build-up to the invasion of North Africa, MI5 tried to gull the Germans into thinking that an invasion of both Norway and northern France was about to take place; in 1943 the London Controlling Section's 'Cockade' plan again tried to divert German troops to Norway, and in 1944 Operation Fortitude North was an attempt to fool German commanders into thinking that a British Fourth Army of some 100,000 troops was about to invade Norway. Yet by February 1942 the idea was an original one.

No less attractive was the impact of Pyke's plan on Germany's economic and industrial capacity. Norway produced 30,000 tons of aluminium per year from just six plants, each connected to an HEP station. Pyke's scheme would knock out some fifty HEP stations, including these.

Though it would not have been discussed at this meeting, his plan would also allow the Allies to stunt the growth of Germany's atomic programme. The year before, a tenfold increase in the production of heavy water (deuterium oxide) had been reported at the Vemork HEP station in southern Norway. This was the first step towards building an atomic weapon. Vemork was another of Pyke's targets.

But there were problems with his proposal. The all-important snowmobile had not yet been invented. There was no exit strategy with which to remove these elite guerrillas from Norway. And of course there was the man behind it: a odd-looking civilian with no military experience at all.

When Mountbatten asked for a show of hands, the result was unanimous: Pyke's scheme was judged to be practicable and worthwhile, and it was agreed that the force he had proposed and their snowmobiles should be developed by Combined Operations without delay. Twenty-one months after its inception, this plan had arrived in the right hands at the right time. Committees were appointed to deal with staffing and resources and the meeting drew to a close, at which point Mountbatten asked Pyke to join him in his office for what was to be their first full-length conversation.

Mountbatten's rooms were probably in the basement of No. 1a Richmond Terrace, spacious without being large, well lit, and with a bed in the corner or next door. No doubt the CCO looked as he usually did, 'handsome and breezy, like Brighton at its best'.

Pyke was a mess. His shirt was neither crisp nor clean and if there were creases in his trousers they were not of the military variety. There was no pomade in what was left of his thinning hair and his goatee had become overgrown and shaggy, looking like seaweed on a rock. His eyes spoke of a frenetic, restless energy. One man who met him around this time described them as 'unusually expressive'; for another they were 'thoughtful and serious'; while the poet and biographer Peter Quennell called them 'burning eyes'.

The two men sat down on either side of a desk and, as legend has it, Pyke fixed the CCO with those burning eyes and said: 'Lord Mountbatten, you need me on your staff because I'm a man who thinks.'

Pyke would often start conversations like this. He was 'trying to size you up by your reaction. If he felt you were sympathetic he took you into his confidence' – which was what he did to Mountbatten. Within this opening salvo were two questions to which he had an answer. He asked what Combined Operations lacked, and what he could provide. This command needed more innovators, problem-solvers, free-thinkers or in-house dissidents, and this was a part that Pyke could play with distinction.

Perhaps to test this, Mountbatten asked him to solve a military problem that was troubling him. The mighty German battleship SS *Tirpitz* had recently left the Baltic and was now at anchor in a Norwegian fjord. It was imperative that the *Tirpitz* did not break out into the Atlantic. Mountbatten asked Pyke what to do.

'The untidy man with the beard hesitated a moment, and then said: "Lower the density of the water around her." He demonstrated his point by calling for a bucket of water and a small model of a ship. It certainly sank.' Whether or not he actually performed a demonstration – perhaps he added alcohol to the water to lower the density – what mattered was the speed with which he had come up with this counter-intuitive idea. The *Tirpitz* was not sunk by lowering the density of the surrounding water, yet this was precisely the kind of radical, innovative thinking that Mountbatten wanted on tap.

Initially he had been wary of the man about whom Amery had raved. 'I must confess, though, that after Pyke came and showed his very original turn of mind I began to appreciate the unusual qualities of that mind. I liked his mind,' wrote Mountbatten, 'and I was prepared to support him.' He saw Pyke as 'a chap with no scientific qualifications, but a crazy, independent thinker, and something of genius'. Everything about him appealed to Mountbatten's character-istically Hessian affinity for those who thought beyond the bounds of convention. When asked about Pyke long after the war 'there was genuine affection, as well as genuine respect, in Mountbatten's voice when he shook his head and murmured: "Clever chap, Pyke. *Very* clever chap . . ."'

Pyke was no less taken by the CCO, an affinity seen most obviously in the breathless rhythm of their conversations. 'I fell into the habit straight away with you of talking and writing on what the US telephone system terms a "person to person" basis,' he told Mountbatten, adding elsewhere: 'You always rush me off my feet, we both think – and talk – so fast.' He found the CCO 'as receptive as a sponge and as quick as a knife', and congratulated him on running a command which had taken just three weeks to accept a proposal that had been ignored by rival organisations for almost two years.

'What I've done,' replied Mountbatten, 'is to take ordinary Service material, and make them more afraid to reject an idea than to accept it.' Hearing this, for Pyke, was like discovering that they were related. 'In face of a new idea,' he had once written, 'oughtn't we to ask . . . "What is *right* with it", *before* asking "What is wrong with it"?' Here were the seeds of an unlikely friendship.

Towards the end of that interview, on 23 February 1942, Mountbatten did something unusual: he offered Pyke a job at Combined Operations. As well as pushing ahead with Pyke's proposal for a force of snow-borne guerrillas, Mountbatten wanted him on hand to solve other problems and help foster a new spirit of creative innovation. His title was to be 'Director of Programmes' but really, as Pyke explained, he would be a 'Suggester of Programmes'.

He accepted, but on the condition that the new force 'be prepared with the same thoroughness, drive and imagination as the Germans would do it'. Then there was the question of payment. In his memorandum 'Pyke on Money' the new Director of Programmes told Mountbatten that he was willing to work for nothing but, if he was to be paid, it must be at the top rate.

'My dear fellow, I am on your *side*,' replied Mountbatten, before asking him to name his price.

Pyke consulted Bernal who suggested a ridiculous sum: £3,000 a year. Mountbatten pointed out that he himself was earning just £1,977 a year. They compromised on £1,500, making Pyke one of the highest-paid members of staff at Combined Operations.

So began one of the strangest appointments of the war. For Elias Canetti, the Nobel Prize-winning playwright who had got to know Pyke over the previous year, it was 'an extraordinary, wholly unbureaucratic arrangement, unthinkable in any other country at war'. A suspected communist, with close connections to two men thought to be Soviet agents, had been given the ear of one of the Allies' most senior military figures.

News of the appointment would also come as a shock to those in MI5, where fresh intelligence had just come in about Pyke. It was still not clear to the Security Services whether this man was a patriotic boffin or someone whose first loyalty was to Moscow. There was also the slim possibility that he was in fact both.

PYKE HUNT, PART 3

Milicent Bagot, the most influential woman in MI5, was quick, redoubtable and at times impatient with those who could not keep up. She sang in a choir on Tuesday evenings and would later inspire the Connie Sachs character in John le Carré's 'George Smiley' novels. She was MI5's expert on Soviet espionage and communism and, on 6 January 1942, she received an alarming report.

On the day that 75,000 people piled into Wembley to watch England play football against Scotland, with the proceeds going to Mrs Churchill's Aid to Russia Fund, an SIS report on the inner workings of Moscow's Comintern arrived at MI5. The report confirmed what she had suspected: Hitler's invasion of Russia had done little or nothing to change the scope or intensity of clandestine Soviet activities in Britain. The report also suggested that there was a Comintern propaganda bureau operating right under her nose in London. Bagot belonged to F.2b, the section responsible for monitoring Comintern activities.

The Comintern, or Communist International, had been set up in 1919 by Lenin with the task of destroying capitalism. Over the next two decades its headquarters in Moscow opposite the Kremlin had become a haven for international dissidents and political refugees, many of whom went on to study at the Comintern's Lenin School where revolutionaries were taught the finer points of Marxian dialectics, tradecraft, sabotage, agitprop and secret communication. The brightest and best, including Pyke's friend Percy Glading, were cherry-picked to join the NKVD or GRU before being sent back to their native countries, sometimes under assumed names, to help local Communist Parties carry out Moscow's bidding.

Bagot had known for years about the threat posed by the Comintern. As early as 1933, MI5's then Deputy Director of B Branch, Guy Liddell, wrote that 'the Comintern remained a more serious problem than the Nazi regime'. Since then, MI5 had intercepted a glut of wireless traffic between the Comintern headquarters in Moscow and the CPGB, via the 'MASK' decrypts. More recently, an MI5 informant had expressed his amazement at 'what a complicated and detailed *Apparat* the Comintern is building for itself and consolidating in England' and 'what vast sums of money it must have at its disposal'.

Yet the Security Service was thin on detail. Bagot could only guess at the extent of Comintern operations, which was why the latest report from SIS was so interesting. As well as revealing the existence of an undercover Comintern propaganda bureau in London, it suggested that one of its employees was Rolf Rünkel, and that he worked under a senior Comintern operative who went by the cover name 'Professor P'.

Bagot was determined to unmask 'Professor P'. She began by working through MI5's voluminous card index. Her colleagues could look through the same material, yet none had the ability to process what they saw in quite the same way. Since 1931, when her position at Special Branch was transferred to MI5, Milicent Bagot had developed an intuitive understanding of communism. She knew the mindset of a 'fellow traveller' and his or her emotional attachment to the cause just as she recognised the dead-eyed detachment of Party cadres. She had the imaginative capacity to suggest and hold in her mind a bewildering array of connections within this maze of names and incomplete biographies, and to find meaning where others saw mere coincidence. Using her considerable expertise, Bagot reached a conclusion on the identity of 'Professor P'. As she wrote in an internal minute dated 21 January, 'Professor P. is, I think, identical with Geoffrey Nathaniel PYKE.'

He was, in many ways, a perfect fit. A vital clue could be found in Special Branch's investigation of Rolf Rünkel in which the subject was seen to be 'gathering and translating material concerning the evolution of German public opinion' for Geoffrey Pyke. This was the kind of work you would expect to take place in a propaganda bureau. Pyke also sounded like the sort of intellectual who might be given the nickname 'Prof' or 'Professor' by his friends. Further corroboration came from the smorgasbord of foreign Communists he was thought to be in touch with and the belief within MI5 that Pyke's charity had been under Communist control.

Bagot's only concern was that the Special Branch report on Rünkel might have been based on just one source. To clear this up she sent out an internal minute and, not long after, MI5's E Branch, responsible for foreigners classified as 'Alien', provided her with fresh intelligence on Professor P. One of its anonymous sources had recognised the name.

He described Professor P. as 'a very important man in the Comintern who worked on the Continent for a time and also in Germany'. In Berlin, Professor P. was part of what appeared to be an 'economic and scientific bureau' run by Professor Varga, later known as 'Stalin's Economist', but was actually a 'large and comprehensive *Weitverzweigte* [wide-ranging] *Apparat*' where Comintern propaganda was prepared and distributed and counterfeiting took place. Of Professor P.'s work in Britain, the source warned that he 'is doing the same job today as he used to do in that *Apparat*, provided of course, that he is identical with the person I have in mind'.

Bagot's mental picture of this figure was filling out fast. But did any of this new intelligence rule out an identification of 'P.' as Pyke? It depended really on whether Pyke could have been living in Berlin while Varga's bureau was active, between the mid-1920s and 1933.

There was nothing to rule this out. MI5's biography of Pyke contained a gap which stretched from the Great War through to 1937, easily encompassing the period when Professor P. was said to have been in Berlin. Even today there is a similar fog in the middle of Pyke's story, from his breakdown in 1929 through to the start of his work on anti-Semitism in 1934. While there are scraps of evidence here and there to suggest that during these years he was living in a tumbledown cottage in the Devil's Punchbowl, long periods remain unaccounted for. So for Bagot in 1942, as much as for any researcher today, it was at least possible that Geoffrey Pyke had spent some time in Berlin during the early 1930s. The only question that remained was whether this identification of Professor P. as Pyke made sense.

Very much so. It is hard to imagine anyone grasping the murderous potential of Nazi anti-Semitism as early as he did without the kind of affinity for a society which comes from having lived within it. There were other details that Bagot was unaware of which would only have strengthened her conviction. As well as the selection of Comintern agents with whom Pyke was in touch, such as Percy Glading and Claud Cockburn, the first two people he sought out in Paris, during the summer of 1939 – Richard Kisch and Frederick Fuller – were also Comintern agents.

If there were others whom Bagot suspected of being Professor P.

their names have not been released by MI5. By the middle of February 1942, just before Pyke was offered a job by Mountbatten, Bagot suspected this man of running an undercover Comintern propaganda bureau. All she needed now was proof.

HOW TO CHANGE THE MILITARY MIND

Lieutenant-General Archie Nye, a former barrister and favourite of Churchill's, was surprised to see Mountbatten arrive with a dishevelled civilian in tow. It was early March 1942 and in a matter of days Nye was due to chair a meeting of the Vice-Chiefs of Staff at which Pyke's proposal would be on the agenda. Too often in the past senior army officers had taken one look at this plan and dismissed it as a trussed-up proposal for a snowmobile. Mountbatten was determined that this should not happen again, and had engineered this meeting with Nye so that Pyke could talk him through his idea for a snow-borne guerrilla force operating with specialist snowmobiles behind enemy lines in Norway. Nye was quick on the uptake and grasped the potential of the plan almost at once.

Several days later, during the crucial meeting, Nye won over his fellow Vice-Chiefs of Staff to the benefits of the scheme. As if reading from a script prepared by Pyke – indeed, it was not uncommon for civil servants actually to prepare a script, so he might have been literally reading from Pyke's notes – he insisted that producing the snowmobile 'was only part of the problem'. No less important was 'the tactical and strategical employment of this particular weapon'. It was agreed that the War Office should look into its implementation. Only a month after asking Leo Amery to contact the CCO about his idea, Pyke's plan had been accepted by the Vice-Chiefs of Staff. It was a major coup.

On the same day that Nye made the case for his snow-borne guerrilla force, Pyke was sitting at a desk 300 yards away in Richmond Terrace, revelling in his new career as a highly paid civil servant. The contrast between this new job and his solitary existence in Great Ormond Street could not have been greater.

He was surrounded now by conversations, questions, introductions and new faces. When junior soldiers entered his office they would salute before looking to see who was in there – an experience which never failed to make Pyke laugh. His colleagues in Combined Operations included celebrated figures such as the land speed record-holder Sir Malcolm Campbell, the Hollywood actor Douglas Fairbanks Jr, the novelist and biographer Robert Henriques and the businessman Sir Harold Wernher, who employed his own secretary and walked to work each morning from the Dorchester Hotel.

Indeed, from afar this command sounded like a glamorous, easy-going appointment. Certainly there were, as one member of staff put it, 'handsome social chaps who could always be relied upon to say "The champagne's over here, Dickie,"' men like the Cuban playboy and racing driver the Marquis de Casa Maury, then Mountbatten's head of intelligence. But they were in a minority. The atmosphere elsewhere was busy and sharp. Evelyn Waugh, a liaison officer at Combined Operations, described it as a 'surrealist whirligig'. For the academic, journalist and one-time NKVD agent Goronwy Rees: 'To join this fish-flesh-fowl company was to find oneself almost literally at sea or up in the air; one felt oneself hopelessly earthbound, a clumsy and an ignorant landlubber.'

Pyke experienced no such discombobulation. He was 'excited and elated' by his new surroundings. It was, after all, the job of his dreams. He was being paid to identify and solve problems which might help the Allies in their fight against fascism, and as he settled into his new career he found the range of his thought exploding, swapping 'precaution for the lascivious beauty of progress'.

Word spread fast about Pyke's ability to solve problems. Like schoolboys asking the class swot for help, officers soon started to come to him with their knottiest questions. The afternoon on which the Vice-Chiefs of Staff discussed his proposal was typical in this sense. Pyke had been asked earlier that day to work out 'how a plane can measure its *drift* particularly over enemy country when visibility is such that neither landmarks [n]or stars are visible'. He had no expertise in this, but he had a technique and usually it worked.

He began by stripping the problem back. In the purest sense it involved a human being moving through the air who wants to measure his distance from static and invisible points below. Pyke spun this around. He pictured a static human on the ground trying to measure invisible atmospheric conditions above. The outline of a solution now emerged. Meteorologists on the ground measured atmospheric conditions using a 'ballon sonde', a miniature balloon with a wireless device attached which was sent up into the sky, whereupon it relayed a signal with details of the surrounding weather conditions. By doing the same in reverse, surely one could measure the drift of the aircraft. Rather than use a balloon to send the device up, allow gravity to take it down. Once it had reached the ground it could send up a signal to the plane's radio operator. The difference between its position and that of the plane, given its speed, would allow for a calculation of the drift. 'Prof J. D. Bernal FRS of the Ministry of Home Security, etc. etc. etc. thinks I have solved the problem,' Pyke enthused to Mountbatten, 'so does a Squadron Leader of the R.A.F.'

But he did not stop there. Pyke's style was to develop his fantasies in full before paring them back. He went on to imagine what would happen to this reverse ballon sonde after it had served its primary purpose. How should it be disguised? What would a German farmer make of it? How long before the enemy designed one itself? Was it possible to drop dummy versions over England to see how long it would take before concerned members of the public handed them in to the authorities, to get a sense of their likely fate in Germany? As well as allowing his fantasies to play out *in extenso*, Pyke understood the value in innovation of conducting as many small-scale experiments as possible.

When not dealing with other people's problems, Pyke took on questions regarding his proposed force. One of these was about how this unit could strike the oilfields near Ploesti in Romania. It was typical of Pyke that this not only triggered a flood of ideas, but that he wanted his colleagues at Combined Operations to understand how he had arrived at them. Rather than circulate a précis of his proposals he had a long diary-entry typed up and passed around. Few people in Combined Operations had ever read anything like it. His paper was described as 'ingenious', its ideas 'an advance on any other means known to us' and it was agreed that 'energetic and immediate support' should be given to them and that a full-time Planning, Research and Development body should be established to investigate these suggestions further. This diary included plans for training St Bernard's dogs to take alcohol up to bored sentries, exhausts fitted to snowmobiles in order to sound like barking dogs and guerrillas who would enter oil refineries disguised as firemen who would carry hoses capable of propelling explosive elements as well as water. There were references to detective stories, thrillers, humorists, lawyers, a short film Pyke had recently seen, an Admiralty handbook, the endemic fondness for dogs in rural Romania and, of course, there were references to the works of Shaw. What this text also provides is a complete example of what Pyke meant by his 'auto-Socratic' technique.

This was when Pyke tackled a problem by conducting either on paper or in his head a conversation between two voices. One was imaginative and full of fantasy, the other more considered, polite and wise – the Socrates figure, who rarely interrupted and would try to allow each fantasy to play out in full, always asking what was right with the idea before moving on to what was wrong. It was a difficult trick, but one which seemed to unlock Pyke's creativity and, now that he had a receptive audience for these thoughts, new ideas came tumbling out of him as never before.

By late March 1942 Pyke was 'bombarding all of us' with proposals and 'if he couldn't get us to listen by writing formally in the ordinary way, he'd write a memorandum or a letter that would compel your attention because it was so damned funny and so damned serious at the same time'. Of these the most widely read was almost certainly 'Mr Pyke's Second and Third Thoughts. A Recantation', soon to be known as: 'Latrines for Colonels'.

Pyke protested that this paper 'was not as it unfortunately appeared to some a *jeu d'esprit*, but was a desperately serious attempt by an amateur to work out a solution to a military tactical problem. The appearance of levity is due to two beliefs still to be disproved: (i) that a certain lightness of thought often enables one to jump over obstacles [. . .] (ii) that the Germans are on their guard against everything but the undergrad spirit.'

That 'military tactical problem' was how many troops each of his snowmobiles should carry. Pyke had initially suggested three – two to perform the act of sabotage, one to guard the vehicle – only to see that he had made a 'colossal blunder'.

> Let us visualise the situation. Our third man, our sentry is to *guard* the machine. Guard it against whom? Germans. German soldiers. Now if no German soldier does in fact appear we have wasted about 3 dwt [deadweight tonnage] of carrying capacity of the machine, a corresponding amount of aeroplane capacity,

etc. etc. Should German soldiers come across our machine what would be the situation? They will see a man. They will think him a fellow soldier, a Norwegian, or an enemy. There are no other possibilities. By custom and duty they will at once challenge him. They will flash a torch on him. Whatever our men wear as a white covering there can be no question to my mind that they must wear uniform. In a few seconds, therefore, our 'guard' and 'sentry' will be discovered as an enemy.

Now what are the alternatives to having our machine guarded while our 'sappers' are on the job? Obviously to leave it unguarded. But that is not enough. We can largely discount the consequences of the machine being discovered by a Norwegian. *For he will think it a German machine.* This, I submit, is a clue to a solution, and our efforts should henceforth be largely devoted to its perfection. The solution is:- *We must make the German sentry think it is a German machine.* The principle by which this force fights must be: 'Never take to Norway any man or machine to perform a function which *we may be able to make the enemy perform for us.'*

So how to make the German sentry believe that the snowmobile was German?

He must be *told* that it is German. A hierarchical civilisation tends to encourage passivity of mind and to inhibit scepticism expressing itself in action. He must be *forbidden* to touch the machine or to attempt to investigate it. He must be induced not to report and if possible not to talk about what he has seen.

The obvious solution might be to place a tarpaulin over the machine with a sign which said 'VERBOTEN', or something like:

Gestapo Research and Development Institute
SPECIAL DEATH RAY DEPARTMENT

Any soldier happening on an installation of the Gestapo
Research Institute who makes any mention of it will be
relentlessly dealt with with true National Socialist ruthlessness.
Countersigned: Gottfried Hecht, Commandant Gestapo.

There are two ways of procuring silence. One is to make a thing
so extraordinary, so terrifying that no one dares mention it; the
other is to make it so ordinary as to make it not worth mentioning.

Perhaps they should erect a canvas tent over the vehicle with a
sign saying:

OFFICERS' LATRINE
For Colonels only.
Latrine Accomodation for other Ranks is provided
2km. to the South.

We now have two tentative solutions: the Secret Research
Insititute Death Ray Department, and the Latrine. Can they be
combined?

Easily. Put one inside the other. If a sentry was brave enough to
venture inside this Colonels' latrine he would find an object covered
with a tarpaulin marked 'Death Ray Installation'. His response, surely,
would be to exit the tiny structure immediately, chuckling perhaps
at the cunning of the Gestapo.

To prove the principle, they could erect similar tents in Britain,
cover each with two layers, one prosaic, the other forbidding, and
see how long before they were entered by placing a telephone number

inside which should be called on discovery.

> If we are to beat the Germans we must, I submit, either be *overwhelmingly* more powerful – ten of everything to their one – OR we must be *at least* a little novel in our methods. That, I submit, is principle number One. To achieve the latter we must accept ancestral ways of doing things *only* after scrutiny, and only because this re-examination shows them to be the ways most suited to the specific occasion, and never because we have been influenced unconsciously by ancestor worship in the design of action.

You can sense here something of the mission Pyke felt himself to be on. 'Ancestor worship' was, for him, doing things in a particular way because that was how they'd always been done. He was not just providing answers in Combined Operations but imparting principles. 'I can teach anyone how to devise schemes for latrines for Colonels, only if they are sufficiently young-minded.' This was all he asked of his new colleagues.

Whether or not he was in contact with a Soviet handler, passing on information, or trying to influence policy along Soviet lines, Pyke was also determined to *awaken* these military minds. At Malting House School his guiding principle had been that each of us is born inquisitive and rational. In Richmond Terrace he wanted to reconnect the men around him to their instinctive curiosity. One must 'never, NEVER let up in the attempt to insinuate into the minds of our elders that nothing is so cheap, and nothing so profitable as a good idea. They may ask for authority for this improper remark. Let them ask Hitler. Or General Jodel. Or let them ask our Russian Allies, who starting from scratch only 20 years ago, are able now to be aggressive to the Germans because for so long they have been aggressive towards the unknown.' In Whitehall, he complained, it was as though in every room the writing was on the wall, not 'mene, mene, tekel, upharsin' but 'nothing should ever be done for the first time'.

After just ten days in Combined Operations Pyke distilled his concerns about this military attitude towards new ideas into a paper called 'New Ideas for the Army'. 'There is, at present, ample evidence to show that the Army lacks many of the right types of technical weapons necessary to conduct a successful campaign. There has never been any shortage of new ideas, but the fact remains, that practically the only progress made during the first 2½ years of the present war, has been a belated imitation of the Germans. The object of the following notes, is to try and show in the case of the War Office and the Ministry of Supply, why new ideas are impeded and how this extremely serious position, which threatens our very existence, can be speedily rectified.' He called for Development Boards to oversee the production of weapons prototypes, greater autonomy for junior officers, a more constructive attitude to problem-solving, more civilians in positions of executive responsibility and a greater emphasis on looking for ideas beyond the military. 'It would be contrary to common sense and to the experience of the Russians to believe that among civilians mine is the only head into which good ideas may fall.'

'Much is very true,' responded Mountbatten. Inspired by this, less than a fortnight later he asked a senior government scientist, Sir Henry Tizard, for the names of two scientists to join his staff. Tizard suggested Solly Zuckerman, the Oxford primatologist, and Pyke's old friend J. D. Bernal. Pyke's ideas were being acted upon faster than ever before, and in this case his suggestion had brought into Richmond Terrace two men who would make crucial contributions to the planning of D-Day.

J. D. 'Sage' Bernal   Solly Zuckerman

A leading crystallographer and jack of many scientific trades, Sage Bernal was known to friends and lovers alike for his 'beautiful, humorous, hazel eyes', his distinctive mane of hair and – to some – for his early advocacy of free love. 'Three in a bed, even when it is two beds placed close together, is always a complicated matter,' began one memorable diary entry for 1924. Bernal and Zuckerman were both cosmopolitan and ambitious, they had grown up on the cultural periphery of the British Empire – Bernal in Ireland, Zuckerman in South Africa – and like Pyke each one was either Jewish or of Jewish ancestry, as well as openly left-wing. Bernal had for many years been a member of the Communist Party.

During the early years of the war Bernal and Zuckerman had been carrying out experimental work together at the Research and Experimental Headquarters, part of the Ministry of Home Security, where they measured bomb impacts using shelters occupied by themselves or some of Zuckerman's monkeys (none of whom were injured). By early 1942, when they received the call from Mountbatten, they had become, according to Bernal's biographer Andrew Brown, 'the boffin equivalent of Gilbert and Sullivan'.

Both were deeply disillusioned by the failure of the British military to make adequate use of the country's scientific talent. After several impressive turns on the *Brains Trust*, a new BBC discussion programme, Bernal wrote an article on this in which he bemoaned the reluctance of the 'British ruling class' to 'press things unduly, they will not take risks, they will not demand the impossible'. He was promptly struck down by the commentator's curse. Mountbatten, a prominent member of the ruling class, offered him the role of Scientific Adviser at Combined Operations. Bernal accepted, on the condition that Zuckerman came too. Unknown to him, an identical letter had already been sent to his friend.

Soon Bernal and Zuckerman were installed at Richmond Terrace, and along with Pyke these three became known as the 'Department of Wild Talents'. For one of Mountbatten's biographers 'it is a reasonable assumption that a scouring of the free world at that time could not have turned up a more valuable trio'.

Mountbatten was soon telling stories to his cousin, King George VI, about his Department of Wild Talents. The King's 'two favourites were a long-haired Irishman and a bearded Jew [Bernal and Pyke]; indeed so familiar did these characters become that the King would refer to them by gesture – either sweeping his hand through his hair or stroking an imaginary beard – as his cousin regaled him with their latest madcap activities.' The monarch was intrigued. Eventually he paid Richmond Terrace a visit. 'Mountbatten introduced us each in turn describing our activities in a fairly flippant manner,' recalled Sir Harold Wernher. Zuckerman was introduced as 'Monkey man'. Pyke was away, yet Bernal was present and with his hair in a state of characteristic disarray.

'Where in the hell did you come from?!' enquired the King.

Bernal was taken aback by this and began to stammer.

This had the effect of setting off the King, which in turn made Bernal's stammer worse.

For a moment the two men were caught stammering at each other, as if communicating in human Morse code, before Mountbatten intervened.

While most in Combined Operations were bemused by the Department of Wild Talents, some were wary. Bernal, Zuckerman and Pyke spoke differently from their colleagues, dressed differently, laughed at different jokes, had few friends in common with anyone else in the building and were evidently of the Left. It was partly their presence which encouraged Evelyn Waugh to describe a fictionalised Combined Operations as a blend of officers, 'experts, charlatans, plain lunatics and every unemployed member of the British Communist Party'. All three members of Mountbatten's 'Department of Wild Talents' had Personal Files at MI5, and, unknown to anyone in the building, just days after all three were in place, one of this trio was placed under surveillance by MI5.

From 18 March this individual was followed to work each day by two ordinary-looking men, 'watchers' from MI5's B.6 section, who lingered outside Richmond Terrace until the end of the day. They never went inside, nor did they ask about their subject's job. Instead their task was to follow this man through London's public spaces and observe the people he met, where he went and any suspicious behaviour.

Their reports were dispassionate and precise but far from exhaustive. In 1951, after the defection of the Soviet agent and 'Cambridge Spy' Guy Burgess, an insider's account of a secret meeting in Combined Operations was found in Burgess's flat. It had taken place just days after the MI5 observation had begun and was attended by two members of the Department of Wild Talents. This raises the possibility that one of these three might have been passing intelligence to Moscow.

The meeting in question was on 19 March 1942 and had been called to discuss further details of Pyke's project. It was chaired by Mountbatten and included representatives of the Special Operations Executive (SOE) and each of the three services. Bernal was there, along with Pyke, who, before his presentation, had asked for blackboard, chalk and 'the largest *physical* map of Norway which you have got. Ditto Europe. Ditto Arctic Russia', as well as 'say 6 copies of the *table of gradients*' and 'umpteen drawing pins'. Everyone present was sworn to secrecy before Pyke gave an account of his idea and what had happened to it so far.

There followed a lengthy discussion in which it was agreed that the idea remained 'desirable and practicable' and that the force should be ready for the winter. Sub-committees were formed to develop the vehicle, study weather conditions in Norway and Romania and design suitable explosives; this last sub-committee included representatives from SOE and MD1, also known as Churchill's Toy Shop on account of the strange – and often deadly – devices that it produced. But there were some on these sub-committees, and elsewhere, who had begun to worry that this force would not be ready by the end of the year.

On Saturday, 28 March, the morning after a heroic Commando raid on the dockyard at St Nazaire, Mountbatten and his wife went to Chequers. At some point over the next few days the CCO told the Prime Minister about Pyke's project. Churchill leapt at it.

As Pyke recalled, he 'displayed his real qualities by his immediate and enthusiastic acceptance of the Plan. I think his reaction should go on the record. He saw the strategic significance of the Plan in a flash. He no more cared what *sort* of machine did the trick, than I did.'

Almost everything about the idea appealed to the Prime Minister. It echoed T. E. Lawrence's Middle Eastern campaign during the last war – Churchill had described Lawrence as 'one of the greatest beings alive in our time' – and its focus was Norway, which for him represented unfinished business following the defeat of British forces there in 1940. He wanted 'to roll the map of Hitler's Europe down from the top', which meant starting with Norway. Pyke's plan was also emphatically Churchillian: brains would save blood, to borrow from one of his speeches. Yet for all his enthusiasm the Prime Minister could not change Britain's strained industrial capacity. Pyke's plan made sense, but there seemed to be insufficient British resources to have it developed.

It is unclear whether Pyke, Mountbatten or Churchill came up with the idea, yet in the days after that conversation at Chequers it was suggested that these snowmobiles should be designed and manufactured in the United States. This was without precedent. Churchill had sent Sir Henry Tizard across the Atlantic earlier in the war in order to strengthen Anglo-American ties and draw in the American scientific community, but until then a British military concept had never been outsourced like this to the United States.

Pyke suggested taking things further. Why not bring in other Allies and set up a 'United Nations snow-warfare board'? Norwegians, Canadians, Americans, British and Russians would all work together to create an international guerrilla force. His plan was welcomed in Combined Operations, save for the inclusion of the Soviets. This was not the first time that Pyke had pushed for greater collaboration with Russia, nor would it be the last.

Pyke knew somehow that in July 1941 the Soviet Union had ordered three Armstead snowmobiles, and felt 'they are sure to be at work on them'. The Russians had greater experience of snow warfare, he went on, and could easily supply logistical support for assaults on Romania and Norway, as well as summer training grounds in Novaya Zemlya, Franz Josef Land and Spitzbergen. 'We are now at the 59th minute of the hour!' he told Mountbatten on 2 April. 'I submit most urgently that:- 1. We go *at once* to the Chiefs of Staff [. . .] 2. We then go at once to Maisky [the Soviet ambassador], telling him the whole story frankly, putting every card on the table. [. . .] Once satisfied of our good faith – AND of our security – Maisky, I am advised, would probably wire Stalin or Vorosholiv at once; and you'd get an immediate reply.' The phrase 'I am advised' was striking. In case his opinion was unclear Pyke called in the same letter for 'a 101% honest and persistent effort be made to secure the cooperation of the Russians', adding that they were bound to like Combined Operations for it was 'a small, vital, growing (if delicate) organisation. The Russians have a slogan:- "We are always on the side of the embryo."'

Mountbatten and Wildman-Lushington felt otherwise, and had heard about the legendary reluctance of Soviet commanders to collaborate with their allies. They were more interested in gaining American support, and it is possible that they were aware of the imminent visit of two high-profile Americans to whom the idea could be proposed.

Harry Hopkins was a farm boy from Iowa who was later described by Churchill as 'the most faithful and perfect channel between the President and me'. Hopkins was President Roosevelt's right-hand man, confidant and adviser. He was a tenacious negotiator, a Washington insider who drank too much coffee and was often at his best at a negotiating table with an agenda and a deadline. He had been dispatched over the year before to see Churchill. Now he had been sent to London again, accompanied this time by General Marshall, US Army Chief of Staff, in order to discuss the Allied invasion of Europe.

On arrival the two men went to Downing Street where they made the case for opening a second front against Germany right away. 'I doubt if any single thing is as important as getting some sort of a front this summer against Germany,' Hopkins had told the President. The Americans outlined two plans: Round-Up and Sledgehammer. The first was an all-out assault on Europe by forty-eight infantry divisions to begin in a year's time, while Sledgehammer involved a smaller force mounting a heavy raid against a single French port. This was to happen by September 1942 and would, it was hoped, divert German troops from Russia.

The response at Downing Street was opaque, yet at dinner that evening, as Churchill got drunk and told stories about the American Civil War, Field Marshal Brooke explained to Hopkins and Marshall that it would be impossible to launch a major assault on Europe so soon due to a lack of landing craft and the necessary intelligence about their targets.

This was not the response that either had been hoping for, and the following morning Hopkins met Churchill alone to stress again the need for prompt action. 'Churchill took this very seriously and led me to believe that he didn't fully take in before the seriousness of our proposals.' But the Prime Minister remained non-committal.

While Hopkins was at Downing Street, Marshall had gone to see the British Chiefs of Staff and was won over by the youngest: Mountbatten. Churchill had appointed him as the fourth Chief of Staff only the month before, much to the annoyance of those he had leapfrogged and two of the three existing Chiefs. While Air Chief Marshal Sir Charles Portal welcomed his arrival, Sir Dudley Pound, a fellow naval man, resented it. 'Rather doubtful how that business will run!' wrote Field Marshal Brooke, later describing Mountbatten's appointment as 'a snag'.

General Marshall, on the other hand, harboured none of their prejudices and was drawn to Mountbatten's can-do spirit. At the end of this meeting he arranged to visit Combined Operations.

'This is amazing,' Marshall was reported to have said as he was shown around Richmond Terrace. Like most senior American officers he had never seen members of all three services working together like this.

'Well, after all, we all speak the same language,' replied Mountbatten. 'Come to think of it, so do you and we. Why don't you send me some American officers?' Less than a month later, nine American officers were installed in Richmond Terrace.

During this brief tour of Combined Operations, General Marshall was also introduced to Pyke. As prompted, the suspected Soviet agent told the US Army's Chief of Staff about his plan. Though bemused by his appearance, Marshall was intrigued by what he had described and left the building with a twelve-page memorandum explaining the project in more detail. This document was among Marshall's papers as he travelled to Chequers the next day.

With just four days to go, the Americans had so far failed to pin down the British. Both knew the importance of returning to the US with cast-iron commitments, and in the less formal setting of

Chequers they hoped to get them. Hopkins, for one, was inspired by his surroundings. 'It's only when you see that country in spring,' he recalled, 'that you begin to understand why the English have written the best goddam poetry in the world.' Nor was he feeling the cold at Chequers as much as he had done on his last visit, having remembered to pack some heavy underwear. While it was doing its job of keeping him warm it was, as he cabled Roosevelt that night, 'itching like the devil'.

There followed on that first morning in Chequers an event which would have made Hopkins forget all about his underwear: the British suggested a new offensive against the Germans.

In the presence of Hopkins and Marshall as well as Churchill, Nye and the ever-present Lindemann (now Lord Cherwell), Mountbatten proposed that the Americans take on Pyke's scheme. The US Army could develop the new snowmobiles and train up a specialist guerrilla force to use them. What was now known as the 'Plough' project – a code name Pyke had insisted upon to disguise the fact that these new snowmobiles would skim over the surface of the snow rather than plough through it – would be responsible for an operation in Norway before the end of 1942. Plough would be a snow-borne Sledgehammer, only less suicidal and far more damaging given its capacity to knock out HEP stations such as Vemork where heavy water was being produced.

Plough was not what Marshall had come for, and nor had the man Churchill liked to call 'Lord Root of the Matter', Harry Hopkins. But they needed to go home with something.

They accepted. As the minutes of this meeting show, 'it was agreed that the United States authorities would undertake to develop and manufacture the necessary armoured fighting snow vehicles (to be known by some suitable "cover" title, such as "snow ploughs"). It was further decided that Mr Pyke, the originator of the scheme, with one or two assistants should be flown to the United States as soon as possible after General Marshall's return and work under his general direction.' The Norwegians and Canadians would be asked to send an officer with experience of snow warfare to work alongside Pyke, and it was also agreed that Churchill would ask Stalin to send over a Russian officer.

This was staggering. Three months earlier Pyke had been bed-ridden, unemployed and in possession of a proposal that had been dismissed by Churchill's scientific adviser as 'pretentious nonsense'. Now, with that same adviser in the room, it had been taken up by some of the most powerful men on Earth.

At Churchill's suggestion, Pyke was to be sent to the US to see his idea through to completion. Enormous sums would be poured into its development. Men's lives would be risked on the basis of his logic. It was the kind of plot twist that would feel contrived in many a novel, and for Pyke it was evidence of the 'ferocity of purpose' at government level that he had always craved – the decisive, sudden and emphatic backing for a new scheme which he had once believed to be impossible outside a country like the Soviet Union.

Seeing that Pyke was to go on a 'most secret' overseas mission Mountbatten had his salary transferred to SOE, sometimes known as Churchill's 'Secret Army', and from late April he was officially employed by this rival organisation and lent to General Marshall's staff through Mountbatten. A new passport was made for him and towards the end of April this most unusual SOE operative was ready to leave.

Unlike others employed by this organisation, he would not be parachuted into enemy territory to help bring supplies and exper-tise to the local resistance. Instead he was destined for Washington DC, where there was perhaps less desire to be given advice by the British.

'I have a feeling that perhaps the USA Army may not be altogether our cup of tea,' Pyke confided to Mountbatten before his departure. 'Military people, if I may say so, don't really *plan* at all. What they call planning is trying to adapt what they were taught in youth, with the minimum of alteration, to what they can see. That's why they see so little.'

This was the military approach that Pyke had battled against during the last two months in Richmond Terrace. He had suggested improvements to nearly every aspect of Combined Operations, from its administrative structure and the way it might impede fresh ideas through to the choice of newspapers in the officers' club. His thoughts were not always welcomed, but on many colleagues he had made a positive impression. In a six-side parting note to Mountbatten, accompanied by Shaw's (almost) complete works for the Combined Operations HQ Library – 'I hope that the interest in them will be such that by the time I return they will all have been stolen' – Pyke described the changes he had observed. While the George Medal was awarded to civilians for gallantry, he suggested a counterpart for 'Distinguished Courage at the Desk'. The first medals, he told Mountbatten, should go to three majors in Combined Operations, including a Major Wyatt, about whom he wrote, 'I tremble for his future. Only by sending him back to his regiment will he be saved from becoming a Bloomsbury intellectual.'

Pyke also reminded Mountbatten of the moment during a critical meeting when he had thanked Pyke on behalf of the three services 'for introducing a new idea'. This had left him speechless. 'For not far off half a century I have been on this unhappy planet. During, probably, all of that time I have been asking, "Why?" – "What for?" "So what?" and "Why do you do like that, why do you not do like this?" I have put forward a certain number of new ideas. Your remark at this meeting was the first occasion in my life when I have been thanked for introducing a new idea. Hitherto my experience has been to be heartily kicked in the pants for doing so. I was completely taken aback at the time, so that I could not even say "Thank you"; you must allow me to do so now.'

This passage reveals something of the powerful bond that had formed between the two men. Mountbatten not only listened to Pyke's ideas but thanked him for putting them forward and did his utmost to have them realised. By offering him a job at Combined Operations he had brought Pyke, for the first time in his life, into the establishment, a feeling which resonated with a man who sometimes craved acceptance. Indeed, the tie between them was so close that Pyke had even begun to refer to Plough as a joint creation.

'Whatever may happen to our scheme now, something, I feel, has already been achieved, and that is that the whole Department is now conscious of the fact that new ideas do exist outside, amongst the general public, and that the Department has the power to appreciate them and to drive them through all resistance to the highest authorities.' It was another iteration of Pyke's most radical idea: there is no such thing as a genius for new ideas, and that with care and hard work anyone could do what he did. With that, Geoffrey Pyke set off for the United States, unaware that MI5 had just contacted Mountbatten about his new Director of Programmes.

PYKE HUNT, PART 4

On 19 March – the day that Combined Operations agreed to go ahead with the Plough scheme – Special Branch filed a new report casting Pyke in a suspicious light once again. They had learnt of a covert organisation called the Inter-States Committee of Communist Groups in Great Britain (ISC), later described as a 'hush-hush body' that was 'shrouded in secrecy'. Chaired by Harry Pollitt, the restored head of the CPGB, it was a 'channel through which the different refugee communist groups have contact with Moscow' and, as one man close to it observed, it 'came near to being a little Communist International in itself'. For Special Branch, the existence of this body was evidence of just what 'a dangerous experiment' it had been during 1939 to allow 'so many leading Czech, German and Austrian Communists – many of them being the most experienced and trusted Communists of Central Europe, while others were for years the frontier workers of the Comintern's illegal groups – to find a refuge in England'. These communists were now laying the foundations for a post-war Europe that was in thrall to Moscow. They saw themselves as 'the rulers of tomorrow', and were 'closely in touch with London Soviet circles, who saw their importance at a time when others thought that they counted for little'.

One of the ISC's strategies was to set up émigré organisations called 'Free Movements' in the style of the Free French movement. These were designed to look and sound like governments-in-waiting, in the hope that the Allies would instal them after the defeat of the Axis powers. In reality they were under hidden Communist control.

In late 1941 the German communists in Britain were instructed to start a Free German Movement. The only problem was that their arch-rivals, the German socialists, had got there first and were now on the verge of setting up their very own 'Free German Committee'. The communists decided to launch a smear campaign.

'THE "FREE GERMAN" TRICK' was the headline splashed over the front page of the left-wing *Sunday Dispatch* on 8 February 1942, followed by a virulent denunciation of this socialist-backed Free German Committee. 'The men concerned must be watched,' the article fumed, 'and their activities curbed.'

Special Branch was curious to know who had placed the article, as this would obviously lead them to the ISC. They soon had a name. One of their informants assured them that the individual behind this *Sunday Dispatch* article was also 'said to be in charge of Communist "action propaganda"'. His name was Geoffrey Pyke.

Pyke in the 1940s

Could this be true? Was Pyke both 'Professor P.' and the man in charge of CPGB action propaganda?

During the first two years of the war, before joining Combined Operations, Pyke had certainly been an active journalist. By looking at what he wrote and when, and those times when he suggested an article or pushed for a particular book to be published, it may be possible to see if he was working as a communist propagandist.

Early on in the war Pyke wrote a string of articles on one subject: the need to dig deep air-raid shelters in the seams of chalk outside the capital. Tunnelling through chalk was relatively easy and in very little time vast underground dormitories could be made to house the population of London each night. As early as May 1939 Pyke had called for a Royal Commission to examine the question. Public inquiries like this usually happened in response to an outcry – but 'it is not *essential* to have the disaster first'.

Between December 1940 and late April 1941 Pyke followed up with a flurry of further articles about the need for deep chalk shelters – 'Perfect safety for a million in six months', 'Cheaper than Andersons', 'Experts Back "Safety in Chalk" proposals' and 'Build Chalk Shelters Now, Mr Morrison' – all of which appeared in the left-wing weekly *Reynolds News*. He gave an impassioned speech on the subject at a public meeting of Democratic Movement and he persuaded an Oxford statistician, E. J. Buckatzsch, to write a piece in an academic journal in support of them. He also tried to get an article in *The Times* but was turned down on the grounds that 'it played straight into the hands of the Communists'.

The chalk-shelter campaign had by then been taken up with great enthusiasm by the CPGB. It had 'everything to it from our point of view', explained Douglas Hyde, then News Editor of the Moscow-backed *Daily Worker*. 'It had the appearance of being a crusade for greater safety for the common people, whilst at the same time it spread alarm about the provisions already made by the authorities.

Moreover, it gave us an opportunity to use many of our crypto-communists on public activity.'

These undercover communists included Dr Allan Nunn May, later imprisoned as a Soviet agent for betraying atomic secrets, as well as J. B. S. Haldane and Ivor Montagu, both friends of Pyke who were later revealed to have been Soviet agents, belonging to the 'X-Group', a GRU espionage cell.

And then there was Pyke.

As well as campaigning for deep chalk shelters, we know that before the war he also went to great lengths to encourage the publisher Victor Gollancz to put out the anti-appeasement pamphlet *THEY Lied*, and the following summer lobbied him to lower the proposed price of *Guilty Men*, a book-length denunciation of British appeasement written pseudonymously by Michael Foot, Frank Owen and Peter Howard. He had even persuaded the editor of *Tribune* to pressure Gollancz into doing this, and at one point had lined up Allen Lane at Penguin to take on the book in case Gollancz pulled out. In the end it was published through the Left Book Club at the price Pyke had pushed for and did more than any other publication to shape the British understanding of 1930s appeasement.

We also know that Pyke tried to persuade Allen Lane to publish a book by Professor Alfred Meusel, alleged by SIS to have once been Chief of the German Communist Party and a key member of the Communist 'anti-war' campaign. As well as the chalk-shelter pieces, Pyke wrote numerous articles which more or less echoed the Party line, whether on the subject of interned refugees or appeasement.

Even more suggestive were his frequent meetings with Sydney Elliott, Editor of *Reynolds News*, and especially those moments when their relationship no longer resembled that of a typical freelance journalist and his editor. On the day of the Molotov-Ribbentrop Pact, for example, while his conversationalists observed the giddy reaction in Germany, Pyke noted in his diary that this was 'a most brilliant move which will, I think, in the long run result in the fall of Chamberlain', adding 'I must make a good effort to persuade Sydney Elliott to this view before he writes his leading article for *Reynolds* on Sunday. [. . .] Sydney is smart but influenced by the last person he has talked to and I suspect that the Labour Party people have been talking to him.' Pyke appears to have been more interested in which line Elliott took than whether he himself would be commissioned to write an article.

There is also the mystery of what was going on in Pyke's flat. Around the same time that MI5 was told about the unusual noises sounding like Morse code we know that he had apparently 'transformed the whole of his top floor into a monitoring station for collecting radio messages from Resistance Movements all over Europe. He had gathered a substantial staff of refugees who could cope with the range of languages and dialects involved, and had organised all the necessary receiving equipment to enable him to edit a daily bulletin of news items from various corners of the Continent.'

What was more, he appeared to have a second office, or propaganda bureau, in Piccadilly. The Special Branch report alleging that Pyke ran Communist 'action propaganda' also stated that he and Rünkel, 'a Communist agent with an unsavoury reputation among refugees', operated out of a Piccadilly flat 'filled with newspapers and files of every description', including some which they thought might have been used for the hatchet job which appeared in the *Sunday Dispatch*.

The Piccadilly flat in question was not Cyril Ray's, but one several hundred yards away on St James's Square. It belonged to Leo Myers, a wealthy Old Etonian who had recently converted to communism. Just as Myers probably gave money to the Party he also offered Pyke money and a space in which to work. When Pyke was in the flat Myers 'paid all his expenses – rent, lighting, telephone, etc.', and according to MI5 'also paid Pyke's personal bills, such as the milk bill'.

For all this, having a wealthy Marxist pay for his milk, writing articles in support of deep chalk shelters or gathering news from around Europe is not proof that Pyke was a crypto-communist. In no way does his journalistic record reveal him to have been running 'action propaganda' for the CPGB. Articles calling for chalk shelters appeared in more right-wing papers such as the *Daily Mail* or *Evening Standard*. What was more, Pyke's first offering on deep chalk shelters was published well before the communist campaign began – indeed, his original article was probably where their idea came from.

Elsewhere he wrote or suggested articles about the need to remove the 'railings from not just some London squares but all of them and in perpetuity'; and called for a more equitable system to determine which children should be evacuated to the United States. In other words, his views were socialist and Fabian as much as they were communist. They spoke to a broader sensibility which came alive in the wake of Dunkirk but is rarely stressed in popular accounts of that period.

In the early summer of 1940, with a Nazi invasion seemingly imminent, British society began to bank to the left. There were many of those outside the Communist Party who called for radical social change. Captain Tom Wintringham, expelled from the Party two years earlier, argued for the creation of a 'People's Army' under a government which was unafraid of revolution. George Orwell, like Pyke a friend of Wintringham and Leo Myers (who had also offered him money and a space in which to work), saw the summer of 1940 as 'a moment at which the willingness for sacrifice and drastic changes extended not only to the working class but to nearly the whole of the middle class, whose patriotism, when it comes to the pinch, is stronger than their sense of self-interest'. For men like Orwell, Wintringham and Pyke, establishing socialism was not an alternative to winning the war but a prerequisite. 'Only revolution can save England, that has been obvious for years, but now the revolution has started, and it may proceed quite quickly if only we can keep Hitler out,' wrote Orwell, adding famously: 'I dare say the London gutters will have to run with blood. All right, let them, if it is necessary. But when the red militias are billeted in the Ritz I shall still feel that the England I was taught to love so long ago and for such different reasons is somehow persisting.' As Pyke's friend Sir Stafford Cripps wrote to Sir Walter Monckton in September 1940, Russia and Germany seemed to represent 'an attempt to get away from an effete civilisation which the countries we represent are desperately trying to cling on to and to revivify. It is indeed a revolutionary war and we are on the side of the past – for the moment [. . .] it will be more difficult then to make any change without a revolution [. . .] if only we would act in time to create a new order. But why preach to the converted?'

These views were not communist *per se*, but cut from the same cloth. They were inspired both by a socialist ideal and by the fear that the war might lead, ironically enough, to a more right-wing or even fascist government in Britain. While none of Pyke's articles established him as a communist propaganda chief it seems that during the early stages of the war he, like so many others, experienced a shift to the left which resulted in him pushing for more radical social reform.

Yet for MI5's Milicent Bagot, the idea that he might be responsible for communist 'action propaganda' was enough. It tallied with her earlier suspicion that he was Professor P. and she decided to act.

On 15 March 1942, just as Pyke was joined at Combined Operations by Bernal and Zuckerman, Bagot wrote to Harry Hunter, head of MI5's B.6, asking him to have Pyke placed under surveillance. Only a handful of MI5 suspects could be shadowed like this at any time. As Bagot knew, it was an expensive procedure. But the evidence against Pyke had become much too strong to ignore.

★

Just three days later, on an overcast Wednesday in London, two MI5 'watchers' took up position outside No. 19 St James's Square. They had no photograph with which to identify their subject, just a written sketch:

'Height: 6'1". Hair: black. Eyes: brown. No distinguishing marks. Has been described as Jewish in appearance and "a rather grubby-looking little man with a black beard."'

Given Pyke's height, the phrase 'little man' is striking. Along with 'Jewish in appearance' it was there to tell the two watchers that their man would stand out in this elegant pocket of London. Today it reads as something else: a reminder of MI5's Achilles heel. For many of the staff at the Security Service the calculus of suspicion was calibrated by class. Secrecy and trust could be assumed within the upper reaches of society, so that anyone who spoke right, acted right and had gone to the right schools was beyond suspicion – just one of the reasons why the Cambridge Spies got away with so much. The Security Service was hamstrung by this mawkish deference to the upper echelons. Jewishness, however, seemed to scramble their calculations of class. Though Pyke came from a distinguished family, had gone to Wellington and Cambridge and sounded 'right', being both Jewish and 'Jewish in appearance' placed him outside MI5's traditional understanding of social background. Worse than that, it seemed to suggest for some of them that he should be watched more carefully.

At a quarter past nine, a man matching Pyke's description stepped out of the house – a 'tall, thin-bearded man, the kind of hatless, rapidly moving vagrant, who, wherever he goes and whatever the season, besides a bundle of papers beneath his arm, is always carrying a heavy knapsack'. He proceeded north towards Piccadilly. Invisibly, separately, the two watchers began their pursuit.

His first stop was Piccadilly Circus Tube Station where he bought two newspapers – that day's and the previous day's copy of *The Times*

– all of which was carefully noted down and the transaction scruti-
nised for clandestine exchanges. Nothing. Pyke continued east, past
the spot where Eros had stood before the war and on to the iconic
Lyons Corner House at the start of Coventry Street. It was large,
noisy and welcoming, a labyrinth of cafés and restaurants all exuding
a cosmopolitan classlessness. The subject made his way to the Old
Vienna Café on the mezzanine floor and ordered breakfast from a
'nippy' waitress. Perhaps he was about to be met by a contact? Or
was the waitress communicating in some kind of code? He met
nobody. His interactions were unremarkable. After a solitary breakfast he returned to St James's Square.

There followed forays to nearby bookshops, lunch alone at the
Chantecler Restaurant on Frith Street, then popular among scientists
and engineers, a trip to Boots the chemist and tea at a nearby Chicken
Inn, one of his favourite haunts. At about six the two watchers called
it a day, as they did each evening. Pyke's night-time activities would
remain a mystery.

On Thursday, after his customary breakfast at the Old Vienna,
Pyke worked from home until lunchtime when he shot out of the
house and got into a taxi. The watchers did likewise. Curiously,
Pyke's cab pulled up on Frith Street, just ten minutes' walk from his
home. He must have been late for lunch – but with whom?

MI5's men followed him into Mars Restaurant and took a table
nearby, confident that Pyke would not have recognised them. Each
of these MI5 watchers had been chosen for his chameleonic ability
to disappear into most crowds and, as their boss later wrote, for
'looking as unlike a policeman as possible'. One of the two men made
a note of Pyke's companion, a shortish man in his fifties with blond
hair and a moustache. He wore a brigadier's uniform and medals
suggesting he had fought in the last war. But the watchers were too
far away to overhear their conversation.

After the meal they followed them outside, at which point the brigadier took a cab towards Whitehall and Pyke disappeared. Not for the last time, the watchers had lost their target.

The next day they picked him up again as he took his breakfast at the Old Vienna Café and trailed him to Richmond Terrace where they spotted the same brigadier from the lunch in Soho. On another occasion they trailed their man to the Ministry of Economic Warfare, where he was seen with an RAF officer before carrying on to the Ministry of Information where he spent more than an hour. After this he rushed out into the street and hopped into a taxi before again being 'lost to observation'.

Bagot's job when picking over the minutiae of these reports was to pinpoint the salient detail, the unremarkable fragment which might unlock a more suspicious pattern of behaviour. She knew by now that Pyke had contacts in what she presumed to be the Cabinet Office, the Ministry of Economic Warfare and the Ministry of Information. Discreet enquiries could be made to determine the identities of the brigadier and the RAF officer. For now the Ministry of Information employee would remain unknown. Naturally she was frustrated by the lack of observable links between Pyke and any foreign communists, and she might have begun to doubt her instincts. Perhaps this man was merely a well-intentioned left-winger 'along *New Statesman* lines', as one MI5 report suggested, who possessed a strange ability to attract suspicion wherever he went. It was too early to say. Bagot decided to keep the observation going.

The following Wednesday, having lost Pyke twice the day before, the two watchers had their first triumph. They saw him have lunch with a woman they knew to be a contact of Rolf Rünkel, and who was now working as a secretary to David Astor. The next day they produced an even more valuable nugget of intelligence.

They had followed their subject to King's Cross where he had lunch with a new contact. This man was trailed to a house near Golders Green. They described him as: 'Age 38, 5'10/11", good build, dark hair, sallow complexion, large hooked nose, clean shaven. Jewish appearance. Dress grey suit and overcoat, black soft felt hat. Carries a portfolio. Speaks with a pronounced foreign accent.' Bagot identified him immediately.

The man Pyke had met for lunch was Jürgen Kuczynski, leader of the illegal German Communist Party in exile and one of the most important Soviet agents in Britain at that time. During the war he passed on information to the NKVD, the GRU and the Soviet Embassy and, notoriously, helped to smuggle British atomic secrets to Moscow. Once the physicist Klaus Fuchs had decided to spy for the Soviet Union, he went first to Kuczynski, and it was Kuczynski who later brought in his sister, Sonya, a GRU officer, to run this prize asset. When working for the OSS, the precursor of the CIA, Kuczynski again supplied valuable intelligence to his sister who later became an honorary Colonel in the Red Army and remains the most decorated female agent in Russian history. Indeed, the work carried out by the two Kuczynski siblings in Britain changed the shape of the Cold War.

We will probably never know what Jürgen Kuczynski and Geoffrey Pyke discussed over lunch, only that Pyke would have looked forward to the conversation. After their initial meeting he described Kuczynski as 'intellectually of the first order' and 'resembling Frank Ramsey in his method of approach'. We also know when that first meeting took place: when Pyke flew out to Paris in July 1939 he had gone to meet Jürgen Kuczynski.

In the months that followed they saw each other frequently in London. 'I found our conversation of to-day most interesting and stimulating,' wrote Pyke to Kuczynski in late 1939. 'I hope I shall see you again. I may ring you up in the next few days.' They also had at least one mutual friend in Leo Myers, who sent money to Kuczynski as well as Pyke, and in 1941 Kuczynski's wife, Marguerite, had begun to work for Pyke as a researcher.

Though they were connected in many ways, that lunch in King's Cross was the first that Bagot knew of the relationship between Pyke and Kuczynski. While she had numerous reports from SIS, Special Branch and MI5 describing Kuczynski as 'a rabid Communist' known to be doing 'espionage work among refugees', and who was 'a direct agent of Moscow', she was also aware of just how hard it was to pin this man down.

Early on in the war MI5 had managed to get Kuczynski interned on the basis that he was spreading communist propaganda geared towards impeding the war effort – one anti-fascist German émigré described his internment as 'a very good stroke of work'. Around the same time SIS reported that Kuczynski 'has brought out of Germany the whole funds of the German Communist Party. It is a very important sum.' Allegedly £200,000, roughly £6 million today, this money had apparently been transferred to a Dutch bank account accessed by Kuczynski, his father and Professor Meusel – whose manuscript Pyke had offered to Allen Lane – and between them they were rumoured to have invested it in American securities. SIS concluded that the profits were used to fund communist propaganda in Britain such as the anti-war publication *Inside Nazi Germany*, edited by Heinz Kamnitzer. But almost as soon as Kuczynski's internment had begun letters poured in to the Home Office, pushing for his release. They came from members of the Communist Party, fellow-travellers, and MPs such as Geoffrey Mander, Richard Acland, Vyvyan Adams and G. R. Strauss. Even the 'Red' Dean of Canterbury weighed in, as well as the Queen's cousin Lilian Bowes-Lyon. Pyke was another of those who petitioned for Kuczynski's release. The Home Office succumbed to this pressure and he was freed – much to the annoyance of Bagot.

In the months that followed MI5 continued to receive reports describing him as an 'extreme Communist and fanatically pro-Stalin', 'one of Moscow's most brilliant and dangerous propagandists' and a man who was 'in illegal contact with the Soviet Secret Service'. But they had no proof.

Rather than focus on Kuczynski, Bagot tried to identify the government contacts with whom Pyke had met during the days leading up to his lunch in King's Cross. Guy Liddell tracked down the RAF officer. Colonel Lennox chased up the blond-haired, moustachioed brigadier – who turned out to be Mountbatten's Chief of Staff, Wildman-Lushington; yet for now the contact at the Ministry of Information could not be identified.

Bagot also delved deeper into Pyke's history. She read about his father, the brilliant QC who had run for Parliament, and about his escape from Ruhleben which had led to suspicions in MI5 that he was a German agent. Nothing she found ruled out the possibility of Pyke being 'Professor P.', not least his application for a passport to travel to Europe in 1927. But there was no definitive detail, and in a note to Special Branch she betrayed a flash of doubt. Bagot referred to the source which had linked Pyke to the Comintern bureau in Berlin as one which in the past 'has not always proved reliable'.

Nonetheless, the consensus in MI5 was that Pyke should have no further involvement with Combined Operations, where, they presumed, he was merely being consulted from time to time. It was hard to imagine that he could have been offered a job.

Colonel Lennox spoke to Mountbatten over the phone and told him that Pyke was 'possibly a knave and definitely a fool' and should be dropped. His timing was unfortunate. Several days earlier Mountbatten had introduced Churchill to Pyke's proposal and already plans were afoot to have it developed in the US with Pyke overseeing its progress.

Lennox knew nothing of this, and nor did he read his audience at all well. He told Mountbatten that Pyke should go, largely on the grounds of his left-wing political outlook, but had failed to grasp the extent to which these views were shared by Mountbatten himself.

At the time one of the closest friends and advisers to the CCO was the committed Marxist Peter Murphy; Mountbatten's wife was receptive to the Left and had become increasingly pro-Soviet; it has even been suggested that Mountbatten was a keen student of the *Week*, edited by Comintern agent Claud Cockburn, and in 1936 had read excerpts to the King, Edward VIII, stressing the perils of Nazism. A call from MI5 to say that one of his most intelligent, creative and industrious employees had communist sympathies was never going to scare him off. If anything, it might have endeared him to Mountbatten, who was ever the contrarian.

The CCO ignored MI5's suggestion that Pyke should be dropped. He was under no legal obligation to act on this advice; and, anyway, he was under the impression that a separate branch of MI5 had given Pyke security clearance. Instead, he did everything to ensure that his trip to the US got off to a good start. The scheme which had been proposed by this civilian – their scheme – could change the shape of the war and Mountbatten was not prepared to let the unsubstantiated concerns of the Security Service get in the way.

HOW TO SUCCEED IN AMERICA

From the signs in restaurants and cafés inviting you to drink as much coffee as you liked, through to the unbombed majesty of the city's ramrod-straight avenues, Washington DC had an unreal and at times magical quality for anyone who had spent the early years of the war in London. There was a weightlessness to life without air raids, rationing or the threat of Nazi invasion. The city looked healthier and more affluent than the British capital. Its people were better dressed and rosier in the cheek, their way of speaking was more confident and direct, and so was the mood, as Geoffrey Pyke discovered on arrival towards the end of April 1942.

General Marshall, Harry Hopkins, Churchill and Mountbatten had agreed that if Pyke was to be taken seriously by the US Army he would have to be accompanied by several British Army officers. One of the men chosen was Major E. A. M. Wedderburn of the Royal Scots – Sandy to his friends – a barrister in peacetime who suffered from a weak heart, asthma, bronchitis and gastric ulcers. In spite of all this, remarkably, he was a formidable mountaineer and one of the most respected instructors at the Winter Warfare School in

Lochailort, Scotland. Though Pyke found Wedderburn initially distant, he soon warmed to this perspicacious Scot, praising his 'intelligence' and 'absolute integrity'.

The third member of the party was altogether different. Just days before they left for the US, Averell Harriman, Roosevelt's Special Envoy to Europe, had shared with Mountbatten his fear that a temporary officer like Wedderburn would not pack enough of a military punch on the other side of the Atlantic. Though a businessman in peacetime, Harriman understood the shibboleths of the American military all too well. This third man should be 'preferably from the Royal Tank Corps and of a rank not less than Brigadier'.

By coincidence, just two weeks earlier Brigadier Nigel Duncan had joined Combined Operations from the Royal Tank Corps. He was a slender, upright individual who spoke in short, stammered bursts. For Pyke he was both 'War Office *par excellence*' and '"Staff College" *par excellence*. He is not even aware of this quality. To change him, he would have to be born again, and born different.'

Duncan seemed to be a perfect fit and was hastily attached to the British mission just days before its departure for the US. Efforts were made to bring the Sandhurst-schooled brigadier up to speed. He was given papers to read and told by General Nye – no less than Vice Chief of the Imperial General Staff – that the Plough project 'may shorten the war by years'. But there was only so much he could take in.

In Washington DC the three Britons spent their first night in the luxurious Wardiman Park Hotel, one of the largest hotels in the world, before moving the next day. Perhaps one of them had pushed for a more central location, as for the rest of their stay they operated out of the air-conditioned Sheraton Lee Hotel, on 17th and L, two minutes from the White House. It was also one block from the Soviet Embassy.

Pyke was thrilled by the sights and sounds of the American capital, even if he found the latter somewhat muted. Since crossing the

Atlantic in 'the bomb rack of a bomber' he had become 'slightly deaf'. It was as if he was hearing everything through a fine layer of cotton. In conversation he had always prided himself on his ability to read his audience and adjust his message accordingly, yet now that the need to do so was greater than ever he felt himself to be at a small disadvantage.

Perhaps this did not matter. He was in the American capital on a secret government mission which had backing at the highest level. He had never felt so relevant. Among his papers were letters of introduction to Harry Hopkins, also known as the 'Assistant President', and to William Stephenson, the British spymaster and head of British Security Coordination (BSC), who was to devise 'adequate cover' for Plough. Another letter was to Captain John Knox, Combined Operations Liaison Officer in the US, to whom Mountbatten stressed 'the great importance which the Prime Minister and Mr Averell Harriman attach to this scheme which, indeed, has grown in importance in their minds since the departure of General Marshall and Mr Harry Hopkins'. In 1929, during Pyke's bankruptcy hearings, one of the examining barristers had referred witheringly to the Malting House School as the bankrupt's 'great scheme'. Now Mountbatten described Plough using the same phrase. 'If Mr Pyke's great scheme comes off,' he continued, '"never in the history of human conflict will so few immobilise so many" (to paraphrase the Prime Minister).' Such is the nature of 'great schemes'.

Pyke's task was simple. He would have to win over the American military to this new idea. For the first time it seemed as though this restless, industrious innovator had been handed the chance to shape history.

Three days after their arrival the three members of the British mission made the short journey through the mounting heat of the day to the War Department. They were led past armed sentries to a room containing fifteen US staff generals and colonels, including the Deputy Chief of Staff, Lieutenant-General Joseph MacNarney who was there to preside over the meeting, as well as General Eisenhower, Assistant Chief of Staff and head of Operations Division, who had brought along 'all the officers of my staff immediately concerned'. There were also officials from the Office of Scientific Research and Development (OSRD), a powerful new government agency coordinating war-related scientific research and industrial engineering. It was a mighty display of military and scientific capital and, as requested, Pyke got up to introduce Plough.

Nobody in the audience was used to being addressed by someone looking like this. The battered glasses, scraggly facial hair, lack of uniform, the more expressive and at times musical delivery – all this set Pyke apart. But they had been warned. General Marshall had circulated a note about the project, describing the man behind it as 'a very odd-looking individual' who 'talks well and may have an important contribution to make'.

'No one, except Hitler, has ever spoken to so many generals for so long,' Wedderburn later wrote of Pyke's performance. Others referred to him 'lecturing' the room and resisting attempts by others to interrupt. He had a lot to get through, certainly, and as well as introducing the generals to the scheme he tried, no doubt, to describe the broader philosophy behind it. The gadfly Pyke was forever happy to make a fool of himself and elicit laughter, confusion or anger if – and only if – it challenged the preconceptions of his audience. Yet by his own admission, on that day he 'spoke badly' and did not endear himself to everyone in that room.

His partial deafness might have played a part; he might have been nervous. But what really threw him was the growing sense as he spoke that the room was not with him. When he described the importance of international collaboration and wide-ranging scientific research, he looked out onto a sea of blank faces. It seemed that the

US Army was enthusiastic about Plough but wanted the project for itself. He worried that the generals had failed to grasp the strategic concept behind it, not because it was too complex but, rather, 'because the idea is too simple'.

In spite of his shaky performance, by the end of that session, wrote Eisenhower, 'a working committee was organised, which will start on the task of developing snow-sleds without delay'. Days later Project Plough was divided in two. The elite Plough force would be trained up by the War Department's Operations Division under General Eisenhower, while Brigadier-General Raymond W. Moses, Assistant Chief of Staff and head of the Army's Supply Branch, would oversee the development of the snowmobile by OSRD.

'Things had to happen fast, and they did,' began Dr Vannevar Bush, head of OSRD. '[Palmer] Putnam carried the ball throughout, and he certainly made it move.' Under Putnam were the likes of Hartley Rowe and Sherman Warner, experienced industrial engineers who would later play key roles in the the atomic-bomb research programme, the Manhattan Project, at Los Alamos. The Plough snowmobile was in safe hands and, as Pyke wrote to Mountbatten, 'despite hirsute appearance of your Director of Programmes' the project had been taken up with genuine enthusiasm. General Moses confirmed on 3 May that the Plough force would be operational by the end of the year, replete with snowmobiles each capable of carrying two men, food for thirty days, fuel for 250 miles, 600 rounds of ammunition, two rifles, one automatic weapon and 100 pounds of explosives.

It was a thrilling claim, and of a piece with the contagious confidence of the US Army which Pyke had begun to relish. 'Because of the American attitude to the unknown and to the impossible, even in Army circles, I find myself more at home here than at home,' he told Mountbatten in the first of a long series of letters back to London. Provided the US Army's 'hostility to basic research' could be overcome, 'we may be ready in time with [a] practicable venture'.

The Plough project was swimming in optimism, and it seemed as though Pyke had more or less succeeded in winning over the American military. Indeed, after that first week in Washington DC it was hard to see how anything could really go wrong.

Several days after these confident assessments of the project, Sandy Wedderburn arrived at Soda Springs Ski Resort, in northern California, where he expected to find Pyke. It was the first day of a week-long set of tests on different snowmobiles to determine which one should be adapted for the new Plough vehicle. By the end of the fourth day most of the project's key players had arrived in Soda Springs. But there was still no sign of Pyke.

Wedderburn was told that Pyke was finding the heat in the capital 'trying' and had decided to stay where he was rather than endure higher temperatures on the West Coast. It was an unusual explanation. In fact, it barely made sense: a Californian ski resort was much less humid than Washington DC. But Pyke was known for idiosyncratic decisions like this.

Those who did make it to California were given demonstrations of the various snowmobiles. First the Eliasson motorised toboggan – dismissed by Wedderburn as 'little more than a winter sports toy' – followed by track-laying vehicles, a single-screw snowmobile and the Burgess, similar to the Armstead that Pyke originally favoured in that it was propelled by twin Archimedian screws. Yet this particular Burgess had not been used all winter and the sprockets of the chain drive had warped, meaning it would need to be repaired.

Rather than wait to have this done, the assembled party discussed the vehicles they had seen and agreed that the new Plough snow-mobile should be track-laying and amphibious, similar to the Tucker 'Sno Cat'. Pyke's idea of using an Archimedian screw was, they felt, a distraction. Too little was known about it.

Once this discussion had ended Colonel Hoag formally instructed

OSRD to 'design, develop, build and test one or more pilot models of a track-laying, airborne, amphibious snow vehicle, to carry a payload of 1200 lbs up a 25-degree slope in deep snow, and have a maximum speed on level packed snow of 35 mph'. The DNA of the new Plough snowmobile had been decided. Two days later Pyke found out.

'I wish to submit my resignation from this mission and work in connection with my project,' he cabled Mountbatten (note that it was no longer 'our' project). 'I ask you to have me returned to London by air within some reasonable time as agreed.'

The idea that he had been unable to cope with the Californian heat was an invention. Pyke had been kept away from those tests by design.

What infuriated him about this was that he knew more about the evolution of snowmobiles over the last twenty years than perhaps anyone else in North America, possibly the world. He had studied every snowmobile patent ever filed and during his months of intensive research had compiled a list of small-scale experiments to help determine which of the existing vehicles should be adapted. Yet rather than have the tests observed by an expert like Pyke they were overseen by the former Chief Engineer at the United Fruit Company, a naval architect, and two senior military men who between them had no experience of snow warfare and knew almost nothing about snowmobiles. It was like organising a Combined Operations conference on polo without inviting Mountbatten. Brigadier Duncan saw things differently.

Shortly before setting off for the West Coast he had sent Pyke an apparently artless note promising to return his copy of Shaw's *Major Barbara*, which he had now read three times, adding that he would be sightseeing the next day and, finally, 'I am off this week.' He did not explain where to.

With Machiavellian efficiency this upright, unassuming soldier had taken control of the British Mission. As Duncan saw it, he was the senior officer on a military project which, by some oversight, still had a civilian attached – a troublesome one at that. Keeping Pyke away from Soda Springs was, for him, no more than an expression of rank.

'I am sure Duncan sincerely believes he was sent out here to carry out my ideas at *his* discretion, according to *his* method,' Pyke complained to Mountbatten, 'and that, as we don't agree, *he* had the authority to arrange things without reference to me, including the authority to think me unable to endure the heat of the snow fields. Brigadier Duncan would, I am sure, lead his tanks into battle with bravery and efficiency. He is, I have no doubt, a good officer in peacetime. But in my opinion he does not possess the qualities requisite for helping to bring my ideas into being.' The problem, he went on, was 'that Duncan not only does not believe in my policy; he does not begin to understand it, and does not really understand that there are two policies'. Duncan was 'in fact so contra-suggestible that he would not understand anything I were to say. When I demur to his statements that 2 and 2 are 5, he thinks me no gentleman because I won't agree they are 4½.' This was not to say that Duncan was at all slow: his attitude was 'due to rigidity of intellect, not lack of it'. He possessed 'both the extreme cunning and the extreme simplicity of a child', both of which he had employed to force Pyke's resignation.

But Pyke had no intention of actually resigning. You do not need to look hard between the lines of his resignation letter, all 3,000 words of it, to see that this was a bluff. He wanted Mountbatten to choose between him and Duncan, yet the CCO had other ideas.

'Once a civilian has joined a fighting organisation and involved his country in a major project in war he loses the ethical right of withdrawing,' came the reply, testier than usual. Bernal was more direct.

'Don't be a bloody fool,' he wrote. 'Your resignation disastrous not only to scheme but to whole of scientific collaboration in war effort. [. . .] I can help on scientific side if you let me know what problems are.'

Yet neither Mountbatten nor Bernal was responding to Pyke's 3,000 word exposition of the situation. Instead they had been sent a crude précis written by Captain Knox, through whom most of Pyke's messages went. As he must have known, no cypher clerk would be prepared to encrypt a 3,000 word text. Instead Knox had cabled over to London what he felt was the salient point: 'Pyke's grievance is based entirely upon differences with Duncan.'

Mountbatten thought it ridiculous that Pyke should 'allow personal grievances to interfere with the major project' and asked Knox to 'smooth out differences between Duncan and Pyke and get team spirit into them. Surely Pyke realises that only real hope of getting his own scheme through is by using British Brigadier. Advise Duncan to be above board with Pyke. I wish them to be friends and co-operate closely.'

The following night Knox took Pyke out to dinner and 'during three and a half hours discussion, I appealed to Pyke from every point of view, but failed to alter his decision, which he states is taken on fundamental differences and not on personal grounds'. Pyke then wrote to Mountbatten describing himself as 'anxious and distressed lest you continue to think I am or would let either you down or what became of our joint concept'. 'If irritation and impatience were adequate causes for chucking this project, it would never have survived its first 20 months,' he added. 'Put briefly, my reason for resignation is this: I am a drag on Duncan's policy; he is a drag on mine. [. . .] I am not chucking the job, it has chucked me. There is no question of dropping the pilot, only of discarding the mascot. I am not a mascot. In London you generously let me be the pilot.'

Pyke's task in the US had changed. The Plough vehicle and the Plough guerrilla force looked set to go ahead. It was up to him to ensure that both lived up to their promise, and to do this he had to wrest back control of the British Mission. Otherwise there was a danger that Plough would end up as a confused and watered-down translation of his original idea and as such would be militarily useless. Rather than withdraw his resignation, Pyke decided to hold out for a change of heart in London. As he waited, Brigadier Duncan ran amok.

'Macbeth', as Pyke and Wedderburn now referred to him, spent the days that followed travelling up and down the East Coast making uninformed decisions on snowmobile design. Earlier it had been agreed that the vehicle must travel at 35 mph on level packed snow. Duncan approved plans for a vehicle with a maximum speed of just 20 mph. The difference did not bother him. He described the inferior specifications as 'good enough for the very good reason that I do not think anything better can be obtained'. There is no more accurate expression of the difference between Duncan and Pyke when faced with the mechanically unknown.

The week after Pyke's letter of resignation, Duncan approved OSRD's proposal to produce an amphibious snowmobile and later that day the contract to build these machines was given to Studebaker. General Joseph T. McNarney and Henry Stimson, the US Secretary of War, then approved Eisenhower's suggestion that the War Department build 860 of these new Plough vehicles, all designed to Duncan's specifications, adding that these should be ready 'by the early fall of 1942'.

Men from OSRD now scoured the Americas for suitable test sites, travelling as far afield as Chile and Alaska, while the snowmobile acquired a new name. It would be called the 'Weasel' after a description of this mammal as 'very active, bold' and known to 'turn white in winter'.

From a distance, the Weasel appeared to be on schedule. But, in their rush to produce these vehicles, OSRD had failed to investigate alternative snowmobile design or tackle basic questions like whether these vehicles could actually fit into the planes that would carry them. 'The Americans are remarkable,' wrote Pyke, 'but many are rather in love with the process of production for its own sake.' Things were moving too fast, and there was a danger that the Weasel might become a white elephant.

Pyke was desperate to be involved in the design process – asking questions, teasing, testing, probing, pushing for further research – but with Duncan in charge he was powerless. Instead he and Wedderburn stewed in their room in the War Department. They would 'sit day after day and sometimes literally all day, with nothing to do'. In the heat of the capital, Pyke's mind wandered to other more radical ideas. Occasionally they received a note from Duncan to say how well his work was going. Pyke's response was to fire off another letter of resignation to London.

'I've made no mistakes,' he complained to Mountbatten, on the same day that Churchill asked for a progress report on Plough, 'because I've not had the chance to do anything. Your assumption "Pyke is the only person capable of seeing it through", "Pyke is indispensable" is a bitter joke to us at this end. Could you have been an invisible witness of what has happened you would realise it. What has happened is that Pyke, far from being "indispensable", has in *fact* been dispensed with . . . gradually, skilfully and indisputably.'

Knox believed that 'Duncan had behaved outrageously'. Field Marshal Sir John Dill, head of the British Joint Staff Mission and the most influential Briton in Washington DC, 'was shocked and said that Duncan ought to be sent home at once' – though Dill did little to bolster Pyke's credibility by ribbing General Marshall whenever he saw him for listening to Mountbatten's 'tame lunatic'. Only when a glut of delayed letters from Pyke reached the CCO in London, including his initial letter of resignation, did the situation clear up.

'At last understand position,' sighed Mountbatten, before ordering Duncan back to London, promoting Wedderburn to Lieutenant-Colonel and declaring that 'Pyke is now my sole representative of Snow Plough scheme'. He even followed up on Pyke's reminder to bring in the Russians and obtained 'sympathetic support' for Plough from Molotov, the Soviet Foreign Minister. 'In spite of my somewhat petulant telegrams,' he assured Pyke, 'I have not lost faith in you and I feel that the misunderstandings that have cropped up are already disposed of.'

At a stroke, control of the British Mission was back with Pyke. The Russians might be coming in. Relations with Mountbatten were restored. Pyke's mood soared.

Several days later, however, it emerged that Mountbatten had put these sweeping decisions on hold. Rather than dismiss Duncan by telegram he would come out to Washington DC to sort things out in person. Perhaps he had also heard about the security matter concerning Pyke: some of his secret papers, including a report on the Inner Front in Norway, in an envelope marked 'On His Majesty's Service', and a diary on Romania labelled 'Secret – for Mr Pyke only', had gone missing. Though they had been under lock and key in the capital's Grafton Hotel, they had since 'vanished into thin air'.

Mountbatten boarded a plane for the the United States on 2 June 1942, where, it was noted at Richmond Terrace, 'he will be dealing with the matter of Mr Geoffrey Pyke and Brigadier N. W. Duncan'. Yet there was another objective he had been given for this trip.

On arrival, Mountbatten went to General Eisenhower for an update on Plough. The two men had hit it off in London and by that stage of the war Eisenhower was pushing for Mountbatten to become sole commander of the Allied invasion of Europe, such was his faith in the CCO. No doubt he wanted to give him good news. But this would not be easy.

Earlier that day, Eisenhower had received a sobering and detailed report on Plough from an officer in Operations Division which concluded that the prototype Weasel did not meet the necessary specifications, on balance it would probably be easier to ask the Norwegian resistance to carry out the proposed sabotage work, and that the US Army should have nothing to do with Plough.

'I can't sign that report,' Eisenhower had complained to the author, Lieutenant-Colonel Robert T. Frederick.

'Why not, General?'

'Because I told them in London that we were going ahead full speed with this project.'

Though Eisenhower might have mentioned this damning report to Mountbatten he did not dwell on it and instead whisked his visitor and Lt-Colonel Frederick off to the Russian Embassy where they met Litvinov, the Soviet ambassador. There followed an 'animated discussion' about Plough with Litvinov expressing a strong desire for the Soviets to have some of these new snowmobiles once they were ready.

The following day, 4 June 1942, Mountbatten met Duncan and Pyke separately. He concluded that the former had '(a) failed to ensure that the machine being designed could be carried in any existing form of aeroplane; (b) failed to press for more than one type of machine to be investigated; (c) failed to press for the formation of a Planning Staff to plan the project; (d) failed to press for the establish-ment of an Intelligence Department to collect and collate all the topographical and other intelligence of the area in which operations were to take place.' Indeed, Duncan had behaved 'just like a schoolboy', he told Pyke. 'The Service is full of them. They become greybeards but they remain schoolboys. They don't grow up.' Pyke coined a term for this condition: 'Duncanitis'. Symptoms included a tendency to be 'charming, moderately sincere, sometimes energetic, but simply behind the times'. Though a curable disease, it seemed that most sufferers refused treatment. Brigadier Duncan was sent back to London.

Later that day there was a meeting on Plough in which Mountbatten explained to Eisenhower, McNarney, Frederick and several US staff colonels that from now on Pyke would be his sole representative on Plough. This was a risky move. Replacing a senior army officer with an irreverent civilian was never going to endear Mountbatten to the US military, and nor did the gentle criticism of the War Department's approach to Plough that he then delivered, with Pyke chipping in occasionally.

'If I'd known you could do as well as that, I'd never have hung Duncan on you,' said Mountbatten afterwards of Pyke's performance in that meeting. 'If I may say so,' replied Pyke, 'we have dropped into the habit of playing doubles together, and know without thought which shots to take and which to leave to the other fellow.' Yet for his visit to the White House five days later, the meeting that would define his trip, Mountbatten was on his own.

Churchill had given Mountbatten two tasks in the US. He was to get Plough back on track and to persuade Roosevelt, Hopkins, Marshall et al. that an all-out assault on Europe before the end of 1942 was unrealistic. The two were entwined. Ideally Mountbatten would channel American enthusiasm for Round-Up and Sledgehammer into Plough and Jupiter – this being Churchill's plan for the invasion of northern Norway. It was, reflected Mountbatten, 'probably the most important job I had to do in the war'.

There are no minutes of the conversation between Roosevelt, Mountbatten and Hopkins – it was not the President's style to keep precise records of meetings like these – but we know that they spoke for five hours and that the tone would have been sympathetic. Roosevelt was fond of the CCO, having got to know him the year before. Indeed, Mountbatten was just the kind of Englishman that most Americans would take to – he spoke clearly, was good-looking, of royal birth and possessed an American sense of optimism. Mountbatten's stock had risen considerably since his last visit to the US, and on the day of the meeting his portrait adorned the cover of that week's *Time* magazine. But when it came to watering down the American enthusiasm for a major amphibious assault on occupied France before the end of the year he proved to be no match for the President and Harry Hopkins.

Though he won them over to Plough – Roosevelt even asked to meet Pyke – the President maintained that US soldiers must see action in Europe before the Plough force would be ready. In Mountbatten's account of the meeting, Roosevelt reminded him of Churchill's assurances that 'in the event of things going very badly for the Russians this summer, a sacrifice landing would be carried out in France to assist them'. This was the Sledgehammer plan mooted by Hopkins and Marshall in London. Following his talks the week before with Molotov, the Russian Foreign Minister, the President was more determined than ever to make this happen.

Mountbatten assured him that the British would be 'ready to follow up a crack in German morale by landing in France this autumn', and that such an operation could be launched at two months' notice. Just over two months later, Mountbatten oversaw Operation Jubilee, the disastrous Allied raid on Dieppe. It was Sledgehammer in all but name and resulted in no territorial gain, limited enemy losses and the death or capture of more than half of the 6,000 Allied troops involved, most of them young Canadians. Even if the mistakes made at Dieppe would go on to inform the landings on D-Day, this failure haunted Mountbatten for the rest of his life.

★

Possibly uneasy at the assurances he had given Roosevelt, Mountbatten set off the next day by train for Montreal. He was due to meet the Canadian General Staff before flying back to London. In the carriage next to him was Geoffrey Pyke, bearded and talkative, and the author of the damning report on Plough, Lieutenant-Colonel Frederick, who was by contrast quiet and well turned out. Frederick was perhaps the last person you might have expected to have on this trip – indeed, it made no sense for him to be there – but for General Eisenhower's decision the day before to put him in charge of the Plough force.

'I was shocked,' Frederick confessed. 'It was beyond my comprehension that I should be the man picked.' He was a staff officer in his mid-thirties with no experience of combat, working in a job which 'carried the rating of a glorified chief clerk'. Now he was to build from scratch a force of elite guerrillas before leading them into battle at the end of the year.

Most historians of the Plough force agree that the idea for this unlikely appointment came from the British camp. Of those who go further, the consensus is that Mountbatten was responsible. But it seems that Pyke was the one who put this idea in his head.

Not only did the idea of appointing a scheme's strongest critic as its chief advocate have an unmistakably Pykean ring to it – he often described the need to 'embrace your defects and proclaim them virtues' – but in a letter from Pyke to Mountbatten he referred to himself, in relation to Frederick's appointment, as 'Warwick the Kingmaker', the 16th Earl of Warwick famous for his manoeuvring behind the scenes during the Wars of the Roses to set up or bring down several English monarchs. Having got rid of Duncan, Pyke, it seems, had put Frederick on the throne.

'Bob' Frederick turned out to be an inspired choice. He would go on to become one of the great military commanders of the Second World War. For now, just one day into his new job, he faced the monumental challenge of recruiting, training and leading a force which existed only on paper. He did not have the necessary infantry training, knew little about parachuting, mountaineering or winter warfare, and needed to win over colleagues who had read an unrelentingly negative report on this proposed unit – which he had written.

In Montreal the three men sat down with the Chief of the Canadian General Staff, Lieutenant-General Kenneth Stuart, to whom Mountbatten outlined the idea behind Plough. He then handed over to Pyke and Frederick and made to leave. Before he could go Pyke asked for a word in private.

Either in the corridor or perhaps in a room next door, Mountbatten's Director of Programmes explained that he was working on a new idea that was bigger than Plough, and perhaps the biggest idea of the war. He would send over a detailed proposal once the results of certain tests had come in. The CCO said that he would be happy to look at it.

As he left the building, Mountbatten was met by 'a battery of press cameras'. We know this from the diaries of Guy Liddell, MI5's Director of Counter-Espionage, who happened to be walking past at that moment. On several occasions over the last few years he had gone through Pyke's Personal File, but Liddell had no inkling that the same man had just been in conversation with Mountbatten. Very few people knew that Pyke was in Canada just then, let alone why.

As Pyke and Frederick explained to General Stuart, they had come to discuss the prospect of bringing in the Canadians on Plough. Over the coming days the American colonel and the British inventor endured a barrage of meetings, explaining the idea to soldiers, politicians, civil servants and scientists. Although there were moments when the Canadians seemed unsure what to make of this gregarious civilian – during one meeting a Canadian general passed a note to Frederick, while Pyke was holding forth, saying 'What the hell does he want?' – generally the idea was received with enthusiasm, and in the days that followed a landmark decision was reached. It was agreed that this new military unit should be a joint American-Canadian force. This was without precedent, and would not have happened but for the intervention of a rule-breaking Englishman.

Though there had been an agreement earlier that year between Combined Operations and the Canadian General Staff that several Canadian officers would work on the project, Duncan had failed to follow up on it. When Pyke discovered his oversight, he decided not to go to the US Army, for fear that they would merely sit on it, but to contact the senior Canadian officer in the US, Major-General Pope and arrange a meeting with the General Staff. He had ignored the proper channels. But he was determined to turn Plough into a multi-national and collaborative enterprise, even if it meant breaking protocol. He was driven as much by his internationalism as a more practical sense that Canadians were 'experienced cold-weather people' and would probably take to this scheme well, as they did.

In between their Canadian meetings, Pyke told Frederick about how this new force should operate. Though Frederick was receptive to these ideas, there were times when the man behind them became too much. 'The son of a bitch won't let me alone,' he groaned. 'I'm with him all day and he talks, talks, talks. Almost everything he says makes sense but after a while my ears close up. I stop listening because I get numb and although I'm sure that the things he is saying are brilliant, I just can't absorb them any more.' This was not the only time in his life when Pyke displayed an on-the-spectrum inability to know when to stop.

Frederick returned to Washington DC alone on 13 June with a to-do list from Pyke that was almost comic in its length. As with the volunteers of VIAS, staff at Malting House School or his conver-sationalists in Nazi Germany, Pyke assumed that everyone he worked with would share his own extraordinary work ethic. Several days later Pyke arrived in the capital and was pleased to find the Plough force shaping up as he had hoped. The fate of the Weasel was less clear. As before, he was finding it difficult to discover how things were progressing. His calls were rarely returned, access was often denied and there were times, now that 'Macbeth' had gone, when his ghost seemed to linger. Or was there someone else now working against him behind the scenes?

Vannevar Bush

Dr Vannevar 'Van' Bush was, by 1942, America's most senior government scientist. He ran OSRD, the department responsible for producing the Weasel, yet by his own admission was 'naturally sceptical' of Pyke's project and later described it as merely 'an instance of Churchill's unbridled enthusiasm'. On Pyke, he conceded that this man 'had lots of ideas, some of them superficially brilliant and intriguing' and was 'a consummate salesman of a sort', but felt that he was 'short on physics, especially short on engineering judgment'. This is a reminder that in America, especially in the sciences, higher academic qualifications mattered more than they did in Britain at the time where Pyke's lack of formal scientific training might more easily be overlooked. This was just one of the reasons why Van Bush began to turn against this unqualified Englishman.

In the weeks before Mountbatten's visit Pyke had complained to two OSRD employees about the development of the Weasel, a conversation which had left Bush incensed, less for what Pyke had said than the fact that he was even speaking to a member of his staff. Vannevar Bush was a stickler for organisational protocol. He argued that as his department and the British Mission were both attached to the US Army, like two tributaries of the same river they must never meet. He was all for 'working through channels'. Pyke was not. He believed in intellectual cross-fertilisation and stressed the importance of seeking out those working beyond one's official milieu. In many companies you will find similar attitudes, with some calling for greater interaction between departments while others might prefer compart-mentalisation, but rarely are these opposite views held with such intensity by two senior figures on the same project.

Bush labelled Pyke a 'tyro' – someone who 'has a contempt for channels of authority and ducks around them. [. . .] Everyone who has ever worked in a complex pyramidal organisation recognises that there occasionally appears somewhere on the ladder of authority a dumb cluck who has to be circumvented if there is to be any progress whatever. [. . .] He can throw any organisation, civilian or military, into confusion. His breed should be exterminated for the good of society.' Bush was referring specifically at this point in his memoirs to Pyke.

Shortly after Pyke's unauthorised conversation with one of his staff, he did the same thing again with another employee. This time Bush went to General Moses to complain, pepping up his account of what had happened with phrases like: 'I judge that Mr Pyke's conversation was interspersed with many references to people in high places and that there were scarcely veiled threats involved.' Moses, sensibly, took no action.

Bush returned to OSRD where he ordered his staff to have 'no formal contact whatever with this particular British Mission'. Indeed, if any of them so much as spoke to Pyke they were 'to put in my file promptly a full memorandum on the conversation'. It was one of the only times in his life when Bush issued such an order and, as he later wrote, 'it is fortunate that I did'.

Soon after Mountbatten's arrival Bush heard a more startling claim about Pyke. A newly promoted and perhaps over-confident Sandy Wedderburn had told a member of Bush's staff that Pyke was 'now sitting pretty with a direct liaison to the President' and that 'if the project did not move as Pyke wished, heads would roll'. Wedderburn had also claimed that Pyke had placed an 'explosive charge' under Bush, and that if Plough did not move in the right direction he would light the fuse. Bush reiterated to his staff that they must keep away from this man, which was why Pyke found the reception so frosty on his return from Canada.

Unaware of what Wedderburn had said, let alone Bush's reaction, Pyke found himself in a quandary. He could ignore this reception, resign for a second time, or he could play his trump card: he could explain the situation to an acquaintance of his at the White House.

Seen in these terms it was not a difficult decision to make. Pyke was starting to understand the subtleties of people's resistance to new ideas and the importance of having support at the highest level. So far he had failed to get the backing of Bush. It seemed that the only way to get Plough moving in the right direction was to win over an even more powerful body. The danger was that by going to the White House he might also alienate the US Army, and ultimately that would have repercussions for both him and the man who had shown such faith in him over the last five months: Mountbatten.

Pyke sat down for lunch with the Economic Adviser to the President, Isidor Lubin, on 22 June 1942. Mountbatten had told him to 'be frank both with the President and his advisers', and at lunch that day Pyke held nothing back. Disregarding everything Bush had ever said about 'working through channels' he explained to Lubin what had happened with Plough, concluding that 'the organisational level of the American Army at this stage of its evolution is not adequate to the working-out of such a project as I've put before them'. Though Pyke was fulsome in his 'appreciation of the treatment we have received from every officer in the War Department and the US Army with whom we have had contact. From me as a civilian such acknowledgement is particularly due. Every kindness has been shown us,' he went on, but 'they don't understand war. They will win, of course, but by weight of numbers and material. And but for the Russians, they'd lose even then.'

Lubin listened at length, was silent and at last proposed a solution. 'For one so imperturbable he then became quite enthusiastic and emphatic,' recalled Pyke. Lubin's plan was bold. He suggested that the British Government ask the Office of Lend-Lease Administration for assistance with Plough. Lubin's friend there, Oscar Cox, could allocate the necessary funds for experiments and production costs, and the mistakes of the last two months could be rectified. In other words, Lubin and Cox would help Pyke take Plough away from OSRD and the US Army and have it developed through Lend-Lease instead.

The ramifications of this slowly dawned on Pyke. 'It meant a *Caste War*. For no caste ever gives up the slightest of its privileges without a struggle.' By agreeing to Lubin's plan he would initiate a battle between the White House and the War Department, and 'was almost certain to be a war casualty in that fight'. It was, however, a risk he was prepared to take in order to save his project. Lubin picked up the telephone, called Cox and arranged for him to see Pyke.

Oscar Cox was a bright-eyed, hard-working lawyer from Maine of whom it has been said that 'in this big, husky Maine lawyer, Harry Hopkins had found his own Hopkins'. More importantly, when it came to rescuing scientific projects that had run aground in the military shallows, Cox had form. Back in May 1940 he had arranged a meeting between Hopkins and a scientist in need of state funding for atomic research – Vannevar Bush. That meeting led to the creation of OSRD and helped accelerate progress towards the Manhattan Project. Now Cox was being asked to take a different scheme away from the same scientist he had once helped, on behalf of a fast-talking Englishman.

Pyke explained to Cox 'with complete frankness our experience of the American Army, and of the sabotage efforts of G-4 in particular'. If he was worried about how Cox would respond, he need not have been. Cox was 'receptive and enthusiastic' and agreed with Lubin's suggestion to 'set up a parallel organisation which would act competitively on the Army'.

The following day Cox called Lubin. 'There is a lot to what he says,' he began. 'The problem is, how far it's gone and what can be done about it.' They agreed that the problem with the Army handling Plough was that 'nobody wants to take it on because it is controversial and it will get them into trouble'. Although they found Pyke 'fascinating', or as Cox described him, 'amazing', both men could see how he 'would drive the Army nuts'.

They agreed that Lubin should explain the situation to Hopkins, while Cox would buttonhole John J. McCloy, Assistant Secretary of War, and push to have a scientist placed in the War Department to get things moving from the inside. Pyke then sent Lubin and Cox copies of his damning report on the US Army's handling of Plough, which he had recently submitted to Mountbatten. This was another dangerous move. 'I am doing this after thinking thrice. My Chief, I *believe*, showed it to one or two high authorities, but you will appreciate that if it were known or even suspected that I had shown this to you or anyone else, the complications would be serious.' Or as he told Cox, 'you realise, I hope, that this is high explosive, and should be handled gently. It is best dealt with in the dark in solitude.'

Later that day two of Cox's young assistants, both lawyers, visited

Pyke in his hotel room. One was George Ball, who would go on to be Under-Secretary of State for Economic and Agricultural Affairs; the other was Eugene Rostow, later appointed by President Lyndon Johnson as Under-Secretary of State. It was another sweltering evening in the capital, and by midnight the three men were still talking. 'We "clicked" in the first ten minutes,' wrote Pyke. 'I applied my usual tests on them to see what they laughed at' and concluded that they were 'our sort'. The two lawyers were no less taken with Pyke, seeing him as 'an unusually gifted and attractive Englishman'. 'Pyke could not write or talk without skyrocketing wit, interlarded with quotations from Shaw, Churchill, Tolstoy, the Bible, or whatever apt epigram he might dredge from his vast arsenal,' wrote George Ball, adding, 'it did not endear him to the soldiers'.

His room that night was an echo chamber in which everyone seemed to agree on the Army's anti-scientific bias, its resistance to new ideas and the absurdity of Bush's insistence on Pyke having no contact with OSRD engineers. In the heat of it all, Pyke made a throwaway remark. He said that things were so bad that there should be an official investigation into the methods of the War Department. It was a comment that would come back to bite him.

Over the coming days, Cox and Lubin interviewed some of those working on the project. They learnt that the design of the prototype Weasel was so bad that the snowmobile could not steer. An expert in tank production told them that the ideal design should involve Archimedian screws, as Pyke had suggested. But before they could put together a report, Vannevar Bush heard of these White House enquiries. He also discovered that they had originated with Pyke.

Immediately Bush went to the US Secretary of War, Henry Stimson, an indomitable seventy-four-year-old Republican who was, by that stage of the war, less than enamoured with the British, and handed him his docket of papers on Pyke and his contacts with

OSRD. Some of these reports were tendentious, others riddled with exaggerations and omissions. Yet the gist of what they said was accurate: Pyke was deeply critical of the War Department's handling of Plough; he had expressed these concerns to those at the White House; and had at one point suggested that there should be an official investigation into the methods of the War Department. These documents also indicated that there were security concerns regarding Pyke.

Stimson was livid. He summoned Field Marshal Dill to say that Pyke's behaviour was 'seriously upsetting friendly relations between the US and British Armies'. This man must 'go home immediately'. As one of Cox's assistants remarked: 'The Weasel business has taken a turn for the acute.'

Mountbatten's representative was now treading water. He sent another long letter to his boss telling him how much he was looking forward to receiving a cable from London to say that he had been sacked. He would throw 'a large and riotous dinner here to celebrate my dismissal, inviting to it foe and friend alike, all united in common rejoicing, where I should dance on the table among the champagne glasses'.

All he really wanted to do just then was to work on the radical new idea which he had mentioned in Canada. By his nature, Pyke was forever more interested in the solution of fresh problems than the slogging and scheming required to steer a project like Plough through to completion. Yet to carry on with his new work he needed emotional assurances from the CCO. 'It is very very difficult to think if you are feeling angry and aggrieved,' he told him. 'The elan vital gets drained off. You may be a bit staggered by this letter. "*More Pykerie.*" But this psychological fact is the basic one. Part of the difficulty is that while I can blow off steam to you about other people, I've no one to whom I can blow off steam about you.'

With his world starting to collapse around him, Pyke was reaching out to the man to whom he had come to feel closer than perhaps any other. In Richmond Terrace this proximity had been a source of occasional resentment. Shortly before Pyke's departure, several officers had even gone to the trouble of disabling the magnetic lock on Mountbatten's door because they were annoyed about the amount of time the Director of Programmes was spending in there. If there were moments when Pyke saw himself as the Figaro-figure in this relation-ship – nominally junior yet essentially in control – there remained a genuine camaraderie between the two and mutual admiration, all of which meant that Mountbatten would go to great lengths to resist having him dismissed.

In the thick of this, unaware of the crisis, Churchill cabled Hopkins. 'I am anxious to know what the prospects are of carrying out Mountbatten Plough Scheme this winter and would be grateful to hear how development and planning are progressing.' Plough was in disarray, Hopkins might have replied. There was no snowmobile, no guerrilla force and those involved in the project were busy casting about for scapegoats. Pyke had rounded on a Norwegian officer involved in the project. Cox's two assistants thought *'Putnam Must Go'*, a reference to an OSRD employee. Bush and Stimson were convinced that Pyke was the problem. Cox and Lubin, meanwhile, described Pyke as 'the red herring of this affair', which in their opinion had become an unflattering reflection of the War Department's approach to scientific development.

Several days later Bush's department launched a fresh attack on Pyke. One of its employees circulated a punishing account of Pyke's behaviour and character that was passionate and detailed, yet failed to make several valid criticisms.

Over the last month in the US, Pyke had allowed the power given to him by Mountbatten to go to his head, often coming across as obstreperous and brittle. Temperamentally he was better suited to roaming about within an organisation – suggesting, provoking, making people laugh, solving problems, coming up with ideas – than ordering others around. The court jester had become king and, as almost everyone agreed, this had been a mistake. Knox described Pyke in the wake of Mountbatten's visit as puffed up 'with the impression that he was to run the show and could boss anyone about'. As if to prove this, Pyke then referred to Knox in a cipher telegram to London as 'that damned old woman'. This message passed through SOE's headquarters on Baker Street and 'caused so much amusement on arrival', wrote Mountbatten, 'that I actually had my leg pulled by people in the London office before the telegram reached me! Your telegram unfortunately tickles their sense of humour.' Knox was less amused.

Pyke also had a tendency, Mountbatten observed, to rush 'to the conclusion that everyone is out to be an obstructionist, or, until they prove themselves otherwise, are congenital idiots'. His technique of opening a conversation with a blast of provocative remarks did not always bring out the best in those he spoke to. 'Most of the people he comes into contact with are all very busy,' a friend of Mountbatten's explained, and to them 'his opening gambits are often frivolous, and, to the uninitiated, pointless; that is half the trouble.'

'I have not gone deeply into pros and cons of case,' Field Marshal Dill told Mountbatten, 'but Harry Hopkins has taken full story as prepared by War Department and will, I know, ask you to recall Pyke before he further disturbs Anglo-American relations.' Yet four days later, somehow, Pyke was still clinging on. 'You don't sack me now only out of obstinacy,' he teased Mountbatten. 'You are gambling on my pulling something off somehow, sometime, where-upon you reckon to turn round in glee on all your critics.' But the pressure soon became too much.

'It has been made absolutely clear to me that your particular scheme will probably best be served by your running it from here,' Mountbatten told him. First General Marshall and then Hopkins had explained that if he did not have Pyke recalled they would force him out. 'I know both of them well enough to realise that this was a polite way of giving me an opportunity of "withdrawing my son from school before he was sent down".'

The top line of the charge against Pyke was serious. As a guest of the US, he had initiated a White House investigation into the methods of the War Department. Yet Mountbatten did not have him sacked. He merely asked him to return to Richmond Terrace to continue his work on Plough from there and, in the meantime, as a personal favour, 'to avoid entangling us any further'.

Pyke felt a lift of relief. In spite of 'the unspeakable misery of seeing the beautiful and delicately balanced plan I had taken so long to create crushed in the clumsy and unthinking hands of the Duncans, Hoags, Putnams etc.,' he told Mountbatten, 'I am like a soldier at the front delighted that having been wounded he is at last being sent home.' He was also grateful for not being dismissed from Combined Operations. 'This is your usual – your constitutional generosity – crystallised, maybe, round a seed of amour-propre to show the Americans that though you can be compelled to recall, you cannot be compelled to sack me.'

It had been a strange three months. Pyke had gone to America to win over the US military and shepherd Plough through to its conclusion. He had certainly failed in the first of these challenges, and in the process caused a contretemps between the White House and the US Army which had threatened to disturb Anglo-American relations, but his efforts had been worthwhile. In the months after his removal from Washington DC, his ideas would flourish.

The Weasel, as we shall see, became a huge success and, around the time that Pyke was recalled, training began for the Plough guerrilla force. Renamed the First Special Service Force (FSSF), this unit was a faithful rendering of Pyke's blueprint. FSSF recruits were selected on their ability to hold their own in the wild and were 'trappers, guides, cowboys, lumberjacks, etc'. Rather than sections, there were 'war parties'; platoons were 'bands'; battalions 'tribes' and as one FSSF document added, this elite new force might 'possibly bring back a few "scalps"' – a detail which later inspired the film-maker Quentin Tarantino to centre his 2009 film *Inglourious Basterds* on an imaginary FSSF that literally collected German scalps. For its brand of guerrilla warfare, its unconventional recruits and the sight of Canadians fighting in the same unit as Americans, the FSSF was unique. Against a backdrop of bitter personal antagonism and inter-departmental strife, Frederick's leadership and Pyke's imagination, as well as his persistence and propensity for breaking protocol, had all combined to produce a legendary military unit. It is seen today as the father of both the US Special Forces and their Canadian equivalent. Geoffrey Pyke, the creative, opinionated and sometimes childlike Englishman, had left his mark on North American military history.

PYKE HUNT, PART 5

It was only after Pyke flew to the US that MI5 realised he was on the staff at Combined Operations. This was a shock, especially in light of the latest intelligence to come in from one of their most reliable sources – 'Kaspar', the code name for the Austrian aristocrat Josef Otto von Laemmel. Just two weeks after Pyke had left for America Kaspar supplied further clues to suggest that he was a communist propaganda chief.

'PYKE is said to be mainly concerned with a Cutting Office which distributes to its contributors cuttings from newspapers of all kinds, above all economic ones, from all parts of the world,' ran the summary of what had been heard. 'He combines with this communist propaganda work and perhaps also passes on information. At any rate he is in contact with a number of officials of the German Communist Party.' This was not the kind of individual MI5 wanted to have employed by Combined Operations, let alone sent to the US on a secret government mission.

'It would seem that Pyke was taken on without any previous consultation with us,' wrote one MI5 officer to Major Bacon of C Branch, the MI5 section responsible for vetting candidates with jobs involving the Official Secrets Act. 'I should be interested to know how this could happen.'

'We have only just started vetting the staff of Combined Operations,' replied Bacon, 'and have no trace of Pyke's name being submitted to date.' An earlier note from Richmond Terrace suggested that Pyke's name had been submitted and later cleared. Someone, somewhere, had slipped up.

Milicent Bagot was more interested in how Pyke had come to be offered this job in the first place. 'Our records gave no indication that he has been trained for such work.' She asked Bacon for 'a copy of the curriculum vitae which was presumably put up when he applied for this employment or, failing that, to discover the grounds for his selection?' Bacon would search in vain, for Mountbatten had never asked Pyke to submit a formal application.

These MI5 officers were not the only ones intrigued by Pyke's appointment. While he was away in the US, an MI5 listening device picked up a suggestive conversation between the leader of the CPGB, Harry Pollitt, and Wilfred Macartney, one of the first British communists convicted of espionage and a trusted member of the Comintern. Macartney had said to Pollitt that Pyke – who was known to both of them – 'has got the left ear of Louis Mountbatten'.

Pollitt already knew. 'I hear it's amazing, what they take from him,' he replied. 'He's the fellow down there. I hear it's amazing the influence he's got with Mountbatten.'

One of Pyke's neighbours later claimed that Mountbatten and Pyke were so close that the CCO 'was unhappy if he didn't have the daily stimulus of a conversation with him' and would often come to visit Pyke in Hampstead 'in a dull mood' and 'without any escort'.

Pollitt was right. Pyke's influence with Mountbatten *was* amazing, but it was hard to say whether Pollitt's and Macartney's reaction indicated that Pyke might be a senior Comintern official, or were they simply bemused by the incongruity of this pairing? It was equally hard to place another exchange in this conversation. One of the two had asked whether Pyke was in America, to which the other had replied that it would be 'very interesting' to know.

Was Pyke engaged in undercover activities in the US? The answer to this, sadly, must remain a mystery. Given the FBI's limited capacity for domestic counter-intelligence at that time, they did not have a file on Pyke. Although we know, as Christopher Andrew has it, that 'every section of the wartime administration of Franklin D. Roosevelt had been penetrated by Soviet intelligence', including the various government departments with which Pyke worked, it is impossible to say whether he was involved. The precursor of the CIA, the OSS, was 'the most penetrated intelligence agency in American history' and would later be infiltrated by Pyke's friend Kuczynski. More recently it has emerged that as the USSR and the US forged closer diplomatic ties, between 1942 and 1945, Soviet intelligence-gathering activities escalated. But the names of many of those involved remain hidden in closed Russian archives. Rather than drown in a sea of speculation we are left with what can be proved, namely, that by the time Pyke had been recalled from Washington DC MI5 had worked out what to do with him.

The month before his return, one of the only MI5 officers who knew him personally, Victor Rothschild, 3rd Baron Rothschild, an accomplished jazz pianist, scientist, collector and MI5's expert in counter-sabotage, had been asked for his opinion on Geoffrey Pyke. What followed would prove decisive.

'He is a rather brilliant and persuasive talker,' began Rothschild. 'In fact he persuaded me to give him some money for what I now realise was a most fantastic project.' This was either Malting House School or, more likely, Pyke's scheme to explode the myth of anti-Semitism, yet given the latent anti-Semitism in some parts of MI5 it is unsurprising that Rothschild chose not to elaborate on this. 'He is eccentric and erratic. He is clever, though he has little judgement.'

He had strong left-wing sympathies as well, yet 'it would be idle for this office to try and prevent near-Communists from obtaining scientific posts in Government departments, even if it was considered desirable. Many scientists, particularly those who are still young, have very Left views, and so many of these are already in Government departments that to attend to any particular one would not only be pointless, but would also bring a certain amount of opprobrium on to MI5, as so many people are only too ready to accuse us of being Blimps. On the other hand, I feel that somebody who combines extreme Left views with an erratic character should not be at Combined Operations headquarters which must, owing to the operational nature of its activities, be one of the most secret government departments.' Bernal should also be dropped, Rothschild went on, to avoid a situation in which 'somebody whose first loyalty may be to Moscow rather than this country is in a position where he may well get information of considerable interest to Moscow and which the Government may not wish them to have at the moment'.

The irony of all this was that Rothschild's close friend Anthony Blunt, whom he had helped to bring into MI5, was at that time passing titantic quantities of information to Moscow. Rothschild had been blinded by both friendship and class. Pyke exuded 'Soviet spy' in the way that Blunt never would. Indeed, Rothschild was so convinced of his judgement on Pyke that he took it up with Lord Cherwell, Churchill's scientific adviser, who agreed that something must be done about him. Ultimately it was decided that MI5's Director-General, Sir David Petrie, should contact Mountbatten and pressure him into dismissing both Pyke and Bernal.

This was hardly an ideal moment for Pyke to show the CCO his radical new proposal. By then he had caused him major embarrassment in the US, threatening to upset Anglo-American relations, and now MI5 wanted him dismissed. But for Pyke there was no choice. His new scheme had the potential to change the shape of the war, and perhaps the future of warfare itself. 'Either it is a washout,' he told Mountbatten, 'or it is of vastly greater importance than the Plough scheme could have been at its most successful. I hope it is a washout.'

HOW TO WIN THE WAR WITH ICE

During the summer of 1942, in the tight and swampy heat of the American capital, Geoffrey Pyke came up with a plan to end the war by using ice. There were just two problems. One was that he might be sacked at any moment, the other was that too many people might hear the idea and laugh.

For many of us, laughter is an involuntary response to an idea or situation which challenges our understanding of how things should be while, at the same time, poses no threat. A joke is a 'safe shock', and throughout the history of invention some of the boldest and brightest ideas have been met with laughter. Pyke knew that he would be up against his 'old enemy' – 'the appearance of absurdity'. His only chance of having this proposal taken seriously was to win over a man like Mountbatten who understood that new ideas could be both useful and funny.

In the weeks after being ordered back to London, Pyke disappeared. He did not return to Britain, and in OSRD a rumour circulated about him being holed up in a New York hotel, hard at work on some mad new scheme. Another story was that he had checked himself into a 'mental institute'.

Instead he began to shoot up and down the Eastern Seaboard like a man who had lost something. He ate solitary meals in hotels, exchanged telegrams with an Austrian polymer scientist living in America and tracked down obscure texts on the properties of ice. He made at least one trip to Lake Louise in Canada and on two separate occasions went to the Mayo Clinic in Rochester, Minnesota, complaining of chronic exhaustion.

Again he had been poleaxed by his mystery illness, but after numerous tests the doctors could find nothing wrong with him. They concluded that he was in fine physical condition for a forty-nine-year-old, apart from a gum infection which would require the removal of two teeth. To alleviate his condition he was prescribed a mild amphetamine and a phenobarbiturate. The latter was mildly addictive, sometimes known as 'a doctor's best friend', and at the same time a drug often found to have to been taken in lethal quantities in cases of suicide.

On his second visit to the Mayo Clinic, in September, Pyke stayed for several weeks, and as he slid between the extremes of complete exhaustion and a blissed-out chemically induced high, he finished his proposal. Given the need for secrecy, he had asked William Stephenson of British Security Coordination to supply a trusted secretary, who now took his finished proposal to New York where it was sent to London by diplomatic bag. On 24 September an enormous, book-length dossier arrived on Mountbatten's desk from the Mayo Clinic.

'It may be gold: it may only glitter,' read the note stapled to the cover. 'I have been hammering at it too long, and am blinded.'

Pyke knew that in the past the CCO had asked junior officers to go through his proposals, especially the longer ones, and present him with a summary. He did not want him to do the same thing now. 'You have an able and admirable staff,' he warned, 'but of those I've met you are the only Promethean. They can read, but not with your eyes.' 'You promised me half an hour of your time,' he went on. 'I

330

don't ask so much to begin with. Read only the first 33 pages. If you find it no good, so be it. Chuck it away. But if you find the basic ideas new and good and important to the war, *then* you must read on to the end of the half hour.'

Mountbatten was busy and might have put this vast memorandum to one side had it not been for its epigraph, taken from one of his beloved G. K. Chesterton 'Father Brown' stories.

> Father Brown laid down his cigar and said carefully: 'It isn't that they can't see the solution. It is that they can't see the problem.'

This intrigued Mountbatten. Perhaps more than any other pair of sentences it seemed to embody one strand of his intellectual outlook. He turned the page and began to read.

How to Win the Battle of the Atlantic with Ice

Churchill would describe the Battle of the Atlantic as 'the dominating factor all through the war. Never for one moment could we forget that everything happening elsewhere, on land, at sea or in the air depended ultimately on its outcome.' Pyke's proposal described how the Allies could win it.

He began with a series of stark assertions: Britain's ability to wage war depended on the millions of tons of vital supplies it received across the Atlantic; most of these were transported using unarmed ships manned by civilians; there were not enough Allied warships to protect them all; over parts of the ocean there was no air cover; Allied ships were being sunk in the Atlantic faster than they could be replaced.

Few military strategists would argue with any of this. June 1942 had been the worst month yet in the Battle of the Atlantic, in which a staggering 652,487 tons of Allied shipping had been sunk, most of it by submarines marauding in a hitherto anonymous strip of ocean now known as 'U-Boat Alley'. It was impossible to win the war without victory in the Battle of the Atlantic. No less important was the ability to mount attacks on enemy supply lines. Allied efforts fell short on both due to a lack of air cover. In each of the major naval exchanges of the war – whether it was the attack at Pearl Harbor or the sinkings of the *Prince of Wales*, the *Repulse* or the *Bismarck* – aircraft had played the decisive role. Only now was it becoming clear that control of the seas depended upon mastery of the air. So how to achieve this over the Atlantic?

In an imaginary world Churchill might have waved a magic wand to conjure a fleet of new aircraft carriers, each vessel magically immune to torpedoes, comfortable in rough seas, requiring very little steel to build and capable of accommodating long-range bombers and fighters. This was fantasy, of course. There seemed to be no realistic solution to these strategic problems other than building up Allied military strength using existing weaponry until victory was assured by weight of numbers. Pyke proposed something else. He had found a way to turn fantasy into reality.

His starting point was a dog-eared 1924 copy of the *National Geographic Magazine* which contained an account by Captain Zeusler of the North Atlantic Ice Patrol of what had happened when his men fired six-pound shells at an iceberg. Rather than shattering into icy smithereens, as you might expect, given that ice is brittle, these bergs absorbed the shells. None penetrated more than a few inches while some failed to explode. Zeusler had been bemused. Pyke was intrigued.

The article also touched on the history of collisions with icebergs, stressing that the sinking of the *Titanic* was not an isolated incident but one of hundreds of encounters between boat and berg in which the vessel would always come off second-best. Pyke asked himself a silly-sounding question: was it possible to harness the colossal strength of icebergs to the Allied war effort?

While Pyke had been left to stew in the capital as Brigadier Duncan made uninformed decisions on Plough, he had begun to track down historical references to ice including the story of an American businessman who wanted to tow an iceberg from Alaska to Los Angeles to make ice cream. It had come to nothing and, besides, the iceberg would have melted after reaching more temperate waters – but the story planted in Pyke's mind the idea of moving these apparently unsinkable objects.

At this point, Pyke had a fortuitous conversation with an old friend of Bernal, Professor Herman Mark, a charming Austrian scientist in his late forties who would later become known as one of the pioneers of polymer science. He had taught in Vienna before moving to New York at around the time of the *Anschluss* (his father was Jewish), since when he had built up a laboratory at the Brooklyn Polytechnic Institute. Earlier that year Pyke had got him involved in the Plough project, for Mark knew more about ice than almost any other practising scientist – though this was faint praise. By 1942 astonishingly little was known about the physical properties of this ubiquitous material.

During their conversation Mark showered Pyke with information about ice, including the fact that it melts at a much slower rate when insulated. Were you to place a cube of ice some 300 feet wide in water heated up to 52° F., it would melt in less than a week. Surround that block with a wall of wood just one foot thick and it would lose no more than 0.9 per cent of its volume in 100 days.

This appeared to change everything. Pyke pictured an Alaskan iceberg insulated by wood and hollowed out to store military materiel. Knowing that planes had performed emergency landings on the tops of icebergs in the past, perhaps the cap of the berg could be levelled off to form a runway? Effectively this would create a floating airfield. Tow one of these into U-Boat Alley, in the mid-Atlantic, and aircraft based on it could lay waste to nearby enemy submarines. Better still, it could be done at a fraction of the cost of building a new aircraft carrier from steel. Given that ice was so cheap, why not build an archipelago of these customised floating islands?

'The war can be won *either* by having ten of everything to the enemy's one (including the ships to carry it),' he wrote, '*OR* by the deliberate exploitation of the super-obvious and the fantastic.' Pyke had combined three 'super-obvious' ideas: icebergs are hard to destroy; ice melts slowly when insulated; ice is cheap.

It is also brittle, which was why a customised iceberg along these lines could never work. It lacked the necessary crush resistance to withstand powerful mid-Atlantic swells and would break up after reaching U-Boat Alley. The resistance of a material that could cope, such as high-grade reinforced concrete, was 4,000 pounds per square inch (psi). Ice, at best, had a resistance of 1,300 psi, making it significantly weaker than even low-grade reinforced concrete.

This would have been a good moment to abandon this train of thought and return to Plough. Many of us, at this point, might have done so. Pyke had checked his fantasy against reality and found it to be unworkable. But he did not let go. He saw this as the kind of setback one should expect when tackling a problem of this magnitude.

Instead he took a step back and tried to unbutton his mind. He had to distance himself from every assumption that he had ever held about ice, to banish from his imagination the traditional uses of ice and to think of this material instead as if he were a scientist who had discovered it for the first time.

What had happened to most other new materials following their initial discovery? Iron had been alloyed with other materials to produce steel; wire had been added to concrete to make reinforced concrete; raw copper, as he knew from his days as a copper investor, had been smelted and refined. In other words, each of these new materials had been artificially strengthened. Why not do the same to ice?

Earlier that summer Pyke had picked up a copy of the forbiddingly titled *Refrigeration Data Book of the American Society of Refrigeration Engineers* and had read that 'frozen sand is harder than many kinds of rock'. The implications were fascinating. It seemed to suggest that you could strengthen ice by adding materials such as sand to the water before it is frozen.

At this point Pyke had a rare stroke of luck. He asked Professor Mark to carry out several experiments into reinforcing ice, only for this Austrian scientist to say that he had already begun.

'I told him that when I worked in a pulp and paper mill in Canada, we found that the addition of a few per cent of wood pulp greatly increased the strength of a layer of ice.' Not only was Pyke right about strengthening ice but he was speaking to perhaps the only man in the world to have already begun experiments along these lines.

Breathless at the thought of what might be just around the corner, Pyke asked Mark to conduct fresh investigations into the properties of ice made from water to which sawdust or cork had been added. The results were extraordinary. This reinforced ice was not only stronger than pure ice but the wood pulp formed a soggy protective layer which slowed the speed at which it melted. Two birds had been killed with one stone. Mark's team was now producing reinforced ice which melted slowly and had a crushing resistance of 3,000 psi – a greater tensile strength than many varieties of reinforced concrete. A square column of this strengthened ice, measuring just one inch across, could support a medium-sized car.

These were only the initial results. In time Mark's team was bound to find more fecund combinations of water and wood-pulp. 'The possible repercussions of having a material of this quality that can be made in any desired shape, uniform and monolithically *AND* which floats, are obvious.'

Just before Mountbatten ordered him back to London, Pyke's iceberg scheme underwent its final evolutionary leap. Rather than customise a natural berg, Pyke proposed to build an artificial one using reinforced ice. Just as a refrigerating ship is kept cool by a series of ducts webbed out over its hull this man-made berg would contain ducts capable of keeping the temperature of the ice low enough for it to sail through tropical waters.

The document he sent to Mountbatten seven weeks later was summarised by its title: *Mammoth Unsinkable Vessel with functions of a Floating Airfield*. This 'berg-ship' made out of reinforced ice would be cheap to build and, on account of its gargantuan size, would be capable of accommodating even modern fighters and bombers. It would measure at least 2,000 feet from bow to stern, making it twice as long as the ocean liner *Queen Mary* and twice as wide; this would be the largest vessel ever made by man. What was more, it would be unsinkable.

Water weighs eight times less than steel but is heavier than ice. A berg-ship *could not be sunk*. To destroy it, an attacker would need to break the vessel up into thousands of tiny pieces, all of which would float, and do this before the initial holes in the hull could be patched up. Here was another startling claim: 'A battleship, when hit, has to go into port for repair. There is no such need for the berg-ship. The damage done by projectiles can be repaired at sea and in a very short time. All damage will be made good by filling the hole with about five-sixths crushed ice and water replacing the refrigerating pipes (made of cardboard) and refreezing.'

The berg-ship, in theory at least, was an astounding improvement on the modern aircraft carrier. Each one would be cheap, unsinkable, capable of carrying heavy bombers and equipped with one of the most powerful secret weapons in any war: surprise. Until then, most major breakthroughs in naval design had occurred in peacetime, and as a result of this few sides had ever gone to war with a telling technological advantage over the other. The berg-ship was different in that it had been conceived during a war. Weapons designed to sink ships of steel would have little or no impact. Magnetic mines would drift harmlessly past; torpedoes would perforate the ship without sinking it. 'Its adoption by one side will give advantages of surprise that have, I believe, never accompanied the introduction of a new strategic material.'

The rest of Pyke's proposal was an imaginative journey into a world in which one side had mastered the military potential of ice before the other. It is unlikely that Mountbatten read these latter sections. They contain colourful descriptions of what Pyke called Super-Cooled Water, or Liquid Ice, being sprayed onto enemy coastal defences before being used to form icy barricades around cities like Genoa, Naples and Hamburg. There are ice floes and dummy ice floes, each with tricksy neon-lit messages for Luftwaffe pilots, such as 'This is a real floe. Please waste bombs on it.' Pyke envisioned hundreds of berg-ships lumbering around the world and into enemy ports, where they could merrily 'smash up every ship to be found there'.

Lacing the proposal together were broader ideas about deception, the need to take ground without holding it and the importance of winning civilian hearts and minds. Some of this extraneous material has since been dismissed as science fiction, which it was, in the purest sense. But to understand Pyke is to realise that every idea he had was science fiction – science in the fictional stage of its development. This is the passage through which every scientific idea must travel before it can be subjected to rigorous experimentation. What set this proposal apart was the extent to which Pyke had allowed his imagination to race beyond the point at which most scientists would stop. This is why some of it felt outlandish or silly. 'One way to beat the Germans is precisely by being – not *merely* funny – but funny, *and* as thorough as the Germans are. Do you think the men who conceived and built the Trojan Horse were stiff and solemn men?' Again he was pointing Mountbatten towards something more than cunning and intelligence or what the Ancient Greeks called *metis*. His emphasis was on laughter, the gateway to deception, which 'destroys German morale'. The goal should be not just 'to beat them but to make fools of them in beating them.' Again there are echoes here of his childhood, of being chased down the corridor at Wellington and the realisation that the only way to really get back at his bullies was by making them look ridiculous.

For all its flights of fancy Pyke's scheme contained a brilliant military innovation. It proposed an unsinkable aircraft carrier made out of a cheap new material that could be produced quickly. Yet his paper was merely a starting point, 'a catalyst of the ideas of other people. NO idea is a good one which does not breed its own successors.' It was up to Mountbatten to grasp its potential. If he did and was able to press it upon Churchill with characteristic gusto then the scheme might survive its infancy. More likely was that Mountbatten would chuckle at this latest instalment of 'Pyke's Nonsense' and set it aside to focus on more urgent and realistic plans.

Pyke's only chance of beating his old enemy, the appearance of absurdity, was by winning over Mountbatten, which was why the proposal was aimed specifically at him. Its jokes and references, even the declarative nature of its sentences, all were tailored to the CCO. 'My style is a reflection, not of me, but of the man I am writing to,' Pyke had explained to him. 'That is why my letters and memoranda to you have been what they are.' 'That I do this is your fault,' he wrote elsewhere. 'You egg me on. You don't suppose I write like this to other people – or do you? I am not clear in what leadership consists, but I know – to my cost – that you are a born stimulator of men.' Mountbatten had become both patron and muse, which was why Pyke chose 'Habakkuk' as a cover-name for this proposal (misspelt by his American secretary as 'Habbakuk', the spelling that stuck).

Habakkuk was the Old Testament prophet who had warned: 'Be utterly amazed, for I am going to do something in your days that you would not believe, even if you were told.' There is also a

Donatello sculpture of the same name, a hollow-eyed Habakkuk who seems to stagger under the weight of his prophecy, and who bears an uncanny resemblance to Pyke. But the intended reference was to what Pyke imagined to be Voltaire's line on Habakkuk: '*Il était capable de tout.*' So was Mountbatten. From a hospital bed in the Mayo Clinic, his mood mediated by powerful drugs, Pyke began to wait for a response.

Within three hours of reading Pyke's proposal, Mountbatten had arranged a conference in Richmond Terrace to discuss the practicality of the scheme. He was captivated. His staff went over Pyke's document and agreed that it was 'both sound and brilliant'. The problem was that Mountbatten might not be in a position to do anything about it.

The CCO's reputation was at a wartime low. Two weeks after ordering Pyke back from the United States, Mountbatten had overseen the 'sacrifice' landing discussed with Roosevelt, the disastrous Commando raid on Dieppe. While the blame for the scale of the defeat was not entirely his — he had called for a pincer attack rather than Montgomery's frontal assault — Dieppe was seen as his 'show' and in the weeks that followed he was openly rebuked by the Chief of the Imperial General Staff, Field Marshal Sir Alan Brooke, and the Prime Minister had demanded a full explanation.

But it was not yet clear whether the fallout from Dieppe had fundamentally changed the dynamic between Mountbatten and Churchill. At the heart of their relationship had been a weakness for bold, daring ideas, the kind of schemes that made them gasp. Churchill wanted proposals from inventors with 'corkscrew minds', and was open to all but the unlikeliest suggestions from his effervescent Chief of Combined Operations. In the past, when they had sat down to discuss these ideas, a curious thing had tended to happen. Usually two people who know each other this well will assume complementary roles, so that if one has a habit of getting carried away, the other is there to apply the brakes. Yet during a conference of 'Mahomet' and 'God Almighty', as they were known in Combined Operations, the opposite was often true. Mountbatten and Churchill had a habit of pushing each other skywards, which was why Brooke and his fellow Chiefs of Staff had come to dread Monday-morning meetings after one of Mountbatten's weekends at Chequers.

Churchill and Mountbatten in Casablanca in 1943

Over the weekend of 5 December 1942 Mountbatten introduced Churchill to the most daring scheme yet from 'John the Baptist' – Pyke's nickname in Combined Operations. The US Ambassador John Winant was also staying, along with Cherwell and Roosevelt's special envoy, Averell Harriman, but Mountbatten would have explained this idea to Churchill alone.

He jumped at it. Indeed, by the end of their conversation the Prime Minister had been won over with the force of an infatuation. Churchill was entranced by the idea of a floating airfield made of ice. It was just the kind of spectacular technological innovation that he would find irresistible throughout his premiership. The atomic bomb, for example, might possess more destructive force than any other weapon but it remained, for him, just a bomb. He was more intrigued by proposals which possessed a paradoxical elegance and ingenuity, and in this sense the idea that Mountbatten had just explained was without equal.

Early on Monday morning Churchill issued an emphatic Personal Minute to his Chiefs of Staff. 'The advantages of a floating island or islands are so dazzling that they do not at the moment need to be discussed,' he began. 'I attach the greatest importance to the prompt examination of these ideas, and every facility should be given to CCO for developing them. He will report to me weekly on the setting-up of the organisation and the preliminary work.' Pyke could not have hoped for more.

In the same minute Churchill gave a detailed account of how he felt these berg-ships could be built. Either Mountbatten had slightly misunderstood the proposal or various elements had been lost in translation at Chequers, for Churchill described customising an existing iceberg. This would never have worked. 'Bombs and torpedoes would crack it, even if they could not sink it,' wrote one scientist, 'and natural icebergs have too small a surface above water for an airfield, and are liable to turn over suddenly.' That was not the point. What mattered was that Churchill's impulsive and romantic imagination had been seized by the idea of creating these mammoth airfields out of ice.

Lord Cherwell was the first to try to talk him down. As well as having a track record of rubbishing every scheme associated with Pyke, Cherwell had recently urged MI5 to have him dismissed. So his hostility was to be expected. In a long letter to Churchill he explained that Habbakuk should be abandoned because too little was known about ice. Couldn't they use concrete instead?

'*Prof*,' came the reply. 'I have long thirsted for the floating island (see backpapers). It was always broken down. The ice scheme must be reported on first. Don't stand in its way.'

Though Pyke was never aware of it, there was further good news in the days that followed: the Security Service was no longer angling for his immediate dismissal. As MI5's Roger Fulford explained to Milicent Bagot, 'on strictly security grounds' it was no longer 'practicable to ask for Pyke's removal from CCO, since he was not for certain a member of the CPGB'. They remained confident of being able to get him out, but not now. 'Mountbatten is liable to sudden enthusiasms for unorthodox recruits to his staff, and at the moment he has this enthusiasm for Pyke and Bernal,' their source in Richmond Terrace explained. 'It will not last.' Once this moment had passed, MI5's contact would gently suggest that work be found elsewhere for Pyke. 'I think that this is all we can do for the moment.'

Pyke, meanwhile, was busy anticipating the reaction to Habbakuk from the 'collection of fools on whom Churchill had to rely for the conduct of the war', also known as the Chiefs of Staff. He worried that they would take one look at this proposal and brand Mountbatten 'brilliant, but unsound', or they might resent him 'for having gone with his suggestion direct to the Headmaster without consulting the Prefects'.

Pyke was right to sense that it required unusual conviction from his chief to propose an idea as radical as Habbakuk. Mountbatten's reputation remained fragile. As well as the ignominy of Dieppe, some had called his character into question following the release of the film *In Which We Serve*. This was a fine piece of wartime propaganda starring Noël Coward as a fictionalised version of Mountbatten during his command of the destroyer HMS *Kelly*. Yet for the Canadian newspaper proprietor Lord Beaverbrook, among others, it smacked of vanity. After the film's release he had staggered up to Mountbatten at a party and told him that he was finished. He disliked the film's simpering portrayal of Mountbatten's abilities as a naval commander as well as the sight of Coward – for Beaverbrook a 'pansy' and 'war slacker' – playing the war hero. No less irksome was the moment in the film when the camera zoomed in on the 1 September 1939 edition of one of Beaverbrook's papers, the *Daily Express*, carrying the headline 'There will be no war this year'.

Beaverbrook's outburst was just one instance of the burgeoning resentment some felt towards Mountbatten. While he remained as decisive and charming as ever, enjoying the continued loyalty of his colleagues, by December 1942 the ranks of those waiting for him to make a mistake had grown insidiously. His decision to back one of the wildest schemes of the war was a mark of supreme confidence in both Pyke and his own judgement. The last thing he could afford was a costly fiasco.

The response to Habbakuk at that first Chiefs of Staff meeting was cautiously enthusiastic. 'Discussed Winston's new project of making battleships and aircraft carriers out of ice!!' wrote a bemused Field Marshal Brooke. The next day the same group looked at Pyke's plans in more detail, and by the end of that session Habbakuk had been given an amber light. 'In discussion the strategical value of this project was freely accepted,' ran the official account, 'but it was considered premature to go into questions of planning and construction until we were satisfied that it was in fact a practicable proposition.'

Further research was needed, for which the Habbakuk Directing Committee was formed. It met just three days later.

In a more dispassionate world none of the men who attended that session would have arrived with fixed views on the practicality of the scheme. All would have waited for the results of the scientific research. Instead they followed their gut instincts. While for some the idea felt fascinating, others found the notion of a ship of ice hard to stomach. As many studies have subsequently shown, how we feel about an idea is more than capable of overpowering what we know.

Mountbatten was at the forefront of those in favour, such as Pyke and Bernal, as well as scientists and engineers from the advisory panels including Professor Pippard, then working on the 'dambuster' bomb with Barnes Wallis. The opposition clustered around Lord Cherwell, unsurprisingly, as well as Sir Charles Goodeve from the Admiralty and Brigadier Sir Harold Wernher of Combined Operations, who felt that Habbakuk went 'against Nature' and later confessed that he 'had no faith in it or its promoter and considered that it was a waste both of time and energy'.

Notwithstanding this antagonism, the Habbakuk Directing Committee agreed that reports and experiments were needed and that one or two 'enthusiasts' like Pyke should go to Canada to investigate the properties of reinforced ice and whether a berg-ship was practical. With the backing of Mountbatten and Churchill, and the cautious enthusiasm of the Chiefs of Staff, the project was starting to gather momentum.

On New Year's Eve 1942, in a high-ceilinged bedroom just a stone's throw from the gentle thrum of Piccadilly, an unusual meeting began. Propped up in bed amid a jumble of papers, ashtrays and empty milk bottles was Geoffrey Pyke in a pyjama coat. In a courtly semi-circle around him were a Vice-Admiral, a Brigadier and two wild-haired scientists. One of these, Solly Zuckerman, recalled Pyke at the heart of this 'extraordinary conference [. . .] looking, with his strange beard, like some jaundiced Christ'.

His illness had struck again, but rather than delay any Habbakuk discussions, Mountbatten, Wernher, Bernal and Zuckerman had come to see the Director of Programmes in the Albany bedroom he had borrowed from his friend Cyril Ray. Though Ray had been out of the country when Pyke returned from America, he had managed to let himself in and had since taken over the main bedroom. Ray found the whole incident amusing and was happy for him to stay on.

Bernal began by stressing that in his opinion the possibility of success justified all risk of failure, for the introduction of just one berg-ship could transform the Battle of the Atlantic, and as such the Canadian trials should begin right away. The next report they considered, from an elderly engineer named Mr Spanner, was altogether more dour. Pyke and Bernal groaned as Mountbatten read out his pessimistic conclusions, protesting that Spanner had shown 'a complete lack of imagination throughout his investigations'.

Mountbatten agreed. For him 'the success of a project of this nature was dependent on how determined one was to do it. If Mr Spanner was too old to tackle such a problem, he should be paid for his services, and a man with a more fertile brain should be asked for an opinion.' This was what they agreed to do.

Yet it was not enough to lift Pyke out of his darkening mood. Propped up in bed like a dying patriarch surrounded by his family, his words still slurred following the operation on his gums in the Mayo Clinic, he complained that too many of those working on Habbakuk had no faith. 'Mountbatten tried to assure him that work was proceeding as fast as it possibly could,' recalled Zuckerman. 'Pyke was not satisfied. "Without faith," he kept protesting, "nothing will come of this project." "But I have faith", replied Mountbatten. "Yes," said Pyke, "but have the others got faith?", and turning to

Harold Wernher he asked solemnly, "Have you got faith, Brigadier?" Poor Wernher did not know what to say.'

The following week Cherwell launched a fresh attack on Habbakuk that would again test the faith of those behind it. At this critical meeting the Prime Minister's scientific adviser produced a steamrollering display of destructive criticism. Each point was countered by Bernal or a convalescent Pyke – until Mountbatten snapped. As the minutes reveal, the CCO 'outlined the state the war had now reached, stressing the seriousness of the U-boat campaign. He pointed out that when a scheme was presented which might relieve this stalemate, it should not be turned down out of hand through incredulity and natural antipathy, but every facility should be given to prove its worth.'

It is easy to forget when looking back at the period which stretches from the British victory at El Alamein in 1942 through to D-Day two years later, that during the early months of 1943 the outlook for the Allies was bleak. In very few theatres of war did they have control of both air and sea, and during the last year they had lost 7.8 million tons of shipping, most of it in the Atlantic. There were few indications that this would change. 'The only thing that ever really frightened me during the war,' wrote Churchill, 'was the U-boat peril.' Mountbatten's words proved decisive, and Cherwell backed down. It was also agreed that given the urgency of the scheme they would need Churchill to help get things moving in Canada.

On 14 January 1943 a Canadian civil engineer named Jack Mackenzie received a call from his Prime Minister, who had just got off the phone with Churchill. He wanted his help in developing a top secret British scheme.

Mackenzie was 'small in stature and quiet of mien' with a head that rose up out of his shoulders like a block of weathered stone. When he first heard about Habbakuk his reaction was cool, to say the least. 'This is another of those mad, wild schemes that we come in contact with frequently,' he grumbled in his diary. 'While one cannot say that it is not practicable I am quite sure that if it were suggested in normal circles here we would not have the ghost of a chance of getting it before even a minor official.'

This was ominous. As Acting President of the National Research Council of Canada, Jack Mackenzie was one of the few Canadians who could give Habbakuk the energetic push it so needed. Of course he was quite justified in dragging his heels. Little was known about either ice or reinforced ice. Again, it was a question of imagination as well as faith.

Four days later, having inspected the plans, Mackenzie and his colleagues mellowed. 'The soundness appeals more to us as we get deeper into the problem.' Perhaps Habbakuk could work. Certainly he appreciated the jaw-dropping nature of Pyke's scheme and that if this was going to happen, work had to begin immediately.

Mackenzie set off right away for the blinding, snowy wilds of Western Canada to get the necessary experiments started. He knew better than to issue orders from Ottawa and instead met the relevant engineers and scientists in person. Soon the Canadian side of 'Project Habbakuk' was under way. The Canadian Department of Finance approved a budget of £150,000 for Habbakuk's development, largely due to Mackenzie's lobbying, and in Banff and Jasper National Parks the first experiments began. Scientists from the universities in Winnipeg, Saskatoon and Edmonton began to direct teams of conscientious objectors in their investigations into the effects of stress or enemy fire on giant blocks of ice and reinforced ice. On a frozen lake in a remote part of the Canadian Rockies work would soon begin on a scaled-down model of the first berg-ship.

None of this was made any easier by the sapping wintry conditions. 'When I tell you that at Banff we have to open up a road forty miles through the mountains with snow ten feet deep, take in supplies, secure ice-cutting equipment, and all accommodations for a staff of twenty or thirty which we hope to assemble, you will see that we have to move rapidly,' wrote Mackenzie.

No less remarkable was the level of security. The Canadians went to great lengths to keep the project secret. Each Habbakuk research site was guarded by Mounties, while none of the conscientious objectors labouring in the cold on Pyke's *chef d'oeuvre* were told what they were working on. Most were tough young Mennonites and Doukhobors unable to fight for religious reasons. While they knew their scripture and could tell you about the biblical Habakkuk, none would hear about a 'Habbakuk' berg-ship. For many months, nor did the other scientists working on the project, including Max Perutz.

By that stage of the war, Perutz could be forgiven for having something of a persecution complex. This bespectacled crystallographer, who would go on to win a Nobel Prize for Chemistry, had left his native Austria partly on account of his Jewishness, which had limited the number of academic positions open to him, before finding a place at Cambridge. Here he had excelled, first under Bernal and later Sir Lawrence Bragg. He was awarded a Ph.D. and relished 'the stimulus, the role models, the tradition of attacking important problems, however difficult, that Cambridge provided. It was Cambridge that made me, and for that I am for ever grateful.' By April 1940 everything seemed to be going right in his life. He had a girlfriend. His parents had made it safely out of Austria to England. The stars in his life had aligned and, just as it seemed that nothing could go wrong, it did — and spectacularly so.

In May 1940 Max Perutz was called before an Enemy Aliens Tribunal to determine whether he was sympathetic to the Nazi regime. To his astonishment he was judged to be a 'Category B' alien: 'absolute reliability uncertain'. It is hard to imagine why. If Perutz's criminal record played a part, we can only presume that the actual offence was never revealed. One night in Cambridge he had been arrested for riding his bicycle without lights.

To keep Britain safe from Nazi Fifth Columnists this twenty-six-year-old Jewish crystallographer was shipped off to Quebec, strip-searched, relieved of his possessions and deposited in a detention camp that looked out over the St Lawrence River. He gave lectures, became the 'doyen of the camp's scholars' and was taught theoretical physics by fellow detainee Klaus Fuchs, the man who later went to Jürgen Kuczynski to start passing atomic secrets to the USSR.

Perutz was not released until the following year when he returned to Cambridge to resume his work on the structure of haemoglobin. It left him feeling detached. 'Nobody wanted my help for anything related to the war except fire-watching on the roof of the laboratory at night.' All this changed in the Spring of 1942 when he received a call from a man with a 'gentle, persuasive voice' who wanted advice on tunnelling through glacial ice. It was Pyke, then exploring an icy version of the Trojan Horse ruse in which the Plough force would pretend to withdraw from Norway but instead hide deep within a glacier. Later that year Perutz was contacted again by Pyke.

'This time, he sized me up with a volley of provocative remarks, and then told me, with the air of one great man confiding in another, that he needed my help for the most important project of the war.' Perutz dropped his haemoglobin work and agreed to conduct experiments for Pyke into the properties of reinforced ice. To do this he was given the use of a secret laboratory five floors below London's Smithfield Meat Market.

His new workplace had once been a refrigerated meat store and was lit by blue fluorescent lights, which gave it an eerie, futuristic atmosphere. Perutz and his six assistants, each one a muscular Commando, went about in electrically heated flying suits, while the soundtrack in this subterranean lair was the rhythmic grind of a generator, a wind tunnel and the concrete mixer which stopped the pulp composite from drying out. It was like something out of a science fiction novel – and so was the material they were working with.

Perutz was fascinated by the properties of the strange new substance, even if he did not yet know what it was for. 'It can be machined like wood and cast into shapes like copper; immersed in warm water.' It was buoyant and cheap and very strong. By freezing a mixture of water and 4 per cent wood pulp, Perutz was manufacturing reinforced ice that was 'weight for weight as strong as concrete'. This gave him and Lieutenant Commander Douglas Grant, one of the Combined Operations officers assigned to the project, an idea for what to name it. 'In honour of the originator of the project, we called this reinforced ice "Pykrete".'

Mountbatten was eager to see this material for himself, so a visit was arranged to Perutz's laboratory. Wearing civilian clothes to make sure they did not arouse the suspicions of the local meat porters, Mountbatten, Wernher and the Canadian High Commissioner were driven in an unmarked van from Scotland Yard to Smithfield Market where they were taken underground and shown into Perutz's lair. The balding Austrian scientist led them over to two blocks of ice, one pure, the other Pykrete and produced a hammer. He then asked one of his guests to smash the blocks.

The clearer of the two shattered easily enough. That was ice. Yet when the hammer struck the Pykrete it pinged off the icy compound and fell to the floor.

Seeing is believing, and for many this demonstration was an epiphany. Not so Sir Harold Wernher, however – indeed, he was so determined to prove the material's inherent weakness that he took out his pistol and fired at the block of Pykrete. Still it did not shatter. As Perutz's Commandos had recently discovered, a bullet fired from a rifle into a Pykrete block one foot thick merely formed 'a little crater and was embedded without doing any damage'. Ironically, given his reasons for producing the gun, the effect of Wernher's bullet was only to harden the faith of those in the room. The Canadian High Commissioner, Vincent Massey, now called for construction on the first berg-ship to start immediately. Mountbatten agreed, but understood that for this to happen the project needed another push from up on high. He filled a thermos with one of Perutz's samples and set off for Chequers.

There was a large party staying that weekend, with guests ranging from the Duke and Duchess of Marlborough to 'Bomber' Harris and the Turkish Ambassador. When Mountbatten arrived, shortly before dinner, he was told that the Prime Minister was in the bath.

'Good, that's exactly where I want him to be,' he replied, before bounding up the stairs into Churchill's room. He called through to the bathroom: 'I have a block of a new material which I would like to put in your bath.'

It is unclear whether Churchill was still in the bath when Mountbatten strode into the room. Either way, the CCO went over to the tub and launched a block of Pykrete into the warm water. Apparently Churchill complained that this would make the bath cold, which suggests that he was either already soaking himself or planned to be doing so very soon. Perhaps this is the image we want, that of Churchill in his bath, face full of wonder as a miniature version of Pyke's artificial iceberg bobs about between his legs. In the bath or out of it, on the weekend of 18 March 1943 the Prime Minister saw for himself the magical sight of Pykrete afloat in warm water.

'I must tell you about our wonderful new plan,' he had told the US President in Casablanca earlier that year. Admiral King, the Commander-in-Chief of the American fleet, also heard of the scheme while in Morocco, and said that if Habbakuk was feasible it would 'win the war at one blow'. Now that he had seen Pykrete for himself, Churchill was more determined than ever to bring this extraordinary scheme to fruition. It would become something of an obsession.

That month he and his Minister of War Production, Oliver Lyttelton, were shown a cross-section of a proposed berg-ship. They were 'both enthusiastic and anxious to know the approximate earliest date [by which the] first ship [was] likely to be complete'. Thousands of miles away, on a frozen lake in Canada, the author of this scheme was trying to find out.

Soon after the decisive Habbakuk meeting at which Mountbatten had clashed with Cherwell, both Bernal and Zuckerman had set out for North Africa to investigate why the RAF had failed to inflict greater damage on Rommel's retreating Afrika Korps. This was 'operational research', the marriage of scientific analysis and military practice which Bernal had been calling for since 1939. He was in his element. But almost as soon as they landed in Cairo, Bernal was handed a telegram calling him away from his work.

Mountbatten knew all too well what had happened the last time Pyke had gone to North America on a secret military project. He had also come to believe that Habbakuk might be 'the most important single idea of this war', and at the last minute had decided that Bernal must join Pyke in Canada. It was a canny move: Pyke listened to Bernal, who was also far more sensitive in his dealings with others.

Yet Bernal turned a blind eye to this telegram and instead accompanied Zuckerman to Tripoli. They spent the next week inspecting RAF bomb craters, and their work was going well until the night when Bernal sat down with Zuckerman to announce that he was leaving.

'He had been just as nervous about telling me as he always was when making a break with one of the many women who used to fall in love with him,' fumed Zuckerman. 'I was appalled at the thought of being left alone, with the responsibility of carrying out not only the enquiries for which I had become trained, but also those that he would have done. I spent hours that evening, pleading with him by candlelight – there was no electricity in the hotel – not to go, saying that *Habbakuk* was nonsense'.

Zuckerman accused Bernal of being an emotional and scientific dilettante who was incapable of commitment. The same thing would happen with Habbakuk, he warned. Bernal would give himself to it until the situation became more serious, when he would run away. 'Des became more and more silent as, in desperation, I added accusation to accusation. But all to no avail.' Bernal had been asked to decide between Canada and Libya, experimentation and analysis, Pyke and Zuckerman. He had chosen the former in each case. Zuckerman would never forgive him. 'Habbakuk, or rather Pyke, proved the beginning of the parting of the ways for Bernal and me.'

From a khaki tent in the Libyan desert Des Bernal was driven to Cairo where he took a plane to Accra and spent the night in a stable with a shipwrecked sailor. On Ascension Island he swam off a bone-white beach in shark-infested waters and by night drank whisky with American servicemen. There followed a forced landing in the Amazonian forests of British Guiana, a cricket match in Trinidad, and lunch with his old friend Professor Mark in sub-zero New York. Here he found Pyke, who had also found crossing the Atlantic harder than expected, and the next day the two friends flew north to Ottawa.

Jack Mackenzie, the Canadian civil engineer, was unsure what to make of them. 'Bernal and Pyke are a queer-looking team,' he tried, describing Pyke as 'a most unusual type', adding 'most people think he is absolutely mad. He is not mad. He thinks in a most unorthodox way.' Mackenzie enjoyed Pyke's account of getting into and out of Germany, calling him 'a bit of a psychological expert' whose 'advice on commando tactics is very useful'. But he could not understand his wardrobe. 'He lands in this country without any gloves and with only a light raincoat to embark upon a trip into the Arctic weather.' Not to be outdone, Bernal was apparently 'dressed like a tramp' in 'a little pair of corduroy trousers with a belt halfway down from the waist, and a blue and green shirt like a lumberman's'.

Mackenzie was to escort the British mission, two-thirds of Mountbatten's Department of Wild Talents, out to the experimental sites in western Canada, a job he found initially exhausting. 'Travelling with Pyke is like travelling with a small child', he complained, for he 'can never find anything [. . .] He just goes through his pockets and the most unusual things come out – memos, tickets, dollar bills, etc.' It came as no surprise on the train out of Ottawa that Pyke had lost his ticket. Mackenzie had to buy him a new one, muttering to his diary, 'I am still perfectly sure that his ticket to Jasper will turn up some day.'

The mood changed once they arrived at the first of the Habbakuk experiments. Over the next few days, covering vast distances in between, the three men witnessed tests into how Pykrete bonded with pure ice, the rates at which mixtures of water and wood pulp could be frozen, and the extent to which Pykrete displayed plastic flow or 'creep'. Everything was progressing at remarkable speed, as it needed to.

It had taken sixty years of scientific tests and experiments to establish beyond doubt the fundamental properties of concrete. The Habbakuk project demanded an equivalent understanding of Pykrete in less than a year and for this knowledge to be incorporated into the design of the world's largest ship. This was research and construction on an almost Soviet scale, which was perhaps why it appealed so much to Bernal and Pyke. It was daunting, certainly, a project of brazen ambition, but from what they had seen so far it might just be possible, a belief that was only strengthened by what they saw next.

Over the past few weeks the frozen surface of Patricia Lake had become an outdoor factory. On this picturesque lake in Jasper National Park labourers were now working round the clock on a scaled-down model of the Habbakuk berg-ship. They had begun by laying out a wooden floor on the ice in the shape of a vessel sixty feet long and thirty feet wide. While this was not the 1:10 model requested by the British Admiralty (it would have needed to be 140 feet longer for that) it would at least answer the question of whether a self-refrigerating berg-ship made from ice was at all practicable.

Once the floor had been laid out it was sealed with pitch before work began on the walls. Tinsmiths installed a web of refrigerating ducts sandwiched between blocks of ice, which would stop the ship from melting in warmer waters. Originally brine coolant was to be pumped through the ducts, but some of these had been damaged en route to the site so cold air was pumped through instead. With the ducts sealed in place, just days before the arrival of Pyke, Bernal and Mackenzie, the outer blocks of ice were moved into position.

It was a thrilling sight. The icy vision which had come to Pyke in the pummelling heat of Washington DC in the summer was materialising fast, and the construction proved to be rapid and intuitive. 'They are working in the most primitive way using wheel-barrows, etc.,' Bernal reported to London, adding that a 1,000 ton model would probably take no more than fourteen days to build, confirming Pyke's assertion that unskilled labourers with little specialist equipment could make these vessels in very little time.

Perhaps the only danger was that some of the labourers might learn that they were building the model of a ship designed to carry bombers and other weapons of war. When the nature of this project, known to them at the time as 'Noah's Ark', was revealed many years later at least one of these pacifist Mennonites and Doukhobors felt that 'his principles had been violated in the name of science'. But security was tight and it remained a secret. That same pacifist remembered the day when the site was visited by two Englishmen including one with a goatee beard, thin coat and pork-pie hat who apparently inspired among the labourers a lot of 'humorous talk'.

On 8 March 1943, the day after they had inspected the model at Patricia Lake, Mackenzie and the two-man British mission arrived at Lake Louise in Banff National Park, a place of astounding natural beauty. Valley walls slid into the water at graceful intervals while, beyond, a majestic vista swept off into a blueish distance. Yet when Pyke and Bernal arrived the tranquillity was shattered repeatedly by the sound of enormous explosions. A team of scientists and labourers was busy blowing up sections of ice and Pykrete to see how the berg-ships would respond to enemy fire. As before, progress was better than expected. 'The Lake Louise outfit has done a remarkably good job,' concluded Mackenzie. 'Very valuable information has been obtained.'

Work on Habbakuk at Lake Louise

Further work on Habbakuk at Lake Louise

Their work had been done and the three men were due to return to Ottawa, when Mackenzie noticed that the two British boffins had begun to gaze longingly at the snow-covered mountains around the lake.

'Hope I live long enough to ski once again,' Pyke had written the year before. On that morning both he and Bernal decided that they would go to see the nearby glacier.

Mackenzie, as ever, could not understand what they were wearing. 'At ten o'clock they got on their skis and their spats and started for Victoria glacier without a watch or any method of knowing what time it was,' he wrote, before describing Pyke's get-up as 'the most grotesque outfit – a little hat on top of his head with his muffler and raincoat and a pair of spats'.

Later it seemed as though this lack of suitable clothing had been his undoing. Bernal had reappeared two hours later by himself. 'We thought probably Pyke had collapsed as he had not been feeling very well. However, Bernal said the only reason Pyke was not there was that he could not get him to come back. He was going on for another hour and should be back about two. Actually he showed up just at train time and looking very fit.'

It turned out that Pyke was an 'excellent mountaineer' – one of the last things you would expect of a bookish forty-nine-year-old who was often so ill that he could not get out of bed. It suggests that his illness was periodic and did not make him generally infirm. On the train back from Lake Louise, Pyke reminisced to Mackenzie about skiing in Switzerland during the 1920s, in the days before his bankruptcy, and the occasion when he had rescued a party of stranded skiers by skiing down a mountainside during a snowstorm. Were it not for those skiing holidays, paid for with the profits from his speculation, Pyke's interest in snow and ice might never have taken hold. Now he was caught up in another life, a more impoverished life, and yet one that could include the sight of hundreds of men labouring in the freezing cold to realise one of his contributions to the war against fascism.

On their return to Ottawa, Bernal sent an effusive telegram to London describing the 'great energy and enthusiasm' everywhere they had been, and how 'on a number of occasions work on the Habbakuk experiments had continued all night'. No major obstacles had been encountered, excellent progress had been made. They had also learnt that blocks of Pykrete were essentially self-adhesive: you had only to place them next to each other at suitably cold temperatures for bonds to develop, a discovery which might save thousands of man-hours when building the full-scale vessels.

The only problem was the unknown nature of 'creep'. Creep was the rate at which Pykrete, or any other material, changed shape – and the extent of that change – when exposed to consistent pressure. With little or no research into the rates of creep in pure ice, let alone Pykrete, this was one of several questions that required Habbakuk scientists to steer out into uncharted waters. While it was possible to estimate the compressive, tensile and flexural strength of both pure ice and Pykrete, the rate of creep would take much longer to understand as one needed to measure the effect of sustained pressure over a matter of weeks. While it might be possible to build an enormous berg-ship, until the issue of creep had been resolved there was a danger that this leviathan might start to sag under its own weight once it had put out to sea. This was a problem, but Pyke saw no reason to think that it might be insoluble.

In London the mood was becoming impatient. By late March 1943 the Battle of the Atlantic was going so badly that some in the Admiralty had proposed abandoning convoys altogether. The Canadian High Commissioner asked Mountbatten to draw up a shortlist of possible sites for the construction of the first full-scale berg-ship. His concern was that this ship would not be finished by the end of that year 'unless the necessary organisation is set up at once and proceeds to act in every way as if success were assured'. He was calling for a mental adjustment. 'If a thing is sufficiently badly needed, the risk of failure due to incomplete knowledge can well be taken.' Even if Habbakuk might prove to be impossible, 'the attempt would have been worth the cost'.

Mountbatten showed this note to Churchill, who cabled the Canadian Prime Minister the following day. 'I am very much interested in the project called Habbakuk,' Churchill reminded him, 'and am most anxious to have your vehement support. The Chief of Combined Operations is arranging to send Mr Pyke and Professor Bernal to you to tell the whole story. This is for you alone as the utmost secrecy is indispensable.'

On the same day, Churchill wrote to his Chiefs of Staff with news of the progress from Canada and his wish that an order for the first berg-ship be placed 'with the highest priority and for arrangements to be made for further ships to be built without delay should it appear that the scheme is certain of success.' Towards the end of a month in which more than 100 Allied ships were lost, the Chiefs of Staff duly instructed the Admiralty to 'initiate action in accordance with the Prime Minister's instructions'.

Admiral Sir Charles Kennedy-Purvis, the Deputy First Sea Lord, then met his Director of Plans to discuss Habbakuk. Until then the Admiralty had been lukewarm on the scheme, yet in light of the initial reports from Canada their position changed. On 27 March, Kennedy-Purvis agreed that 'fundamentally, Habbakuk is practical politics', and that three berg-ships might be ready in little over a year, each expected to cost about the same as a standard destroyer. With the Admiralty apparently behind the scheme, one of the last obstacles to Habbakuk's development had been removed.

The following day Jack Mackenzie had dinner in Ottawa with Pyke and Bernal, who were to tell the Canadian Prime Minister 'the whole story', as per Churchill's telegram, and on 29 March they went to meet him.

'Mr Chamberlain has sent me such a nice letter about you,' began the Prime Minister. It is not clear whether he realised his gaffe, only that the next awkward remark in that meeting came from Pyke. He drew the Prime Minister's attention to his own trouser fly. It was open. In an attempt to smarten up for this meeting Pyke had bought a new suit the day before which came with the latest advance in fly design – a zip. Perhaps feeling anxious before the meeting, Pyke had popped into the nearest restroom only for his fly to become stuck (apparently this was not the first time that something like this had happened to him). The root of the problem, he explained to the Prime Minister, was shoddy Canadian engineering.

In spite of this, the meeting was thought to have gone well. The Canadian government formally agreed to take responsibility for the construction of the first Habbakuk berg-ship and for further research related to Pykrete. Their only conditions were that the British Admiralty should supply naval architects and that Pyke and Bernal should remain attached to the project. These terms were readily accepted, and the Canadian War Committee approved the expenditure of an initial $1 million on a full-scale berg-ship (roughly £6 million in today's money) with Mackenzie in charge.

Mackenzie approached the Montreal Engineering Company, which agreed to carry out the work at no cost beyond their expenses, and during the weeks that followed, in April 1943, work on Habbakuk accelerated. Communications zinged back and forth between London, Cambridge, Ottawa and the five research stations in Western Canada about how much steel and pulp would be required, where to source it, how this would affect costs, the ideal distance between refrigerating ducts in the walls of Pykrete, the size of the bulkheads and how to improve the ship's manoeuvrability. A mechanical spreader was designed to speed up the manufacture of Pykrete in industrial quantities. Explosives tests continued in Canada. Perutz worked out the ideal ratio of wood pulp to water. At Patricia Lake the finished model was cut away from the ice and showed no signs of melting. Potential construction sites were whittled down to one in Newfoundland and another on the St Lawrence River, and it was agreed that the stern and bow of the ship must be made from wood. Spaced out along each side of the vessel would be twenty-six enormous propeller units. While Pyke had argued that these obviated the need for a rudder – to steer the ship one could vary the propulsive strength on either side – the Admiralty insisted on having one. It was also during April 1943 that Max Perutz tackled the problem of creep.

Pykrete was robust in response to a sudden application of pressure, like the impact of a hammer or bullet, but when compressive force was applied over a long period it had a tendency to sag. Although the rate of creep was less pronounced in Pykrete than in ice – and after the first two weeks it tended to stabilise – a solution was needed. Perutz consulted Sir Lawrence Bragg at Cambridge, took a well-earned break and at last solved the problem. He discovered that at temperatures below freezing Pykrete's rate of creep was greatly reduced. He concluded on 4 May that 'at -15°C. creep will be no obstacle to the safety of the vessel'. This temperature was easily achieved in refrigeration boats, and there was no reason to think that the hull of the proposed berg-ship could not be cooled to the same extent. This was a critical advance, but not one that Pyke and Bernal were able to enjoy for long.

The day after Perutz announced his solution to the problem of creep, the Admiralty received a preliminary report on the viability of Habbakuk from two naval architects. Churchill's instruction had been to place an order for the first berg-ship *should it appear that the scheme is certain of success*. Rather than wait to hear the answer from Canada, the Admiralty had sent out two of its own men to investigate. Mountbatten would have objected, had he known, but he was on sick leave for the first time since taking over Combined Operations. 'During the illness of CCO I require weekly reports on "Habbakuk",' Churchill had informed his Chiefs of Staff. However, nothing was sent to Downing Street which mentioned the Admiralty's decision to carry out its own study.

The two naval architects concluded that 'it will be impossible to complete the project next year', before going beyond their engineering brief to suggest that the project would also be over-budget. Pyke and Bernal were furious. They protested to Mountbatten that this conclusion 'has in our opinion and as almost admitted by them, been arrived at by means of feeling [. . .] rather than by QUANTITATIVE investigations'. The risk of failure in Habbakuk was no more than was 'customary in sound commercial engineering enterprises'.

The clash here was between two different engineering philosophies. The Admiralty wanted to follow the proven peacetime method of starting with research before moving on to design and finally construction. Pyke and Bernal called for all three stages to run in parallel, 'to design without an exact knowledge of the properties of the material and to plan construction without a detailed design'. Owing to the pressure of time, and the lives this new invention could save, 'the procedure for tackling this job successfully will have to be different from anything that has been undertaken before'.

They dispatched the telegram and set out for London, urging Mountbatten not to make any Habbakuk decisions until they were back. There followed a 'nightmare journey' across the Atlantic 'in an unheated bomb bay' in the company of the British film-maker and secret agent Sir Alexander Korda. On arrival, Bernal was asked by a reporter from the *Evening Standard* what he had been up to in North America. 'I wish I could tell you,' he replied, 'but I can't.'

What he might have said was that he had been working on the strangest and most ambitious idea of the war, one which appeared to have been delayed by a critical Admiralty report, and was now back in London to fire up his boss, Lord Louis Mountbatten. On the day of their return Pyke and Bernal had lunch with the CCO – only to be joined by an uninvited guest, Evelyn Waugh, then a Liaison Officer to Combined Operations, who 'arrived rather tipsy' and by his own admission 'behaved rather badly'. Waugh noted that, with Pyke and Bernal back in the office, Richmond Terrace was once again 'a nest of Communists'. Yet over the weeks that followed Mountbatten's faith in the project was renewed. Pyke and Bernal, working now as a team, wrote a detailed rebuttal of the report from the Admiralty. But they could not undo all the damage that it had done.

In a meeting of the Habbakuk Standing Committee on 3 June it was agreed that the project was still feasible, but there was a new note of caution in the projected timings. It was no longer thought that a berg-ship could be ready by the end of that coming winter. There was, at least, full agreement on the strategic need for these vessels, particularly in the Pacific, and the importance of getting

American planners involved. Habbakuk had regained some of its drive. But for Churchill the progress was still too sluggish.

'Well, Lord Louis, what is the situation?' the Prime Minister had asked at the start of a meeting in Downing Street called to discuss Habbakuk. Cherwell was on his right. Elsewhere in the room were Mountbatten, Sir Stafford Cripps, Kennedy-Purvis, Bernal and Jack Mackenzie, who described the Prime Minister on that day as 'a little old man in a zippered suit with a big cigar in his mouth. Incidentally he does not smoke – he chews about half a cigar, smokes one inch, throws it away, takes out a gold case and starts the proceeding over again.'

Churchill at 10 Downing Street in his bespoke zippered 'siren' suit

Mountbatten explained that the berg-ships would not be ready that year, at which 'Churchill showed very definite annoyance. He said he did not care whether the equipment would last over a month if he could get it on the coast of Norway. He went on a long dissertation on the value of having Habbakuks which was all very sound. He said it was impossible to invade Europe without a fighter cover, that where a fighter cover was now possible the defences were impregnable, that if he had Habbakuks he could get into Norway and the Bay of Biscay, etc., all of which we knew.' Mountbatten 'danced around' and agreed that Combined Operations should draw up a report on the idea of building modified Habbakuks from wood which would not be designed to last for long. Churchill also wanted a report on whether these Habbakuk berg-ships could be used as part of his Jupiter plan for attacking northern Norway.

It fell to Pyke to produce this report, a task he did not appreciate. He continued to believe that the idea of occupying northern Norway was *fundamentally fallacious* [. . .] I trust I may not appear critical of the authors of the Jupiter Memoranda. To a layman these appear a most competent solution of a problem. But it is the wrong problem.'

Days later, just after the start of the Allied invasion of Sicily, Churchill returned to the idea of using Habbakuks in an invasion of Norway. He told his Chiefs of Staff that if a cross-Channel invasion of northern France was impossible for May 1944 'then Operation Jupiter must be in place, and that for this "HABBAKUK" would be an invaluable aid, and it would seem prudent in view of all the uncertainties ahead to make the wooden "HABBAKUK" at a cost of £2 millions now.'

That was not the end of it. The Prime Minister had suggested at the recent Trident Conference in Washington DC, on the question of invading Japan, that '"HABBAKUK" in one of its ice forms might play a very important part'. Churchill would not let go of this idea and asked for his last note on Habbakuk to be passed on to the Deputy Prime Minister and the Foreign Secretary. General Ismay assured him that answers to his questions would be ready in time for the Quadrant Conference, in Quebec, where Habbakuk would be officially presented to the Americans for the first time.

In early August 1943, the *Queen Mary* set out for Quebec carrying a precious cargo: Churchill, Mountbatten, various British Chiefs of Staff, several Cabinet ministers and more than 200 military officials. The fact that this journey could even be contemplated was a sign of just how much had changed in the Battle of the Atlantic.

Over the past twelve months a raft of small improvements in Allied weaponry and tactics had tipped the balance in this theatre of war. Aircraft could now travel further and some were equipped with Leigh Lights, connected to centimetric radar. Escort ships had become more numerous and better equipped, with HF-DF masts and 'Hedgehogs' to launch depth charges fore and aft. A growing number of Bogue-class escort carriers allowed for greater aerial cover, while new anti-submarine tactics devised by the likes of Captain 'Johnnie' Walker, an expert U-boat hunter, were helping to turn the tide. Bletchley Park had gained the upper hand over B-Dienst, its German equivalent, giving the Allies better intelligence on the location, size and direction of U-boat wolf packs. No less significant was the recent renewal of a treaty between Britain and neutral Portugal which allowed the British to operate an airbase in the Azores, an archipelago in the heart of the Atlantic. In exchange, the Portuguese government received six squadrons of Hawker Hurricanes. Britain had effectively gained possession of a large and unsinkable aircraft carrier in a key strategic location, so perhaps they no longer needed one made out of ice.

This string of small victories – diplomatic, tactical, technical and industrial – had combined to change the complexion of the Battle of the Atlantic, and by September 1943 Allied shipping losses were ten times fewer than during the same month the year before. Indeed, by the end of the year Admiral Karl Dönitz, Grand Admiral of the German Navy, ordered all German U-Boats away from the North Atlantic. All this meant that Habbakuk was no longer needed to win the Battle of the Atlantic. Instead it had been given a new purpose.

During the early stages of the Quebec conference there were detailed discussions about Operation Overlord and a nuclear agreement was signed. Yet on several issues the British and American delegations found themselves far apart. Tempers were getting short, as they had done in a meeting of the Combined Chiefs of Staff on 19 August. Field Marshal Brooke suggested that the sixty or so junior staff officers present be asked to leave the room so that the senior Allied commanders could speak off the record.

This seemed to work, and the discussion became smoother. Mountbatten then went up to Brooke to remind him that he had promised to allow him to introduce Habbakuk. Brooke duly gave him the floor.

'Dickie now having been let loose gave a signal, whereupon a string of attendants brought in large cubes of ice which were established at the end of the room,' wrote Brooke. 'Dickie then proceeded to explain that the cube on the left was ordinary pure ice, whereas that on the right contained many ingredients which made it far more resilient, less liable to splinter, and consequently a far more suitable material for the construction of aircraft carriers.'

Churchill also recorded the scene: 'He invited the strongest man present to chop each block of ice in half with a special chopper he had brought. All present voted General Arnold into the job of "strong man".

General Henry H. Arnold

'He took off his coat, rolled up his sleeves [in another account Arnold spat on his hands], and swung the chopper, splitting the ordinary ice with one blow. He turned round, smiling, and clasping his hands, seized the chopper again and advanced upon the block of

Pykrete. He swung the chopper, and as he brought it down let go with a cry of pain, for the Pykrete had suffered little damage and his elbows had been badly jarred. Mountbatten then capped matters by drawing a pistol from his pocket to demonstrate the strength of Pykrete against gunfire.'

Brooke recalled that once Mountbatten had produced his pistol 'we all rose and discreetly moved behind him. He then warned us that he would fire at the ordinary block of ice to show how it splintered [. . .]. He proceeded to fire and we were subjected to a hail of ice splinters! "There," said Dickie, "that is just what I told you; now I shall fire at the block on the right to show you the difference." He fired, and there certainly was a difference.' Rather than become embedded in the Pykrete the bullet ricocheted off.

Accounts differ as to precisely what happened next. In Churchill's version of events the bullet narrowly missed Air Chief Marshal Sir Charles Portal. In another it nicked Admiral King. One has the bullet landing in Mountbatten's stomach, elsewhere it takes a lump of plaster off the wall. Another account has General Hollis diving for cover under a table, where he 'collided, skull to skull, with [Field Marshal] Alan Brooke, approaching from the opposite direction'.

'Dickie, for God's sake, stop firing that thing!' cried Brooke.

'The waiting officers outside,' Churchill went on, 'who had been worried enough by the sound of blows and the scream of pain from General Arnold, were horrified at the revolver shots, one of them crying out, "My God! They've now started shooting."'

Calm was soon restored. Thankfully Pykrete had not been responsible for the death or injury of any senior Allied commanders. Instead this incident seemed to enliven the mood and there followed a constructive discussion of Habbakuk. Though the original purpose of Pyke's ships had been to win the Battle of the Atlantic, in Quebec they were presented to the Americans as offensive vessels which were cheap and unsinkable and could be used in operations against Japan and occupied Europe. The consensus was that if further experiments could show that these berg-ships were both practical and cheap then they should be built without delay.

By the end of the conference the British Chiefs of Staff had agreed to construct two of the smaller berg-ships for use in the Pacific theatre and to continue experiments on a larger vessel. It was also decided that the Habbakuk project would become an Anglo-American-Canadian venture and that the London team of Habbakuk engineers and scientists should be flown over to Washington DC.

Mountbatten also introduced two other proposals from his 'lunatic asylum' on Richmond Terrace: the concept of a floating harbour which could be towed to northern France on D-Day; and the idea of laying an oil pipeline underneath the Channel to supply the Allied forces. Better known as Mulberry and PLUTO, they would become two of the best-known inventions of the war. And yet, of the three ideas from Combined Operations, Habbakuk was seen by many of those in Quebec to be the most realistic prospect.

None had been quite so gripped by these ideas as Churchill, who now began to suggest building Mulberry floating harbours out of Pykrete. Pyke, Perutz and others would soon draw up plans for D-Day landing stages and breakwaters constructed from Pykrete, code-named Gog and Magog, as well as small non-propelled vessels made from Pykrete to be known as Monitors.

At last it seemed that Pykrete's potential as a cheap, buoyant and revolutionary material had been recognised. Almost a year after Pyke's proposal had first arrived on Mountbatten's desk,

Habbakuk, or at least the basic concept behind it, was set to play a major part in the closing stages of the war. That was the good news from Quebec. The bad news took a little longer to reach London.

HOW TO SURVIVE

By the time he boarded the *Queen Mary*, before it set sail for Quebec, Mountbatten had become restless. He longed for another naval command and over the next five days, as the ship zigzagged across the Atlantic, he tried to corner the First Sea Lord, Sir Dudley Pound. 'I followed him like a shadow, pacing the decks for exercise, or up on the bridge. He always seemed to be talking to someone. It never occurred to me that he might be avoiding me. Then one day I did catch Pound alone. "I've finished my work at Combined Operations," I said, "and I think it's about time I went back to sea." He did not seem to take any interest at all.' This was because he knew what was in store for Mountbatten.

Soon after this encounter Churchill told the CCO that he was to become Supreme Allied Commander, South-East Asia. His appointment would begin in less than two months. Not only was Mountbatten to be denied his naval command, but Habbakuk was set to lose its most energetic advocate.

Although Admiral King had been impressed by the Habbakuk idea when he had heard about it earlier that year, now that it was to be developed jointly by the US, Canada and Britain he wanted a detailed assessment and asked a team of US naval engineers to go over the project in detail. This was when things began to fall apart.

They objected to the lumbering speed of these berg-ships as well as the amount of steel required to build them, given that large refrigeration plants would need to be constructed to produce the Pykrete. Beneath these concerns lay a more stubborn and irrational reluctance. The naval engineers disliked the idea of building an aircraft carrier out of ice. Often the greatest challenge faced by an innovator is not the conception of a new idea but, rather, persuading others to overcome their often automatic preference for the status quo. Another problem was Pyke.

Jack Mackenzie, now directing the multinational Habbakuk project, knew that Pyke's reputation in America after Plough was so noxious that he must be kept away. Mountbatten was given the unfortunate task of telling his Director of Programmes not to come out to Washington DC, adding that he had 'consulted Bernal who entirely agrees'. 'We are both so sorry.' The idea of Bernal and Mountbatten combining like this to keep him away from Habbakuk flattened Pyke. Indeed, his relationship with Bernal would never recover.

In spite of Mackenzie's best efforts, Pyke's original connection to Habbakuk soon became known and, as he had feared, it did nothing to endear the project to the Americans. Even Vannevar Bush, the head of OSRD, heard about Pyke's involvement and later told Roosevelt, when asked for his opinion of Habbakuk, 'I think it is the bunk.' In his memoirs he also described the moment when the two men behind the scheme came to him for help.

'Mountbatten and Pyke walked into my office,' he began. 'They had evidently just come from the White House, there was no presentation of a proposal, no request that OSRD should study one and advise on it. Rather, Pyke told me the plan was approved and just what OSRD was now to do about it. [. . .] Mountbatten looked embarrassed but not nearly enough so. I listened. Then I told Pyke, no doubt with some emphasis, that I took orders from the President of the United States and from no one else, and that ended the interview.'

One of the most interesting features of this conversation is that it never took place. At no point during the development of Habbakuk were Pyke, Mountbatten and Bush in the same country. Bush had contrived to imagine this encounter, and as a pure fantasy it is revealing. The emphasis on taking orders from the American President, rather than these interloping Englishmen, is telling. It is a reminder of the resentment that some Americans felt towards the idea of being told to work on a British idea like Habbakuk.

Another reason why Pyke's involvement in the project was so troublesome was that he continued to be seen as a security risk, thanks to the cartoon character Superman. In late March 1943 an exciting new plot-line had emerged in the Superman daily cartoon strip, then syndicated to newspapers throughout North America and read by millions. Just as the Habbakuk prototype neared completion, the Man of Steel encountered a strange-looking iceberg.

Superman ™ and © DC Comics, 29 March 1943

The following day the attack began.

Superman ™ and © DC Comics, 30 March 1943

Luckily Superman was on hand to put an end to these 'fiendishly clever' 'floating fortresses'.

Superman ™ and © DC Comics, 31 March 1943

The similiarity between these floating fortresses and Habbakuk was astonishing. One of the Canadian engineers working on Habbakuk saw the cartoons and immediately sent copies to Jack Mackenzie. The chances of this being coincidence seemed to be infinitesimal. Earlier that year Pyke had been in New York, where those behind the comic strip lived – a detail which did nothing to remove any lingering suspicion about the man responsible for Habbakuk.

Yet it was Bernal who delivered the coup de grace. Admiral King's engineers had given their cautious assessment of the project to the new American-Canadian-British Habbakuk board, after which Bernal was called upon to counter their criticisms. He did no such thing.

'Bernal, who had become so expert in proclaiming the points in favour of Habbakuk, now, with his Jesuitical mind, volunteered to produce all the points against it as well,' explained Mountbatten wearily. 'The criticisms of the project were so powerful that they turned the scales against it.'

It was not that Bernal had lost faith in Habbakuk, but that he had become impatient and wanted to be back in London during the build-up to D-Day. Perhaps Zuckerman was right. Bernal really did find it hard to see a project or relationship through to the very end. News of his performance even reached Churchill who told Mountbatten that, in future, 'you must not bring your Scientific Advisers' to such meetings.

Habbakuk remained 'practical politics', as the Admiralty had put it, but the momentum behind it had evaporated. The projected cost of the scheme, the amount of steel required and the war's adjusted strategic aims all militated against it, and so did the identity of its author. With Mountbatten gone, Pyke excluded and Bernal bored, it had lost three of its most passionate supporters, and by January 1944 the British Admiralty and US Navy had ceased all work in connection with Habbakuk. What might have been the most ambitious ship ever produced by a nation at war, the world's largest vessel, would remain *in utero*. For the moment Pyke did not have time to digest the scale of this defeat – his more immediate concern was surviving at Combined Operations now that his great supporter had left.

In the weeks after Mountbatten's departure, Pyke circulated papers around Richmond Terrace on seemingly everything from the ideal width of a typescript through to the need for a handbook of '*ruses de guerre*' culled from history and literature. 'If professional historians were too busy, school-boys should be invited to undertake the task and thus to play, intellectually, a real and early part in the war by remedying the omission of their elders.' He proposed having an actor dress up as Hitler to trick German units into withdrawing from small Mediterranean islands. He submitted plans for gravity-propelled ball-bombs to be rolled down beaches onto coastal defence walls. He sketched out plans for different vessels made from Pykrete. He returned to the 'Trojan Horse' idea of tunnelling through glaciers. But the idea into which he devoted most of his energy in this frenzied post-Habbakuk period was reserved for Mountbatten in his new role as Supreme Allied Commander, South-East Asia.

Pyke understood that one of the great problems that Mountbatten now faced was moving men and materials either from ships to the shore or across paddy fields and through dense jungle. He proposed large-bore pipes through which cylinders could be pumped containing either supplies or troops, with each soldier breathing from a hand-held oxygen canister as his cylinder was shot down the tube. These pipelines could run from warships to islands or across inhospitable terrain, and would be called Power-Driven Rivers, as he explained in the 50-page proposal he sent to Mountbatten in India. 'Like Plough, but unlike Habbakuk, it is both new and orthodox,' he went on. 'So orthodox and obvious that everyone will say "Poof, I could have thought of that" and from that they'll slide into saying they did think of it (almost), and start on the reasons why nothing should be done about it.'

But Power-Driven Rivers was not in the same league as his two earlier schemes, and Mountbatten was 'perhaps not so obviously enchanted with the idea as he was with Plough and Habbakuk', as Wildman-Lushington delicately put it. It was also turned down by the British Chiefs of Staff, following a presentation by Pyke and Bernal. But it was Mountbatten's rejection which had stung the most.

Pyke struggled to reconcile himself to not being invited out to South-East Asia, especially after learning that both Bernal and

Zuckerman had been asked to go. His letters lost their verve. 'Dear Mountbatten,' began one, 'Do the old terms still apply?'

His former boss had not lost faith in Pyke or his abilities, and in the coming months he wrote to Sir Charles Lambe, Director of Plans at the Admiralty, describing Pyke as a man possessing 'a brain twenty or thirty years in advance of any scientist's and one that is particularly suitable for planning'. He urged Lambe to keep Pyke 'in fullest touch with the various plans in my own field of operations, to be able to see the relevant papers and intelligence, and to communicate to me directly, any suggestions he may have to make on this and other subjects'. But he did not want Pyke to join his South-East Asian Command.

The truth was that Mountbatten had by then received far too much criticism for his decision to recruit Pyke in the first place. As Wildman-Lushington reminded his boss, firmly, 'I do not think you want him out here.' The issue had nothing to do with Pyke's irreverence or moments of eccentricity but with his inability to work easily in a group. Pyke's emotional fragility and heightened sensitivity to being sidelined appeared to make this impossible. When he felt himself being marginalised he had a tendency to self-destruct, and would either cast around for a scapegoat or become difficult and behave, as one colleague put it, like an 'awkward cuss'.

A typical example was his reaction to the news that he was not to attend a key Habbakuk meeting at Downing Street shortly before the Quebec conference. Pyke had rounded on the officer he felt was responsible, the news of which soon reached Mountbatten. 'I share with Professor Bernal the highest possible opinion of your brain,' he told him, 'and have often wondered that a man of such outstanding intellect should be unable to guide his everyday life in such a manner as to avoid friction for himself and all his supporters.'

Pyke's reply came in the form of a mocked-up 'Obituary Notice of Lord Louis Mountbatten', dated to 2001, in the British Socialist

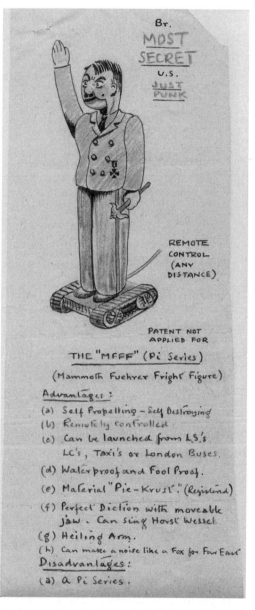

A sketch passed around Combined Operations in 1943,
probably drawn by Sandy Wedderburn (note the sole
disadvantage, 'Pi' being shorthand for 'Pyke')

Republic of the USSR (which he imagined coming about after a Communist uprising in 1949–50). It contained a long and playfully absurd confession from 'our beloved Comrade and Commissar – habitually so calm, so benign, so dialectical' – Mountbatten. 'I had belonged to a set within a caste within a class which lacked the experience of frustration,' Pyke has him say. 'We had only to see to desire, and had only to desire to obtain or to do. Sensations poured down the gullet of experience, and yet left the whole body thirsty and exhausted.' There followed a detailed critique of the way Mountbatten ran Combined Operations, in which Pyke called him decisive without being reflective. 'You are too arrogant to refuse to apologise . . . You are the living dialectical reverse of Bluntschli in "Arms and the Man": and the Chocolate Soldier: – you *always* apologise. It is part of your technique.' Nor was he 'sufficiently hard-boiled'. At one point Pyke imagined Mountbatten describing himself as having 'something of the innocent in me. [. . .] My technical advisers even referred to me, among themselves, as Peter Pan. They were right. It was a Peter Pan age. One of the most vital accusations against the Capitalist system is that under it, it was for everybody so very, very difficult to become truly adult.' This was the sort of letter you might write in the heat of the moment but never send. Pyke, of course, sent it. He had to, such was the power of his self-destructive impulse in moments like this.

To his credit, Mountbatten took this obituary notice well and later joked with Pyke about it. He was certainly used to these epistolary outbursts. As Pyke reassured him: 'I have always been, as I think you know, one of your, I hope, most discerning critics, and at the same time one of your greatest admirers.' But it is hard to imagine an episode like this doing anything to improve Pyke's chances of being invited out to India.

★

Though Mountbatten left Combined Operations in October 1943, Pyke managed to hang on for more than a year in Richmond Terrace. Soon after D-Day he was told by the Admiralty, on whose books he had been since they had assumed responsibility for Habbakuk, that his pay would be halved. Pyke protested to the Association of Scientific Workers, and to Bernal, Amery and Mountbatten – to whom he was, as usual, at his liveliest. 'Though – damn it – I *want* to work on war problems, and think I still have something to contribute, I am not accepting a reduction in salary for two reasons: private and public. One, that over the last 30 years I have given away to public causes three inheritances and also what I have made [. . .], in all, a considerable packet. For health and other reasons I have now got to bother about my future. (The right time to bother about one's future is, of course, when one has no future to bother about.)' Yet Mountbatten did not intervene and, because Pyke refused the pay cut, he was now out of a job. Though he stubbornly went in to work each day, in spite of receiving no salary, by the end of 1944 the sentries guarding Combined Operations were instructed not to allow him back into the building. One of the strangest Whitehall appointments of the Second World War had come to an end.

Geoffrey Pyke's career as a civil servant – to add to those as war correspondent, amateur spy, magazine publisher, advertising copy-writer, educationalist, metals-market speculator, pioneering charity worker, pollster, suspected propagandist and military inventor – had been provocative and productive. He was responsible for a glut of ideas including, it seems, one of the inventions most often associated with D-Day.

The traditional story of PLUTO – the oil pipeline laid beneath the English Channel to supply the invading Allied forces – goes roughly as follows: in 1942 Mountbatten was asked to provide a list of items he required for the Normandy landings, and in April of that year he told Geoffrey Lloyd MP, Minister in charge of the Petroleum Warfare Department, that he would like an oil pipeline under the Channel. Several years later this was what he got. But was this idea originally Mountbatten's?

It appears not, based on the fact that Pyke had had precisely the same idea in 1934. 'I put it up to one of the big oil companies [Shell] suggesting not that they should build one straight away, but that they should appoint a small bureau to collect the results of any research which might be relative to its eventual construction and, perhaps, to subsidise and stimulate such research.' Nothing came of it, nor does this prove definitively that Pyke conceived PLUTO. However, given his desire to regale Mountbatten with every passing idea of his, and the amount of time he spent talking to him during and before April 1942 – so much that colleagues tampered with the locks on the CCO's door – it seems more than likely that he would have mentioned the idea to Mountbatten shortly before it was put forward.

Pyke's greatest achievement in Combined Operations, about which there is no question of authorship, was Plough. This scheme led to the formation of the American-Canadian First Special Service Force (FSSF), later described as a 'group of individualists and outcasts [and] probably the best fighting force this continent ever produced'. Mountbatten told Pyke at one point that they had 'become such a vital necessity in the coming stage of the war that General Eisenhower and the C-in-C. Middle East are vying between them to try and obtain the services of this force', later praising Plough as 'probably the most bold and imaginative scheme of this war'.

The FSSF was an elite, maverick unit capable of demolition work, amphibious warfare, mountain warfare and operations on snowy terrain. It first saw action on the Aleutian Islands and more famously in Italy and southern France. In the winter of 1943 the

FSSF broke the German's 'Winter Line' by capturing Monte La Difensa. They were legendary night-fighters, known for operating behind enemy lines with a minimum of equipment. Faces blackened, they would attack using knives and their bare hands and leave 'death stickers' bearing the unit's insignia on the foreheads of their victims – a red spear with the words USA and CANADA entwined – above the legend *DAS DICKE ENDE KOMMT NOCH!* – roughly, 'the worst is still to come'. During one of these night-time operations a diary was found on a dead German officer in which he had written: 'We never hear these black devils when they come.' This provided the unit with its nickname, 'The Devil's Brigade', also the title of the 1968 Hollywood film telling a version of their story.

Even the Weasel, or M-29 Tracked Cargo Carrier, a watered-down version of the snowmobile that Pyke had first envisaged, made workable thanks to his protests, was considered a success. Weasels were used in 1944 to keep the Nijmegen bridgehead open and, when German forces flooded the Ardennes to halt the Allied advance, the first vehicles to get through the German lines were Weasels. Even Vannevar Bush admitted that this machine 'accomplished fine things' and by the end of the war 12,000 had been built with plans for a further 10,000.

Yet one of the most important contributions Pyke made in Combined Operations was the least tangible. On their return from an inspection of the D-Day landings, Churchill, Brooke, Marshall and King had collectively cabled Mountbatten: 'We realise that much of this remarkable technique and therefore the success of the venture has its origins in developments effected by you and your staff of Combined Operations.' They were referring to the ingenious inventions which had come out of Richmond Terrace, such as the Mulberry harbours and PLUTO pipelines. What they may not have known was that most of these innovations were conceived during a surprisingly short period.

The M-29 Weasel in action

'It is true to say that almost every novel idea which was later used in "Operation Overlord" [. . .] originated in COHQ during April 1942', wrote Captain John Hughes-Hallett, Naval Adviser at Combined Operations.

April 1942 was the golden age of Pyke's career in Richmond Terrace. It was the apogee of his efforts to get his colleagues to look at the world upside down, ask pertinent questions, think more about anything which made them laugh and otherwise be imaginatively iconoclastic towards every sacred cow. He became, in some ways, the flintlock in this firing mechanism, constantly solving problems and imparting his principles of radical innovation. Without this, some of those 'novel ideas' which played a part in D-Day might not have come about when they did, or at all.

Though Mountbatten assured Pyke 'that the original thoughts which you have contributed to the Headquarters have been of the utmost value to the war effort' this strand of his work would never lend itself to blue plaques, statues or street names. The history of invention is less interested in those who produce ideas and open the minds of others than the individuals who finish things off. We are not taught in school about Paolo Toscanelli, the mathematician and astrologer who had the idea of sailing across the Atlantic to reach the East Indies, but, rather, the explorer who acted on Toscanelli's letter, Christopher Columbus. Douglas Engelbart was the visionary who came up with the idea of a computer mouse, but the man famous today for turning it into a successful commercial product is Steve Jobs. The victors in the history of innovation are the Columbuses and Jobses, not the Toscanellis, Engelbarts and Pykes. While one can talk about the FSSF, PLUTO and Weasel as palpable results of Pyke's innovation in Combined Operations, it is the invisible fruits of his labour which are so remarkable – the creative atmosphere he encouraged as well as his creation of Habbakuk.

In an alternative world, one in which we celebrate spectacular ideas whether or not they are seen through to completion, where there would be no end of streets, avenues and cul-de-sacs named after Geoffrey Pyke – especially cul-de-sacs – Habbakuk would be seen as his wartime masterpiece. In the real world, its legacy was more troubled. Indeed, Pyke never really came to terms with what he saw as his failure to turn Habbakuk into a military reality and the fact that it had taken him until 1942 to come up with the idea.

HOW TO LIVE

On a dry Spring morning in 1945 a man in Primrose Hill left for work, unaware that he was being followed. His pursuer was used to ghosting after Londoners as they made their way through the raggedy, bomb-scarred streets of the capital, past craters that had become overgrown since the Blitz and the fresher, deeper holes where a V1 or V2 had arrowed recently into the ground. He found it easy to tell if his quarry was familiar with basic counter-surveillance tradecraft. He or she might stop suddenly, forcing him to continue past, or turn back on themselves and otherwise take circuitous routes. The man ahead of him did none of these things. Of course, there was always a chance that this in itself was a small deception.

As the two men continued towards Chalk Farm Tube Station in lonely procession, the pursuer made a mental sketch of his subject. He was taller than average, of medium build and carried a brown leather briefcase. He had several newspapers under his arm, including the *Daily Worker*, and wore a belted, teak-coloured raincoat, dirty flannel trousers and a grey Homburg. Below the brim you could see his ears protruding like handles on a trophy, and when he turned it was possible to glimpse horn-rimmed spectacles, a longish nose and the tuft of a goatee beard.

Geoffrey Pyke got off the Tube at King's Cross, after which he was seen to act suspiciously. He paced up and down the platform, looking beneath the carriages as they rattled past, before moving upstairs to the overground station. Again he took an unusual interest in the rolling stock. His ghost remained close. Pyke left the station and continued on foot to Stratton Street, in Mayfair, where he entered the offices of the Ministry of War Transport. The Special Branch officer who had been in pursuit began to wait outside.

At 5:30 p.m. Pyke reappeared and was followed back to No. 30 Steele's Road where Heinz Kamnitzer also lived. Several days later the same thing happened — same officer from Special Branch, same journey, same interest in trains — and not long after, in early April 1945, a report on Pyke's movements was passed on to the Security Service. MI5 had rediscovered its interest in this itinerant innovator and possible Soviet agent.

Pyke had a number of homes during the war. He had based himself in Great Ormond Street, Albany, St James's Square and now Steele's Road, but perhaps the happiest building he had inhabited was the Hampstead home of Margaret Gardiner, a former Cambridge Heretic and more recently Bernal's lover. Like many affluent Londoners without vital jobs, Gardiner had moved out of the capital and in her absence No. 35 Downshire Hill had become an upmarket hostel for her acquaintances and friends. Pyke had spent the middle years of the war here in what was the prettiest house he would ever live in, as well as the most sociable.

Not since his days as a Cambridge undergraduate had he had so many friends nearby, including several with young children. Indeed, there were times in the long, slow months which followed the demise of Habbakuk when it seemed that he was at his happiest ambling around a garden with an infant in his arms, or having pillow fights with older children. Among the stream of visitors to Downshire Hill were Bobby and Deborah Carter and their houseguest Rolf Rünkel – living in nearby Keat's Grove – as well as the playwright Elias Canetti, then having an affair with one of Pyke's housemates, Friedl Benedikt. Canetti called on Pyke when he came to see his mistress and remembered him being forever caught up in his work and battling an illness, yet always eager to talk. 'He was a clever and articulate speaker, who liked to regale me with literary ideas of a satirical-didactic nature,' recalled Canetti. 'His voice had a mellifluous quality that only became apparent when he was quoting from Shaw. It was as though – in this refined way – he was acting as a sort of agent on Shaw's behalf, which, at this time of his greatest fame, Shaw certainly didn't need.' Canetti went on: 'There would be a torrent of ideas about Shaw, or some comparable idea of his own. Friedl listened, you couldn't interrupt him. She was mesmerised by his voice, and his paradoxes made her laugh. Without any access to science herself, she could still sense his mind and his inventiveness. Then, after about ten minutes, he would suddenly interrupt himself, and she would step away. He never asked her into his room. When he was lying ill in bed, he would allow food – very little – to be brought to him. But, as she said, he always kept his frontiers.'

Canetti went on to suggest that Pyke had an 'insuperable' suspicion of women, which could be traced back to the breakdown of his marriage. This was not quite right. He was merely suspicious of falling in love. He continued to hold Margaret, his wife, in the highest esteem and they never divorced. In New York, before going to observe the Canadian Habbakuk experiments, he had bought her cosmetics and clothes, and on her fiftieth birthday sent her a note calling her 'innately beautiful' and 'the handsomest woman of your decade due to your inner magnificence'. He kept up long correspondences with Margaret Edwards, Margaret Lloyd, Elsie Myers and Maud Joachim, the one-time militant suffragette, and had at least one sexual relationship during the war which only reinforced his wariness of allowing himself to be hurt. In his notebook from September 1940 Pyke sketched out an angry letter to his lover, accusing her of having 'something which compels you to bite people who try to help you', adding that 'it takes time to make love' and that 'I have one desire only – to clear you *completely* out of my life and for ever'.

Life on Steele's Road was different from what he had known on Downshire Hill. He did not have such an easy rapport with Kamnitzer, the devout Stalinist, and geographically was that little bit further away from many of his friends. With his hearing in decline, he became less sociable.

'I now restrict myself to those friends to whose voices I am accustomed, leaving others – if they are sufficiently interested – to obtain news of me from gossip,' of which, he added, there was always plenty. Yet by 1945 many of those whose voices he recognised had either left London or were in the process of doing so.

David, his son, would soon be in Germany to complete his national service as an Army physician; German communist friends such as Rünkel and Kuczynski were about to return home; the Carters would move to Paris; while one of his closest friends, Leo Myers, had recently committed suicide. 'Several times I had imaginary conversations with him,' he wrote to Myers's widow, Elsie. 'He would just hit the nail on the head as easily as he would write a good sentence. An added pleasure was that we both laughed at the same jokes, even though the jokes were silly jokes. Indeed, that made them all the funnier.' Nor did he see Bernal any more, not because he had moved away or died but because a bitter feud had broken out between them.

There had always been an intense rivalry simmering just below the surface of their relationship, but for years it had been sublimated into lively exchanges on science, war and the future of society. When Bernal agreed with Mountbatten in 1943 that Pyke should not come out to the US, before turning against the scheme entirely, this tension exploded. Although Bernal let it be known that he considered Pyke 'the greatest inventive genius of his time', his former friend was convinced that he had harboured a grudge for years. He accused Bernal of needing to be 'number one man' and '"telling stories" about my past – true, distorted and invented for the purpose of satisfying your ignoble psychological desires'. In one letter Pyke referred to a writ for libel that he had issued in the late 1930s about a defamatory story which he was now certain had originated with Bernal. Pyke blamed him for his dismissal from Combined Operations HQ – it was Bernal who had advised him not to accept the pay cut – and began to shut him out of his life. This was not enough. Pyke later threatened to kill himself in Bernal's garden shed, to which he retained a key, prompting Bernal to change the lock.

For all this, he never stamped out what remained of his friendship with Pyke, and nor did Margaret Gardiner, who had come to accept his capacity for turning on those closest to him. 'I have a very vivid picture of you walking about the garden of 35 with the six-months-old Martin [Gardiner and Bernal's son] in your arms, showing him things – and it is that picture and all that it implies that I try to hold in my mind during the violent squalls and buffetings that, it seems, must inevitably be encountered in the course of a friendship with you.'

As he was being shadowed around London towards the end of the Second World War, Geoffrey Pyke was increasingly alone. This may explain something of the intensity with which he threw himself into his new project. When Margaret Gardiner asked him to move the last of his furniture out of Downshire Hill now that her friend, the artist Ben Nicholson, wanted to use his room as a studio, Pyke's response was blunt and a little pompous. His new work must take precedence. 'It is out of the question to put my personal interests or I fear yours before a public interest of such importance and urgency.' Once more, Pyke had foreseen what appeared to be an epic disaster to which he hoped to find a solution.

★

Shortly before coming under surveillance by Special Branch, Pyke had thought about the possible effects of Hitler's defeat on a war-ravaged European continent. Based on extensive research he estimated that in the coming winter there would be a major shortage of coal that would put countless lives at risk. Pyke then persuaded Philip Noel-Baker, a Labour MP who became the only man to win both an Olympic medal and a Nobel Peace Prize, to lend him a desk in the Ministry of War Transport where he could solve the problem.

Though he was not being paid for this, every day he made the journey from Steele's Road to his temporary office to pore over statistical data concerning the European consumption and use of fuel, food, fats and rolling stock (which explains his interest in trains when he was under surveillance). He also conducted experiments with the help of barrow boys in Covent Garden into how much weight they could move in a day.

At the time, as a British child, you would be taught in school that there were three main sources of power: coal, oil and hydroelectric. But, as Pyke explained in an *Economist* article published four days before V-J Day, there was a fourth source of power 'on which the world wholly relied in previous ages and which even before the war represented a far larger proportion than most people know. That source is muscle – animal and human. The widespread and inarticulated assumption that this source of power was, or is, negligible is a myth.' The human body was capable of turning food into energy far more efficiently than a steam locomotive converted coal. Efforts should be made now, Pyke argued, to ensure that during the coming crisis caused by coal shortages there would be equipment in place allowing people to make up some of the energy shortfall using muscle-power.

One of the ways to do this, he went on, was by using pedal-powered machines. Rolling stock could be moved with 'Cyclo-Tractors': pedal-powered locomotives employing twenty to thirty men operating a series of cycles. Pedal-powered dynamos could be installed in homes. Fields could be ploughed using pedal-powered tractors. Pyke had identified a problem before it turned into a crisis and now, in the summer of 1945, he had what appeared to be a solution. Yet he faced a familiar struggle, both to convince others that there was a problem and that he had a solution.

In the weeks after the end of the war, he launched a one-man campaign to promote 'the utilisation of muscle'. As well as his article in the *Economist* he wrote a letter to *The Times*, a trio of articles in the *Manchester Guardian*, another in the *New Statesman and Nation*, several articles in the monthly magazine *Cycling* and gave an interview to the *Daily Mail* (which resulted in an error-strewn account that left Pyke furious). All made a detailed case for embracing muscle power in the face of the looming energy crisis.

Winter came, and with it some of the coal and food shortages that Pyke had predicted. He continued to busy himself around Whitehall, pressing his idea on officials from the Ministry of Supply and the Colonial Office. But nothing happened. From start to finish, this experience was a drawn-out reminder of his newfound impotence and just how hard it was for a private citizen to persuade those in government, during peacetime, to adopt an unusual idea. As he explained to a friend, he was engaged once again on 'the uphill task of innovation, trying to put over a perfectly simple policy which has somehow been missed, without the help of my old ally . . . – not Mountbatten, but Hitler, the threat of disaster – . . . It is a long story, and I am keeping daily notes as material for the "study in the dynamics of innovation" which ought to be written one day. I don't think I am going to meet with success. But I feel I ought not to give it up completely, until I know it to be completely hopeless.'

In late 1945 Pyke turned for help to what he presumed would be two sympathetic bodies, the Fabian Society and the Association of Scientific Workers – then paying him a small unemployment benefit.

He was hoping that one might commission him to write a fuller report on this problem and his proposed solution. The response, however, was tepid. Bosworth Monck, General Secretary of the Fabian Society, admitted to Pyke: 'The truth is that the Society has a reputation for being a hive of long-haired intellectuals, and I am reluctant to put forward anything which might lay us open to the charge of being cranks.' There followed a lively correspondence inspired by this line about the fear of being taken for a crank. For Pyke this illustrated why so many radical ideas went unrealised. 'What's the use of having ideas in a civilisation where you need the force of a sledgehammer to get them looked at?' Of course, once they had been looked at there was always the chance that they would be ridiculed by those who did not fully understand them – as Pyke was now reminded.

'FLOATING AIR STATIONS OF ICE', ran *The Times* headline; 'GIANT ICEBERG SHIPS PLANNED AS BASES' roared the *Express*; 'THE MOST STAGGERING WAR PLAN OF ALL' exclaimed the *Mirror*; while for the *Sketch*, Habbakuk was 'H. M. S. ICEBERG (UNSINKABLE)'. In early 1946 the Admiralty issued a press release outlining the story behind Habbakuk, and for a moment, in the days that followed, it was as if everyone Pyke knew had either read about his idea or heard of it. While the reaction he personally experienced was positive, many of these articles had an incredulous and at times mocking tone. Pyke was happy to be laughed at, but he wanted to be laughed at for the right reasons. He complained to the *Chronicle* for describing Habbakuk as a 'failure'. The plan had been sound, he told them. What had gone wrong was that the Battle of the Atlantic had gone right.

No less upsetting was the timing of the Admiralty press release. It had come after a flurry of letters from Pyke asking for the patent rights to Pykrete. By releasing the story in full, the Admiralty had effectively destroyed his patent rights, an ugly gesture which caused Pyke to turn in on himself. In letters to friends he was now 'at war' with the Admiralty, an institution he described as 'the enemy', and in his spare moments he continued to ruminate on his failure to come up with the idea for Habbakuk sooner.

So it came as a relief after months of thankless campaigning – for the patent rights to Pykrete and the utilisation of muscle-power – when John Cohen, a quantitative psychologist at the Cabinet Office, invited Pyke to take part in a very different project.

During the run-up to the 1945 General Election each of the major British political parties had pledged to create a national health service based on earlier proposals set out by Sir William Beveridge. In the wake of Labour's landslide victory a Working Party was set up to establish a new system of nurse recruitment, nurse training and nurse pay. Cohen, who was attached to this body, decided in 1946 to find a non-civil servant to provide a sweeping analysis of nurse recruitment. Pyke's name had come up. The unemployed former civil servant had little hesitation in accepting.

He soon learnt that the system of nurse recruitment in Britain was haphazard, antiquated and poorly documented. Rates of pay varied throughout the country along with supply, hospital size and standards of care. Job retention was low, owing to the sometimes appalling working conditions, and by 1945 the shortage of nurses, according to the Minister of Health Aneurin Bevan, was very nearly a 'national disaster'. From a distance this was ideal Pyke-territory. There would certainly be no battle to have his opinion heard as for once he had been asked for it. But his progress was slow, and before he could reach any final conclusions the Working Party published its initial report.

In vague terms it proposed a new system of nurse recruitment, not so very different from what had gone before, that could be adapted to future health policy. In no way was this the result of a rigorous scientific analysis, nor did it suggest a list of concrete improvements. Pyke wanted nothing to do with the report, and nor did Cohen, who refused to sign it. Instead he promised a Minority Report with an Appendix by Pyke.

At last, in 1947, Pyke slipped into gear, attacking the subject from first principles and identifying five key questions: What was the proper task of a nurse? What training was required to equip her for that task? What annual intake was needed and how could it be obtained? From what groups of the population should recruitment be made? How could wastage during training be minimised? Before the war, health policy had been governed by the need to establish the minimum health conditions. Now it was time to identify the optimum. Pyke sought out fresh data wherever he could find it, writing letters to hospitals and borrowing so many library books that he had to put up new shelves in Steele's Road.

But still this subject did not yield to his analysis. The work left him feeling weary and spent and he began to describe himself as 'tired, suffering from melancholia, falling asleep after meals, often silent'. His decision-making could become impaired, as it did when he spent hundreds of hours devising a formula for the ideal division of national income between capital expenditure and consumption in the hope of reaching a conclusion on health expenditure, only to realise that the ratio must shift with time, making his formula useless. He took on a secretary to do twenty hours of typing each week, yet this only seemed to make matters worse. At a time when he should have been condensing his notes, the towers of paper around his rooms only became taller.

After months of procrastination, Cohen became anxious. 'Unless our document is published in time for public discussion before the summer, we shall have completely missed the bus. That is what I am beginning to fear,' he told Pyke in January 1948. 'I should hate to think I was harassing or rushing you in any way. I am fully aware of your health troubles. But are there not degrees of "perfection"? Could the level of aspiration not be somewhat reduced?'

By then the problem had as much to do with perfection as paranoia. A misplaced pronoun from Cohen – he had referred to 'my report' rather than 'our report' – had left Pyke convinced that he was secretly planning to take the credit for their joint efforts. 'I have thrown everything into this work,' he told him, 'and gone short of *food* to pay the serious incidental expenses over this long period.' He even demanded written assurances from Cohen that he would not pass off their research as his own. But this was a distraction, really. Unable to finish the report, he had looked for a scapegoat. In the past he had rounded on his mother, his brother, Susie Isaacs, Duncan, Wernher and more recently Bernal; now it was Cohen's turn.

At a loss, Pyke explained his inability to finish this paper to the psychoanalyst Edward Glover, brother of James (who had long ago attempted a psychoanalysis of Pyke). Glover's reply was acute. 'I can see only one practical way of bringing the jam to an end soon; it is to sacrifice the narcissistic desire to finish your own work yourself – or at any rate to submit to the challenge of having someone else finish it for you which might mobilise in you a desperate last attempt to complete it without help.' Cohen was of course the man to do this, and yet, 'it is not what he does (by way of cutting and completing) that matters but the narcissistic threat to you of his attempting to do so'.

Glover knew Pyke well enough to hint at another mental block. 'You hang on to immortality by being the eternal son. To admit that the future generation is a future generation excludes your privilege of taking part in it. So you won't tell them anything. Well. Tell them. As you are working on sound principles you can't be so *very* far wrong.' Though Pyke would often refer to Mountbatten as a Peter Pan figure, there was also a part of *him* which refused to grow up. His outlook had been forged in that youthful moment in his life when the enemy seemed to be the stolid assumptions of an older generation, to the extent that he was unable to imagine himself belonging to that group. There were other anxieties also weighing down on him which he did not share with Glover, ones that troubled him more deeply in the days after reading this letter.

For some of those in London who had lived through the war there was a loneliness that came with peace. By 1948 the country had entered an age of austerity. Wartime amateurs were being replaced by peacetime professionals, some of the old divisions of class were coming back and the country looked dingier, shabbier and more worn than it had done before the war. Rationing was still in place, unemployment was creeping up, and with the return of the soldiers, many of them brutalised by service, Britain had become a more violent place. This was the country that Pyke woke up to on the morning of Saturday, 21 February 1948, the society which George Orwell had spent the past few months abstracting as he wrote *Nineteen Eighty-Four*. It was, in many ways, a more lacklustre place than it had been during the war, and on that particular day it was also bitterly cold, with snow covering large swathes of the country.

Pyke was bedridden again. He was depressed by the thought of tackling the NHS report as well as the uncertainty of what would follow. There were also times when he became gloomy about the society in which he lived, and in particular its attitude towards new ideas. 'Bad manners to new ideas, to new suggestions, are sabotage – as they are in war, they are a Public Offence,' he had recently told his listeners in a BBC broadcast entitled 'The Dynamics of Innovation'. Bad manners towards new ideas were 'an offence against the possibility of more food, more housing, more fun, more expansion of the personality, much as music: – *That is to say* – like bad manners towards children – they are an offence against the *possibility of better people*. That, pragmatically, is the only immortal sin. No matter that the idea to which we are bad-mannered may prove impractical, or not the most economic, or even fundamentally fallacious, – any more than it matters that a person to whom we are bad-mannered may not be first-class, may be a dud. If you are well-mannered only to the successful and to those you like, then you are a snob, and deserve the penalties you may get from your mistakes.'

Years of frustration seemed to coalesce in this grievance about society's attitude towards innovation. In a letter to *The Times* published in December 1947, several months after that BBC talk, Pyke went further by suggesting that the nation was enslaved to its past. He had called for the abolition of the death penalty, insisting this was not about the merits of capital punishment as a deterrent, but whether, in England, 'we have the decency, the dignity, the self-respect, and the courage to live out our lives without this real or imaginary protection. This has nothing to do with the question of whether human life should be regarded as sacrosanct. But if MPs vote for the preservation of the death penalty it will be a vote for the preservation into the future of the beastliness and barbarity of eighteenth- and nineteenth-century English civilisation, and will show that we as a nation are slaves to our social inheritance, for evil and for good.' Shortly afterwards Parliament would vote for the preservation of the death penalty (it would remain in place until 1965).

The following month he wrote again to *The Times*, this time about the government's decision not to contribute to UNICEF. He found this unforgivable, especially in light of the contributions made by poorer nations. 'Can we not pull our socks up? Do we agree with the refusal made in our name? If not, are we to allow it to stand? Our boast of democracy is at stake. What have the churches to say? Will they remain silent, inactive at this blasphemy in action (the only real blasphemy) against "Suffer Little Children to Come unto Me"? What have parents to say? And the Trade Unions? What have decent people of all parties to say to their MPs?' His conclusion was desolate. 'Actions like this, which suggest that we are condemned to perpetuate the evils in our past against our better but impotent judgement, unconsciously persuade men that there is nothing to be done with such a civilisation but to destroy it as thoroughly and rapidly as possible.'

Pyke was arguing himself into a corner, walling himself in until he could only see a society doomed to repeat into perpetuity the mistakes of the past. This civilisation was apathetic and toothless. It was in thrall to its elders and snobbish towards new ideas, and as such it had become unworthy of his improving attentions; much easier to 'destroy' everything 'as thoroughly and rapidly as possible'.

Both of these letters had been sent to Donald Tyerman, Assistant Editor at *The Times*, with whom Pyke had corresponded for several years. In late February 1948 Tyerman replied with a more personal letter than usual. It began with praise for a paper that Pyke had sent him. Then Tyerman delivered his broadside. 'What is wrong with Pyke? Why hasn't he written the great book? Why is it that after reducing our problems to simple questions he can then never finish the answers? Why does every memorandum of his, which sets out to be constructive, end in becoming an unfinished encyclopaedia? I get the impression that all your simple shrewd questions lead in the same direction – in the direction of the Book to end all books which, by its nature, will never be written – which is a pity. There is a case, I think, for asking your next simple shrewd question about yourself, because your inability to impress people with the practical rightness of your views isn't *entirely* due to their imperviousness to new ideas. Even if you had your way and got a community open to innovation, there would still be the problem of Pyke to solve.'

It was a problem which he had tackled repeatedly, one that was as familiar to him as the smell of his sheets, and on the day that Tyerman wrote this letter Pyke set in motion what seemed to him the only solution to the 'problem of Pyke'.

On the night of Saturday, 21 February Geoffrey Pyke placed a note on his door which read 'Please do not wake me'. He shaved off his beard and sat down in a chair by the window. Next to him were headed notepaper, a pen and a container full of commercially available barbiturates.

He took the pills.

Knowing that he had probably less than half an hour to live he began to write. One of his first messages was to his wife.

> Dear Marge,
>
> I write to you after I've taken the poison to die. I have become too tired to go on and have now been swindled of my ideas by one Cohen. I can now do no more than send you my love and best wishes,
> Your Geoff.

Another was to his son David. The Janet he refers to was Janet Stewart, whom David would later marry.

> My darling Sonny,
>
> I cannot help myself. I am too tired; too exhausted, and I have been swindled again, by a man Cohen who has taken my ideas. I die loving you and Mummy and Janet; my heart's best wishes go out to you. I cannot explain the misery of my life. There would be no purpose in the attempt to. I cannot go on. This last blow finishes me.
> Your loving Daddy.

The third was to Elsie Myers, whose husband Leo had killed himself in 1944, also with an overdose of barbiturates.

Dear Elsie,

I have had to go the same way as Leo. – I can't help myself – I've been robbed of my ideas by Dr Cohen at the last moment. This – I am already about dead – is to beg you in the name of our deep friendship – to leave David in your will what you can *so that he may be able to have children more and sooner*, in memory of me.

Best, best wishes to you.

Yours

Geoff.

He wrote so quickly that there was time for more. Pyke's last words, more revealing than the other notes, were to his son:

The thing to do is to be as detached as you can about my death. This may seem a strange thing to say, but I've taken the poison and in the ½ hour or so left am trying to find things to say of use. You will feel I've deserted you. It is true, but it's beyond me to endure more. This last blow has been more than I can stand. Mummy does not know how much I have loved her and how faithful my heart has always been to her. But I have been of no use to her and she should for her own well being, which is what I care about, forget me as soon as possible. It is easier for a wife than a son to do this. But you will be able to do it in time. Do your best for your own sake. It is over negative feelings to me which are perhaps buried and which death tends to bury deeper.

The all-important thing is children. I beg you do not call any of them, I hope there will be many, after me – I'd like everything concerning me to be destroyed and to be forgotten as if I'd never lived. I shall live in all the children I've had to do with, and shall fade away as they grow up and shed (to the extent they do) their early experiences.

I hesitate even now to interfere – and fear I have done so too much

– but keep left. Let me advise you to read Shaw several times. You can short-circuit the job of buying the wisdom of experience – I've only a few minutes left – and obtain generalities for which life is not long enough to do by observation.

I'm now going under . . .

I find great difficulty in thinking and . . .

. . . love you and good wishes for you and Mummy. Remember, take your children as serious as you do grown-ups – and *beware* your social inheritance – the . . . assumptions, indecisively imbibed from environment. [. . .] *Don't attend my funeral* – silly business, *no fuss or ceremony*. As I say below have me cremated. I found my mother's funeral a shock, that's why. I've forgotten so much I wanted to say. *Sorry. Sorry. Sorry.*

Pyke's writing deteriorated and his pen fell to the floor.

Mrs Hopkins, the daily help, was the first to find the corpse, while it was Mrs Mendelsohn, the landlady, who called the police. The operator at the local exchange must have put a call through to the press, for there were reporters at Steele's Road before anyone else arrived. The next day news of Pyke's death appeared in the *Evening Standard*, the *Daily Express* and the *Daily Graphic*.

'Pyke of the Back-room' had taken his own life. Elsewhere he was referred to as 'one of the most famous "back-room boys"'. There followed articles in the *New York Times*, the magazines *Time* and *Discovery*, and fuller obituaries in *The Times* and *Manchester Guardian*. Death became him; the superlatives flowed. Pyke was a 'genius', a 'pioneer', an 'organiser of thought' and for Max Perutz 'one of the most original characters in this country'. He had an 'almost over-developed sense of social responsibility' and an intellectual approach which was 'not only free from accretions of ordinary human prejudice but disregarded their existence'. Later that year the BBC would broadcast an appreciation of Pyke in which Lancelot Law Whyte compared him favourably with Frank Whittle and Albert Einstein.

Yet none of these accounts dwelled on the reasons why he might have killed himself, for they remained something of a mystery. The Coroner, Bentley Purchase, ruled that Pyke had committed suicide while of 'unsound mind'. At the time suicide was a criminal act, so coroners frequently arrived at this verdict on the basis of scant evidence. Most obituaries alluded to his depression; some suggested he had been overcome by work. A biography of Pyke published nine years later, by the American military historian David Lampe, described his suicide as 'an act of intellectual frustration'. Yet a letter subsequently written to Lampe challenged this. It seemed that there might have been another factor in his death, one that was unknown even to Pyke.

The letter had come from a doctor at the Middlesex Hospital who had read Lampe's book and noticed that Pyke had appeared to display almost every symptom of Addison's Disease, right down to a fondness for fried chicken and sardines – low sodium levels brought on by Addison's will often result in salt cravings. By causing him so much pain during his life, this chronic condition would have certainly played a significant part in his decision to kill himself.

Addison's Disease is a rare adrenal disorder that reduces the sufferer's ability to produce the steroid hormones cortisol and aldosterone, making it harder to fight inflammation, move nutrients around the body and regulate blood-flow. It can lead to prolonged periods of lethargy and long-term pain. Those afflicted will also find it hard to deal with stress, either physical or mental, and may produce less of the sex hormone DHEA, thus lowering their sex drive. Addison's usually follows on from an initial failure of the adrenal glands caused by an illness such as tuberculosis. Again this feature of the disease matches Pyke's history. In the freezing loft of the Jewish barrack in Ruhleben he was said to have experienced 'pneumonia' in both lungs, which might have been *tuberculosis* pneumonia. The onset of Addison's is insidious, so Pyke would not have been aware of his condition immediately and, even then, relatively little was known about this disease during his lifetime – which would explain why it was not spotted by the doctors at the Mayo Clinic. It is certainly possible that Pyke suffered from a mild form of Addison's and, as Lampe replied to the endocrinologist at Middlesex Hospital: 'If all of Pyke can be explained by Addison's disease, then we must all revise our theories.'

Yet the consensus among modern-day specialists in the disease as to whether Pyke had this illness is less conclusive. 'I cannot say that Pyke did not have Addison's,' says Professor John Monson, Emeritus Professor of Clinical Endocrinology at St Bartholomew's Hospital. 'It is conceivable, but by no means probable.' This is a view shared by fellow endocrinologists at Charing Cross Hospital in London.

Much easier to establish is that Pyke suffered from frequent depressive episodes. By his own admission, if each of us experiences variations in mood, or cyclothymic tendencies, 'I was more subject to them than most.' The music of his life takes us from all-conquering crescendos in which it seemed for him that anything was possible – that he could prevent a war, end anti-Semitism, earn a fortune, rewrite the rules of education or win the war with a single invention – down to those muffled, more subdued passages during which he found it hard to get out of bed. It is tempting to take this further and reach for a modern term such as bipolar disorder. There were certainly intense, near-manic periods in his life when he seemed to understand the world with mystic clarity and could think exceptionally fast. But ideas often appear to have come to him whether or not he was 'up', and in none of the many descriptions of Pyke are there clear suggestions that his speech was manic or frenzied; nor were there repeated spending sprees or bouts of hypersexuality. Then again, these symptoms are rooted in a modern understanding of this condition, so it is probably best to avoid this term and instead repeat his own analysis: that while we all experience variations in moods, he was much more prone to these than most.

The extent to which he suffered from depression, Addison's, or both – and whether the two compounded each other – will always be unclear. But we can be sure that during the last years of his life he was in pain, both mental and physical.

Unaware of the source of this discomfort, knowing only that it was starting to overpower him, he appears to have tackled this problem as he would do any other some six months before his suicide. In his diary for August 1947 he described a physical 'trough' which lasted two days and left him feeling 'very empty, exhausted "post sick"' and unable 'to get the machine going'. After this he applied himself to 'the way out', or 'the working out of the D. Problem'. 'D' might have been 'Depression' or just 'Death'.

Although he did not spell out his conclusion, we know that he felt 'shock, relief, almost happiness' at the thought of it, sensations which were 'those of a man relieved of a thematic condemnation. And that of course is what has happened.' While intellectual frustration and the pressure of work certainly played a part in his suicide, this entry suggests that he had made the decision to kill himself long before his death and that his suicide had more to do with the nagging, persistent pain he had lived with for so long than the frustration of not being able to finish the nursing report.

There remains another loose end: the question of whether Pyke was working for Moscow. He described himself after the war as a Marxist who had lost faith in the Soviet Union. 'None of us can be trusted with victory,' he had written earlier, and 'Communist Russia has not yet been tested in this respect.' By 1948 it had – and had failed, the iron curtain having descended across Europe.

Was his sense of despair deepened by the failure of the USSR to live up to the ideals he had once invested in it? Or had he really been, as MI5 and Special Branch suspected, a senior Comintern figure? For if so, he would have been living in fear of exposure, which again casts his suicide in a different light.

PYKE HUNT, PART 6

On a Friday evening in May 1951 two British diplomats, Guy Burgess and Donald Maclean, abandoned their car by a Southampton dock and raced to the ferry, one of them shouting over his shoulder 'We'll be back on Monday!' They never returned. From France they were escorted to the Soviet Union where they spent the rest of their lives. Both were NKVD agents who for years had supplied high-grade intelligence to Moscow in prodigious quantities: between 1941 and the end of the war Burgess alone passed on 4,605 documents.

This defection marked the first instalment of the 'Cambridge Spies' espionage saga, which would go on to scandalise British society and undermine some of the foundations of trust within MI5, MI6 and the Foreign Office. For many this was evidence of the worst kind of complacency: a clubbish lack of imagination in which a man who appeared to be 'one of us' was incapable of either treachery on this scale or political radicalisation in the service of what Orwell had once called 'that un-English thing, an idea'. But it would be years before the extent of this deception emerged. In the days after Maclean and Burgess's defection very few people knew what had happened, and MI5 wanted to keep it that way.

Rather than obtain a warrant to search Burgess's flat, MI5's Guy Liddell contacted Anthony Blunt, the former intelligence officer who had since become Surveyor of the King's Pictures and Director of the Courtauld Institute, and asked him to track down a set of keys to Burgess's flat. Liddell knew that Blunt was a close friend of Burgess – but had no inkling then that he might also be a Soviet agent. Before his sudden departure Burgess had been seeing Jackie Hewit, a chorus boy from Gateshead who had also had an affair with Blunt before the war. Blunt borrowed a set of keys from Hewit and accompanied two MI5 officers to Burgess's flat.

Blunt later claimed that as the three of them moved through Burgess's rooms he managed to remove any incriminating papers from under the noses of the MI5 men, yet this is unlikely. Calm and quick-fingered as he might have been, it seems that Blunt had given the flat a quick sweep beforehand. But he did not look everywhere.

Beneath Burgess's bed was a guitar case that contained a treasure trove of letters and papers which cast suspicion on Blunt, Kim Philby and John Cairncross, all NKVD agents, as well as on Peter Astbury, who had passed information to Moscow via Dave Springhall, a CPGB member jailed in 1943 for offences under the Official Secrets Act. Burgess's guitar case also contained documents relating to Geoffrey Pyke. In November of that year more of Burgess's correspondence was found at the Courtauld Institute and again there were references to Pyke.

For more than half a century these papers would remain classified – until 2009 when MI5 released most of its material on Pyke. Four of the documents that were made public then had been found either under Burgess's bed or at the Courtauld. They are the most important pieces in the puzzle of Geoffrey Pyke and his political loyalties.

★

Two of the four documents were extracts from longer reports – not official government papers but chatty, informal accounts of political gossip including profiles of key political figures. The emphasis throughout was on developments that might concern the USSR. One had been written in late April 1942, the other a month before.

The earlier extract began with a detailed biographical sketch of Pyke before telling of a secret meeting in Richmond Terrace to discuss the Plough scheme. It provided a full account of the project, the role envisaged for Russia, its military impact vis-à-vis a second front and Pyke's attempts to push for more Russian involvement. The fact that Mountbatten was initially sceptical about reaching out to the USSR was also mentioned. Pyke, it went on, urged him to push for direct liaison with the Soviets and to send British troops to participate in Russian guerrilla warfare. 'Mountbatten showed keen interest and sympathy for this idea, said he would raise it with the P.M.'

From the wording of this report it was almost certainly the result of a long conversation with Pyke. Less clear is whether he knew that what he was saying might end up in Moscow: did he understand that the man or woman he was speaking to might be a Soviet agent, or had he been gulled into giving this information?

It is impossible to say without identifying his interlocutor. The obvious candidate is Guy Burgess, given that these reports were found among his papers. Burgess was, as the historian Nigel West has written, 'assiduous in cultivating sources'. By early 1942 Burgess was passing vast quantities of intelligence on to Moscow. Even so, we can rule him out, largely because of Milicent Bagot's fortunate decision in March 1942 to have Pyke shadowed around London.

One of the Pyke reports found among Burgess's correspondence was dated 22 March and described a meeting held on 19 March. Since this report was based on a verbal account, and the fact that no Soviet agent would gather this kind of intelligence over the telephone, we can be reasonably sure that Pyke must have spoken to the author of this report in person at some point between 19 and 22 March. By then Bagot had Pyke under MI5 observation, so we know where he was for most of this period, as well as when he ate, what he wore, how long he spent in particular buildings and, crucially, the people he spoke to.

Because it was such a long report, we can discount anyone whom he saw only briefly. This leaves us with just three names (if we disregard those he spoke to inside Richmond Terrace). One was Mountbatten's Chief of Staff, Brigadier Wildman-Lushington. Another was an RAF officer, Squadron Leader Dudeney, then at the Ministry of Economic Warfare. The third was Peter Smollett, who had recently become Head of Soviet Relations at the Ministry of Information.

Of these three, one was revealed after his death in 1980 to have been a Soviet mole code-named 'ABO' and later described by a KGB defector as more 'significant' to Moscow than any of the Cambridge Spies. This man was not unmasked during his lifetime, and instead enjoyed a successful post-war career as a respected *Times* correspondent and was even awarded an OBE. His name was Peter Smollett and he was almost certainly the Soviet agent to whom Pyke supplied details of the meeting in Richmond Terrace.

Smollett was held in high regard by Moscow not only because of the intelligence he provided but also because of his propaganda work in the Ministry of Information. It constituted what KGB defector Oleg Gordievsky called 'the NKVD's most remarkable "active measures" coup'. Smollett would exaggerate Soviet concerns, refuse to give in to them and then suggest as a quid pro quo a more Soviet-friendly stance on other issues. He maintained, for example, that the Soviets were exceptionally thin-skinned and, as such, no stories about Stalinist persecution could be broadcast. Smollett encouraged the BBC to run stories that exaggerated the revival of the Russian Orthodox Church in the USSR and to have these translated and broadcast to Eastern Europe – a major coup, given the anti-religious reputation of the Soviet regime and the high standing of the BBC in Europe. Elsewhere Smollett pushed the idea that after the war the USSR would be too weak to do anything other than rebuild. He organised the legendary 1943 Albert Hall meeting to celebrate the Red Army's twenty-fifth anniversary and, in one month alone, September 1943, as Christopher Andrew has shown, under Smollett 'the Ministry of Information organised meetings on the Soviet Union for 34 public venues, 35 factories, 100 voluntary societies, 28 civil defence groups, 9 schools and a prison; the BBC in the same month broadcast thirty programmes with a substantial Soviet content'.

It worked. Even British communists were taken aback by the 'red haze' which swept across Britain after the entry of the USSR into the war. None of this of course would have been possible without the heroism of the Russian people. This sympathy was inspired by much more than Smollett's propaganda. Yet he helped to blur the line between the heroic Russians and the brutal Soviet regime. It was, as the historian Steven Merritt Miner has written, 'propaganda beyond price'.

At the same time Smollett was busy passing intelligence to Moscow – as he had been doing since the start of the war and perhaps earlier. Initially he had reported to the Soviet agent Kim Philby, but after he joined SIS Philby began to distance himself from Smollett, feeling that he had become, as the BBC's Gordon Corera has put it, like 'the embarrassing friend from school who followed you to university and knew you were not quite what you pretended to be'. Instead Philby handed Smollett over to Burgess, who was impressed by his new sub-agent and mentioned him to the illegal NKVD resident in London, Anatoli Gorsky – who was furious. By taking on a sub-agent without clearing it first with Moscow Burgess had again broken protocol. He was told to drop Smollett. He chose not to. Instead Philby, Blunt and Burgess decided among themselves that Smollett should report to Burgess, who could pass off his material as his own work.

So it seems that the account of the Plough meeting given by Pyke to Smollett was delivered to Burgess who then passed it off as his own to his Soviet handler, before it continued down the chain to Moscow.

The question remains: did Pyke realise when he spoke to Smollett that he was being pumped for information by a Soviet agent?

It seems likely. The length and precision of the report indicate that Smollett was taking notes, which must have raised Pyke's suspicions. Then there is the line: 'No other specific operations were mentioned in Pyke's presence at the conference on March 19th at Combined Operations Headquarters though Mountbatten said something like " . . . of course we have so many other earlier schemes in hand . . ."' This sounds very much like a response to a question such as: *were there any other specific operations mentioned in your presence?* Hardly chit-chat.

More revealing still, Pyke told Smollett that he sought 'co-operation with the Russians because he wanted them to know about all this so that none of these tactical innovations could ever be used against them if there were after all to be a conflict between Britain and Russia at the end of this war. He [Pyke] implied that in such a conflict he would be on the side of the Russians.' What is so revealing here is not that Pyke was pro-Soviet by this stage of the war – we know that – but that he was prepared to say so in these terms to Smollett.

Apart from this report, there are hints that Smollett and Pyke had an understanding which belied their formal relationship. Between them, in 1942, they found a temporary job for Heinz Kamnitzer, the German refugee and suspected NKVD agent, in which he was paid by Combined Operations while being employed at the Ministry of Information. There was also a David Astor connection. Just before Pyke left for the US, Astor decided that Smollett should become the next editor of the *Observer*. At the time Pyke was in contact with two of Astor's secretaries, which raises the possibility that Pyke had been asked to steer Astor towards choosing Smollett.

Even if Pyke had not been told that Smollett was working for Moscow, he might have guessed it. This slightly overweight Austrian gave George Orwell the 'strong impression of being some kind of Russian agent' and otherwise being a 'very slimy person' – words he wrote without knowing that it was Smollett who had persuaded T. S. Eliot at Faber to reject on political grounds his manuscript for *Animal Farm*.

But how does Pyke's decision to pass intelligence to Smollett belong to his broader political evolution? Was Milicent Bagot right to suspect him of being both 'Professor P.' and the man in charge of British communist 'action propaganda'? 'Everything must wear a disguise in order to be real,' wrote John le Carré in *A Perfect Spy*. For much of his life Geoffrey Pyke wore a disguise and here, at last, it can removed.

Geoffrey Pyke did not visit Berlin during the late 1920s or early 1930s; he was not Professor P., the senior Comintern official. Nor did he ever join the Comintern. But in late 1934, as he wrestled with the question of how to end Nazi anti-Semitism, he underwent a powerful political conversion. He became an anti-fascist. This did not involve joining a party, it was a purely personal transformation, and yet it would inform every political decision that followed and ultimately brought him into the orbit of the Party.

After two years spent trying to set up his institute to explode the myth of anti-Semitism, Pyke created Voluntary Industrial Aid for Spain (VIAS), another anti-fascist venture, after which his affiliations became more complex. This was the age of the Popular Front in which the barriers between those on the Left had been either lowered or brought down altogether. Pyke had always felt a strong affinity for the Fabians, and even they were now talking up the 'economic miracle' of Stalin's Russia. So there was nothing unusual about a Fabian like him, one who had voted Labour all his life, recruiting several Party members to VIAS.

He found these men reliable and determined. He was attracted by their internationalism, their political conviction and their European connections (which made it easier to get VIAS ampoules, microscopes, trucks and motorbikes into the hands of the Spanish Republicans). Their links to the American Communist Party might have helped to secure the fleet of second-hand Harley Davidsons that was shipped over from the US.

But to what extent did he allow his charity to be used by the Party? We know that VIAS assisted at least one agent of Moscow, for buried in its records is a note which says: 'Received one packet for Mr Otto Katz'.

Katz was a Communist 'super-agent' with nine cover names. He was an NKVD illegal, a senior Comintern official and a charismatic and talented propagandist who later inspired the Victor Laszlo character in the film *Casablanca*. One of Katz's many poste restantes, it seems, was Pyke's flat.

But this does not make VIAS a communist organisation. Instead, with ties to an array of left-leaning groups, from the CPGB to the Co-Operative Movement, it seems to have been a child of the Popular

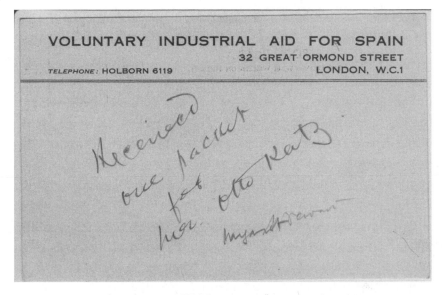

Note found among VIAS papers referring to Otto Katz

Front. In spite of what the insurance agent overheard before going to the police – when Pyke spoke to an empty room about 'attacking' Negretti and Zambra (he was almost certainly speaking into his Dictaphone) – VIAS was not a front organisation and there is no evidence that it was used to obtain industrial or technological intelligence.

Nonetheless, it was around this time that Pyke adjusted his outlook. He read John Strachey's *Theory and Practice of Socialism*, and described its account of the common ground between psychoanalysis and Marxism as 'all that I require'. Over the following months he became convinced, as his idol Shaw had put it, that it was no more possible to produce socialism using the British political machine than it was to get a sewing machine to make a fried egg, and in 1938, having been rebuffed again by the TUC, he decided to abandon the British Labour movement. He felt that its leadership was interested in nothing more than pushing for higher wages and, once these had been won, guarding them 'with caution and jealousy'. 'I became clear that any further ideas that came into my head must not be fed to them.'

So, having decided to carry out a Gallup-style survey of German public opinion, he resolved to work with 'a body of people selected for their political and personal reliability'. This was code for his decision in 1939 to approach the Party for help with his undercover poll, a move born of his anger with the Labour movement as much as his belief that the Party would fight harder in the struggle against fascism.

Over that summer, Pyke was put in touch with senior members of the German Communist Party (KPD). He flew out to Paris to meet Jürgen Kuczynski, and asked him for the support of the KPD.

'I made a report about the matter to our Party leadership in Paris,' wrote Kuczynski. They then sent a message to London instructing KPD cadre Rolf Rünkel to help Pyke, and over the next few weeks Rünkel vetted each of the young conversationalists, none of whom travelled to Germany until either Rünkel or his boss, Wilhelm Koenen, leader of the KPD in exile, was satisfied.

Some of those involved in the survey either belonged to the Party or stood close to it, such as Kenneth Spencer, Fred Fuller and Marjory Watson, who had started out as a Nazi but had since undergone a dramatic political conversion. Eva Webber, the woman in Golders Green whose remark about working with the Secret Service came to the attention of MI5, merely imagined that Pyke's connections to the likes of Vansittart was evidence that this survey was controlled by MI5. It was not. But as a result of Vansittart's connection the crucial survey results were brought out of the country by diplomatic bag. Or, to put it another way, the Foreign Office unwittingly helped the German Communist Party to gather intelligence from Nazi Germany.

Pyke relished that initial experience of working with the KPD. His new friends were serious, politically committed and anti-fascist to the core. He began to inhabit a more communist milieu, until his life was dominated by 'my foreign Communist friends' such as Rünkel, Koenen and Kuczynski. 'I learn more from these German Communists than I do from anybody.' Otherwise he spent time with 'my English Communist friends', who were 'very young members of the Party', and in the wake of the Molotov–Ribbentrop Pact agreed with them that there would be no war because Chamberlain's 'class interest' was so strong that he was bound to make a deal with Hitler. Karl Kneschke – older, wiser and like Rünkel and Koenen a German Communist who had fled Prague – took a more sanguine line. Pyke recalled him saying 'that Hitler and Chamberlain were both in a situation which they could not get out of except by war. I remember asking him, "What do your Moscow friends think?" Elbows on knees, staring at the floor between his feet as if he would find there the words he was looking for, slowly shaking his large head, bald in front but for the wisps of greying hair that had been carefully brushed across the dome in the morning, but which now stood up like Einstein's in a disordered halo, at last he got the words out. "It is coming this time."'

Here is evidence, at least, that Pyke recognised the connection between these German Communists and the USSR. But by then he had made the decision to join them in the fight against fascism and would stand by it. The communist networks to which he now had access provided him with personnel and expertise, and they might have helped with the funding of his survey. The cost of sending his conversationalists to Germany was more than £550, of which £500 came from his friend Leo Myers. Whether or not Myers was given a nudge by the Party is unclear. Much easier to trace is the seismic shift in Pyke's outlook during those heady days just after the outbreak of war and what he did in response.

'I had for many years been convinced that Capitalist civilisation in Western Europe was decaying,' wrote Pyke. 'I took it for granted that the next convulsion was however a decade or two ahead.' Now that war had broken out he began to think that it might come sooner – much sooner. 'We are, I think, approaching one of the greatest and most beneficial crises the species has been through in the last 5,000 years. And everyone should get clear as soon as possible which side he is on. For everyone, as judged by his activities, will *in fact* have to be on one side or the other, whether he likes it or not.' In September 1939 he saw the new conflict with Germany as a prelude to 'the real war, the war against nature, the war to master our environment and the purposeful evolution of the human species. [. . .] We are within easy sight of overcoming the absurd preliminary problem of mere physical want not merely for the upper and middle classes, but for everyone [. . .]. Then we stand a chance of giving science its head.'

Pyke's vision of the future was socialist and anti-capitalist, yet it had virtually nothing in common with the bloody reality of Soviet Russia. He did not long for gulags, purges and a tyrannical secret police. His utopian state was not the architect of aggressive territorial expansion; nor did it tolerate an inefficient economy, wastage, famine, shortages or the stasis of a paranoid and murderous dictatorship.

Instead he envisaged a world in which scientists were given their head, a rational, egalitarian and meritocratic society in which the future was embraced like an old friend. Humans would live without want. The new enemies would be complacency, vested interest and our unthinking resistance to new ideas. Empire, inequality and war would become historical artefacts. Nations would pull together towards a more productive, peaceful and judicious future, all of which, he maintained, could be achieved through socialist revolution.

Here was a worldview anchored so completely in the political idealism of the late 1930s – a period which is, as the biographer Peter Conradi has put it, 'as remote from us as the Romantic Revival two centuries earlier' – that it can be hard to understand today. While none of the individual components of this outlook are either alien or outdated, indeed many have since passed into the political mainstream, what has gone is the sense that all this could be achieved through revolution.

Yet the real tragedy of Pyke's beliefs, at the time he held them, was that he imagined them to be shared by Stalin. He was not alone in willing himself to see the USSR as an embryonic version of a scientific and futuristic utopia. Bernard Shaw and H. G. Wells, for example, felt the same way. When he read that the Russian national income had doubled every six years, he believed it, and was convinced that it was only a matter of time before they overcame 'the absurd preliminary problem of mere physical want'. Pyke now dared himself to believe that he would live to see this new world, and soon after the outbreak of war he resolved to do everything he could to bring this forward. His weapon would be propaganda. 'It is everyone's duty to live as usefully as possible. There is no merit in being shot. But it will be necessary to be ready to be shot, and worse. When the future is only just round the corner, it is worthwhile to sacrifice the present.' The advent of war had had a powerful effect on him, making him more impulsive than ever before.

In the days after the outbreak of war Pyke decided to create a news agency with a hidden communist agenda. Letters written to Kuczynski, which for decades have lain hidden in East German archives, show that this agency was to provide two services. One was a survey of the foreign press to be called *Uncensored News*, inspired by his work with the *Cambridge Magazine* during the previous war. He planned to recruit a team of refugee communists to select foreign-language articles and broadcasts for translation. While the articles were genuine, the choice of which to translate would be partisan.

The other arm of Pyke's agency was to provide reports on public opinion in Germany and other European countries. This was what he was overheard discussing on the telephone with Marjory Watson in May 1940. Men and women from neutral countries such as the US would conduct undercover opinion polls, as Pyke's conversationalists had done the summer before, but now the phrasing of the questions would be geared towards drawing out responses to back the Party line.

These plans faced an array of setbacks. During the Blitz the warehouse in which he had stored twenty-five tons of newsprint for his proposed publication *Uncensored News* went up in flames. He was not given permission to import German newspapers, and in the days when America remained neutral he was unable to get a permit to travel to the US where he hoped to train up conversationalists. But his efforts to get things moving do at least tell us something about the flow of secret information within hidden communist networks at that time.

One of the men Pyke had gone to for help with his news agency was Sir Campbell Stuart, at Department EH, who had looked so unfavourably on Raleigh and Smith before the outbreak of war. This time Pyke told him about his plan to send Americans into Europe. Stuart gave 'every sign of being favourably impressed, but rather distrait', largely because he was off to Paris (to check up on Noël Coward's British Bureau of Propaganda). On his return, Stuart relayed Pyke's plan to the Director of SIS, Admiral Hugh Sinclair, saying 'it might be that some useful information would be gained' and that among others 'Vansittart has commended it warmly'.

'The idea is interesting,' came the reply from SIS, 'and, if properly carried out, might prove very informative.' Neither had any inkling of its hidden communist agenda.

Yet by canvassing political support for his scheme Pyke had destroyed its secrecy and ultimately Stuart rejected it on the grounds that too many people had been informed. He also suggested that this work should only be carried out by professional intelligence agents. The irony here was that Pyke had successfully got his amateurs into and out of Nazi Germany at a time when SIS felt it was safer to watch from the sidelines.

The only reason we know that Sir Campbell Stuart wrote to SIS is because copies of this correspondence were found among Burgess's papers in 1951. When Stuart wrote to 'C', Burgess was working at SIS. Presumably, then, it was Burgess who copied this material. There is also an intriguing possibility that Pyke might have seen it.

Several months after these letters were sent, Pyke mentioned that he had 'excellent reason for believing that' Department EH was 'in favour of the proposal' but that they had had to submit the idea to another department, which he believed to be the Security Service, who had turned it down. It seems that either Burgess had showed the correspondence to Pyke, or it was given to an intermediary who then told him about it, all of which strengthens the idea that Pyke had access to high-powered communist networks during that first year of the war.

We also know that he had a degree of success in running a press-cutting office. For a short period he had installed in his flat a team of refugees and linguists who transcribed and translated foreign radio broadcasts – which explains the strange noises heard on Great Ormond Street in early 1940. Around this time, possibly for no more than a few months, they gathered material from foreign radio broadcasts and a handful of international publications, and at least one of their bulletins was passed on to Tommy Bell, the Comintern agent who administered the Inter-States Committee of foreign communists.

Pyke's propaganda work was not restricted to this news agency. During the early stages of the war he frequently met with Sidney Elliott at *Reynolds News*, badgering him to keep his editorial line to the left. Harry Pollitt once described Pyke as 'working' at the paper with Elliott and 'giving him all his stunt ideas'.

Yet by the summer of 1940, as the threat of Nazi invasion grew, a curious thing happened. Pyke's propaganda work lost its intensity and his position appeared to shift. He confided in a friend 'his terror at the thought of a successful Nazi invasion of Britain', given that he was a left-wing Jew, and began to off-load his political literature. It was also around this time that Pyke had the idea for Plough and set about promoting it with characteristic ardour. In the context of what he had been doing until then, this makes almost no sense.

The Party line was clear: Britain and Germany were engaged in an imperialist war; the British proletariat should rise up against the British bourgeoisie rather than fight the Germans. Pyke's Plough idea flew in the face of this. It was a solution to a military problem faced by the British Army. So why did Pyke press it upon senior political and military figures with such enthusiasm?

This illustrates one of the most powerful contradictions within Geoffrey Pyke. His newfound identification with communism could be at odds with the character he had made for himself over the last four decades. One part of him was internationalist in outlook, radical and all for sweeping, systemic change which might usher in a new world informed by science. Another side of him was more English, if that is the right word – it was in thrall to Shaw, it was non-conformist, inconsistent and incapable of toeing a particular line. He felt the pull of Moscow but at the same time he was determined to tackle the great problems of his age. What made him unusual was his ability to maintain this internal conflict in balance rather than succumb to one part of it. In May 1940 this found him in the bizarre position of being a communist propagandist who was promoting a scheme to help Britain defeat Germany.

The chalk-shelter campaign embodied this paradox. It was a practical solution to an urgent wartime problem which happened to be taken up by the CPGB. For once both sides of his personality were aligned.

Yet even as he began to pull away from his propaganda work, Pyke was either unable or unwilling to divorce himself from the informal networks he had joined, and during the summer of 1940 he appears to have agreed to push for the release of Rünkel and Kamnitzer on behalf of the KPD. At the time it was customary for communists to use 'British subjects to do work which it might be embarrassing for foreigners to handle'; we also know that most Soviet agents dispatched to Britain were assigned a CPGB member.

In this case it seems that they had been assigned a man who 'stood close to the English Party', as Kuczynski put it, rather than a fully fledged member. It is an important distinction. Pyke was prepared to help the Party, just as the Party had helped him, but temperamentally he was unsuited to full membership and never joined.

Any moral difficulties he might have felt during those early stages of the war vanished after Germany's invasion of the Soviet Union in 1941. At last his political consciences were united in the battle against fascism, and he began to promote the Plough scheme again, possibly on the advice of Rünkel, then working for Pyke.

At the time, the USSR desperately needed the British to open a second front against Germany and, given that the Plough scheme was designed to divert German troops away to Norway, it is not inconceivable that Rünkel encouraged Pyke to have another go at selling the idea to the British military. If so, it would seem that the origin of the US and Canadian Special Forces lies in a suggestion made by a Soviet agent.

Having joined Combined Operations, Pyke was candid about his desire for greater collaboration with the Russians – and for this same reason he passed information to Smollett. Just as he never joined the CPGB, Pyke did not become a 'recruited agent' for the Soviet Union. Instead he was merely what was known as a 'confidential contact' of Smollett's and was probably used on just a handful of occasions. In this he was not alone. Following the German invasion of Russia, Moscow was deluged with intelligence from Britain. As Douglas Hyde at the *Daily Worker* wrote, it poured in 'from factories and the Forces, from civil servants and scientists. Those who did it were not professional spies, they took big risks in most cases, received no payment whatever and, this is doubly important, did not see themselves as spies and still less traitors. As Party members they would have felt that they were being untrue to themselves and untrustworthy of the name of communist if they had not done it.' Geoffrey Pyke was one of these men and women – a source of information, but not a spy. The only time he was technically a spy stealing military intelligence from an enemy nation was in 1914 when he slipped into Germany disguised as an American and tried to smuggle a report on enemy troop movements back to London.

Though MI5 later received intelligence to intimate that Pyke might have been given a Party mission to carry out while in the United States during 1942, including an intercepted letter to Otto Katz which referred to 'an English professor of the name of Peake' who had gone to America 'to push the Communist movement there', there is no evidence of Pyke actually doing so. The Superman comic strip featuring a customised iceberg appears to have been a startling coincidence, or, for Pyke, a cute reminder that radical military ideas were not the preserve of military planners.

As his communist activities tailed off, MI5's interest in him bubbled over. They were told that Pyke was a senior Comintern official codenamed 'Professor P.', and that he ran communist 'action propaganda'. Both allegations were untrue. While he might have supplied foreign press cuttings to Tommy Bell and others, there is no evidence that he *ran* CPGB action propaganda, or that he undertook any propaganda work during his time in Combined Operations. Nor was he 'Professor P.' – though he appears to have been in touch with him.

'Professor P.' was almost certainly the man Pyke was seen having lunch with in King's Cross: Jürgen Kuczynski. Kuczynski's cover name in correspondence between senior KPD figures was often 'Peter'. He was an academic, professorial figure, so 'Professor Peter' and 'Professor P.' both make sense as cover names; moreover, Kuczynski was in Berlin when Professor P. was, he was connected to Varga, and was known to be a fine propagandist.

Unaware of this, MI5's suspicions regarding Pyke did not go away, and as late as April 1945 he was under surveillance again. This is a reminder of his uncanny ability to attract suspicion, a trait illustrated so well by Lord Rothschild's judgement and its emphasis on his 'erratic' character. Rothschild's close friend Anthony Blunt, then haemorrhaging secrets to Moscow, never elicited the same kind of suspicion for he did not possess that unbalanced quality which so many saw in Pyke – an electric, frenetic energy which made him stand out in almost any situation and might have been exaggerated by Addison's Disease.

There was also his Jewishness, so prominent in MI5 accounts of him – except for Rothschild's – which for some in the Security

Service only added to Pyke's aura of suspicion. It is interesting that throughout his life most of the men to be won over by him – Teddy Falk, Nathan Isaacs, J. D. Bernal, Leo Amery, Jürgen Kuczynski, Oscar Cox, Isidor Lubin, Max Perutz, Herman Mark, John Cohen – were either Jewish or of Jewish origin, with the notable exception of Mountbatten. Those who found him suspicious or took against him – the Wellingtonians who chased him down the corridors yelling 'Jew Hunt', W. S. Hadley, Vannevar Bush, Lord Cherwell, the MI5 officers who worked on his case – tended not to be.

The English society he inhabited was not exactly anti-Semitic, but it was one in which an individual's Jewishness could become part of the reason why he or she was disliked. As is the case all over the world, those who feel that they have something to lose or are in any way insecure in their social standing tend to be more susceptible to this prejudice – which might explain why Mountbatten, so confident of his aristocratic provenance, seemed incapable of anti-Semitic sentiment. This was also a society which did not lend itself easily to personal reinvention and could be suspicious of those who appeared to disguise their social origins. For some MI5 officers, many of whom did not have Jewish friends, the combination of Pyke's Jewish appearance and his refined English manner would exaggerate any initial suspicions they might have had.

While he helped the Communist Party during the first two years of the war and gave information to a Soviet agent on at least two occasions, Geoffrey Pyke was neither a communist nor a Russian spy. There is just one political conversion which makes sense of the last fourteen years of his life: the moment in 1934 when his analysis of the situation in Nazi Germany convinced him that fascism was the great danger of his age.

After the war, an American journalist contacted him about the story of Plough. In his letter he described Pyke as an 'inventor'. 'This reveals to me that you have got the story wrong,' came the reply. 'I am not in the least interested in inventing. I did not care 2d. what sort of machine would do the work to give us mastery of the snows. For all I cared the thing could hop like a kangaroo.' He did not see himself as an inventor. He did not see himself as a communist. 'I am primarily an anti-fascist.'

EPILOGUE, OR, HOW TO THINK
LIKE A GENIUS

———————

'I'd like everything concerning me to be destroyed and to be forgotten as if I'd never lived,' wrote Pyke in his final letter to his son. Yet David Pyke chose to keep his father's papers. Even if he had thrown them away, it would have been impossible to delete Geoffrey Pyke's imprint on the world, to undo the conversations, speeches, articles and inventions, as well as the universe of ideas which he had sung into being during his fifty-four years, and which had covered such an astonishing range. Pyke's Zelig-like journey through the early twentieth century encompassed a landscape of different fields – from the molecular constitution of ice through to Gallup Surveys, exotic investment models and the application of Freudian psychoanalysis to kindergarten design. He would tackle the problem of European anti-Semitism with the same imaginative, scientific rigour as the question of how to adapt a motorcycle sidecar for the Spanish Republicans. Also he had the remarkable ability to conceive complex technical ideas in spite of having no scientific training. What is interesting today is to see how his various ideas have aged, and the extent to which he was ahead of his time.

Pyke's work on NHS recruitment was included by John Cohen in a Minority Report that went out under both their names and has been described recently as 'one of the most radical critiques of nurse recruitment and education'. It foreshadowed many of the problems which would plague the NHS over the following decades.

His letters to *The Times* about the government's decision not to donate to UNICEF or abolish the death penalty were no less prescient. The latter was abolished in 1965, and today the British government gives roughly 0.7 per cent of the Gross National Income in foreign aid and to organisations like UNICEF.

His hopes for pedal-powered devices and, as he rather clunkily put it, 'the utilisation of muscle-power' are no less relevant today as energy prices soar, along with levels of obesity. Now there are charities and companies which adapt bicycles to power everything from water pumps to threshers, grinders, cinemas, kettles and even laptops. There is also a version of Pyke's cyclo-tractor in use, admittedly not the farm vehicle that Pyke had in mind but a pedal-powered bar in which you and your friends can cycle down the street while getting drunk.

His discovery of Pykrete proved to be a significant development in our understanding of ice, and for Professor Mark the results of the Habbakuk experiments 'have been put to good use ever since in all permanent constructions (roads, airstrips, bridges, and habitats) in Arctic and Antarctic regions.' While the idea of using Pykrete to build an enormous berg-ship has captured many people's imaginations – there has been a radio play on the subject, as well as one book and many television documentaries – to date this ship has not been built. Yet if the price of steel ever again becomes prohibitively high, as it was during the war, we may yet see berg-ships moving cargo around the world.

The Weasel tracked carrier, which emerged from the Plough

proposal, was later used at the South Pole and in Canada's North-western Territories for scientific research and mineral prospecting.

As we know, the First Special Service Force, which also emerged from Plough, later evolved into the Canadian and US Special Forces.

Pyke's idea for an underwater oil pipeline, PLUTO, which he had first proposed in 1934, has since been replicated all over the world.

The pioneering concept behind Voluntary Industrial Aid for Spain of organising groups of factory workers to produce material aid in their spare time remains largely untouched, and in Britain today there are no charities using this model, possibly for a similar reason to the one Pyke encountered at the time: the unions would not stand for it.

The principle behind Pyke's 1936 suggestion of an 'anthropology of ourselves', which resulted in the Mass Observation movement, has since become an accepted and important tool in the way we analyse British society. The Office for National Statistics collects a dizzying range of data on how we live, while the British Social Attitudes survey, among others, gauges our attitudes to major political and cultural questions just as Pyke had once proposed.

A decade after he began to raise money for an institute designed to eradicate anti-Semitism from Nazi Germany, lest there be a genocide on the scale of what had happened to the Armenians in Turkey, the horror of the Nazi Holocaust became clear. Sixty-six years later the Pears Institute for the Study of Antisemitism opened in Britain, at Birkbeck College, University of London, with aims similar to the organisation which had been once proposed by Pyke.

The legacy of Malting House School has since been described as 'out of all proportion to its three-year life span and the limited numbers of pupils with which it dealt'. For Pyke its great achievement was the role it played in raising his son, David, who could later reflect that 'one of the factors of my life has been a distinct absence of revelations. People usually find that some adult experience awakens them to an aspect of life previously closed to them; I have never had that. Everything was always open to me.' Elsewhere it has been suggested that Malting House 'played a key role in contesting and reconfiguring understandings of the "nature" of the English child'. By recording in such minute detail how the children reacted to this unfettered existence Pyke produced a longitudinal study of enormous value. Again, many of the school's underlying principles became widely accepted in educational theory after his death.

Yet the strand of Pyke's thought which has aged better than perhaps any other is one not easily associated with a particular period of his life – it is what he said and wrote about innovation. Inventing radical ideas was his metier. In the millions of words he wrote during his life he was at his most lucid on the history of stunningly original ideas and, as he told Mountbatten and others, he planned to write a history of Habbakuk to serve 'as a serious sociological study of the Dynamics of Innovation in our time'. Right up to his death he was gathering material for this book, focusing on where radical ideas came from and why so many fell on stony ground. 'Should this country go to war again it might be as well that such studies should exist and have been absorbed by both the public and the official mind.' This book was to be the last word on innovation, an exploration of radical ideas written by a man who had been described repeatedly as a brilliant problem-solver. It would be an everyman guide to thinking like a genius – for he believed that anyone could think as he did.

'What made Pyke so extraordinary,' ran his obituary in *Time* magazine, 'was his consistent belief that a human being could reason his way through any problem. That belief rammed Geoffrey Pyke's bald head into – and sometimes through – one stone wall after another.' But like so many books that are described at length by their author before being written, this one never materialised. We can still imagine what it would have contained. If you look at the way Pyke approached problems during his life, whether it was getting out of Ruhleben or winning the Battle of the Atlantic, there are clear patterns that emerge. Rather than waiting for moments of divine inspiration Pyke had a robust problem-solving technique. His method for coming up with radical new ideas can be broken down into a series of stages. They go roughly as follows:

A Pykean Guide to Innovation

His first step, simple as it may sound, was to be adventurous. Adventurousness could be defined as 'a readiness to make a fool of oneself' – something he called 'the first duty of a citizen'. He lived by Dostoyevsky's maxim that 'the cleverest of all, in my opinion, is the man who calls himself a fool at least once a month'. Any mistakes you made were 'the social and purposive equivalent of Nature's mutations', without which there can be no progress. In other words, to be adventurous one must also be prepared to look silly or be laughed at and that requires courage. Without this it is almost impossible to come up with a truly radical idea.

The next step followed on from the first. A by-product of being intellectually adventurous was to develop a more sceptical attitude to what you were told. Pyke trained himself to question accepted truths, and to keep doing so until he had found the one which did not ring true – for there was always at least one. 'It is easier to solve a problem than it is to spot what *is* the problem (as the whole history of science and technology shows). Almost any fool can solve a problem and quite a number do. To detect the right problem – at least so I have found – requires what Wells calls the daily agony of scrutinising accepted facts.' Challenging everything like this was not just a 'daily agony' but a form of impertinence. In Ruhleben it felt rude to question the accepted fact that nobody could escape – rude but essential. 'My technique, whose results sometimes give me a spurious appearance of brilliance, consists of nothing more than having enough intellectual courage to think in terms which *our social environment* has decided are nonsense and to see if after all our epoch is right . . . in every particular. *It is not. And that is all there is* in the trick. And I can teach anyone young enough in heart to do the same.'

Once this 'daily agony' had provided him with an interesting problem, Pyke would pause to refine it. This was a key step, for the wording of the question had to be right. He often found that tiny adjustments to the formulation of a problem could unlock a torrent of fresh ideas. He got nowhere by asking himself what disguise he and Falk should adopt to get from Ruhleben to London undetected; instead the question was how they would like to come across in the eyes of those they encountered. 'The correct formulation of a problem is more than halfway to its solution,' he insisted. 'If anybody says he has nothing to say it only means that the problem has been put to him inappropriately.'

Having refined the question, Pyke would move on to the next stage – research – which saw him head off in two different directions. He would mine the past for historical analogies and lost solutions, for we live in a written culture that encourages forgetfulness. Yet he would also search for scraps of information and inspiration in the world around him, scouring newspapers, journals, films, posters, statistics and surveys, as well as the conversations he had. 'One of my ideas [. . .] came from a music hall song with a line "The Bomb that Found Its Own Way Home.'" In a similar sense, he believed in carrying out small-scale experiments to learn about the problem in hand. His guiding principle here was never to limit research to a single field, which explains the bewildering range of influences behind the Malting House School, for example, from Freud and Rousseau to Montessori, Armstrong and his own childhood. 'We cannot tell where data and ideas will come from, or to whom they will be significant.' Instead he taught himself to look for correlations everywhere. 'EVERYTHING IS IRRELEVANT TILL CORRELATED WITH SOMETHING ELSE.' Identifying those correlations 'is not a question of ability, but of free-mindedness'.

Sometimes this research would provide him with a solution and there was no need to go any further. But for trickier problems Pyke would reach for his 'Auto-Socratic' technique in which he imagined a dialogue between two voices – best described as a wildly inventive teenager and a polite psychiatrist. The teenager represents fantasy, the psychiatrist is reality. One proposes – and takes things to an extreme – while the other scrutinises – and does so graciously. The sober voice of reality does not shoot down ideas for the sake of it but allows the voice of fantasy to finish each train of thought. The dialogue between the two begins always with the patient presenting the problem in its most pared-down form, after which the conversation ferrets off under its own momentum until it produces either a subject for further research or a solution.

There were times when this technique was 'Auto-Shavian' as much as Auto-Socratic, such was Pyke's love of Bernard Shaw's paradoxes and his habit of spinning round every truism, question or statement. Pyke, too, had a pathological weakness for reversal. The Nazis set up an institute to study the Jewish Question; as a Jew he would study the Nazi Question. When in a rush to get to Berlin, he took the slowest train possible. To inflict the greatest damage on an enemy in occupied territory he urged that it be occupied more fully. If for at least one of his critics at OSRD Pyke 'would rather wage a futile campaign with mathematical or psychological elegance than win the war by recourse to vulgar or commonplace weapons or strategems', more often than not these reversals provided Pyke with a way out of any intellectual dead-end.

Another defining element of Pyke's technique was his determination never to become attached to a tentative solution. As he had learnt with Plough and Habbakuk, one must always be ready to try, fail, learn and try again as soon as possible. He also learnt repeatedly and painfully that all innovations must encounter resistance. As he once told Mountbatten, his experience of suggesting new ideas had been 'to be heartily kicked in the pants'. The times in his life when he was most successful were those when he anticipated where the resistance to his idea would lie.

After the war, Pyke complained to Michael Foot, the future Labour Party leader, that 'the sport of shooting down ideas has come to be a substitute for the amusement of shooting down grouse and partridges'. An idea might also be shot down because it was no good. It could be that it threatened the prestige, earning power or autonomy of an individual or an institution. The fear of its unintended consequences, or the suspicion that its benefits had been exaggerated, had the ability to turn people against it. Incomprehension was another reason why some of Pyke's most radical ideas met with resistance. At other times the opposition might stem from a personal dislike of the scheme's author.

But for Pyke, new ideas were usually dismissed because they threatened a tradition or habit. Sometimes he was right. We look for consistency in our surroundings and all too often will turn against an innovation not as a result of a level-headed assessment but purely because of its disruptive nature.

Towards the end of his life Pyke began to appreciate that there were steps he could take to protect his ideas from this kind of opposition, and on those happy occasions when he was successful it was often because he had communicated a clear narrative about what his new idea was and why it was so useful. He would contrast the consequences of developing it with inaction. When convincing those in Combined Operations to take on Plough, he recognised that resistance might be directed against the author of the concept as much as the concept itself, so he worked hard at personally winning over the officers he spoke to. When trying to improve the image of Malting House he understood the importance of showing the radical new ideas it embodied in action, so he commissioned a film about the school. The demonstration of Pykrete which took place in Churchill's bath and in Quebec did more than anything else to convince senior political and military figures that Habbakuk could work (though neither was his idea). But perhaps the most important thing Pyke did when trying to introduce a strange, disruptive idea like Habbakuk or Plough, the reason why he got as far as he did, was that he won over powerful individual supporters.

In today's jargon these are sometimes called 'early adopters'. It is easy to spot a potential early adopter in the top brass of any institution: he or she will be the person who likes to take risks or prides themselves on being outspoken. Once Pyke had identified an early adopter there were various tricks he used to win them over. He would avoid sending over a written summary of his idea before meeting in person. Once he had been granted an audience he would do his best to provoke them and make them laugh, for we become more impulsive when in a good mood. Usually he told them that he only wanted several minutes of their time, or that they need read no more than the first few pages of his proposal. He would appeal to their curiosity by presenting the idea as a story with a beginning, middle and end and, like any skilled storyteller, he tried to vary the scale by moving about historically and remembering to zoom out and in. He would find out about the interests of this early adopter and play to them in his pitch. Where possible he would also appeal to their vanity by implying that they were the only ones with the imagination and foresight to recognise the Promethean brilliance of his new idea. As he did with Mountbatten so often, Pyke tried to extend the ownership of an idea by leaving elements of the plan unfinished. In this way additional details might be provided by Mountbatten and, once he had begun to fill in some of the gaps, Pyke would refer to the proposal as 'our idea'. He would also stress that his radical solution was not the finished one and that others needed to come in – all of which made his ideas appear less dogmatic or intimidating.

The final stage of Geoffrey Pyke's problem-solving technique was to carry out a post-mortem. He would ask himself if there were lessons to be taken from his latest attempt to bring a new idea into the world. Increasingly, towards the end of his life, this was where he went wrong.

When casting his eye back over an unsuccessful campaign he was too quick to blame its failure on society's fear of change. There were times, as Donald Tyerman suggested, that 'even if you had your way and got a community open to innovation, there would still be the problem of Pyke to solve'. Yet to imagine Pyke without 'the problem of Pyke' is a counter-factual too far. The 'problem of Pyke' represents the same disequilibrium that drove him on with the kind of relentless momentum which is so often manifested in those who lose a parent at a young age.

In many ways the shape of his personality was set by the end of the First World War, after which he emerged as a young man suffering from an undiagnosed condition, possibly Addison's

Disease, who carried the scars of an abusive childhood and the complex of having survived a war in which he did not fight – both because he had escaped from imprisonment and was deemed medically unfit for service. He had also written a best-selling book, smuggled himself into Germany, become an amateur spy, faced execution in solitary confinement, converted to socialism and escaped from a German detention camp. All this by the age of twenty-four.

This unique and unlikely set of experiences changed his understanding of what was possible and why change did not happen sooner. Many of us at a similar age might test the boundaries of what we can achieve before undergoing a realignment of sorts. Pyke never experienced that adjustment. He remained in this youthful frame of mind for the rest of his life, unyielding in his determination that no question was beyond him, resistance to new ideas was socially inherited and that each of us can solve any problem we like. Moreover, we have a duty to do so. He was intelligent and comfortable with paradox, and in the English society he inhabited his eccentricities were tolerated – indeed, his character is at times a reflection of this abiding English tolerance for colourful nonconformists.

'Pyke is just a pure English freak,' he imagined Mountbatten telling General Marshall (in a letter Pyke had sent to Mountbatten). 'Of course, most of our freaks are no good. But about one in a thousand is the goods. You know, just like you might have to open a thousand oysters before you get one with a pearl. Though Pyke is not an oyster. For you can't shut him up.' He warmed to his theme of the English and their oddballs: 'We have a very sound method for testing their sense of the practical. If they have got enough sense to force their way through all the barriers of officialdom to the people at the top, then there must be something to them'.

This is a revealing line. It is one of the only times we are given a glimpse of Pyke's ambition. He knew that he was unusual, that some saw him as a 'freak', but he was desperate to prove his worth by having his ideas taken up at the highest level.

During the Second World War this singular Englishman realised his dream by forcing himself and his ideas through to the very top. In the face of the fascist threat he flourished, but there was only so much he could do alone. Throughout his life his most radical ideas depended on the support of others, and his role was simply to propose these ideas. 'I have to behave rather like Nature,' he once wrote, 'throwing up a hundred million pollen on the chance that one may do its duty.' Of course his greatest and most radical idea was that each of us could do the same ourselves.

NOTES

A select bibliography can be found at henryhemming.com.

Where no collection is indicated, the item can be found in the Geoffrey Pyke Archive, housed at the time of publication with Janet Pyke.

'ADM', 'B', 'BT', 'CAB', 'DEFE' and 'KV' – National Archives, Kew
'AMEL' – Churchill Archives Centre, Cambridge
'Cherwell Papers' – Nuffield College, Oxford
'FDR' – Franklin D. Roosevelt Library
'JDB Papers' – Cambridge University Library
'L. H. Myers Papers' – Eton College Library
'MB1' – Mountbatten Papers, University of Southampton
'NRCC' – National Research Council of Canada
'Ramsey Papers' – King's College Modern Archives Centre, Cambridge
'RUH' – Liddle Collection, Leeds University
'SAPMO-BArch' – Foundation Archives of Parties and Mass Organisations of the GDR in the Federal Archives (SAPMO), Bundesarchiv, Berlin

v   epigraph: Socrates, *Defence of Socrates*, 30d–31a, transl. David Gallop, from Plato, *Defence of Socrates, Euthyphro, and Crito* (Oxford: Oxford University Press), 1997, p. 45

Introduction

3   'only unoriginal thing': 'Everybody's Conscience', *Time*, 8 March 1948
3   'one of the most original': 'Mr Geoffrey Pyke', *The Times*, 26 February 1948
3   'Pyke's genius': L. L. Whyte, *The Listener*, 30 September 1948

3   'North Face': John Cohen, 'Geoffrey Pyke: Man of Ideas', *New Scientist*, 23 July 1981, p. 246

3   'the sort of man': David Lampe, *Pyke: The Unknown Genius* (London: Evans Brothers), 1959, p. 10

3   'right-hand men': 'Pyke of Habbakuk', *Evening Standard*, 24 February 1948

4   'immense natural dignity': Cohen, 'Geoffrey Pyke: Man of Ideas', p. 246

4   'Russian princeling': Cedric Hentschel, 'Geoffrey Pyke', *Less Simple Measures* (Berkeley, Gloucestershire: Garratt), 2002, p. 44

4   'Byzantine icon': Elias Canetti, *Party in the Blitz* (London: Harvill), transl. Michael Hofmann, 2005, p. 181

5   'concealed truth': GP Notebook, 9 October 1941

5   'voice of Conscience': Oscar Cox to Harry Hopkins, 13 November 1942

How to Become a War Correspondent

11   'abilities . . . clever': Reginald Drake to R. Banfield, 4 July 1916, 101570/MI5/G, KV 2/3038

13   death of father: Cohen, 'Geoffrey Pyke: Man of Ideas', p. 246

13   'most amazing meetings': *Cambridge Magazine*, 6 June 1914, vol 3, no. 25, p. 708

14   'spellbound . . . every word': Ibid.

15   'log jam': Lampe, *Pyke: The Unknown Genius*, p. 19

15   'firm believer': Geoffrey Pyke, *To Ruhleben — And Back* (New York: Collins Library / McSweeney's), 2002, p. 31

17   Reuters crisis: Donald Read, *The Power of News: The History of Reuters* (Oxford: Oxford University Press), 1999, p. 1

17   Pyke's career as a Reuters correspondent: This episode is not at all well documented — all Reuters telegrams from this period were pulped after the war, and as a String Correspondent Pyke would not have been listed as a Reuters member of staff. But it is unlikely that Pyke would have made such a claim and put it in print, given how easy it would be for Reuters to dispute it.

17   'Reuters' special correspondent': *The Manchester Guardian*, 26 July 1915, p. 4; *The Scotsman*, 26 July 1915, p. 8

18   'Athens . . . intercourse': Geoffrey Pyke, *The Fortnightly Review*, 1 January 1916, p. 35

18   'pointed of questions': Ibid., p. 38

18   'four German destroyers': United States Naval Institute, *Proceedings*, ed. E. J. King, (Annapolis: US Naval Institute), 1914, vol. 40, p. 1566

18   'seedy individual': Basil Thomson to Reginald Drake, 26 June 1916, KV 2/3038

19   no British correspondents: James W. Gerard, *My Four Years in Germany* (London: Hodder and Stoughton), 1917, p. 94

19   'desire . . . Germany': Pyke, *To Ruhleben*, pp. xiii-xiv

20   'censorship': *Daily Chronicle*, 7 August 1914

20—1   'quickly, please': Pyke, *To Ruhleben*, p. 1

21	'crown of ambition': Philip Gibbs, *Adventures in Journalism* (London: Heinemann), 1923, p. 179
21	'absolutely determined': Pyke, *To Ruhleben*, p. 4
22	'procession . . . fun': Philip Gibbs, *The War Dispatches* (London: Anthony Gibbs and Phillips and Times Press), 1964, p. 4
22	'no correspondents in Berlin': Pyke, *To Ruhleben*, p. 5
23	'Glory of glory': Ibid.
24	'fine voice': 'The Union Society', *The Cambridge Review*, 27 Feb 1913, vol. 34, no. 852, p. 320
24	'good elocutionist': *Cambridge Magazine*, 18 October 1913
24	'pleasing song': Ibid., 17 May 1913
24	'spare moments': 'Union Notes', *The Granta*, 10 May 1913, vol. 26, no. 592, p. 319
24	'brilliant . . . ill-balanced': Basil Thomson to Reginald Drake, 26 June 1916, KV 2/3038
24	*Telegraph* scoop: Phillip Knightley, *The First Casualty* (London: Quartet), 1978, p. 87
25	'some knew a little': Pyke, *To Ruhleben*, p. 6
26	'hot iron': Ibid., p. 63
27	'expecting English journalists': Ibid., p. 5
28	'correct formulation': GP to Palmer Putnam, US National Archives and Records Administration, Records of the OSRD, Division 12, Project Records 1940–45, OD-65
28	US consulates: Gerard, *My Four Years*, p. 96
29	birth certificate fee: Bankruptcy Hearing No. 243 of 1928, 'Geoffrey Nathaniel Pyke', BT 226/4520
30	customs shed: Edward Lyell Fox, *Behind the Scenes in Warring Germany* (New York: McBride, Nast and Co.), 1915
30	'The people know': Quoted in De Beaufort, *Behind the German Veil* (London: Hutchinson), 1917, p. 27
30	'people were seized': Gerard, *My Four Years in Germany*, p. 95
31	'He will punish': Peter Englund, *The Beauty and the Sorrow* (London: Profile), 2012, Kindle location 273
31	'divorced . . . breath': Pyke, *To Ruhleben*, p. 9
32	'spitting': Ibid., p. 9
32	'*Ach so*': Ibid., p. 10
33	'horribly uncertain': Pyke, *To Ruhleben*, p. 13
33	'Several times': Ibid.
33	'Suddenly I heard': Ibid., p. 14
33–4	'I saw . . . *Bummelzug*': Ibid., p. 19
34	Berlin: Modris Eksteins, *Rites of Spring* (London: Papermac), 2000, p. 83 with reference to James Steakley, *The Homosexual Emancipation Movement in Germany* (New York: Arno), 1975, pp. 24–27
35	'The first thing': Pyke, *To Ruhleben*, p. 21

36   'I listened': Ibid., p. 22
36   'Do not say "Yes"': De Beaufort, *Behind the German Veil*, p. 49
36   'den of lions': Pyke, *To Ruhleben*, p. 28
37   'packed . . . music': Ibid., p. 34
37   'the booms . . . paper': Ibid., p. 7
39   'It would not be long': Ibid., p. 48
40   'Velazquez': Ibid., p. 50
40   'infantile sparring': Ibid., p. 51
41–2 'Outside I could hear': Ibid., pp. 66–67

How to Escape

44   'terrible mistake': E. M. Falk, 'My Experiences as a Prisoner of War in Germany, and How I Escaped', *Blackwood's Magazine*, No. 1203, Vol. 199, p. 4
44   'specimens': Ibid., p. 11
44–5 'There were whites . . . brothel': Ibid., p. 10
46   'hopeless depression': Ibid.
47   'I would lie': Pyke, *To Ruhleben*, p. 113
47   'loft vibrate': Ibid., p. 123
47   'All night long': Ibid., p. 124
47   'finally vomiting': Ibid., p. xv
48   'only connection': Ibid., p. 71
48   'to think too much': Fyodor Dostoyevsky, *Notes from Underground & The Double*, transl. Constance Garnett (Digireads), 2008, Chapter 2
48   'not the months': Pyke, *To Ruhleben*, p. 61
48   'I could feel': Ibid., p. 56
48   'I could almost hear': Ibid., p. 76
48   'sarcasm of a Voltaire': Ibid., p. 100
49   'with that roll': Ibid., p. 76
49   'real hunger': Ibid., p. 74
49   'rooted objection': Ibid., p. 80
49   'sinking fast . . . creature': Ibid., p. 99
49   Modern studies: See John J. Gibbons, Nicholas de B. Katzenbach, *Confronting Confinement*, The Commission on Safety and Abuse in America's Prisons, June 2006, accessed at www.vera.org on 17 August 2012
49   'mental breakdown': Falk, 'My Experiences', p. 17
49   'jolly evenings': Pyke, *To Ruhleben*, p. 75
50   'moved in the matter': Reginald Drake to R. Banfield, 4 July 1916, 101570/ MI5/G, KV 2/3038
50   'owed my liberation': Falk, 'My Experiences', p. 7
50   'given away': M. L. Ettinghausen, 'Some Extracts from the Memoirs of an Octogenarian Jewish Bookseller', *Transactions: The Jewish Historical Society of England* (London: University College), vol. 21, 1968, p. 194

50   Edward Lyell Fox: Thomas Boghart, *Spies of the Kaiser* (London: Palgrave Macmillan), 2004, p. 63

50   American ambassador intervened: Special Branch would reach a similar conclusion in 1916: 'the American Ambassador was invoked to save his [Pyke's] life if he had been arrested as a spy.' Basil Thomson to Reginald Drake, 26 June 1916, KV 2/3038

51   'overgrown . . . observant': Falk, 'My Experiences, p. 17

51   'pessimist and cynic': E. M. Falk, 'My Experiences During the Great War 1914–1918 as Published in *Blackwoods Magazine* in January 1915 with some Additions', GB 206, RUH 22, p. 25

51   'dirtiest stable': Israel Cohen, *The Ruhleben Prison Camp* (London: Methuen), 1917, p. 46

51   'recoiled . . . shudder': Ibid., p. 50

51   'atmosphere . . . mud': Pyke, *To Ruhleben*, pp. 122–123

51   'its little windows': Cohen, *The Ruhleben Prison Camp*, p. 50

52   'doctor's mentality': Pyke, *To Ruhleben*, p. 128

52   'human kindness': Ibid., p. 145

52   era of daring getaways: GP Notebook, 8 August 1941

53   'Before a problem': GP to Jon Kimche, 14 January 1945

53   'become so garrulous': Pyke, *To Ruhleben*, p. 131

54   'bank holiday crowd': Ibid., p. 116

54   'very gloomy': Ibid., p. 134

54   'insane belief': Ibid., p. 133

54–5   'essentially English': Falk, 'My Experiences . . . with some Additions', p. 25

55   'We were both . . . got out?': Pyke, *To Ruhleben*, pp. 134–135

56   'made no sign': Ibid., p. 136

56   'a little shy': Ibid., p. 137

56   'By admitting': Ibid.

56–7   'artificially calm': Ibid., p. 170

57   'In view of the danger': Falk, 'My Experiences', p. 18

57   'infinitely greater': Ibid., p. 19

57   'Far more courage': GP Notebook, 8 August 1941

57   'a strong presentiment': Wallace Ellison, 'My First Escape from Ruhleben', accessed at http://www.greatwardifferent.com/Great_War/Great_War_Great_Escapes/Great_War_Great_Esc apes_02.htm on 3 November 2011

58   'behaved . . . caddishly': Pyke, *To Ruhleben*, p. 172

58   'make it safe': GP Notebook, 8 August 1941

59   'a natural calm': Pyke, *To Ruhleben*, p. 170

60   'out-manoeuvring': Ibid., p. 142

62   'rattling wires': Falk, 'My Experiences', p. 18

62   'walked on': Ibid., p. 19

62   'depended on lifting': Pyke, *To Ruhleben*, p. 173

63   exercises for a weak heart: Ibid.

63   'elbows aching and brows wet': Ibid.

63 'positive genius': Falk, 'My Experiences', p. 18
63 'sheer hard thinking': Falk, 'My Experiences . . . with some Additions', p. 28
64 'twigs underfoot': Falk, 'My Experiences', p. 19
64 the first fence: Pyke, *To Ruhleben*, p. 174
64 'Seeing him in difficulty': Falk, 'My Experiences', p. 20
64 the third fence: Pyke, *To Ruhleben*, p. 174
64 'great deal of difficulty': Ibid., p. 175
65 heart thumping: Ibid.
65 'I had got to the top': Ibid., p. 176
65 'Was it a constable?': Falk, 'My Experiences', p. 20
66 'rare beatitudes': Draft written in early October 41, GP Notebook

How to Become Invisible

68 'I repeated': Pyke, *To Ruhleben*, p. 142
69 'go forward': Ibid., p. 141
69 'something utterly . . . impossible': Ibid., p. 145
70 'great charm about Arsène': Ibid.
73 'Everything looked different': Ibid., p. 180
73 'Before Pyke could': Falk, 'My Experiences', p. 21
73 'my pocketbook': Ibid., p. 18
74 'great, big fat things': Pyke, *To Ruhleben*, p. 181
74 'whether he had any notion': Falk, 'My Experiences', pp. 21–22
74 'hot coals': Ibid., p. 22
75 Blumenthal and Herr Referendar: Pyke, *To Ruhleben*, p. 166
76 valleys near Goslar: Falk, 'My Experiences', p. 22
76 'a bright sun': Ibid., p. 23
77 forest deserted: Falk, 'My Experiences . . . with some Additions', p. 27
77 'Fugitives please note': Falk, 'My Experiences', p. 26
78 'I lacked the nerve': Falk, 'My Experiences . . . with some Additions', p. 40
78 'extremely addicted': Pyke, *To Ruhleben*, p. 181
78–9 'Burglary . . . catch you': Ibid., pp. 184–185
79 'Red Indian dictum': Ibid., p. 184
79 'In suave tones': Falk, 'My Experiences', p. 29
80 'How our boots': Ibid., p. 26
80 'suicidal, in view': Ibid., p. 27
81 'a buxom dame': Ibid.
82 'Madam, in these days': Ibid., pp. 27–28
83 'that hunted feeling': Falk, 'My Experiences . . . with some Additions', p. 39
83 'respective merits': Falk, 'My Experiences', p. 30
83 factory description: Pyke, *To Ruhleben*, p. 201
84 'end of our journey': Falk, 'My Experiences', p. 29
84 'Get your legs in': Pyke, *To Ruhleben*, p. 202
84 'nothing exciting': Ibid.

85 'frightful Prussian': Ibid.

85 'Section A': Ibid., p. 203

85 'bored young farmer': Ibid.

85–6 'the one wish': Ibid., p. 206

86 'suddenly pitched' and 'I shall never forget': Falk, 'My Experiences', p. 31 and E. M. Falk, undated letter, GB 206, RUH 22, p. 5

87 'for my sight and ears': Pyke, *To Ruhleben*, p. 209

88 'Instead of turning': Ibid., p. 212

89 'until a full stop is reached': Ibid., p. 213

89 'I ached': Ibid.

90 'that red-roofed cottage': Ibid., p. 246

90 'How did you get through': Falk, 'My Experiences', p. 32

91 'To him I feel': Pyke, *To Ruhleben*, p. xv

92 'the joy of that first bath': Falk, 'My Experiences', p. 32

92 'base of German agents': Falk, 'My Experiences . . . with some Additions',

94–7 newspaper headlines: The story even made it to New Zealand and Australia: 'Escapees from Prison Camp', *Hawera and Normanby Star*, 26 July 1915; 'Escapees from Germany, Sensational Adventures', *Poverty Bay Herald*, 27 July 1915; 'Escape from Prison, Wonderful Exploit of Three Englishmen, A Walk Through Germany', *Ashburton Guardian*, 27 July 1915

97 GP and Falk meet Asquith: We know from Teddy Falk's obituary that he met Asquith, and it is reasonable to assume that Pyke would have been invited to Downing Street as well. Falk Obituary, undated, GB 206, RUH 22

Pyke Hunt, Part 1

99 Kell's war: Christopher Andrew, *Defence of the Realm* (London: Penguin), 2010, p. 29

100 Cambridge population. Christopher N. L. Brooke, *A History of the University of Cambridge, vol. IV, 1870–1990* (Cambridge: Cambridge University Press), 1993, p. 331

100 GP mind wandering: Pyke, *To Ruhleben*, p. xvi

100 'not a desirable': Charles Holland quoted in Leonard Dunning to Vernon Kell, 13 December 1915, KV 2/3038

101 'neither included nor': 'Geoffrey Pyke: Thrilling Story of His Escape from Ruhleben', *Cambridge Daily News*, 9 December 1915

101 'You must remember': A. J. P. Taylor, *The Trouble Makers* (London: Penguin), 1957, p. 134

102 case passes to MO5(g): Leonard Dunning to Vernon Kell, 13 December 1915, KV 2/3038/62527

102 warrant for GP's post: Vernon Kell to Charles Holland, 17 December 1915, KV 2/3038/62527

102 'unsettled sort': Charles Holland to Vernon Kell, 19 December 1915, KV 2/3038/63757

102   letters reveal nothing: The only letter kept by MI5 came from Clara Melchior, in Copenhagen, who had taken issue with a point made by Pyke a *Fortnightly* article. Melchior was author of *Familienminder* (Copenhagen, 1915), and may have taken exception to Pyke's claim that 60,000 men guarded the Kiel Canal

102   'manoeuvring, single-handed': Reginald Drake to Chief Constable, County Constabulary, Bodmin, 22 June 1916, KV 2/3038

102   'the day he left': Ibid.

103   'movements and associates': Ibid.

103   'awkward gaps': Ibid.

104   'dirty dog': Letter to Admiral W. Reginald 'Blinker' Hall, quoted in Andrew, *Defence of the Realm*, p. 82

104   'whence he disappeared': Reginald Drake to Basil Thomson, 22 June 1916, KV 2/3038

104   'movements of a boat': It is possible that he was tipped off by the young MI5 officer Hinchley Cooke, later an MI5 interrogator, who was in Falmouth at the time keeping an eye on the flow of German women passing through Falmouth to Holland. Report from District Intelligence Director 'on movements of a boat owned by *PIKE*', 22 June 1916, KV 2/3038

104   'boasts of having': Basil Thomson to Reginald Drake, 26 June 1916, KV 2/3038

105   'dazzling display': Taylor, *The Trouble Makers*, pp. 134–135

105   'enable one to see England': Thomas Hardy, 'Let Us Now Be Praised By Famous Men', *Cambridge Magazine*, 11 November 1916

105   'almost a traitor': GP, proposed broadcast to the German people, 1939

106   'no practical knowledge': R. Banfield to Reginald Drake, 30 June 1916, KV 2/3038

106   'should he transgress': Reginald Drake to R. Banfield, 4 July 1916, KV 2/3038

106   Signals offices contacts MI5: The Chief Officer at the War Signal Station in St Anthony had written to Admiral Denison in Falmouth who wired the MI5 District Intelligence Director, who passed the news on to Drake, 6 July 1916, KV 2/3038

106   MI5 directive: MI5 to all British ports, the Foreign Office, the Home Office, the Permit Office, Scotland Yard, The French High Command (G.Q.G.), Glasgow Police and M.I.1.c., 13 July 1916, KV 2/3038

108   'First World War's best sellers': Knightley, *The First Casualty*, p. 89

108   'writes extraordinarily well': *Punch*, vol. 150, 8 March 1916

108   'narrative . . . thrilling': *The Chicago Tribune*, 29 April 1916

108   'Very exciting': Advertisement, *The Times*, 25 February 1916

108   '"Thrilling" has become': *Country Life*, 26 February 1916, pp. 321–2

109   'too young and too clever': *Punch*, vol. 150, 8 March 1916

109   'irreverent cleverness': *Spectator*, vol. 116, 4 March 1916, pp. 321–2

109   'doggedness' and 'courage': E. M. Falk, undated latter, GB 206, RUH 22, p. 4

109   'pro-German publication': CID to MI5, 22 November 1917

110   RP conscientious objector: Richard Pyke eventually enlisted in the Army on 14 September 1917 before joining the RAF in April 1918. Richard Pyke, *The Lives and Deaths of Roland Greer* (London: Richard Cobden-Sanderson), 1928, p. 118

110 'centre of life': Virginia Woolf, *The Question of Things Happening: The Letters of Virginia Woolf, Vol. 2: 1912–1922* (London: Hogarth), 1976, p. 210. She may have met Pyke in late 1916: 'O my God! what an evening . . . Strange figures . . . Mrs Hannay, an artist – Pike (*sic*) an inventor, Scott a don. Stove smoked, fog thick. Trains stopped. Bed.' Hermione Lee, *Virginia Woolf*, Vintage, 1997, Chapter 21, 'Seeing Life', VW to DG, 17 December 1916

110 'zenith of disreputability': Leonard Woolf, *Beginning Again: An Autobiography of the Years 1911 to 1918* (New York: Harcourt Brace Jovanovich), 1975, p. 216

110 'overpowering aroma': Douglas Goldring, *Odd Man Out* (London: Chapman and Hall), 1935, p. 267

110 'fresh deformity': Virginia Woolf to Lady Ottoline Morrell, November 1919, in Woolf, *The Question*, p. 399

111 GP and Margaret Chubb members of '1917': Richard Pyke talked about his brother and Margaret Chubb belonging to a London circle 'which envious outsiders delight to term a "clique," but which its languid members more often call a "crowd." [. . .] the Bloomsbury crowd whom they so often met', R. Pyke, *Roland Greer*, p. 225

How to Raise Your Child (and Pay for It)

114 'so charmed': As told to Lampe by Mary Pyke and Nathan Isaacs, Lampe in a letter to David Pyke

116 'a hasty temper': R. Pyke, *Roland Greer*, p. 5, p. 8

116 'Myra was consumed': Ibid., p. 9

116 'fist flourished': Ibid., p. 74

116 'irresistibly impelled': Ibid., p. 19

116 'only formidable opponent': Ibid., p. 55

116 'pushed his elbows': Ibid., p. 35

116 'on the side of his head': Ibid., p. 36

116–7 'mother chased them round': Lancelot Law Whyte, *Focus and Diversions* (New York: George Braziller), 1963, p. 92

117 'playing at pork butchers': R. Pyke, *Roland Greer*, p. 67

118 'Not only could': Ibid., p. 63

118–9 'running . . . public school': Pyke, *To Ruhleben*, p. 70

119 'malicious devils': R. Pyke, *Roland Greer*, p. 265

119 when things were at their worst': Lampe, *Pyke*, p. 30

119 'beastly': Audrey Coppard and Bernard R. Crick, *Orwell Remembered* (British Broadcasting Corporation), 1984, p. 23

119 'One ceased so completely': Harold Nicolson, *Some People* (London: Folio Society), 1951, pp. 22–26

119 'blamed the Wellington system': James Lees-Milne, *Harold Nicolson: A Biography, 1886–1929* (London: Chatto & Windus), 1980, p. 12

120 'most dismal period': Evelyn Waugh, *A Little Learning* (London: Penguin), 1990, Chapter 4

120   'an English public schoolboy': Lytton Strachey, *Eminent Victorians*, Kindle locations 2614–2623

122   'a silly business': GP suicide note, 21 February 1948

123   'a real marriage': 60 G. Bernard Shaw, 'Getting Married', *Prefaces* (London: Paul Hamlyn), 1965, p. 30

124   'highly scientific': Bankruptcy Hearing No. 243 of 1928, 'Geoffrey Nathaniel Pyke', BT 226/4520

126   'proprietary rights . . . happy': A. S. Ramsey Papers, Part 1

127   'awfully pleased': 13 January 1923 [incorrect date], F. P. Ramsey Papers, Part 1

127   'wonderful afternoon': F. P. Ramsey Papers, Part 1

127   'Geoff told me': Ibid.

128   GP develops financial model: 'Statement by G. N. Pyke', Bankruptcy Hearing No. 243 of 1928, 'Geoffrey Nathaniel Pyke', BT 226/4520

128   'now made £500': Diary, 8 February 1924, A. S. Ramsey Papers, Part 1

130   'lived almost as one': Institute of Education, London – N1/D/2, p. 7

130   'undoubtedly an educational genius': William van der Eyken and Barry Turner, *Adventures in Education* (London: Allen Lane), 1969, pp. 21–22

133–4   'If we invited': John Cohen quoted in David Lampe, *Pyke*, p. 19

134   average IQ: van der Eyken and Turner, *Adventures*, p. 27

134   'ten most difficult': Ibid.

135   'The method of remaining': Ibid., p. 30

135   'I must say. . . crachat upon her': James Strachey to Alix Strachey, 17 February 1925, Perry Meisel & Walter Kendrick, *Bloomsbury/Freud: The Letters of James and Alix Strachey* (London: Chatto & Windus), 1986, p. 205

135   children building others: School Notes, 10 November 1924

135   'pre-genital brothel': van der Eyken and Turner, *Adventures*, p. 37

136–7   'explicitly requested': Lydia A. H. Smith, *To Understand and to Help* (London and Toronto: Associated University Presses), 1985, p. 69

137   'individual aggressiveness': van der Eyken and Turner, *Adventures*, p. 34

137   'merely a demonstration': J. D. Bernal, *Microcosm*, undated MSS, JDB Papers, B.4.1

137   'a charming and good-natured': Lettice Ramsey Memoir, F. R. Ramsey Papers, 3/1

137   'cured of such wishes': James Strachey to Alix Strachey, 3 November 1924, Meisel & Kendrick, *Bloomsbury/Freud*, p. 107

137   Ramsey resenting GP joking: Frank Ramsey to Lettice Baker, 28 December 1924, F. R. Ramsey Papers, 2/2(2)

138   'a fine exhibition': John Rickman, 'Susan Sutherland Isaacs', *The International Journal of Psycho-Analysis*, vol. 31, 1950, p. 282

138   'Geoffrey turned more': Institute of Education, London – N1/D/2, p. 8

138   'she didn't feel any': Ibid.

138   'very real love': Ibid.

138–9   'blessing and active': Ibid.

139   'he had not been': Philip Graham, *Susan Isaacs: A Life Freeing the Minds of Children* (London: Karnac), 2009, p. 138

139   'rise to the occasion': R. Pyke, *Roland Greer*, p. 155
139   'secret difficulties': Ibid., p. 235
139   'understood too well . . . imparted': Ibid., p. 236
139   'the draw they were exercising': Institute of Education, London – N1/D/2, p. 8
140   GP as one of Cambridge's leading lights: Whyte, *Focus and Diversions*, p. 48
140   'an Assyrian king': Margaret Gardiner, *A Scatter of Memories* (London: Free Association Books), 1988, p. 72
140   'Philosophers have only': Karl Marx, Eleventh Thesis, 'Theses on Feuerbach', *Marx/Engels Internet Archive* (marxists.org) accessed on 24 June 2013
141   undergraduates breaking strike: Charlotte Haldane, *Truth Will Out* (New York: Vanguard), 1950, p. 54
141   'intensely distracted': GP Notebook, 27 August 1941
141–2 an exotic trade: *The Metal Bulletin*, 17 November 1959, p. 13
142   'no longer made any difference': *Bankruptcy Court*, 13 February 1929, p. 3
142   'immensely less speculative': Ibid.
143   over £20,000 trading profit: Based on the National Archives currency converter (measured to 2005): http://www.nationalarchives.gov.uk/currency/results.asp#mid
143   'certainly impressed': Harry G. Cordert to Nathan Isaacs, 10 December 1959, Institute of Education, London – N1/D/3
143   CEI to flush out speculators: Alfred Dupont Chandler, *Scale and Scope* (Cambridge, Mass: Harvard University Press), 2004, p. 126
143   CEI to have greats control of market: Graham, *Susan Isaacs*, p. 134; van der Eyken and Turner, *Adventures*, p. 58
144   'Why do children': Bankruptcy Hearing No. 243 of 1928, 'Geoffrey Nathaniel Pyke', BT 226/4520, p. 12
145   'It fair makes you sick': van der Eyken and Turner, *Adventures*, p. 55
145   'Even Geoffrey Pike': Ibid.
145–7 'Remarkably interesting . . . every child': 'C.S.' review of 'Let's Find Out', *Spectator*, 23 July 1927
147   'Moulds are wrong': Quoted in van der Eyken and Turner, *Adventures*, p. 20
147   children wanting boundaries: 'Memorandum of staff meeting held together with the children on November 11th 1928, 2 p.m.'
148   'irrespective of money': Bankruptcy Hearing No. 243 of 1928, p. 27
148   'imbecility': van der Eyken and Turner, *Adventures*, p. 61
149   'I don't want to hurt you': Institute of Education, London – N1/D/2, p. 32
149   'quite naturally displaced': Ibid., p. 8
149   'I've no resentment': Ibid., p. 6
149   'free play. . . mind': Ibid.
150   claims of £72,701: 'Differentiations in Prices', *Financial Times*, 31 January 1929
151   'possibly the greatest galaxy': van der Eyken and Turner, *Adventures*, p. 64
151   'great scheme': Bankruptcy Hearing No. 243 of 1928, p. 44
151   'never seen so much': E. Lawrence, 'The Malting House School', 1927, unpublished document

151   influence of Isaac's books: Malcolm Pines, 'Susan S. Isaacs', *Oxford Dictionary of National Biography*, 2004

152   influence of Nunn's department van der Eyken and Turner, *Adventures,* p. 66

152   'Quibbling again?': Bankruptcy Hearing No. 243 of 1928, p. 8

152   'tissue of falsehoods': Ibid., p. 63

152   'indisposition': Ibid., p. 20

152   'sudden illness': 'Costs of the Trustee of and relating to the Public Examination of the Debtor', No. 243 of 1928, B 9/1073, p. 11

152–3   GP declares himself ill: Geoffrey Pyke, 19 March 1929, B 9/1073

153   'dangerously ill': H. E. Nourse and C. H. Budd, 22 April 1929, B 9/1073

153   'he will not be fit': Dr Robert Nicholl, 30 May 1929, B 9/1073

153   'bordering upon insanity': 'Costs of the Trustee of and relating to the Public Examination of the Debtor', No. 243 of 1928, B 9/1073, p. 18

154   'her husband died': Jennifer S. Uglow, Maggy Hendry, Frances Hinton, *The Northeastern Dictionary of Women's Biography* (Boston: Northeastern University Press), 1998, p. 441

How to Resolve an Epidemic of Anti-Semitism, a Royal Scandal and the threat of Fascism

158–9   'emotional . . . anti-Semitism of reason': Adolf Hitler to Adolf Gemlich, 16 Sept 1919, quoted in Alan Steinweis, *Studying the Jew* (Cambridge, Mass.: Harvard University Press), 2006, p. 8

159   100,000 Jews in the German Army David Pyke and Jean Medawar, *Hitler's Gift* (New York: Arcade), 2012, p. 12; Phyllis Goldstein, *A Convenient Hatred* (Brookline, Mass.: Facing History and Ourselves), 2012, p. 259

160   'Semitic in its persistency': Pyke, *To Ruhleben,* p. 17

160   GP rows with Jewish barber: R. Pyke, *Roland Greer,* p. 211

160   'I have been told': GP Notebook, c. 1935

161   'the Jews among all': GP to Lord Lytton, c. 1936

161   'zig-zagged across the 1930s': Claud Cockburn, *I, Claud* (London: Penguin), 1967, p. 344

161   'Belief in contemporary Germany': Geoffrey Pyke, 'Politics and Witchcraft', *The New Statesman and Nation,* 5 September 1936, vol. XII, No. 289, pp. 312–314

162   'the guilty were roasted': 'Politics and Witchcraft' unpublished MSS sent originally to R. M. Barrington Ward at *The Times*

162   'one thing is clear': Pyke, 'Politics and Witchcraft', pp. 312–314

163   'perhaps the first result': Ibid.

163   'It is idle to argue': Michael Holroyd, *Bernard Shaw* (London: Vintage), 1998, p. 732

163   'The answer to those': Pyke, 'Politics and Witchcraft', pp. 312–314

163   'people will take': GP to Sidney Webb, c. 1936

163   'Let a man be thought': GP to Lord Lytton, c. 1936

164   'the man who unless': GP to Sidney Webb, c. 1936

164   what made this solution remarkable: Andrew McFadyean to GP, 17 June 1936

164   debts written off: He owed just £4 by January 1935, BT 226/4520

165   'commonsense . . . humour': David Keilin to GP, 13 Feb 1935

165   Marquess of Reading's refusal: Rufus Isaacs to GP, 30 May 1935

165   early backers of GP's plan: Melchett was one of the first to come on board, as he explained in a letter to GP, 2 December 1934

166   'a really good cause': Chaim Weizmann to Jan Smuts, undated

166   'Do you know of any better': GP Notebook, 1935

167   'a mere dreamer': Comments on the Captain of Koppenick, 1942, p. 3

167   'some of us wish': 'True Aspect of the Coronation', *The Telegraph and Argus*, 1 December 1936

167–8   'Society is suspended': Entry for 17 November 1936. A. Duff Cooper, John Julius Norwich (ed.), *Duff Cooper Diaries: 1915–1951* (London: Weidenfeld & Nicolson), 2005, p. 230

168   'there is little doubt': Lord Hardinge of Penhurst, *The Times*, 29 November 1955

168   'with the exception of': Clement Attlee, *As it Happened* (London: Heinemann), 1954, p. 86

168   'I do know public opinion': Cabinet Minutes, 27 November 1936, CAB 23/86 vol. LIII 69 (36)

168   'the Gallup Poll': The Duke of Windsor, *A King's Story* (London: Cassell), 1951, p. 331

168   'it was curious': Duff Cooper, *Duff Cooper Diaries*, p. 236

170   'anthropology . . . anti-Semitism': Humphrey Jennings, Charles Madge, Thomas Harrisson, 'Anthropology at Home', *The New Statesman and Nation*, 30 January 1937

170   'under trained . . . recorded': Evelyn Lawrence, 'The Malting House School', *National Froebel Foundation Bulletin*, February 1949, vol. 56, p. 5

171   'preliminary soundings': GP Notebook, 1937

171   'one of those moments': Martha Gellhorn to Phillip Knightley, quoted in Caroline Moorehead, *Martha Gellhorn* (Vintage), 2011, Kindle location 2376 of 11015

172   'Never has there been': Eric Hobsbawm, *The Age of Extremes* (London, 1995), p. 144

172   'a *de facto* Popular Front': Tom Buchanan, *The Spanish Civil War and the British Labour Movement* (Cambridge: Cambridge University Press), 1991, p. 138

173   'covered . . . song': GP Notebook, c. 1941

175   'failed to respond': GP Notebook, 30 July 1941

175   'complexity . . . Labour movement': GP to J. D. Bernal, 12 April 1937

176   'dangerous precedent': W. J. Bolton, 'Voluntary industrial aid: inter-departmental correspondence', 29 May 1937, Archives of the Trades Union Congress. 292/946/36/23(v)

176   'rather unfortunate': Vincent Tewson, 'Voluntary Industrial Aid: memorandum of interview with Geoffrey Pyke', 12 April 1937, Archives of the Trades Union Congress, 292/946/36/47

176   TUC rejects VIAS: Buchanan, *The Spanish Civil War*, p. 162

176   'complete destitution': GP to J. D. Bernal, 18 April 1937
176   'To forego': 'I Enclose' undated VIAS pamphlet, c. 1938
178   item sent by VIAS: Ibid.
178   details of VIAS cells: Michael Weatherburn, 'Motorcycles, Mattresses, and Microscopes: Geoffrey Pyke, the Communist Party, and Voluntary Industrial Aid for Spain, 1936–9', paper presented to the Voluntary Action History Society Workshop, Southampton University, 10 October 2012 – see also files K91-K94, Joseph Needham papers, Cambridge University Library
178   'real capital': GP, Memorandum to the Spain Campaign Committee of the Labour Party, January 1938, p. 47
178   'starting to understand': Weatherburn, 'Motorcycles, Mattresses, and Microscopes', – see also Arthur Exell, 'Morris Motors in the 1930s. Part II: Politics and Trade Unionism', *History Workshop Journal* 7:1 (1979)
179   'social entrepreneurs': GP, Undated Memorandum on operations of VIAS constructional groups, Sheet 22
179   'not yet trained myself': GP, Second part of Memorandum to the Spain Campaign Committee of the Labour Party, 15 February 1938
179–80 'I am very conscious': GP to J. D. Bernal, 12 April 1937
180   'complete confidence': GP, Second part of Memorandum to the Spain Campaign Committee of the Labour Party, 15 February 1938
181   'one of the most valuable': Sir Edward Ward, 'Report on the National Scheme of Coordination of Voluntary Effort', HM Stationery office; July 1919
181   GP finds forgetting unforgivable: GP, 'Murder and Forgetfulness', 1938
181   moss gathered near Balmoral: Undated newspaper cutting entitled 'Princesses gather moss for bandages', probably late 1940
181   VIAS Vehicles in Spain: *The Times*, 2 May 1938
181   Spanish minister praises VIAS: Weatherburn, 'Motorcycles Mattresses, and Microscopes', – see also Exell, 'Morris Motors'
182   'a country whose deepest': 'I Enclose' undated VIA pamphlet, probably 1938
182   'Wisdom is like gold': GP, 'If I Were A Dictator', p. 14

How to Prevent a War

183   'His quality of mind': Peter Raleigh, 'Communism', unpublished memoirs
183   Raleigh taken aside by Kettle: Ibid.
184   'Mad Scientist': Peter Raleigh, 'Germany', unpublished memoirs
185   'If the main facts': *Manchester Guardian*, 29 August 1938
185   'For me the world changed': GP Notebook, 'July 20 to July 31, 1941'
185   'The civilian population': GP, 'Message to the Workers of Germany Over Hitler's Head', 28 September 1938
186   National Council of Labour releases GP's message: 'British Labour's "Message to German People"', *Manchester Guardian*, 28 September 1938
186   'the common assumptions': GP Notebook, 8 August 1941
186–7 'among the first': GP Notebook, c. September 1941

187   'not only practicable': GP Notebook, 8 August 1941

187   'The fact of the matter': Hugh Sinclair quoted in Keith Jeffery, *MI6: The History of the Secret Intelligence Service* (London: Bloomsbury), 2011, p. 295

188   'by a short head': GP to Vernon Bartlett, 4 October 1939

189   'a drunkard': Passport papers for Watson, 15/11/38, KV 2/3035/25a

189   'a woman suspected': KV 2/3035/24a

189   'unsuitable for employment': KV 2/3035/31a

189   GP gives nothing away: GP, account of Golfing Spies, 1 May 1941

190   'Most of us, I suppose': Patrick Smith, unpublished account

190   Hentschel's poem: Hentschel, 'Geoffrey Pyke', *Less Simple Measures*, p. 44

190   'amply worthwhile': GP to Norman Angell, 27 July 1939

191   'Higgins' in GP's diaries: GP Diary, 1 August 39, first mention of 'Higgins'

192   holidaymakers on Bank Holiday: An Automobile Association official quoted in the *Daily Mail*, 4 August 1939

192   'the attention of the whole world': GP, 'Investigations into Public Opinion of Germany', September 1939

193   'whole nation . . . optimism': 'General Ironside's Report on conditions in Poland, 28 July 1939', PREM 1/331a War Office to PM, August 1939, quoted in Richard Overy, *1939: Countdown to War* (London: Viking), 2009, p. 15

194   'most carefully guarded': GP, draft opening of a lecture, September 1940

194   'a private attempt': GP, draft 'Beginning of Book', copied from Notebook, 26 August 1941

194   'It is true that': GP, draft opening of a lecture, September 1940

195   'Ridiculous': GP, account of Golfing Spies, 1 May 1941

195   'part of the general opinion': GP Notebook, 14 October 1941

195–6   'Quite an interesting': Patrick Smith to GP, via M. Ridley, 5 & 6 August 1939

196   'My dear Cedric': GP to Cedric Hentschel, 12 August 1939

196   'Life continues strenuous': Cedric Hentschel to GP, 10 August 1939

196   'For all their harsh': Patrick Smith, unpublished account

196   'how much they have': GP Notebook, 9 October 1941

196   'I had ridiculously over-rated': Ibid., 14 October 1941

196   'go grumbling . . . every class': Ibid., 21 October 1941

197   raining in Frankfurt': Peter Raleigh, 'Germany', unpublished memoirs

197   'endless coffees': Ibid.

197   'You *are* a disgusting pig': GP to Peter Raleigh, 10 August 1939

198   Raleigh and Smith meet: GP Notebook, 9 October 1941

198   'rasp of the Messerschmitt': Peter Raleigh, 'Germany', unpublished memoirs

198   'as strange as a unicorn': Patrick Smith, unpublished account

198   'It should have been no surprise': Peter Raleigh, 'Germany', unpublished memoirs

199   GP welcomed into Germany: Patrick Smith, unpublished account

199   'I suppose the best': Peter Raleigh, 'Germany', unpublished memoirs

199   'I only once reached': Ibid.

199   'as closely as is possible'; GP, 'Proposed Plan for a One-Time Survey in Germany', March 1939

200   publication of *Britain by Mass-Observation*: Judith Heimann, *The Most Offending Soul Alive* (London: Aurum), 2002, p. 150

200   Germans' views on war: Peter Raleigh, 'Reactions and General Observations', unpublished and undated note

200   'Though they admitted': Ibid.

201   'If that's bad music': Stanley Smith, undated account of his interviews

202   'the Nazi regime itself': GP to Duff Cooper, 12 August 1940

203   'I find it all interesting': Lal Burton to GP, 15 August 1939

203   'memorised perfectly': GP, undated note

204   'All the isms are wasms': As quoted in Cockburn, *I, Claud* p. 206

204   'almost tangible spirit': Watson to GP, 24 August 1939

204   'The word "England"': Watson's account of her interviews, late August 1939

205   'I found him full': GP Diary, 23 August 1939

207   train stops for German police: Peter Raleigh, 'Germany', unpublished memoirs

207   Raleigh evades capture: Ibid.

207   GP's reactions to safe return of team: GP Diary, 25 August 1939

208   report from woman in Golders Green: Copy of Min. from B2b to A.2 giving the phone number of PYKE, 23 August 1939, KV 2/3039/15a

209   'if Pyke was identical': Cross reference to Special Branch report mentioning Pyke, 7 February 1938, KV 2/3039/10a

209   'As I was about to enter': Police telegram re PYKE, 26 February 1938, KV 2/3039/11a

210   'strong autonomous body': GP Notebook, January 1937

210   'particularly anxious': Vincent Tewson, 'Voluntary Industrial Aid: memorandum of interview with Geoffrey Pyke', 12 April 1937, Archives of the Trades Union Congress, 292/946/36/47

210   'closely linked': Tom Buchanan, 'The Politics of Internationalism: The Amalgamated Engineering Union and the Spanish Civil War', *Bulletin of the Society for the Study of Labour History*, vol. 53, Part 3, 1988, pp. 47–55

210–11 'under Communist control': Roger Hollis to David Petrie 'From Box 201, Piccadilly B. O. re INTERNATIONAL VOLUNTARY SERVICE FOR PEACE', 19 December 1941, KV 2/3039/32a

211   'the ablest professional': Kim Philby quoted in Andrew, *Defence of the Realm*, p. 341

211   Sissmore requests GP's passport papers: 'A2c asked to obtain passport papers for PYKE', 2 March 1938, KV 2/3039/12a

211   'Listening in on the telephone': GP Notebook, 21 June 1941

211   '[Soviet] activity in England': Andrew, *Defence of the Realm*, p. 185

213–4 '"pink" Cambridge . . . almost entirely': Campbell Stuart, 'Extracts from FO file re PYKE', 29 April 1940, KV 2/3039/20a

214   'stiff with uniforms': Peter Raleigh, 'Germany', unpublished memoirs

214   results of GP's surveys: 'Investigations into Public Opinion of Germany', September 1939

Pyke Hunt, Part 2

217 'a known Communist': Document dated 18 February 1940, this line added on 22 February 40, KV 2/3039

218 'the habit of listening': 'From Special Branch regarding Morse code signals coming from 32 Great Ormond St', 21 February 1940, KV 2/3039/15b

218 'investigations failed': 'Cross reference re suspected illicit wireless from PYKE's residence', 11 March 1940, KV 2/3039/16x

218 'an interesting, or possibly': Malcolm Cumming to Gilbert Lennox, 27 April 1940, KV 2/3039/19a

219 'on excellent terms . . . propaganda': 20 May 1940, KV 2/3035/51a

219 'In view of this': Malcolm Cumming to Gilbert Lennox, 27 April 1939, KV 2/3035/50a

219 'a short man': Peter Wright with Paul Greengrass, *Spycatcher* (Australia: William Heinemann), 1987

220 'You see some' . . . 'trustworthy': Watson overheard talking to Pyke, 24 May 1940, KV 2/3038

221 SIS's concerns about GP's undercover work: There are several allusions to this, including Leo Amery's letter to Frederick Lindemann, 19 July 1940: 'The secret service branches under the War Office somehow or other think that his investigation would cross their wires. Personally, both the investigation and the kind of people employed would be so entirely different that I cannot imagine that there is any real danger of that happening.'

221 'close to collapse': Andrew, *Defence of the Realm*, p. 222

222 'a much persecuted': Leo Amery to Osbert Peake, 11 July 1940 (mistakenly marked as 11 May 1940)

222 'Depart, I say': Peter Hennessey, *Never Again* (London: Vintage), 1993, p. 20

222 'a strange creature': L. S. Amery, 26 Feb 1948, AMEL 8/66, Churchill Archives Centre

222–3 'the *only* man': GP to Osbert Peake, 17 July 1940

223 Higgins in GP's notebook: GP Notebook, August 1940

223 'deep gratitude': Rolf Rünkel to GP, 4 July 1941

223 GP sends payments to Higgins: Ibid., 10 December 1940

223 'deep sympathy with': GP to Sidney Kraul, 3 July 1940

223–4 'Pyke is well known': MI5 to Sidney Kraul, 9 August 1940, KV 2/3039

225 'all those interested': GP to Rolf Rünkel, 19 July 1941

225 'Higgins all possible': GP Notebook, 9 Feb 1940

225 '*Blonder Hans*': This appears in numerous sources, including the original Gestapo file on Runkel at Reichssicherheitshauptamt (RSHA), Amt IV, A2, Bundesarchiv, Berlin

225 Rünkel recruited by NKVD: Though NKVD personnel files from this period remain classified, the extraneous details about Rünkel's life up to and during this period suggest that he might have been recruited to the NKVD in the early 1930s. We know from his reaction to Special Branch surveillance in 1941 that he was experienced in picking up a tail, and that he was one of the first

Communists to be taken out of Prague in 1938, which attests to his seniority among the many German Communists gathered in Prague at the time. It is also significant that, in spite of this, he was not attached to any Party cell during his time in Britain. Those attached to the NKVD or GRU were customarily instructed to disassociate themselves from Party factions. Looking beyond the war, the lack of an archival trace in the GDR archives is suggestive. In a country where all Party members had voluminous files on them the relative lack of files on Rünkel opens up the strong possibility that the bulk of his papers were taken to the USSR, as happened with those of other employees of the NKVD or GRU.

226   Rünkel on Gestapo's list: RSHA, Amt IV, A2, Geheimes Staatspolizeiamt, Bundesarchiv, Berlin

226   'Certain words were missing': Fred Uhlman, *The Making of an Englishman* (London: Victor Gollancz, 1960), p. 242

227   Rünkel might have spied on Koenen: Documents captured in 1946 at Koethen (soon to be GDR) – Abw, III F. HELMUT WEHR papers on KOMINTERN Agents from PRAGUE, 10 January 1939. According to report i/28 of Helmut Wehr on 10 January 1939, four men were dispatched to London by the Komintern office in Prague, including Wilhelm Koenen and his secretary Hamann, and each one had a 'Labour functionary to spy on them in accordance with Komintern instructions' – one of whom might have been Rünkel, KV 2/2800/278b

227   'banality of evil': Hannah Arendt, *Eichmann in Jerusalem* (London: Penguin), 1994

228   'in the case of all non-Russian': Haldane, *Truth Will Out*, p. 292

230   'the publishing house': KV 2/2357/60a

230   MI5 raises no objection to Kamnitzer's release: KV 2/2883/15a

230   'a fanatical . . . Party work': W. Younger to Roger Hollis, 23 December 1941, KV 2/2883/26b

230   MI5 Suspect Rünkel: 'Information from B2 source 'M/S', 22 December 1939, KV 2/2714/6a

230   'is stated to have been': KV 2/1561/53a

230   Rünkel member of N-Dienst: B.8.c summary of MOELLER-DOSTALI interrogation at the Oratory Schools, 17 February 1941, KV 2/3364/58x

230   GP pays Rünkel's expenses: GP to Bobby Carter, 27 August 1941, Private Collection of Sarah Carter

231   'We know how devotedly': GP to Rolf Rünkel, 19 July 1941

231   'B[obby] and I': Deborah Carter, unpublished reminisces, c. 1989

232   Rünkel pointing out shadows: Author's correspondence with Thomas Rünkel, 10 September 2012

232   policeman suspects stronger connection between GP and Rünkel: Cross Reference to extract from Special Branch report re PYKE and RUNKEL', 22 September 1941, KV 2/3039/30a

232–3   'see to it . . . improved upon': Source: Ri, 17 November 1941, KV 2/1873/172a

233   'I consider this': Ibid.

233   MI5's libertarian approach': Hyde, *I Believed*, 1952, p. 75

234   'complete reliability': 'Photostat copy of letter from Pyke to AWS Dept re RUNKEL', 31 October 1941, KV-2–3039–31a

234   MI5 notes German communists at the BBC: KV 2/2883/30a

How to Defeat Nazism

235   'intensely elitist . . . birth': Philip Ziegler, *Mountbatten* (London: Fontana), 1986, p. 52

236   'how to do something': GP to Jon Kimche, 14 January 1945

237   'The Germans had complete': Ibid.

237–8 'The mathematical physicists': Ibid.

238   'Note the obvious': Ibid.

238–9 *Mastery . . . succession*': GP, 'A Strategic Proposal', revised version, November 1941

239   'The Assyrians': Pyke to Liddell Hart, 15 May 1940, and originally in Byron's 'The Destruction of Sennacherib', *Hebrew Melodies, 1815*

239   'how often could an aeroplane': GP to Jon Kimche, 14 January 1945

239   'Principles of attack': GP to Louis Mountbatten, 7 June 1942

239   'no more an invention': GP, 'A Strategic Proposal'

240   'similar to the adaptations': GP Notebook, December 1941

240   'with relatively slight': GP, 'A Strategic Proposal'

240   'Make every one': Ibid.

240   'Far from wanting': 'Commentary by Mr Pyke on C.O.H.Q.Int./28/15.4.42' S.7.0. North Norway – Large Scale Operation. US National Archives and Records Administration, Record Group 165, Entry 21, 390/30/16/4, Box 968, submitted on 15 April 1942 to Louis Mountbatten

241   'military ju-jitsu': GP to Louis Mountbatten, 7 June 1942

241   'Consider the *political*': Ibid., 4 June 1942

241   'to make a fool': GP to Basil Liddell Hart, 15 May 1940

241   'impressed by': Leo Amery to David Pyke, 11 March 1948, AMEL 2/3/5

241   Amery's patience with GP: Leo Amery, *The Empire at Bay* (London: Hutchinson), 1988, p. 1072

242   'no prospect for Jews': Leo Amery, 26 Feb 1948, AMEL 8/66

242   'the sort of person': GP to Sydney Elliott, 13 November 1939

242   'very naturally appealed': Leo Amery, 'Recollections of Mr Pyke', AMEL 2/3/5

242   'I am bothering': Leo Amery to Walter Monckton, 24 June 1940

242   'it seems to be all': Walter Monckton to Leo Amery, 24 June 1940

243   'others have thought': Frederick Lindeman to Walter Monckton, 10 July 1940, Cherwell Papers, G. 465/3

243   Bourne dismisses snowmobiles: Bourne, 'Response to the proposals to use sledges driven by air screws and aircraft engines for cross country operations in the Narvik area', Combined Operations HQ, 15 July 1940

243   'the circumstances he has': A. V. Alexander to 'Sydney', 17 July 1940

243   'measureless obstructive strength': Evelyn Waugh, *Men at Arms* (London: Penguin), 1967, p. 135

243   'Unless all my skiing friends': Leo Amery to Fletcher, 23 July 1940

243   'a *quality* . . . ends of war': GP, 'A Strategic Proposal'

244   'The worse the weather': Ibid.

244   'You won't get it done': GP, Account of conversation with J. D. Bernal, 23 June 1940

244   'The whole country': GP to Jon Kimche, 14 January 1945

245   Ray 'a Communist': KV 2/3039/102a

245   'perhaps the greatest': Cyril Ray, 'Boat People', *Punch*, vol. 288, 20 March 1985, p. 51

245   'I heard things about him': GP to Jon Kimche, 14 January 1945

245   'I feel that, and I think': GP to Leo Amery, 4 February 1942

245   the 'brilliant' inventor: Michael Harrison, *Mulberry: The Return in Triumph* (London: W. H. Allen), 1965, p. 141

246   'Many of the descriptions': Pyke, Draft Profile of Mountbatten for the *Evening Standard*, September 1943

247   'excite you more': Quoted in Ziegler, *Mountbatten*, p. 112

247   Mountbatten's naval ambitions. Ziegler, *Mountbatten*, p. 36

247   'extraordinary drive': The Duchess of Windsor, *The Heart Has Its Reasons* (London: Michael Joseph), 1956, p. 206

248   'damned annoyed': Harrison, *Mulberry*, p. 15

248   'You fool!': Mountbatten's diary, 25 October 1941, quoted in Ziegler, *Mountbatten*, p. 156

248   'All the other headquarters': Churchill quoted by Mountbatten in Harrison, *Mulberry*, p. 15

249   'When I return': Louis Mountbatten to GP, 8 February 1942

249   'Major Parks-Smith . . . intellect': GP to Amery, undated

249   'Like Mephistopheles': GP to Louis Mountbatten, 26 April 1942

249–50 'They knew, only too well': 'Pyke on How to Sell Pyke', GP to Louis Mountbatten, June 1942

250   'what my biographers': Ibid.

250   'a vast gathering . . . length': GP to Jon Kimche, 14 January 1945

250   GP bad at judging audience: Pyke to Bobby Carter, 10 August 1939

250   'bore himself . . . voice': Cohen, 'Geoffrey Pyke: Man of Ideas', p. 246

251   Japanese rampant in South-East Asia: '*We do not possess enough naval forces, even leaving the barest minimum for our vital commitments in Home Waters, to meet the Japanese forces already in the Indian Ocean, not to mention those which may be brought against us.*' 'Draft Reply to General Marshall', Chiefs of Staff Committee, April 1942, CAB 79/20

252   'handsome and breezy' Goronwy Rees, *A Bundle of Sensations* (London: Chatto & Windus), 1960, p. 145

253   GP's clothes: Maurice Goldsmith, *Sage* (London: Hutchinson), 1980, p. 100

253   'unusually expressive': Cohen, 'Geoffrey Pyke: Man of Ideas', p.246

253   'thoughtful and serious': M. F. Perutz, 'An Inventor of Supreme Imagination', *Discovery*, May 1948

253   'burning eyes': Peter Quennell, *The Wanton Chase* (London: Collins), 1980, p. 30

253   'Lord Mountbatten, you need me': Andrew Brown, *J. D. Bernal: The Sage of Science* (Oxford: Oxford University Press), 2005, p. 209

253   'trying to size you up': Perutz, 'An Inventor of Supreme Imagination'

253   'The untidy man': John Hillary, 'The Ozzard of Whizz', *Public Opinion*, 18 May 1951, pp. 11–12

254   'I must confess': Harrison, *Mulberry*, p. 142

254   'a chap with no scientific qualifications': Goldsmith, *Sage*, pp. 97–98

254   'genuine affection': Harrison, *Mulberry*, p. 39

254   'I fell into the habit': GP to Louis Mountbatten, 6 July 1942

254   'you always rush me': GP to Louis Mountbatten, undated

254   'as receptive': GP to Betty Behrens, 23 January 1946

254   'What I've done': Transcript for 'The Dynamics of Innovation', part of 'We Beg to Differ', BBC, broadcast between 9:40 and 9:55 in between the third and fourth acts of *The Marriage of Figaro*, 25 September 1947

254   'In face of a new idea': Ibid.

255   'Suggester of Programmes': GP to Louis Mountbatten, 3 August 1942

255   'be prepared with': 'Pyke on How to Sell Pyke', GP to Louis Mountbatten, June 1942

255   GP's salary: Mountbatten Papers, MB1/C209

255   'an extraordinary, wholly unbureaucratic': Canetti, *Party in the Blitz*, p. 180

Pyke Hunt, Part 3

257   'the Comintern remained': Andrew, *Defence of the Realm*, p. 190

257   'what a complicated': KV 2/2799/153b

258   'Professor P. is I think': 'Photostat of Minute from Bagot (F2bMJEB) to ADE7, Prof P is Pyke', 21 January 1942, KV 2/3039/33b

258   'gathering and translating': Ibid.

258   'large and comprehensive': Today in the Comintern Archives in Moscow there are more than 407 files under the heading 'Varga Bureau in Berlin'

259   'doing the same job': 'Copy of E.3.(a) report re PYKE', 31 January 1942, KV-2-3039–34a

How to Change the Military Mind

261   Nye supports the scheme: 'Pyke on How to Sell Pyke', GP to Louis Mountbatten, June 1942

261   'tactical and strategic': CAB 79/19, COS (42) 58 (o). 77th Meeting

262   'handsome social chaps': Quoted in Richard Hough, *Mountbatten* (London: Weidenfeld and Nicolson), 1980, p. 148

262   'surrealist whirligig': Evelyn Waugh, Michael Davie (ed.), *The Diaries of Evelyn Waugh* (London: Weidenfeld & Nicolson), 1976, p. 524, p. 533

262   'this fish-flesh-fowl company': Rees, *A Bundle of Sensations*, p. 143

263   'precaution for . . . progress': GP, unpublished manuscript, 12 June 1941

263   'how a plane can measure': GP, 10 March 1942

263   'so does a Squadron Leader': GP to Louis Mountbatten, 1 March 1942

264   'ingenious . . . support': Appendix 'B', minutes of meeting at COHQ in response to Pyke's 'Diary of War Ideas', 27 March 1942

265   'if he couldn't get us': GP to Louis Mountbatten, 'Pyke on How to Sell Pyke', June 1942

265   'was not as it unfortunately': 'Mr Pyke's Second and Third Thoughts. A Recantation', 26 March 1942, US National Archives and Records Administration, Record Group 165, Entry 22, 390/30/16/4, Box 980

266   'a sign which said "VERBOTEN"': This idea can almost certainly be traced back to the following line in De Beaufort, *Behind the German Veil*, p. 25: 'If the notice "Verboten" appears on any door, passage, lawn, railway train, church, or anything else, then in nine hundred and ninety-nine cases out of a thousand it is unnecessary to take any further safeguards. [. . .] A good, law-abiding, respectable German citizen will not dream of passing through that door, gate, field, or step into that railroad train.'

268   'I can teach anyone': GP to Louis Mountbatten, 15 May 1942

268   'never, NEVER let up': GP to Louis Mountbatten, 'There should be more civilians in COHQ', 13 April 1942

268   'mene, mene . . . first time': Solly Zuckerman, *From Apes to Warlords* (London: Collins), 1988, pp. 151–152

268   'There is, at present': GP, 'New Ideas for the Army', 1 March 1942

269   'It would be contrary': GP to Louis Mountbatten, 'There should be more civilians in COHQ', 13 April 1942

269   GP approaches Tizard: Louis Mountbatten to GP, 30 March 1942

270   'beautiful, humorous': C. P. Snow, 'Bernal, a Personal Portrait', *The Science of Science* (London: Penguin), 1966, p. 19

270   'Three in a bed': JDB Papers, 0.23.1

270   'the boffin equivalent': Brown, *J. D. Bernal*, Kindle location 4700

270   'press things unduly': J. D. Bernal, *The Freedom of Necessity* (London: Routledge), 1949, p. 67

270–1   'Department of Wild Talents': Raleigh Trevelyan, *Grand Dukes and Diamonds* (London: Secker & Warburg), 1991, p. 369

271   'it is a reasonable assumption': Hough, *Mountbatten*, p. 148

271   'two favourites': Based on a conversation between Andrew Brown and Martin Bernal, quoted in Brown, *J. D. Bernal*, p. 217

271   'Monkey man': Harold Wernher, *World War II: Personal Experiences* (London: Worrall & Robey), 1950, p. 16

271 Bernal and the king's conversation: C. J. Mackenzie, NRCC/CJM Diary, 1 March 1943

271 'experts, charlatans': Evelyn Waugh, *Officers and Gentlemen* (London: Penguin), 1967, p. 44

272 'the largest . . . drawing pins': GP to Captain Colvin, 18 March 1942

273 Mountbatten at Chequers: Copy of an appointment book for Churchill's weekends at Chequers, kept by Inspector George Scott, Churchill's police escort commander (ref. WCHL 6/43), Churchill Archives Centre

273 'displayed his real qualities': GP to Jon Kimche, 14 January 1945

273 'one of the greatest': A. W. Lawrence (ed.), *T. E. Lawrence by his Friends* (London: Jonathan Cape), 1937, p. 161

273 unfinished business Norway: James A. Wood, *We Move Only Forward* (ST Chatarines, Ontario: Vanwell), 2006, p. 20

273 'roll the map': Winston Churchill, *The Hinge of Fate: The Second World War, Vol. 4* (New York: RosettaBooks), 2002, p. 314

274 'they are sure to be': GP to Louis Mountbatten, 2 April 1942

274 'now at the 59th minute': Ibid.

274 'a 101% honest': Ibid.

275 'I doubt if any single': Memorandum quoted in Robert E. Sherwood, *Roosevelt and Hopkins* (New York: Harper), 1948, p. 519

275–6 'Churchill took this': Hopkins quoted in Sherwood, *Roosevelt and Hopkins*, p. 526

276 'Rather doubtful': Alan Brooke, *War Diaries: 1939–45* (London: Weidenfeld & Nicolson), 2001, p. 236

276 'a snag': Ibid.

276 'Well, after all': Bernard Fergusson, *The Watery Maze* (London: Collins), 1961, p. 150

276 Marshall leaves with memo: US National Archives and Records Administration, Record Group 165, Entry 21, 390/30/16/4, Box 968

277 'It's only when you see': Hopkins quoted in Sherwood, *Roosevelt and Hopkins*, p. 529

277 Hopkins' underwear: Winston Churchill, *The Second World War, Vol. 3* (Boston: Houghton Mifflin), 1948–53, p. 22

277 'itching like the devil': Hopkins to Roosevelt, 11 April 1942, in Sherwood, *Roosevelt and Hopkins*, p. 527

278 'pretentious nonsense': Frederick Lindemann to Walter Monckton, 10 July 1940, Cherwell Papers, G. 465/3

278–9 'I have a feeling that perhaps': '*The Meeting with General Marshall*', GP to Louis Mountbatten, 9 April 1942

279–80 'For not far off': GP to Louis Mountbatten, 26 April 1942

280 'Whatever may happen': Ibid.

Pyke Hunt, Part 4

281   'hush-hush . . . secrecy': Nigel West, *Mask* (London: Routledge), 2006, p. 226

281   'channel through which': 'Photostat copy of S. B. report re German Organisations in this country', 23 February 1942, KV 2/3039/38a

281   'came near to being': Hyde, *I Believed,* p. 203

281   'so many leading Czech': 'Special Branch on CRTF, 28 January 1940, KV 2/2715/19b

281   'the rulers . . . for little': Hyde, *I Believed,* p. 204

282   'the men concerned': *Sunday Dispatch*, 8 February 1942; the following week the same point was made in more detail: 'Refugees welcome the exposure of the "Free German" trick', *Sunday Dispatch*, 15 February 1942

282   'said to be in charge': 'Photostat copy of Special Branch report re. German Organisations in this country', 23 February 1942, KV 2/3039/38a

283   'it is not *essential'*: GP, 'Let Raid Shelters be Probed in Public', *Reynolds News*, 21 May 1939

283   GP's articles on chalk shelters: GP, *Reynolds News*, 22 December 1940, 29 December 1940, 12 January 1941, 27 April 1941

283   piece in academic journal: E. J. Buckatzsch, *Institute of Statistics, Oxford*, 17 May 1941, bulletin vol 3, no. 7

283   'played straight into the hands': GP Notebook, 5 May 1941

283–4   'everything to it': Hyde, *I Believed,* p. 94

284   GP pushes anti-appeasement book: GP Notebook, July 1940

284   GP pushes Meusel book: Incidentally, Allen Lane told GP that if he could write an account of sending his pollsters into Nazi Germany he'd publish it 'like a shot'. GP Notebook, August 1940; 'anti-war' SIS report CX/12650/5274/V, 9 April 1940, KV 2/1872/87a; 'Chief of Communist Party' Captain Derbyshire to V. Vivian, 22 April 1940

284   GP campaigns for interned refugees: The CPGB also ran a campaign pushing for the release of anti-fascists interned as Enemy Aliens with Tommy Bell writing articles on this and helping to put together a book called *Morrison's Prisoners*. At the same time GP pitched a piece to Kingsley Martin at *The New Statesman and Nation* railing against the internment of enemy aliens such as Higgins. Martin felt it was 'too violent' and might do his cause 'more harm than good'. GP Notebook, 17 August 1940

284–5   'a most brilliant move': GP Diary, 24 August 1939

285   'transformed the whole': Nares Craig, *Memoirs of a Thirties Dissident*, online memoir accessed on 9 April 2012 at http://www.narescraig.co.uk/memoirs/index.html#TOC. Craig does not appear in P's notebook until April 1940, and his sight of this flat may have been as late as that

285   Myers gives GP money: 'I shd like you to meet him and some day when all this is over I think Iris (and you) will be satisfied that the money I gave him were well spent.' Myers to Bayard James, intercepted, passed to MI5, 4 July 1942. KV 2/3039

285 'also paid Pyke's personal bills': 'E.7. note (Source Kaspar) re PYKE and MYERS', 4 August 1942, KV-2–3039–75a

286 'railings from not just': GP Notebook, 6 July 1940

286 'a moment at which': George Orwell, 'Our Opportunity', *The Left News*, No. 55, January 1941

287 'I dare say the London gutters': George Orwell, 'My Country Right or Left', *Books v. Cigarettes* (London: Penguin), 2008, p. 48

287 'an attempt to get away': Andrew Roberts, *Eminent Churchillians* (New York: Simon & Schuster), 1994, p. 247

287 Bagot writes to Hunter: 'F2b note to B6 asking for observation to be kept on Geoffrey Pyke', 15 March 1942, KV 2/3039/36a

288 'tall, thin-bearded': Quennell, *The Wanton Chase*, p. 29

289 'looking as unlike': 'B.6 report on the operations of the section during the war 1939', 1 March 1945, KV 4/443

290 'lost to observation': 'B.6. report further to 37a re Geoffrey PYKE', 27 March 1942, KV 2/3039/38a

290 GP seen having lunch with woman: Ibid.

290–1 'Age 38, 5'10"': KV 2/3039/38a

291 Fuchs and Kuczynski: Robert Chadwell Williams, *Klaus Fuchs* (London: Harvard University Press), 1987, p. 33

291 Kuczynski supplies intelligence for sister: David Burke, *The Spy Who Came in from the Co-op* (Woodbridge: Boydell Press), 2008, p. 110

291 'intellectually of the first': GP Notebook, 26 July 1939

291 'I found our conversation': GP to Jurgen Kuczynski, 9 October 1939, Kuc2–1–P1402–P1413_0007

291 Myers sends money: Myers sent JK £100 with a view to sending another £100, 8 May 1940, KV 2/1872/86b

292 'rabid Communist . . . refugees': B4b Minute, 22 November 1939, KV 2/1871/37

292 'a direct agent': 'M/S report on an interview with EICHLER', 20 Feb 1940, KV 2/1871/69b

292 'a very good stroke': Ibid.

292 £200,000: KV 2/1873/185a

292 petitioners for Kuczynski's release: Lilian Bowes Lyon to Marguerite Kuczynski: 'I have rung up a friend of mine who is going to get in touch if possible, through an influential friend of his, with Sir Robert Vansittart. I won't go into details but both these people are well known to your husband and great admirers of his anti-Hitler work.' The 'influential friend' was probably Pyke. 26 January 1940, KV 2/1871/63a

292–3 MI5 reports on Kuczynski: Source: Hi, 'Report No. 38 re. Free German League of Culture', 25 February 1941, KV 2/1872/128x

293 GP's 1927 passport application: Milicent Bagot, 'Note re Geoffrey PYKE', 8 April 1942, KV 2/3039/45a

293 'not always proved': Milicent Bagot to Deputy Assistant Commissioner, Special Branch, 'Letter to S. B. re PYKE's career', 19 April 1942, KV 2/3039/53a

293 'possibly a knave': Milicent Bagot, MI5 Internal Minute, 7 April 1942

294 Mountbatten reads the *Week*: Cockburn, *I, Claud*, 1967, p. 158
294 Mountbatten believes GP has security clearance: Letter from Combined Operations to Lt-Col Clarke of MI14 says that Pyke 'has already been vouched for by many people in responsible positions, but I am arranging double check with M.I.5, just to make sure.' In handwriting after that: 'This has now been done and is alright'. 28 March 1942

How to Succeed in America

295 Wedderburn's health: A. M. Greenwood, 'E. A. M. Wedderburn', *Climbers' Club Journal, 1945–1946*, F. A. Pullinger (ed.), (London: The Climbers' Club), Vol. 8, no. 1, no. 71, 1946, pp. 72–74
296 'intelligence . . . integrity': GP to Louis Mountbatten, c. June 1942
296 'preferably from the Royal': Louis Mountbatten to John Dill, 24 April 42, DEFE 2/883
296 'War Office *par excellence*': GP to Louis Mountbatten, 19 May 1942
296 '"Staff College" *par excellence*': Ibid., 11 May 1942
296 'may shorten the war': Ibid., 4 June 1942
297 'bomb rack': John Cohen, 'Geoffrey Pyke: Man of Action', *New Scientist*, 30 July 1981, p. 303
297 'slightly deaf': GP to John Knox, 7 July 1942
297 letters of introduction to Hopkins: Louis Mountbatten to Harry Hopkins, 24 April 1942, DEFE 2/883
297 'adequate cover': Louis Mountbatten to William Stephenson, 24 April 1942
297 'The great importance': Louis Mountbatten to Knox, 24 April 1942, DEFE 2/883
298 'all the officers': Dwight D. Eisenhower to Louis Mountbatten, 19 April 1942, *The Papers of Dwight David Eisenhower: The War Years*, Alfred D. Chandler ed., (Baltimore and London: Johns Hopkins Press), 1970, p. 274
298 'very odd-looking individual': George C. Marshall, quoted in Robert Adleman and George Walton, *The Devil's Brigade* (Annapolis, Maryland: Naval Institute Press), 2004, p. 2
298 'No one, except Hitler': GP to Jon Kimche, 14 January 1945
298 'spoke badly': GP to Louis Mountbatten, 29 April 1942, DEFE 2/883
299 'the idea is too simple': Ibid.
299 'a working committee': Dwight D. Eisenhower to Louis Mountbatten, 19 April 1942, *The Papers of Dwight David Eisenhower*, p. 274
299 'Things had to happen': Vannevar Bush, *Pieces of the Action* (London: Cassell), 1970, p. 126
299 'Because of the American': GP to Louis Mountbatten, undated
299 'we may be ready': Ibid., 2 May 1942
300 GP finds heat 'trying': Pyke later heard this from 'a third party', almost certainly Wedderburn, GP to Louis Mountbatten, 21 May 1942
300 'little more than': E. A. M. Wedderburn, 3 May 42, DEFE 2/884
300 Burgess needs repairing: Ibid.

301   'design, develop, build': Development of Weasel, 1 July 42, US National Archives and Records Administration, Records of the OSRD, NC-138, Entry 1, Office of the Chairman, NDRC, and the Office of the Director, OSRD: General Records, 1940–1947, Box 55

301   'I wish to submit': GP to Louis Mountbatten, 12 May 1942

302   'I am sure Duncan': Ibid., 21 May 1942

302   'Duncan not only': Ibid., 19 May 1942

302   'in fact so contra-suggestible': Ibid., 15 May 1942

302   'due to rigidity of intellect': Ibid., 19 May 1942

302   'both the extreme cunning': GP to J. D. Bernal, 22 May 1942

302   resignation letter: GP to Louis Mountbatten, 11 May 1942

302   'Once a civilian': Louis Mountbatten to John Knox, 20 May 1942

303   'Pyke's grievance': John Knox to Louis Mountbatten, 12 May 1942

303   'smooth out differences': Louis Mountbatten to John Knox, 13 May 1942

303   'during three and a half': DEFE 2/883

303   'anxious and distressed': GP to Louis Mountbatten, 16 May 1942

303   'If irritation and impatience': Ibid., 19 May 1942

304   Duncan runs amok: GP to J. D. Bernal, 22 May 1942

304   'good enough': Nigel Duncan to E. A. M. Wedderburn, 16 May 1942

304   Duncan approves OSRD's proposal: Palmer Putnam to Hartley Rowe, 18 May 1942

304   'by the early fall': US National Archives and Records Administration, Record Group 165, Entry 21, 390/30/16/4, Box 968

304   'very active . . . winter': From OSRD Confidential History, US National Archives and Records Administration, Record Group 227/NC-138/Entry 106/ Box 8, Chapter 4

305   'The Americans are remarkable': GP to Louis Mountbatten, 19 May 1942

305   GP resigns again: John Knox to Louis Mountbatten, 16 May 1942, DEFE 2/883

305   Churchill asks for report: 'The Prime Minister has asked Lord Cherwell to keep him informed of the progress of Pyke's scheme.' Louis Mountbatten to Robert Neville, 21 May 1942

305   'I've made no mistakes': GP to Louis Mountbatten, 21 May 1942

305   'tame lunatic': John Knox to Louis Mountbatten, 21 May 1942

306   'At last understand': Louis Mountbatten to John Knox, 26 May 1942

306   Duncan ordered back to London: Mountbatten checked with General Nye that Duncan's military career would not suffer as a result. Louis Mountbatten to Archie Nye, 26 May 1942

306   'Pyke is now my sole': Louis Mountbatten to John Knox, 26 May 1942

306   'sympathetic support': Ibid.

306   'In spite of': Louis Mountbatten to GP, 28 May 1942

306   details of missing papers: E. A. M. Wedderburn, 'Note on Missing Papers', 18 May 1942

306   'vanished into thin air': E. A. M. Wedderburn to Nigel Duncan, 16 May 1942

306   'he will be dealing': N. T. P. Cooper to First Canadian Army, 3 June 1942

307   Operations Division report on Plough: Robert T. Frederick, 'Memorandum on Plough Project for the Chief of Staff', June 1942
307   'I can't sign that report': Adleman and Walton, *The Devil's Brigade*, p. 29
307   'animated discussion': Ibid., p. 30
307   '(a) failed to ensure': Louis Mountbatten, 'MEMORANDUM BY CHIEF OF COMBINED OPERATIONS ON THE SNOW PLOUGH SCHEME'. Undated.
307   'just like a schoolboy': GP to Louis Mountbatten, 7 June 1942
308   'charming, moderately sincere': Ibid.
308   'If I may say so': Ibid.
308   'probably the most': Hough, *Mountbatten*, pp. 152–3
309   Mountbatten on *Time* magazine: It went on sale on 8 June 1942 bearing the legend: 'Mountbatten of the Commandos: His boys in blackface will see the day of wrath.'
309   'in the event of things': Louis Mountbatten to Franklin D. Roosevelt, 15 June 1942, FDR, Harry Hopkins Papers, Container 194
309   'ready to follow up': Ibid.
310   Frederick in charge of Plough: Robert T. Frederick to Robert D. Burhans, 10 September 1942, quoted in Wood, *We Move Only Forward*, p. 26
310   'I was shocked': Ibid.
310   'carried the rating': Adleman and Walton, *The Devil's Brigade*, p. 33
310   'embrace your defects': 'Pyke on How to Sell Pyke', GP to Louis Mountbatten, June 1942
310   'Warwick the Kingmaker': GP to Louis Mountbatten, 21 June 1942
311   'a battery of press': 11 June 1942, Guy Liddell, Nigel West (ed.), *The Guy Liddell Diaries, Vol. 1* (Abingdon: Routledge), 2005
311   'What the hell': This was Major-General J. C. Murchie, Canadian Vice-Chief of the General Staff, Adleman and Walton, *The Devil's Brigade*, p. 35
312   a joint American-Canadian force: GP to Louis Mountbatten, 16 June 1942
312   'experienced cold-weather': Robert T. Frederick to Robert D. Burhans, 10 September 1946, quoted in Wood, *We Move Only Forward*, p. 27
312   'The son of a bitch': Adleman and Walton, *The Devil's Brigade*, p. 38
313   'an instance of Churchill's': Bush, *Pieces of the Action*, pp. 126–7
313   'lots of ideas . . . judgement': Vannevar Bush, *Atlantic Monthly*, March 1965
314   'working through channels': Ibid.
314   'has a contempt': Bush, *Pieces of the Action,* p. 121
314   'I judge that': Vannevar Bush to Raymond Moses, 3 June 1942
315   'it is fortunate': Ibid.
315   'now sitting pretty': 'Notes on Certain Phases of the Development of Weasel (With excerpts from the Project Log)', 13 July 1942, US National Archives and Records Administration, Records of the OSRD, NC-138, Entry 1, Office of the Chairman, NDRC, and the Office of the Director, OSRD: General Records, 1940–1947, Box 55
315   'be frank both with': GP to John Knox, 7 July 1942
316   'the organisational level': GP to Louis Mountbatten, 21 June 1942
316   'appreciation of the treatment': Ibid., 7 June 1942

316   'It meant a *Caste War*': Ibid., 3 August 1942
316   'in this big, husky': Thomas Parrish, *To Keep the British Isles Afloat: FDR's Men in Churchill's London, 1941* (New York: Smithsonian), 2009, p. 233
317   'with complete frankness': GP, 'Interview with Mr Oscar Cox, Assistant Solicitor General: Director under Mr Stettinius of Lend-Lease', 23 June 1942
317   'amazing': OSC Daily Calendar, 24 June 1042, FDR, Cox Papers, Box 143
317   'I am doing this': GP to Isidor Lubin, 24 June 1942
317   'you realise, I hope': GP to Oscar Cox, 24 June 1942, DEFE 2/884
318   'an unusually gifted': Eugene Rostow to Bob Bryce, 31 March 1943
318   'Pyke could not write': George W. Ball, *The Past Has Another Pattern* (London: W.W. Norton), 1982, p. 25
318   Stimson's feelings towards British: Louis Mountbatten to GP, 25 July 1942
318–9   Bush gives Stimson reports on GP: Bush, *Pieces of the Action*, p. 128
319   'seriously upsetting': E. A. M. Wedderburn, Notes on a conversation with Knox, 1 July 1942
319   'the Weasel business': Daily Calendar, 2 July 1942, FDR, Cox Papers, Box 143
319   'It is very, very difficult': GP to Louis Mountbatten, 30 June 1942
320   'I am anxious to know': Winston Churchill to Harry Hopkins, 7 July 1942, Prime Minister's Personal Telegram no. T.960
320   '*Putnam must go*': Eugene Rostow and George Ball to Oscar Cox, 'Memorandum to be read prior to seeing Lubin and Hopkins', 8 July 1942
320   'the red herring': 'MEMORANDUM PREPARED BY LEND-LEASE ADMINISTRATION', 3 July 1942
321   'with the impression': 'Note on Conversation with Captain Knox, R. N., C. O. L. O., in his office on 20 June, 1942'
321   'that damned old woman': GP to Louis Mountbatten, 19 June 1942
321   'caused so much amusement': Louis Mountbatten to GP, 23 June 1942
321   'Most of the people': Ibid., 'Phillips, on "How Not to Sell Pyke"', 6 July 1942
321   'I have not gone deeply': John Dill to Louis Mountbatten, 17 July 1942
321   'you don't sack me': GP to Louis Mountbatten, 20 July 1942
321   'It has been made': Louis Mountbatten to GP, 23 July 1942
322   'I know both of them': Ibid., 25 July 1942
322   'to avoid entangling': Ibid.
322   'the unspeakable misery': GP to Louis Mountbatten, 3 August 1942
322   'This is your usual': Ibid.
322–3   'trappers, guides': E. A. M. Wedderburn, 'Notes on Conversation with Lt Col. Frederick', 25 June 1942
323   'possibly bring back': Undated memorandum, US National Archives and Records Administration, Record Group 165, Entry 22, 390/30/16/4, Box 980

Pyke Hunt, Part 5

324   'PYKE is said': 'Kaspar', 10 May 1942, KV 2/2883/39a

324   'It would seem that Pyke': Roger Fulford to Major Bacon, MI5 Internal Minute 68, 29 June 1942

325   'We have only just started': Major Bacon to Roger Fulford, MI5 Internal Minute 69, 6 July 1942

325   'Our records gave no': Milicent Bagot to Roger Fulford, MI5 Internal Minute 71, 9 July 1942

325   'I hear it's amazing': 'Extract from Y.2127 re PYKE Geoffrey', 15 September 1942, KV 2/3039/76b

325   'was unhappy . . . escort': Canetti, *Party in the Blitz,* p. 181

326   'every section of the wartime': Andrew, *Defence of the Realm,* p. 366

326   'most penetrated': Ibid.

326   Soviet activity between 1942 and 1945: John Earl Haynes and Harvey Kiehr, *Venona, Decoding Soviet Espionage in America* (New Haven: Yale University Press), 2000, p. 337

327   Petrie to contact Mountbatten: Victor Rothschild, 19 June 1942, KV 2/3039/65a

328   'Either it is a washout': GP to Louis Mountbatten, 3 August 1942

How to Win the War With Ice

329   'the appearance of absurdity': GP, War Diary, 1942

329   'mental institute': John Knox to GP, 31 August 1942, DEFE 2.883

330   'It may be gold': GP to Louis Mountbatten, 23 September 1942, covering note on Habbakuk Memorandum

330   'You have an able': GP, Habbakuk Memorandum, September 1942

331   'the dominating factor': Winston Churchill, *The Second World War,* (London: Vol. 5 Cassell & Co), 1952, p. 6

332   'U-Boat Alley': John Costello and Terry Hughes, *The Battle of the Atlantic* (New York, The Dial Press), 1977, pp. 304–305

335   'I told him that when': Herman Mark, *From Small Organic Molecules to Large* (Washington DC: American Chemical Society), 1993, p. 100

338   'to beat them but': GP to J. C. Haydon, 20 October 1943

338   'My style is a reflection': GP to Louis Mountbatten, 13 November 1942

338   'That I do this': Ibid., 20 July 1942

339   'both sound and brilliant': J. D. Bernal quoted by GP in a letter to Kingsley Martin, 10 March 1946

340   Monday-morning meetings: Ziegler, *Mountbatten,* p. 178

341   'The advantages': Winston Churchill, Prime Minister's Personal Minute, D. 7 December 1942, 212/2, Cherwell Papers, G. 237/8

341   'Bombs and torpedoes': Max F. Perutz, *I Wish I'd Made You Angry Earlier: Essays on Science, Scientists, and Humanity* (New York: Cold Spring Harbor Laboratory Press), 1998, p. 89

342   Churchill's imagination seized: J. D. Bernal to C. P. Snow, JDB Papers, J. 217, 11/4/61

342   '*Prof*, I have long thirsted': Frederick Lindemann to Winston Churchill, 10 December 1942, Cherwell Papers, F. 168

342   'I think that this is all': Roger Fulford to Milicent Bagot, MI5 int. min. 83, 11 November 1942

342   'collection of fools': Perutz, *I Wish I'd Made You Angry Earlier*, p. 82

342   'for having gone': GP to Godfrey Wildman-Lushington, 10 December 1942

343   'Discussed Winston's new project': Brooke, *War Diaries*, p. 347

344   Habbakuk Directing Committee formed: Chiefs of Staff (42) 195th Meeting (o), 11 December 1942, ADM 1/15236

344   'against Nature': GP Notebook, recollection of J. D. Bernal's account of a conversation with Harold Wernher, 28 December 1942

344   'had no faith in it': Wernher, *World War II*, p. 28

345   'extraordinary conference': Solly Zuckerman, *From Apes to Warlords* (London: Collins), 1988, p. 159

345   Bernal Presses for trials to begin: J. D. Bernal, 'General Conclusions', 31 December 1942

345   'the success of a project': GP, 'Meeting at Albany, Piccadilly – 31 December 1942', 4 January 1943.

345–6   'Mountbatten tried to assure': Zuckerman, *From Apes to Warlords*, p. 159

346   'outlined the state': 'Draft Minutes of Meeting of the Directing Committee', 7 January 1943, ADM 1/15236/23

346   'The only thing': Winston Churchill, *The Second World War*, Vol. 2 (London: Cassell & Co.), 1949 p. 529

346   'small in stature': R. F. Legget, 'Charles Jack Mackenzie, 10 July 1888 – 26 February 1984', *Biographical Memoirs of Fellows of the Royal Society*, Vol. 31, November 1985. Royal Society, pp. 410–434

346–7   'This is another of those': C. J. Mackenzie, NRCC/CJM Diary, 14 January 1943

347   'The soundness appeals': C. J. Mackenzie to A. M. Laidlaw, 4 February 1943, ADM 1/15236/36

347   budget of £150,000. Lorne W. Gold, *The Canadian Habbakuk Project* (Cambridge: International Glaciological Society), 1993, p. 16

347–8   'when I tell you that': C. J. Mackenzie to A. M. Laidlaw, 4 February 1943, ADM 1/15236/36

348   'the stimulus': Max Perutz in Pyke and Medawar, *Hitler's Gift*, p. xii

349   Perutz sent to Quebec: Perutz, *I Wish I'd Made You Angry Earlier*, p. 76

349   'doyen of the camp's': Ibid., p. 82

349   'Nobody wanted my help': Ibid., p. 82

349   'gentle, persuasive voice': Ibid.

349   'This time, he sized': Ibid.

350   'It can be machined: Ibid., p. 89

350   'In honour of': Ibid., p. 83

350   Mountbatten's visit to Perutz' laboratory: Edward Gardner, 'The World and His Wife', BBC, No. 8, 4 March 1946

350   'a little crater': Perutz, *I Wish I'd Made You Angry Earlier*, p. 83

351 'I have a block': Lampe, *Pyke*, p. 137

351 Churchill complains his bath will get cold: Harrison, Mulberry, p. 143

351 Churchill in the bath: It would not have been out of character for Churchill to receive Mountbatten in the bath – he was happy to talk to President Roosevelt while wrapped in his bath-towel. Sherwood, *Roosevelt and Hopkins*, p. 442

351 'I must tell you about': GP Diary, 2 Feb 1943

351 'win the war at one blow': Ibid.

352 'both enthusiastic': Louis Mountbatten to GP, 3 March 1943

352 'the most important': Ibid., 12 February 1943

353 'Des became more and more silent': Zuckerman, *From Apes to Warlords*, p. 164

353 'Habbakuk, or rather Pyke': Ibid., p. 161

353 'Bernal and Pyke': C. J. Mackenzie, NRCC/CJM Diary, 1 March 1943

353 'He lands in this country': Ibid.

353–4 'dressed like a tramp': Ibid.

354 'Travelling with Pyke': Ibid.

354 'I am still perfectly sure': Ibid.

355 'They are working': J. D. Bernal, 'A Brief Summary of Progress of Research Work in Canada', 13 March 1943, ADM 1/15236/49

355 'his principles had been violated': A. J. Dick, interviewed for Bill Waiser, *Park Prisoners* (Saskatoon & Calgary: Fifth House), 1995, p. 163

356 'humorous talk': 'Ship of Ice', documentary broadcast in December 2009, part of *Clive Cussler's Sea Hunters*, Season 5, Episode 7

357 'The Lake Louise outfit': C. J. Mackenzie, NRCC/CJM Diary, 8 March 1943

357 'Hope I live long enough': GP, Earlswood Deary, 16 January 1942

357 'At ten o'clock': C. J. Mackenzie, NRCC/CJM Diary, 9 March 1943

357 'the most grotesque': Ibid., 1 March 1943

357–8 'We thought probably Pyke': Ibid., 9 March 1943

358 'on a number of occasions': J. D. Bernal, 'A Brief Summary of Progress of Research Work in Canada', 13 March 1943, ADM 1/15236/49

358 no major obstacles encountered: Ibid.

359 proposal to abandon convoys: Ben Wilson, *Empire of the Deep* (London: Weidenfeld & Nicolson), 2013, p. 609

359 'the attempt would have been worth': Vincent Massey to Louis Mountbatten, 20 March 1943, PREM 3/2/ 16/6

359 'I am very much interested': Winston Churchill to Mackenzie King, 21 March 1943, PREM 3/2/ 16/6

360 'fundamentally, Habbakuk': Meeting convened by the Dep. First Sea Lord and Director of Plans at the Admiralty, 27 March 1943, DEFE 2/1087, H696

360 'Mr Chamberlain has sent': Perutz, *I Wish I'd Made You Angry Earlier*, p. 84

360 Pyke's fly sticking: 'p.s. I hope you have had no more trouble with your new "zipper" trousers!' Louis Mountbatten to GP, 23 July 1942

360 shoddy Canadian engineering: Zuckerman, *From Apes to Warlords*, p. 158

362 'at -15°C.': This work prefigured later discoveries about glacial flow. 4 May 1943, ADM 1/15236

362 Admiralty sends two men: 9 April 1943, ADM 1/15236

362   Mountbatten on sick leave: Louis Mountbatten to Winston Churchill (draft), to say that he planned to have 'a very small operation about the 10th April and expect to be on the sick list for about ten days.' DEFE 2/844

362   'During the illness of CCO': Winston Churchill, *The Second World War, Vol. 4* (London: Cassell & Co.), 1951, p. 848

362–3   'to design without . . . before': GP and J. D. Bernal, 3 May 1943, ADM 1/15236.

363   GP and Bernal urge Mountbatten to wait: 5 May 1943, ADM 1/15236

363   'nightmare journey': Bernal 'A framework for his own autobiography', JDB Papers, O.1.1.

363   'I wish I could tell you': 'Sealed Lips', *Evening Standard*, 24 May 1943

363   'arrived rather tipsy': *Diaries* Waugh, p. 538

363   berg-ship not going to be ready: 'Minutes of COS (43) 51st Meeting', 22 March 1943, CAB 78/11

365   account of Churchill and Mountbatten meeting: C. J. Mackenzie, NRCC/CJM Diary, 10 June 1943

365   *'fundamentally fallacious'*: GP to Louis Mountbatten, 'Jupiter-Habbakuk', 1 July 1943

365   'then Operation Jupiter': Winston Churchill, "HABBAKUK" Prime Minister's Personal Minute, 19 July 1943, D.134/3, CAB 121/154/1

365–6   '"HABBAKUK" is one of': Ibid.

366   Churchill asks for his note to be passed on: 22 July 1943, CAB 121/154/8a

366   Ismay's response: Hastings Ismay to Winston Churchill, C.O.S. (43) 170th Meeting. (o), Min. Y., 23 July 1943, CAB 121/154/7

367   September 1943 shipping losses: Costello and Hughes, *The Battle of the Atlantic*, pp. 304–305

369   Arnold spits on hands: Harrison, *Mulberry*, p. 144

369   'we all rose': Brooke, *War Diaries*, pp. 445–446

369   Churchill's account: Winston Churchill, *The Second World War, Vol. 5, Closing the Ring* (London: Cassell & Co.) 1952, p. 81

369   'collided, skull to skull': Harrison, *Mulberry*, p. 144

369   'Dickie, for God's sake': Ibid.

369   'The waiting officers': Churchill, *The Second World War, Vol. 5*, p. 81

370   Habbakuk seen as most realistic prospect: Harrison, *Mulberry*, p. 145

How to Survive

372   Mountbatten tries to corner Pound: Hough, *Mountbatten*, p. 162

372   'I followed him': Mountbatten quoted in Hough, Ibid.

373   'We are both so sorry': Louis Mountbatten to GP, September 1943

373   GP's connection becomes known to Americans: Wernher, *World War II*, p. 27

373   'I think it is the bunk': Bush, *Pieces of the Action*, p. 124

373–4   'Mountbatten and Pyke walked': Ibid.

374   Superman cartoon: By late March 1943, when the storyline appears, Jack Schiff was playing a more prominent role in choosing the storylines and the principal

writer, Jerry Siegel, had been drafted into the US Army. Wayne Boring was one of the ghost artists around this time

375   cartoons sent to Mackenzie : A.E. Macdonald to Jack Mackenzie, 5 April 1943

376   'you must not bring': Louis Mountbatten, 'Memories of Desmond Bernal', in D. M. C. Hodgkin, *Biographical Memoirs of Fellows of the Royal Society*, Vol. 26, 1980, p. 193

376   'If professional historians': GP to Godfrey Wildman-Lushington, 18 December 1943

377   'Like Plough, but unlike Habbakuk': 8 June 1944, Mountbatten Papers, MB1/C209

377   'perhaps not so obviously': Godfrey Wildman-Lushington to GP, 7 July 1944, Mountbatten Papers, MB1/C209

378   'Do the old terms still apply?': GP to Louis Mountbatten, 8 June 1944, Mountbatten Papers, MB1/C209

378   'a brain twenty': Louis Mountbatten to Charles Lambe, 26 June 1943

378   'in fullest touch': Ibid., 2 October 1943

378   Mountbatten rejects GP for South-East Asian Command: Mountbatten Papers, MB1/C51/8

378   'I do not think you want': He went on to say: 'I must confess that I'm not too happy about the revival of this connection. I am afraid if the First Sea Lord gets hold of it that this may tend to discredit you in his eyes and I do not think you can afford to lay yourself open, gratuitously, to his ridicule.' Godfrey Wildman-Lushington to Louis Mountbatten, 7 July 1944, Mountbatten Papers, MB1/C209

378   'an awkward cuss': Harrison, *Mulberry*, p. 39

378   'I share with Professor Bernal': Louis Mountbatten to GP, 17 June 1943

378–80   Obituary Notice quotes: GP, Mountbatten Obituary, 13 June 1943

380   'I have always been': GP to Louis Mountbatten, 30 July 1943

382   'Though – damn it – I *want*': Ibid., 14 July 1944, Mountbatten Papers, MB1/C209

382   Mountbatten asks Lloyd for pipeline: Interview between Geoffrey Lloyd and Robin Tousfield, *Transcripts*, Vol. II, pp. 60–61; A. J. Clements, *Operation 'Pluto' 1942–45* (Porthcurno: Cable and Wireless Porthcurno and Collections Trust), 2005, p. 3

382   GP had idea in 1934: 'I do remember your Pluto scheme for the Atlantic. I think the date must have been 1934/5' – Jack Beddington to GP, 24 January 1946

382   'I put it up to one': GP to Ray Murphy, 25 July 1946

382   'group of individualists': Adleman and Walton, *The Devil's Brigade*, p. 21

382   'probably the most bold': Louis Mountbatten to GP, undated farewell letter on his departure from COHQ

383   FSSF unit: Brett Werner, *First Special Service Force 1942–44* (New York: Osprey), 2006, p. 13

383   'the worst is still to come': Ibid., p. 22

383   'We never hear these black devils': Ibid., p. 23

383   M-29 Tracked Cargo Carrier considered a success: While it did not live up to Pyke's original expectations the Weasel was faster on snow than he had thought it might

be. When the OSRD set up a race between a pack of Weasels and skiers from the 87th Mountain Infantry in the hills above, the skiers did not catch the Weasels over three miles. From OSRD Confidential History – US National Archives and Records Administration, Record Group 227/NC-138/Entry 106/Box 8, Chapter 4: 'The Weasel'

383   'accomplished fine things': Bush, *Pieces of the Action*, p. 127

383   'We realise that much': Ziegler, *Mountbatten*, p. 215

384   'It is true to say': Papers of John Hughes-Hallett, Churchill Archives Centre, HHLT, p. 145

385   'the original thoughts': Louis Mountbatten to GP, undated farewell letter on his departure from COHQ

How to Live

388   'He was a clever and articulate': Canetti, *Party in the Blitz*, p. 182

388   'There would be a torrent': Ibid., pp. 181–3

388   'the handsomest woman': GP Notebook, 1943

389   'something which compels . . . for ever': Ibid. September 1940

389   'I now restrict myself': GP to Gordon Schaffer, early 1946

389   'Several times I had': GP to Elsie Myers, 17 February 1946, L. H. Myers Papers, MS 447/01

390   'the greatest inventive': Canetti, *Party in the Blitz*, p. 180

390   '"telling stories" about my past': GP to J. D. Bernal, 16 February 1946

390   Bernal changes lock on shed: Brown, *J. D. Bernal*, p. 293

390   'I have a very vivid picture': Margaret Gardiner to GP, c. 1945

390   'It is out of the question': GP to Margaret Gardiner, c. 1944

391   'on which the world wholly relied': GP, 'The Mobilisation of Muscle', *Economist*, 11 August 1945

392   letter: GP, *The Times*, 21 September 1945

392   trio of articles: GP, 'Europe's Coal Famine: The Problem Analysed', 20 August 1945, 'Europe's Coal Famine: A Solution Outlined', 21 August 1945, 'Europe's Coal Famine: The Organisation of Muscle-Power', 24 September 1945, *Manchester Guardian*

392   several articles: GP, 'Utilisation of Muscle', *Cycling*, 5 September 1945

392   interview: *Daily Mail*, 22 September 1945

392   'the uphill task of innovation': GP to Betty Behrens, 23 Jan 1946

393   'The truth is that the Society': Bosworth Monck to GP, 20 August 1946

393   'What's the use': GP Notebook, c. 1939

393   newspaper reports: Press release issued by the Admiralty on 28 February 1946 in Washington, Ottawa, and London

394   'national disaster': *Lancet*, 1945, vol 2, p. 413

395   'tired, suffering from': GP to Elsie Myers, 17 February 1946, L. H. Myers Papers, MS 447/01

395–6 'Unless our document': John Cohen to GP, 5 January 1948

396   'I have thrown everything': GP to John Cohen, c. January 1948

396   'I can see only one': Edward Glover to GP, 9 January 1948

397–8 'Bad manners . . . mistakes': Transcript for 'The Dynamics of Innovation', part of 'We Beg to Differ', BBC, 25 September 1947

398   'We have the decency': GP, *The Times*, 3 December 1947

399   'Actions like this': Ibid., 18 January 1948

399   'What is wrong with Pyke?': Donald Tyerman to GP, 23 February 1948

402   GP's waiting deteriorates: *The Times*, 26 February 1948

402   'Pyke of the Back-room': 'Pyke of the 'Pyke of Habbakuk', *Evening Standard*, 24 February 1948

402   'one of the most famous': 'Last Idea of Mr Pyke, the "Boffin"', *Daily Graphic*, 26 February 1948

402   article: *New York Times*, 26 February 1948

402   'one of the most original': M. F. Perutz, 'An Inventor of Supreme Imagination', *Discovery*, May 1948

402   'not only free from': *Manchester Guardian*, 24 February 1948

402–3 BBC broadcast: Whyte, *Focus and Diversions*, p. 93

403   'an act of intellectual': Lampe, *Pyke*, p. 213

404   'If all of Pyke': David Lampe to Nathan Isaacs, 11 January 1960, Institute of Education, London – N1/D/3

404   fellow endocrinologists: These include Dr Amir H. Sam MRCP, PhD, Director of Clinical Studies at Charing Cross Hospital and his colleagues there. Professor John Monson also took the time to look at what we know of Pyke's medical history and discuss this over the phone.

404   'I was more subject': GP, unpublished manuscript, 12 June 1941

405   'those of a man relieved': GP, note on depression, 30 August 1947

405   GP as Marxist who has lost faith: GP to John Lloyd Lampe, *Pyke in*, p. 198

405   'Communist Russia has not yet': GP, 'Russell', c. 1936

Pyke Hunt, Part 6

407   'We'll be back': Andrew Boyle, *Climate of Treason* (London: Hutchinson), 1980, p. 403

407   4,605 documents: Miranda Carter, *Blunt* (London: Pan), 2002, p. 268

408   Blunt sweeps flat: Ibid., p. 346

410   'ABO' more significant to moscow: This was the opinion of the KGB defector Oleg Gordievsky. Steven Merritt Miner, *Stalin's Holy War: Religion, Nationalism, and Alliance Politics, 1941–5* (London: University of North Carolina Press), 2003, p. 278

410   'the NKVD's most remarkable': Christopher Andrew and Oleg Gordievsky, *KGB* (London: Hodder & Stoughton), 1990, p. 265

410   Smollett exaggerates Soviet concerns: Steven Merritt Miner, *Stalin's Holy War: Religion, Nationalism, and Alliance Politics, 1941–45* (London: University of North Carolina Press), 2003, pp. 246–247

411   Smollett maintains USSR is weak: Anthony Glees, *The Secrets of the Service* (London: Jonathan Cape), 1987, p. 197

411   'the Ministry of Information': Christopher Andrew, *The Mitrokhin Archive* (London: Allen Lane), 1999, p. 158

411   'red haze': Hyde, *I Believed*, p. 123

411   'propaganda beyond price': Miner, *Stalin's Holy War*, p. 272

411   Smollett initially reports to Philby: Some have suggested that Smollett was recruited by Philby during the mid-1930s – Chapman Pincher, *Their Trade Is Treachery* (London: Sidgwick & Jackson), 1981, p. 114. Gordievsky and Andrew think he moved to London in 1933 'probably at Maly's instigation, as an idealistic young NKVD illegal agent working under journalistic cover for a Viennese newspaper'. Christopher Andrew and Oleg Gordievsky, *KGB* (London: Hodder & Stoughton), 1990, p. 334

411–2   'the embarrassing friend': Gordon Corera, *The Art of Betrayal* (London: Weidenfeld & Nicolson), 2011, p. 19

412   Burgess told to drop Smollett: MADCHEN, file no. 83792, vol. 1, p. 216, quoted in Nigel West and Oleg Tsarev, *The Crown Jewels* (London: HarperCollins), 1998, p. 157

412   'cooperation with the Russians': KV 2/3040/128a

413   GP and Astor connection: Richard Cockett, *David Astor and the Observer* (London: Andre Deutsch), 1991, p. 102

413   'strong impression': George Orwell, 'Orwell's List', FO 1110/189/PR 11/1135G

413   'Everything must wear a disguise': John le Carré, *A Perfect Spy* (Penguin), Kindle version, page 69

414   'economic miracle': Sidney and Beatrice Webb, *Soviet Communism: A New Civilization?* (London: Longmans), 1935 (a book later described by A. G. P. Taylor as 'despite severe competition, the most preposterous ever written about Soviet Russia')

414   possible American Communist Party link: This is based on conversations and correspondence with the historian Michael Weatherburn in early 2014, as well as Michael Weatherburn, 'Motorcycles, Mattresses, and Microscopes', 10 October 2012

414   'Received one packet': The signature is that of Margaret Stewart and was found alongside papers dating from 1938

415   'all that I require': GP Diary, January 1937

415   socialism using British political machine: Bernard Shaw, *Labour Monthly*, 1921

416   'with caution and jealousy': GP Notebook, 14 August 1941

416   'a body of people': Ibid., 'July 20 to July 31, 1941'

416   GP flies to Paris: Contact might have come about through Pyke's friend Konni Zilliacus MP, later described by Jürgen Kuczynski as 'somebody we turned to for various ends'. – 'Protokoll der Befragung des Genossen Professor Jürgen Kuczynski am 20.7.1953', in SAPMO-BArch, DY 30/IV 2/4/123, Bl. 180–205; or perhaps through Pyke's friend Harold Laski, a colleague of Kuczynski's father Rene

416   'I made a report': Jürgen Kuczynski to Hermann Matern, 22 September 1950, SAPMO-BArch, DY 30 / IV 2/4/113, p. 73 (a copy is among the Kuczynski papers held at Zentrale Landesbibliothek Berlin, Kuc8–2-M13)

417   'I learn more from these': GP Diary, 25 August 1939

417   'Hitler and Chamberlain were both': GP Unpublished MSS, 1 May 1941

417   £500 from Myers: GP Notebook, c. August 1939

418   'I had for many years': Ibid., 27 August 1941

418   'the real war': GP Diary, 'War Aims', 12 October 1939, p.18

419   'as remote from us': Peter Conradi, *A Very English Hero* (Bloomsbury), 2012, Kindle Edition, p. 270

419   'It is everyone's duty': GP Diary, 'War Aims', 12 October 1939, p.18

420   GP plans to recruit communist translators: 30 October 1939 – 'My dear Kuczynski, I return to the subject which I mentioned to you at our last meeting of help in a) marking for translation, and b) translating from foreign languages. I am very anxious to secure the help of your friends because at the moment I am getting help from people whose outlook is rather more to the right, and I shall be compelled to rely on people of this sort inevitably, if I cannot get help from people of your sort. I wonder therefore if you could find time to take the matter up with some of your friends?' GP to Jürgen Kuczynski, 1 November 1939: 'I did not make myself quite clear about the translators. I know that many of your friends cannot translate into decent English, but what I want is folk who can *mark* the significant articles in papers, which we can then get translated by those who can translate but have no political background.' Kuc2–1-P1402-P1413_0010.

420   GP's conversation with Watson: Robert Vansittart to Leo Amery, 19 July 1940

420   'every sign of being': GP Diary, 16 October 1939

421   'excellent reason for': GP to Leo Amery, 3 May 1940

422   'giving him all his stunt': 'Extract from Y.2127 re PYKE Geoffrey', 15 September 1942, KV 2/3039/76b

422   'his terror at the thought': Craig, *Memoirs of a Thirties Dissident*

423   'British subjects to do': KV 2/3364/51b

423   'stood close to the English': Jürgen Kuczynski to Hermann Matern, 22 September 1950, SAPMO-BArch, DY 30 / IV 2/4/113, p. 73 (a copy is among the Kuczynski papers held at Zentrale Landesbibliothek Berlin, Kuc8–2-M13)

424   'confidential contact': Corera, *The Art of Betrayal*, p. 262

424   'from factories and the Forces': Hyde, *I Believed*, p. 145

424   'to push the Communist': 'Extract from censors comment mentioning PYKE, Fritz Heine to R. Katz', 14 November 1942, KV 2/3039/84b

425   radical military ideas: GP, 'Commentary on Proposal for the Occupation of Selected German-occupied Islands in the Mediterranean by Bluff', 18 November 1943

427   'I am primarily': GP to Ray Murphy, 7 October 1946

Epilogue, or, How to Think Like a Genius

429   'one of the most radical': Anne Marie Rafferty, *The Politics of Nursing Knowledge* (London: Routledge), 1996, p. 157

429   bicycle-power companies: Electric Pedals: http://electricpedals.com/about-us/ and for the laptop: http://www.alternative-energy-news.info/pedal-powered-laptops-afghanistan/ both accessed on 24 November 2013

429   pedal-powered bar: http://www.lowtechmagazine.com/2011/05/pedal-powered-farms-and-factories.html accessed on 11 March 2014

429   'have been put to good': Mark, *From Small Organic Molecules*, p. 101

429–30   Weasel tracked carries: Ten Weasels were used by a team of Canadian soldiers prospecting for minerals in Canada's North-western Territories, 'Exercise Musk-Ox', *Manchester Guardian*, 22 April 1946; South Pole – Perutz, *I Wish I'd Made You Angry Earlier*, p. 87

430–1   'out of all proportion': Mark Dudek, *Architecture of Schools* (Oxford: Architectural Press), 2000, p. 22

431   'one of the factors': van der Eyken and Turner, *Adventures in Education*, p. 18

431   'played a key role': Laura Cameron, 'Science, Nature, and Hatred: "Finding Out" at the Malting House Garden School, 1924–29', *Environment and Planning D: Society and Space*, Vol. 24, No. 6, 2006, pp. 851–872

431   study of enormous value: Adrian Wooldridge, *Measuring the Mind: Education and Psychology in England, c. 1860–c.1990* (Cambridge: Cambridge University Press), 1994, p. 121

431   'a serious sociological study': GP to Louis Mountbatten, 30 July 1943

431–2   'What made Pyke so': *Time*, 8 March 1948

432   'the social and purposive': GP to Kingsley Martin, 10 March 1946

432–3   'It is easier to solve': GP to Jon Kimche, 14 January 1945

433   'My technique': GP to Louis Mountbatten, 'Cow thesis', 16 April 1942

433   'The correct formulation': GP to Palmer Putnam, US National Archives and Records Administration, Records of the OSRD, Division 12, Project Records 1940–45, OD-65

433–4   'One of my ideas': GP to Louis Mountbatten, 'Comments on Captain of Koeppenick', 30 June 1942

434   'We cannot tell where': GP, 'Notes for Talk to Combined Operations Training School', 21 January 1947

434   'not a question of ability': GP to Louis Mountbatten, 'Comments on Captain of Koeppenick', 30 June 1942

435   'would rather wage': Notes on Certain Phases of the Development of Weasel (with excerpts from the Project Log), 13 July 42, US National Archives and Records Administration, Records of the OSRD, NC-138, Entry 1, Office of the Chairman, NDRC, and the Office of the Director, OSRD: General Records, 1940–1947, Box 55

435   'heartily kicked': GP to Louis Mountbatten, 26 April 1942

435   'the sport of shooting': GP to Michael Foot, 5 September 1945

437   'even if you had': Donald Tyerman to GP, 23 February 1948

439   'I have to behave': GP to David Pyke, 1 February 1947

LIST OF ILLUSTRATIONS

ACKNOWLEDGEMENTS

I still remember the thrill of being shown into the dusty attic, in south London, which contained almost all of Geoffrey Pyke's papers. It was 2008, and by my side was Pyke's daughter-in-law, Janet. The sight before me was a biographer's dream – papers which had not been touched for decades gathered together in bulging bin liners, wasp-strewn trunks and khaki folders fastened long ago with pins. Not only did Geoffrey Pyke write prolifically but he tried to keep everything he put down on paper. My greatest debt in writing this book is to Janet Pyke and her family for allowing me to see these papers and for providing assistance and encouragement over the last six years.

Just months after I decided to write this life of Pyke, MI5 released almost all of its papers on him to the National Archives in Kew. I am grateful both to the Security Service for choosing to do so at this particular moment and to the staff at the National Archives, particularly Ed Hampshire. I'd also like to acknowledge the assistance I received at the British Library, the Lambeth Archive, Nuffield College Library, the new defunct newspaper library at Colindale, Cambridge University Library, the Archive Centre at King's College, Cambridge, the National Archives and Library of Congress in Washington DC and the Franklin D. Roosevelt Presidential Library at Hyde Park,

New York State. Michael Meredith at Eton College Library, Glyn Hughes at the National Meteorological Archive, Catherine Wise at the Cambridge Union Society, John Entwistle at the Reuters Archive, Cindy Tsegmid and Lucy Arnold at the Leeds University Archive, Dr G. E. Edwards at Pembroke College, Steven Leclair at the National Research Council Canada in Ottawa and Katharine Thomson at the Churchill Archives Centre in Cambridge were equally helpful.

Further assistance, for which I am indebted, came from Bernd Barth-Rainer, Peter Morris, Georgina Ferry, Michael Weatherburn, Jeremy Lewis, Paul Collins, Jared Bond, Jonathan Ray, Janet Sayers, Kevin Morgan, Gordon Corera, Thomas Rünkel, Reinhard Müller, Charles Faringdon, John Monson, Amir Sam, John Betteridge, Philip Womack, Lindsay Merriman, Hugo Macpherson, Sarah and Tom Carter, Robin Lane Fox, George Weidenfeld, Artemis Cooper, John Julius Norwich, Leonora Lichfield, Harriet Crawley, Dickie Wallis, Cutler Cook, Alexander Kan, Jeremy Bigwood, Andrew Lownie, Nigel West, Boris Jardine, Nicolas Smith, Karen Ganilsy, Stephen Raleigh, Anthony Hentschel and Charles Leadbeater.

Jonathan Conway showed tenacity and skill in helping to shape the outline of this book. Trevor Dolby at Preface has been hugely supportive throughout and great fun to work with. Will Sulkin was an extraordinarily thoughtful editor. John Sugar and Rose Tremlett at Preface have both been immensely helpful. For this American edition, I'm enormously grateful to everyone at PublicAffairs, including Melissa Raymond, Melissa Veronesi, and in particular, my editor Ben Adams. Thanks also to my dad, for his feedback, and to Bea, my sister, to whom this book is dedicated and who has been, from the start, full of imaginative advice.

Finally my love and thanks to the two women in my life, Helena and our daughter Matilda, the latter for splashing me each evening at bathtime, the former for her unending love, silliness and unconditional encouragement. I can't imagine doing any of this without you – you make the whole thing worthwhile.

INDEX

Entries in *italics* indicate photographs.

INDEX

HENRY HEMMING is the author of four works of non-fiction—
*Together, In Search of the English Eccentric, Misadventure in the Middle
East,* and a monograph on the artist Abdulnasser Gharem—and has
coauthored the visual books *Edge of Arabia* and *Offscreen.* He has writ-
ten for *The Sunday Times, Daily Telegraph, Daily Mail, The Times, The
Economist, FT Magazine,* and *The Washington Post* and has given in-
terviews on Radio 4's *Today Programme* and NBC's *Today Show* and
spoken at schools, festivals, and companies including RDF Media,
The RSA, Science Museum, Frontline Club, The School of Life, Port
Eliot Literary Festival, and Canvas8, where he is a Thought Leader.
He lives in London with his wife and daughter.

PublicAffairs is a publishing house founded in 1997. It is a tribute to the standards, values, and flair of three persons who have served as mentors to countless reporters, writers, editors, and book people of all kinds, including me.

I. F. STONE, proprietor of *I. F. Stone's Weekly*, combined a commitment to the First Amendment with entrepreneurial zeal and reporting skill and became one of the great independent journalists in American history. At the age of eighty, Izzy published *The Trial of Socrates*, which was a national bestseller. He wrote the book after he taught himself ancient Greek.

BENJAMIN C. BRADLEE was for nearly thirty years the charismatic editorial leader of *The Washington Post*. It was Ben who gave the *Post* the range and courage to pursue such historic issues as Watergate. He supported his reporters with a tenacity that made them fearless and it is no accident that so many became authors of influential, best-selling books.

ROBERT L. BERNSTEIN, the chief executive of Random House for more than a quarter century, guided one of the nation's premier publishing houses. Bob was personally responsible for many books of political dissent and argument that challenged tyranny around the globe. He is also the founder and longtime chair of Human Rights Watch, one of the most respected human rights organizations in the world.

.   .   .

For fifty years, the banner of Public Affairs Press was carried by its owner Morris B. Schnapper, who published Gandhi, Nasser, Toynbee, Truman, and about 1,500 other authors. In 1983, Schnapper was described by *The Washington Post* as "a redoubtable gadfly." His legacy will endure in the books to come.

Peter Osnos, *Founder and Editor-at-Large*